GREAT OPERAS

VOLUME II

Volume One of *Great Operas* contains
essays on the following works:

Together, Volumes One and Two consist of thirty unabridged
essays taken from *More Stories of Famous Operas* and *Seventeen
Famous Operas*, originally published by ALFRED A.
KNOPF, INC.

GREAT OPERAS

ERNEST NEWMAN

THE DEFINITIVE TREATMENT OF THEIR HISTORY, STORIES, AND MUSIC

VOLUME

II

VINTAGE BOOKS

NEW YORK

1958

Contents

GREAT OPERAS

VOLUME II

The Seraglio

WOLFGANG AMADEUS MOZART [1756–1791]

PRINCIPAL CHARACTERS

CONSTANZE	*Soprano*
BLONDE	*Soprano*
BELMONTE	*Tenor*
PEDRILLO	*Tenor*
OSMIN	*Bass*
THE PASHA SELIM	*Speaking Part*

1

T is of course impossible for that rather terrible by-product of the contemporary theatre, the producer, to keep his meddling hands off *The Seraglio;* and so we seldom see the charming work given precisely as it is, in spite of the fact that it is virtually the one opera of Mozart's that does not require any rearrangement for the modern stage. There are dull numbers in *Figaro* and *Don Giovanni* to which no amount of piety can induce us to listen with any pretence of rapture, and the conductor or producer who omits these today is doing us in the audience a service. But in *The Seraglio* there is not a single really dull number from start to finish. In his later operas and instrumental works Mozart develops admirable qualities that were not present, at any rate to the same degree, in his earlier ones; but in some of his creations of the period between about 1775 and 1782 there is a peculiar romantic glow that somehow or other faded out of him as he matured.

In 1818 Weber introduced *The Seraglio* to Dresden under his own baton, and in a preliminary article he commended the work to his fellow-townsmen in words that bear quotation today. Weber hit the nail on the head when he said that *The Seraglio* presents us with a picture of " what every man's joyous youthful years are to him, years the bloom of which he will never recapture. . . . I venture to say that in *The Seraglio* Mozart had attained the peak of his artistic experience, to which only experience of the world had to be added later. Mankind was entitled to expect from him several more operas like *Figaro* and *Don Giovanni;* but with the best will in the world he could never have written another *Seraglio.*"

In 1781 Mozart was living in Vienna. He had cut the ties that had so long bound him to his father and his father's employer, the Prince Archbishop of Salzburg, and he had fallen in love with Konstanze Weber, the daughter of a former ticket-seller in the Vienna National Theatre. It was while he was waiting for his father's consent to his marriage that he received a commission for a German Singspiel — the order being given in accordance with the desire of the Emperor Joseph II that his Court Theatre should aim at being more German in its future policy and less Italian. For the text of the new opera recourse was first of all had to the actor Friedrich Schröder; but as he had nothing useful to contribute the commission was turned over to Gottlieb Stephanie (actually Stephan), who figures in theatrical history as Stephanie Junior to distinguish him from his brother. Mozart's father has some nasty things to say about Stephanie in his letters to his son; but to have been disparaged by the envious, suspicious Leopold Mozart is regarded today as more of a testimonial for any man than an indictment of him.

On the 1st August 1781 Mozart wrote to his father, " The day before yesterday young Stephanie handed me a ' book' to compose. . . . It is very good. The subject is Turkish, and is called *' Bellmont* [sic] *und Konstanze, oder Die Verführung* [sic] [1] *aus dem Serail.'* For the symphony [i.e. the overture], the chorus in the first act, and the final chorus I will write Turkish music. . . . I am so delighted with the book that I have already done the first aria for the Cavalieri, that for Adamberger, and the trio that concludes the first act." [2] The music to this act was complete by the 22nd

[1] The ultimate title of the work was *Die Entführung aus dem Serail* (*The Abduction from The Seraglio*).

[2] Caterina Cavalieri was the Constanze, and Adamberger the Belmonte, in the first performance of the opera.

August. Then it was announced that the production would have to be postponed owing to the inability of the Emperor to visit the theatre on the date originally intended. Mozart was consequently able to work in more leisurely fashion at his score, which was finished in June 1782. The first performance took place in Vienna on the 16th July. On the following 4th August Mozart was at last able to marry his Konstanze.

"Turkish" operas and plays and stories were highly popular in the seventeenth and eighteenth centuries, when pirates still made the Mediterranean unsafe for quiet people, and no one undertaking a voyage anywhere between Jaffa and Gibraltar could be quite sure that it would not end, if he were an able-bodied man, in a slit throat or slavery, or, if she were a young and good-looking woman, in a harem. The "Turkish" theme, in fact, communicated to the romantic mind in those days something of the thrill for which the youth of the nineteenth century used to turn to the Red Indian, and the youth of today turns — or did so as late as the day before yesterday — to the American gangster. Of the many previous incursions into the "Turkish" world only one has any interest today in connection with *The Seraglio*. In 1781 there was produced an opera entitled *Belmont und Konstanze*, the text of which was by one Christoph Friedrich Bretzner; this was laid under contribution by Stephanie with the gay nonchalance characteristic of the days when copyright protection for authors and composers was unknown. Bretzner, however, managed to immortalise himself by a communication he sent to a Leipzig journal in 1782: "A certain person of the name of Mozart, living in Vienna, has had the impudence to misuse my drama *Belmont und Konstanze* for an opera text. I hereby protest most solemnly against this encroachment on my rights, and reserve further action." The name of Herr Bretzner thus goes down to history coupled with that of one Franz Schubert, a minor composer of the early nineteenth century, who indignantly protested that *he* was not the Franz Schubert responsible for a certain setting of *The Erl-King* about which everyone was talking. In any case Bretzner had small claim to sympathy on the ground that he had been robbed, for his own work had been the result of all-round pillage: everyone and everything in his *Belmont und Konstanze* is a stock character or a stock situation of the period.

5

2

The main themes of the charming overture — which, with its piccolo, big drum, cymbals and triangle colouring, is in the best vein of eighteenth century "Turkish" music — are the vigorous ones given out in the opening bars:

and its counterpart in the key of the dominant:

but midway in the development of his material Mozart inserts a tender reference, in the minor, to Belmonte's first song, which we shall soon hear in the major:

The overture has no formal close, but runs straight on into the song of Belmonte's just mentioned:

The scene is the terrace of the Pasha Selim's house, overlooking the sea, in which Belmonte believes his long-lost Constanze, who had been taken by pirates, to be a captive. His immediate problem is how to get access to her in the conditions that obtain in the establishment of a Turkish Pasha. While he is thinking this out the Pasha's head gardener and factotum Osmin enters, singing a little love song of his own, for the old curmudgeon, as we discover later, is over head and ears in love with Constanze's maid Blonde, who had been captured with her mistress.

Belmonte thinks that this old fellow may be able to give him the information he wants, but Osmin is too much absorbed in his own lyrical reflections to be open to general conversation. Belmonte has to ask him several times whether this is the Pasha Selim's house:

before he can get an answer. When this comes, it is in a musical form that shows how conclusive a plump drop into the tonic key can be after one has been kept poised for some time on the dominant, as we have been during Belmonte's questions: the tonality of Osmin's reply leaves nothing further to be said on the subject:

It appears, moreover, that the gardener is in Selim's service. In that case, says Belmonte, can he have a word with one Pedrillo, who, he understands, is also engaged there? The knowledge that the young man is a friend of Pedrillo's does not endear him to Osmin, for Pedrillo — a veritable gallows bird, according to him — is his rival in the affections of Blonde: he would have the rapscallion hanged, drawn and quartered if he could. All this we learn in an amusing duet, which ends with Osmin shooing Belmonte off the scene.

Pedrillo now enters, full of an impudence and self-assurance that are especially exasperating to Osmin, because the gallows bird has somehow or other managed to get on the soft side of the Pasha. There is a lively scene between the pair, Osmin swearing by the beard of the Prophet that he will get the better of his saucy young rival one of these days, Pedrillo making him madder and madder by laughing at him. As soon as Osmin has stormed out, Belmonte returns. He and his former servant are rejoiced to see each other again. Pedrillo gives Belmonte all the news. He and the two girls had had the good fortune to be bought from the pirates by the Pasha Selim, whose favourite Constanze has become — though, he hastens to assure Belmonte, there is nothing whatever to worry about on that account. Pedrillo's own poor little Blonde has not done quite so well, for she is daily pestered by the attentions of an ugly old clodhopper to whom the Pasha has seen fit to assign her — the same with whom Belmonte has just been talking, not only the Pasha's gardener but his handy man and spy. Still, taking one thing with another, things might be worse. Thanks to the Pasha's liking for Pedrillo, he is allowed to be about the garden when the ladies of the harem come out to take the air. Belmonte informs him that he has a ship lying just off shore; and Pedrillo, though not underrating the difficulties, thinks they may be able to get the girls away. Then, seeing Constanze and the Pasha in the distance, he hurries away to meet them and, if possible, put in a good word for Belmonte.

The latter, left alone, launches into a song of love to his Constanze:

O wie ängstlich, o wie feu-rig klopft mein lie - be-vol - les Herz,

the orchestral accompaniment to which, as we learn from one of Mozart's letters to his father, is full of touches descriptive of the lover's state of mind. " The throbbing of the loving heart is indicated by the first and second violins in octaves. . . . One sees the trembling, the faltering, the heaving of the breast (expressed by a *crescendo*), one hears the whispering and sighing (first violins, muted, and a flute in unison)." It was doubtless to his own Constanze, as much as to Stephanie's, that Mozart was pouring out his heart in this aria.

Pedrillo comes running back with the news that the Pasha is close by, whereupon Belmonte conceals himself. Selim, who is accompanied by Constanze, lands from a boat, and is greeted with a chorus of welcome from his janissaries:

" As regards the janissaries' chorus," says Mozart in the same letter, " this is all that a janissaries' chorus ought to be — short and merry, and the very thing for the Viennese."

Addressing Constanze in the most courteous fashion, although she is his property, Selim laments that he has not yet succeeded in winning her love. She recognises his nobility and forbearance, but explains that her thoughts always run on the one she loved in the days of her freedom; to him she will for ever be true. Her aria, " Ach, ich liebte " is of the coloratura order and takes her at one or two points up to the high D; but for all that the dominant expression of it is that of grief. When, in the dialogue that follows, she tells the Pasha once again that no one will ever have her heart but the lover from whom she has been torn, his anger rises for a moment. He bids her reflect once more, and for the last time: he will wait for her answer till the morrow. But when she has left him he softens again; never will he employ violence, he says, against one so loving and so lovable.

Pedrillo now approaches with Belmonte, whom he introduces as a friend from Italy who, having heard glowing accounts of Selim's magnificence, has come to offer him his services as architect. The Pasha promises to consider the matter and to see the stranger again the next day. He goes into his palace, and Belmonte and Pedrillo, congratulating themselves on the success of their scheme, are about to follow him when Osmin comes out and bars their way. Neither Belmonte's haughty assertion of his rank nor Pedrillo's gay impudence and his assurance that the stranger is now in the Pasha's service has the smallest effect on the surly Osmin. He knows, he says, how easy it is to impose on the good Pasha, for he is as soft as butter: but he, Osmin, is a tougher proposition altogether. The scene culminates in a lively trio, in the course of which the pair manage to push him aside and run into the palace.

3

The opening scene of the second act, which takes place in the Pasha's garden, introduces us to the sprightly Blonde, who, as the curtain goes up, is telling poor Osmin, not for the first time, apparently, what she thinks of him. It isn't a Turkish slave he has to deal with, she gives him to understand in her aria. It appears that she is English; and English girls don't stand any nonsense from people like him. All this bullying and threatening and sulking and snarling gets a man nowhere: the only things that impress a nice girl like herself are smiles and tender speeches and flatteries:

As none of these happen to be in Osmin's repertory, he tries the high hand with her. Are they not in Turkey? Has not the Pasha given her to him? Is he not the master, she the slave? But Blonde, as a free-born Englishwoman, does not care a rap for any Osmin, Pasha, or Turkey. Let him wait till she knows the place a bit better:

then she will raise the banner of revolt among the ladies of the harem. For her part she is in love with that charming young fellow Pedrillo. At the mention of his detested rival, Osmin, as usual, sees red; but when he threatens violence Blonde reminds him that her mistress is the Pasha's favourite — one word from her, and it's fifty of the best on the soles of Osmin's feet! This cools him down; and after a lively duet, in which the most that Osmin can do is to apostrophise the English race, telling them they must be crazy to give their women so much liberty, she bundles him unceremoniously off the stage.

As she does so, Constanze enters from the opposite side, looking very sad. Blonde feels sorry for her: *she*, at least, can see her Pedrillo by stealth every day, while her mistress can only dream of her Belmonte. Constanze pours out her heart in a melancholy aria, descriptive of her sufferings since the day she was torn from her lover:

Blonde tries to console her: surely, she says, a young man so rich and so resourceful as Belmonte will find some means of rescuing them, even from a Turkish harem. But Constanze has given up all hope.

Blonde retires as the Pasha enters. He woos Constanze once more, and once more is repulsed. Never can she love him, she says; neither the threat of death, nor, what is worse, of torture can shake her resolution. She proudly assures him of this in the long and brilliant aria " Martern aller Arten ":

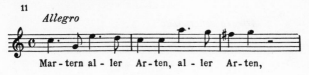

which is laid out on the broadest concerto lines, with four solo instruments and an orchestral introduction of some sixty bars. It is not easy for either of the characters to keep the action alive while this long introduction is playing, or for the Pasha to know what to do while the aria itself is running its lengthy course. That, however, is the actors' and producer's problem; and since Mozart wanted things thus, they had better get their brains to work at it. Towards the end, Constanze approaches the Pasha to hurl her final defiance straight in his face: "Patiently will I bear the worst you can do. Command, storm, rage, do what you will: death will release me from it all."

She leaves him, and he does some thinking. What gives her the courage to defy him like this? Is she planning to escape? No, it cannot be that, otherwise she would take another line with him, and try to put him off his guard by seeming complaisance. But as neither prayers nor threats avail, he must try craft.

Blonde, returning to the scene, is astonished to find neither Constanze nor the Pasha there. Have they come to an understanding at last? she asks herself. This poor mistress of hers is really too faithful to her Belmonte. As for herself, she is fortunate enough to have Pedrillo always at hand. Were it not so, there is no saying what might happen; she might be tempted, as she puts it, to become quite mussulmanised in her way of thinking. Pedrillo breaks in upon these meditations of hers with the news that great plans are on foot — Belmonte has come, he has obtained admission into the palace as an architect, he has a ship waiting in the bay, and he intends to rescue all three of them before many hours are over. At midnight he will be at Constanze's window with a ladder: Pedrillo will be at Blonde's window with another: as for Osmin, Pedrillo is going to put a sleeping-draught into his drink in the course of the evening. Blonde is to give the good news to her mistress. Left to herself, Blonde pauses only long enough to give vent to her feelings in a joyous song:

Lust, herrscht nun-mehr in mei-ner Brust!

and then runs into the palace.

Pedrillo returns to await Belmonte: he has with him a basket containing two flasks of wine, one large, the other small, and a couple of drinking-cups. Now that the hour for action is approaching, the bright little fellow does not feel quite so pleased with himself as he did a little while ago. If only they were safe on the sea with their maidens, never to see this accursed land again! To give himself courage he sings a ditty in which he assures himself again and again that " only cowards are afraid."

Osmin enters, and a richly comic scene ensues between the two. Pedrillo, the soul of gaiety once more, commiserates with Osmin on being a Mahommedan, and so forbidden wine. Bit by bit he manages to overcome the old fellow's suspicions and inveigle him into drinking with him, assuring him that Mahomet, who has long been dead, has something better to do than to bother about Osmin and his drop of wine. The pair sit down back to back, become eloquent on the themes of wine and women, and drain glass after glass, until Osmin is so completely tipsy that he can even address Pedrillo as " brother." He refuses to go indoors, denying that he is sleepy; but Pedrillo scares him by dropping a hint about the Pasha. He somehow manages to prop the bulky Osmin up against a tree and then take him on his own back and drag him off the stage. Then he returns to keep the rendezvous with Belmonte, considerably happier than he was a little while ago. It is only three hours now from midnight, and Osmin can be trusted, he thinks, not to recover consciousness within that time.

Belmonte enters, followed in a moment by Constanze and Blonde. Pedrillo draws the latter on one side and, judging by his miming, gives a humorous account of the trick he has played on Osmin. Belmonte begins to pour out his soul to Constanze, though not, as one might have expected, in an impetuous aria but in an *adagio* one: his first thought is of all they have suffered since their separation. It is only towards the end, when he looks forward to their future bliss, that the tempo changes to *allegretto*. Constanze replies in much more passionate tones, and gradually communicates her ardour to Belmonte. Pedrillo and Blonde, going over the arrangements for midnight, join with the leading pair of lovers in a quartet. This is not without its clouded moments, for Belmonte cannot help expressing a timid hope that Constanze has resisted the Pasha's advances, which emboldens Pedrillo to put a question or two of a similar kind to Blonde. Constanze convinces Belmonte by the simple process of bursting into tears: the indignant Blonde's only argument is a box on the ear for Pedrillo. Each of the lovers thereupon craves pardon for ever having doubted, and is soon forgiven. The curtain falls on their complete reconciliation.

4

The setting of the third act is an open space before the palace, overlooking the sea, with the main building on one side and Osmin's quarters on the other. It is midnight. Pedrillo enters with the captain of Belmonte's ship, one Klaas, who is carrying a long ladder which he places against the wall of the palace. Then he goes back to his ship, leaving Pedrillo to give yet another exhibition of that shrinking from danger that has been one of the characteristics of the comic stage servant from the earliest days of the drama. Pedrillo is a distant descendant of Sosia, for example, the slave of Amphitryon in the comedy of Plautus. These plaguey Turks, according to Pedrillo, have no sense of humour; and though the Pasha Selim is a renegade, when it comes to chopping off heads he is just a Turk like the rest. (This is the first intimation we have had that Selim had changed his religion: it is no doubt inserted here to prepare us for his most un-Turk-like generosity later to a lady who has tried to abscond from his harem).

Klaas returns with a shorter ladder, which, being intended for Blonde, he places against the wall of Osmin's house. Then he goes off to his ship again to make the final preparations for the flight.

Belmonte enters. Pedrillo leaves him in order to take a last look round and see that there are no spies about. Meanwhile, he says, Belmonte is to burst into song, for apparently the inhabitants of the palace in general and Osmin's quarters in particular are so accustomed to hearing Pedrillo serenading Blonde every night that they will suspect there is something wrong if for once some one does not give a recital. So Belmonte launches out into a long aria, "Ich baue ganz auf deine Stärke":

13 Andante

Ich bau-e ganz auf dei-ne Stär-ke,

the burden of which is the power of love to accomplish whatever
it sets its hand to. This finished, Pedrillo returns. He looks at his
watch. It is just twelve o'clock — time for the signal to Blonde.
Bidding his master keep watch on the other side of the stage, he
takes up a position near Osmin's house and sings two stanzas of
a delightful little romance about a pretty maiden who was taken
captive by the Moors and waited and waited till the rescuer came.
Strange to say, this evokes no sign of life from within; so Pedrillo
confides to the night air a further couple of verses, which tell how
the elopement was achieved at precisely twelve o'clock one night.
At last the song awakes Constanze, who puts her head out of an
upper window. Belmonte ascends the ladder, and a moment or
two later makes his exit with her through the palace door. They
disappear into the darkness, leaving Pedrillo, whose heart is in his
boots again, to follow with Blonde when he can. He ascends the
shorter ladder and disappears through the window which is now
opened in Blonde's room.

But his singing has awakened a mute, who in turn has roused
Osmin. Befuddled as the old man still is, he guesses there is something wrong, and comes out to investigate. Soon the mute spots
the ladder in front of Osmin's house. Sending the dumb man to
rouse the guard, Osmin climbs the ladder, and reaches the upper
window just as Pedrillo and Blonde appear at it. They go back
hurriedly into the room, slamming the window in Osmin's face. He
begins to descend the ladder, but so cautiously and clumsily, as
befits a man of his years, that he is only half-way down when
Pedrillo and Blonde come out by the door and escape under his
very nose. As soon as Osmin reaches earth again he is arrested by
the watch under suspicion of having put the ladder where it is.
He is still explaining who he is and what has happened when
Pedrillo and Blonde return in custody, followed a minute or two
later by the captured Belmonte and Constanze.

Pedrillo tries to convince Osmin that he had merely been taking
Blonde for a little walk, seeing that his " little brother " Osmin is

hardly in a condition to do that himself today — a gentle reminder of the episode with the bottles, designed to frighten Osmin, who, as a professing Mussulman, has laid himself open to dire penalties by indulging in wine. But Osmin is not so easily terrified. When Belmonte and Constanze are brought in, he asks ironically if perhaps the Herr Architekt has also been planning to take a walk. Belmonte tries to bribe him, but Osmin prefers his revenge: with Pedrillo in particular he has long wanted to get even. He pours out his detestation of poor Pedrillo in a vigorous aria in which he gloats over the prospect of seeing him and his companion strangled:

14 *Allegro vivace*

Ha! wie will ich tri-um-phi-ren,
Wenn sie euch zum Richtplatz füh-ren,

und die Häl-se schnüren zu, schnüren zu,

The final scene takes place in a hall in the palace, in the early hours of that same morning. The Pasha, who has been awakened from his sleep by the noise, has just ordered his servants to find out the meaning of it all, when Osmin enters, still a trifle heavy from the sleeping-draught that had been put into his wine. He tells the Pasha of the plot of the pseudo-architect and Pedrillo to abduct Constanze and Blonde, a plot which, thanks to Osmin's devotion and intelligence, has been frustrated. Belmonte and Constanze are brought in by the guards. The Pasha reproaches Constanze for her perfidy. She pleads, in excuse, that this " architect " is the man to whom her heart has long been pledged; let the Pasha take her life if he will, but spare her lover's. Belmonte, though it goes against the grain with him, also begs for clemency. He is, he explains, the son of one who will pay anything to free him — a rich Spaniard of the name of Lostados. Selim looks up in astonishment. Lostados? Does Belmonte know a Commandant at Oran of that name? " My father," replies the young man. Thereupon the Pasha rejoices that fate has thrown into his hands the son of his deadliest enemy, the man who had robbed him of his betrothed, ruined and degraded him, and driven him from his fatherland. What would that Lostados do, he asks, if he were now in the Pasha's place?

He will deal with Belmonte, he says, as once Lostados did with him; and he leaves the hall with Osmin, ostensibly to give orders for the torture. Belmonte bitterly reproaches himself for having brought Constanze to this pass; but she consoles him with the assurance that she is willing to die with him. At the conclusion of their long duet Pedrillo and Blonde are brought in by the guards. They too face torture and death with composure, though their views on those subjects are necessarily not expressed at such length and in such elegant language as those of their master and mistress. The Pasha returns. Belmonte defies him to do his worst, but Selim surprises him by telling him that his contempt for Lostados is too vast for him to imitate him in anything, even in revenge. " You are free. Take your Constanze, return to your own land, and tell your father that though you were in my power I set you free, to prove to him that there can be more satisfaction in returning good for evil than in requiting one crime with another." Constanze also, who thanks him and implores his forgiveness, he dismisses with a kindly word. Then Pedrillo, who looks like being forgotten, puts in an appeal for similar magnanimity towards himself and Blonde. This he obtains, in spite of the protests of Osmin at being robbed of his female slave, the Pasha humorously assuring him that it will be better for him too, in the long run, that he shall lose her.

Belmonte begins a little song of praise of the Pasha:

15 *Andante*

Nie werd'ich dei - ne Huld ver-ken - nen,

the final strain of which:

16 *Andante*

Wer so viel Huld ver-ges - sen

kann, den seh'man mit Ver-ach-tung an!

17

is repeated by the whole assembly. Then Constanze takes up the melody, followed by Pedrillo and Blonde in turn, the refrain being repeated each time as on the first occasion. A passing reference of the irrepressible Blonde to Osmin goads the old man into an angry reply, in which he hankers once more after the vengeance that will now never be his. The janissaries sing the praises of the Pasha in a chorus which, like that in the first act, has a pleasant pseudo-"Turkish" touch about it here and there, and the curtain falls with the two happy couples making their way to the ship that is awaiting them.

5

The modern producer, as we have said, cannot keep his officious hands off *The Seraglio;* but the more he tries to re-shape the work as he imagines it ought to be the more convinced we become that it is better as Stephanie and Mozart wrote it. That it has one or two little awkwardnesses and weaknesses of construction cannot be denied; but every attempt to remedy these only substitutes a fresh set of flaws, and a worse set, for the old ones. Several of the so-called "defects" of the opera are more imaginary than real; we cease to be perturbed by them as soon as we try to look at the work from the point of view of its own period and milieu, instead of making it an absurd grievance against the past that it did not shape its theatrical practice in accordance with certain notions of today. Some critics have succeeded in persuading themselves that it is a blot on the opera that the Pasha has only a speaking part — a circumstance said to have been imposed upon Mozart and his librettist by the limited number of singers at their disposal. But for many of us the fact that Selim uses only the speaking voice lends a special interest to the character and confers a peculiar distinction on it. Whatever strict aesthetics may conceive it to be its duty to say on this matter, there can be no doubt that telling dramatic effects can sometimes be drawn from the co-operation of the speaking with the singing voice in opera. In any case, *The Seraglio* is not "grand opera" but a Singspiel. It is only in the more highly-lit emotional moments that the characters break into song: the whole of the action is carried on by means of ordinary speech. It is not, then, as if the Pasha alone spoke always while everyone else always sang; it is merely a matter of his continuing to speak in one or two situations in which the modern theoretician assumes he ought to sing. One critic laments that there is " no musical answer " on the Pasha's part to Constanze's big aria (No. 11 — " Martern aller Arten "). But why on earth should Selim any more reply in music to *this* expression of Constanze's sentiments than he does to so many others? " Martern aller Arten " is a very extended piece of musical design: a musical reply to it on Selim's part would constitute, if short, an anti-climax, while if long it would upset the proportions of the act as a whole. Moreover, since he has so far been able, and later will be able again, to express in speech, with perfect effectiveness, every emotion set up in him by Constanze or anyone else, is there any particular reason why the resources of language should prove insufficient for his purpose in just this one instance?

The experiment has been tried of giving Selim, somewhere or other in the course of the work, an opportunity to sing one of the finest of the many arias — " Per questa bella mano " — written by Mozart for concert room use. But the only result has been to make us feel that a two-dimensional Selim, so to speak, has been arbitrarily substituted for Mozart's one-dimensional Selim without any corresponding gain in psychological verisimilitude or dramatic effectiveness. There is another consideration to be borne in mind. The fact that Selim has not to sing makes it possible to entrust the part to an actor — not a singer — entirely qualified for it by appearance, vocal timbre, and skill in elocution; and no one who has seen the rôle played as it can and should be played can regret that Mozart did not see fit to substitute for this grave, dignified figure — whose curiously dominating intellectual position in the drama is accentuated by his never breaking, like all the others, into song — just one more bass or tenor to add to the evening's tale of technical shortcoming.

Another reproach that is brought against the libretto is that the whole scene of the abduction in the third act is carried on by means of speech alone: no singing occurs between Pedrillo's " Romanze " — " In Mohrenland gefangen war " — and the aria of Osmin — " Ha! wie will ich triumphieren " — after the frustration of the plot. But once more we have to bear in mind the genre to which *The Seraglio* belongs. It would no doubt have been an excellent thing had Mozart's librettist been able to supply him, for the abduction episode, with a text that would have enabled him to cast the whole scene, packed as it is with action, into music from start to finish, in the style that makes the second act of *Figaro* the miracle it is. But it is not easy to see just how Stephanie could have got through all he has to get through in this scene in the way of action and at the same time provide Mozart with a series of opportunities to " spread himself " as a musician. Let us once more accept the fact that *The Seraglio* is a Singspiel — a sublimated specimen of it, thanks to the genius of Mozart, but for all that just a Singspiel, a genre in which music as a matter of course surrenders some of its own claims for the convenience of the drama.

As for the changes that are sometimes made in the disposition of the arias, it can only be said uncompromisingly that they weaken rather than strengthen the action. The only possible excuse that can be put forward for transferring " Martern aller Arten " from the second act to the third is the fact that while in this last act Belmonte, Pedrillo and Osmin all have arias of one kind or another, Constanze has none: she joins the rest of them, of course, in the finale, but apart from that, Stephanie and Mozart make her sing only in the duet with Belmonte — " Welch ein Geschick! " — which follows the capture of the lovers. But to transfer " Martern aller Arten " to this point involves first of all holding up the concluding action of the opera while Constanze tells the Pasha at great length what she thinks of him, and in the second place weakens the effect of the scene between him and Constanze in the second act. " Martern aller Arten " is best left where Stephanie and Mozart chose to put it. So with the cut that is sometimes made in the second act, necessitating the removal of Belmonte's Aria No. 15 — " Wenn der Freude Thränen fliessen " — to the beginning of the third act; and with the experiment occasionally made of leaving No. 15 in its proper place but transferring Belmonte's aria — " Ich baue ganz auf deine Stärke " (No. 17) — from its proper place in the third act to the commencement of that act.

Some sort of case might be argued for modifying the construction of *The Seraglio* were its little peculiarities the result of incompetence on the part of either the librettist or the musician. But they were not: they were merely the result of indifference on their part to considerations that seem more important to us of a later day than they did to them. Mozart, like the other opera composers of his epoch — apart from Gluck — was blissfully free of aesthetic or historical prepossessions: nor did he ever pause to consider whether theatrical humanity a century or two later would approve or disapprove of what he was doing at this moment or that. What he had to do, and all he thought of doing, was a job of work: he had been commissioned to produce an opera, and given a certain local personnel to produce it with; and he would have thought anyone crazy who suggested to him that he had a duty to posterity as well as to himself, and that he must not so much as embark on his share of the work until he was satisfied that psychologically and dramatically Stephanie's "book" would stand the strictest scrutiny by critics and aestheticians to the end of time. The eighteenth century opera audience was completely lacking in our own highly developed historical sense. It knew next to nothing of the remote past of the art, and cared absolutely nothing about its distant future; and Mozart, the least theoretical of musicians, would have been the last to imagine it to be his duty to try to impose a new water-tight, objection-proof ideal of opera on his collaborators and his listeners. He sensibly applied himself not to aesthetic speculation but to throwing himself heart and soul into whatever dramatic character or situation appealed greatly to him, and where the appeal was less strong he availed himself of his unique faculty for turning out, at a moment's notice, and in response to any stimulus or even to no stimulus at all, a piece of music which, if it does not particularly elevate the critical modern listener, at any rate never lets him badly down — music that manipulates the most serviceable clichés of the period with consummate skill and the most perfect taste.

It is true that he generally did some thinking of his own about the subjects and texts submitted to him. But, as the references to *The Seraglio* in his letters to his father are alone sufficient to show, his thinking was that not of an arm-chair theoretician but of a practical man of the theatre. If he thought there was a better way of making a particular episode effective than the one provided by his librettist, he would tell him so. But he would, and could, suggest improvements only within the framework dictated by plain common sense and the theatrical practice of his day; the vast field of speculation lying outside that framework had the minimum of interest for him. Moreover, like other composers of the period, he had perforce to see every work of his in terms of the human material at his disposal for the first production of it; and since a radical change of cast for the benefit of an opera was out of the question, the only thing to do was to shape the work with an eye constantly on the cast allotted to him. The main reason why his Osmin is given so much to sing is that he was a first-rate singer. The original player of the part, Ludwig Fischer, had a bass voice of exceptional tonal range and remarkable flexibility. Considering himself fortunate to have such an asset in his opera, Mozart decided to make the utmost possible use of him; and Osmin becomes a more important character in Stephanie's libretto than he was in Bretzner's merely because Fischer was exceptionally competent in his particular line.

The reader will recall that *The Seraglio* begins with an aria by Belmonte, after which Osmin sings his little ditty, " Wer ein Liebchen hat gefunden "; then comes a longish duet between him and Belmonte. Stephanie had evidently cast this scene, apart from Osmin's song, in the form of spoken dialogue; and it was Mozart who insisted on its being sung throughout. On the 26th September 1781 he writes thus to his father: "The opera [as originally submitted to him] began with a monologue. This I asked Herr Stephanie to make into a little arietta — and further, that instead of making [Belmonte and Osmin] chit-chat together after the latter's little song, they should have a duet. Since the rôle of Osmin is intended for Herr Fischer, who has a really capital bass voice . . . we must make good use of him, especially as he has the great public with him. In the original libretto Osmin had nothing whatever to sing except this *Liedchen* and a share in the trio [3] and the finale. So now he gets an aria [No. 3, " Solche hergelaufne Laffen "] in the first act, and he will be given another in the second." [4] Mozart goes on to say that in the aria in the first act he has taken care to make good use of Fischer's effective deep notes: moreover, he has been so intent on Fischer, rather than on Osmin, that not only did the suggestion for the aria come from himself but he actually wrote the bulk of the music without any text, leaving it to Stephanie to fit words to the melody as best he could later.

Mozart, it will be seen, knew perfectly well what he was doing

[3] I.e., with Belmonte and Pedrillo at the end of the first act.
[4] As a matter of fact Osmin did *not* get an aria in the second act, though he takes part in a duet with Pedrillo.

in *The Seraglio;* and if we have to choose between him and the modern producer there ought to be no hesitation in our choice. We go to see and hear the opera for Mozart's, not the producer's, sake; and it is really much easier for us to make the slight mental effort necessary to listen to the work in its proper historical perspective than to accommodate ourselves to changes in it that have their origin, for the most part, merely in the conviction of the producer that in order to justify his position in the theatre he must at all costs " produce." [5]

[5] It is true that while in the middle of his labours Mozart desired a drastic change in the lay-out of the end of the second act and the beginning of the third; but for one reason or another this was not done. What would have been the final effect on the opera of this re-modelling it is useless to conjecture. The only *Entführung* we have is the actual one bequeathed to us by the librettist and the composer; and the broad fact remains that this is better in the form in which Stephanie and Mozart left it than in any new form imposed on it by the modern producer.

Così Fan Tutte

WOLFGANG AMADEUS MOZART [1756–1791]

PRINCIPAL CHARACTERS

FIORDILIGI	*Soprano*
DORABELLA	*Soprano*
FERRANDO	*Tenor*
GUGLIELMO	*Baritone*
DON ALFONSO	*Basso buffo*
DESPINA	*Soprano*

1

C OSÌ *FAN TUTTE*,[1] which was first produced in Vienna on
the 26th January 1790, was the last but two of the operas
of Mozart's maturity: it had been preceded by *Idomeneo*
(1781), *The Seraglio* (1782), *Der Schauspieldirektor*
(1786), *Figaro* (1786) and *Don Giovanni* (1787), and was followed by *La Clemenza di Tito* and *The Magic Flute* (both 1791).
Its fate has been somewhat peculiar. It has been revived again and
again in the theatre in one form or another during the last century-
and-a-half, and invariably with the same result. People go away
remarking how charming most of it is, and wondering why it is not
given oftener; but after a few performances it again disappears
from the bill for another longish interval. Various theories have
been put forward to account for the work never having become a
real repertory piece. Some have blamed the subject itself, some
the treatment of it by the librettist, Da Ponte: a few, like Wagner,
have been frank enough to admit that the music is not always
Mozart at his best, and have excused him on the ground that even

[1] The original title in full was *Così fan tutte, o sia La Scuola degli Amanti*
(*They All Do It, or The School for Lovers*).

his consummate genius could not always grace a poor text with fine music. This, of course, is really to lay the blame once more on Da Ponte at a further remove. No one explanation, however, will cover all the facts of the case. The fault certainly is not wholly Da Ponte's. Many a composer, including Mozart himself, has written enduring music to an opera " book " no better in essentials than that of *Così fan tutte*. When due allowance has been made for Da Ponte's lapses, there still remains a certain amount of blame to be debited to the account of Mozart. It is just as well for us to recognise frankly that there were limits even to his genius — limits in part personal, rooted in his mentality and his temperament, in part due to the fact that music in general in the eighteenth century lacked the vocabulary and the apparatus for the expression of several things which it was reserved for a later epoch to encompass in opera.

Mozart seems to have received the commission for a new opera in the autumn of 1789 at the instance of the Emperor Joseph II himself, who, it is said, further suggested, as the subject, a story from real life that was amusing all Vienna at that time — the story of two gentlemen who, concealing their identity, had made love to their respective fiancées in other semblances, and had found the fair ones regrettably frail. It may have been so; but scholars hint vaguely at previous stage plays on much the same theme, and industrious research would probably establish the fact that the alleged incident in Vienna, if it ever happened, was merely one more instance of life imitating, or pretending to imitate, art.

In Da Ponte's libretto everything goes in pairs: equilibrating the two sisters and their lovers we have the old cynic who sets the action going and the maidservant who aids and abets him in all his devices. Though the librettist makes an occasional attempt to differentiate psychologically between Dorabella and Fiordiligi, and again between Ferrando and Guglielmo, he often handles each pair as a unity in itself; Mozart has necessarily to follow his lead in this, with the result that on several occasions he has to give up the attempt at individual characterisation and fall back on a generalised kind of musical utterance for each couple — a procedure in which he does not always manage to command our full interest.

No opera of Mozart's has been so persistently and so absurdly overwritten as *Così fan tutte;* and the overwriting has generally sprung from the curious passion of many biographers and critics for crediting Mozart with all kinds of psychological profundities and subtleties of the possession of which he himself was blissfully ignorant. The plot of the opera has been gravely censured for its " improbability and frivolity " — as if the Muse of Comedy were bound to go everywhere with John Stuart Mill's *System of Logic* under one arm and Law's *Serious Call to a Devout and Holy Life* under the other. If we are not to laugh at the improbable, what becomes of *Alice in Wonderland?* If the moralist in us is to frown on the frivolous, which of us can ever again book his seat for *L'Heure Espagnole* or *Die Fledermaus* without a sense of shame?

One odd feature of the *Così fan tutte* matter is that people who raise disapproving eyebrows at the " improbability " of the action are the same people who docilely accept the legend that it was derived from an actual contemporary occurrence, known to everyone in the theatre, in the very city in which the work was first produced! Some of the German commentators assure us, of course, that Mozart, as was his wont, raised this " sordid " comedy into the higher sphere of " universal humanity " by means of his music. The libretto, we are asked to believe, must have been distasteful to him in many respects, because it expected him to find amusement in an exposure of feminine frailty; Mozart's ideal being the Eternal Womanly, it must have gone terribly against the grain with him to associate himself with an irreverent jester of the type of Da Ponte, to whom, for the purposes of comedy, one woman was very like another, and women in general no better than they ought to be. Accordingly, we are given to understand, the divine element in Mozart rose in protest against the immorality of the plot, and this protest took the practical form of his writing serious music for more than one situation in which Da Ponte had seen only humour. Upon all which the only fitting comment is that if Mozart accepted with his eyes open a libretto designed by its author as a comedy, and intended to be listened to as a comedy, and then, because he disapproved of its ethics, deliberately " raised it into a higher sphere " by being serious where his job was to be funny, then Mozart was an ass. But Mozart was very far from being an ass; and if he sometimes fails, as we must frankly recognise, to strike the sure note of comedy in the music of his *Così fan tutte,* that is purely and simply for the reasons given above — that even a genius like his was unable to transcend either its personal limitations or those of the music of his epoch.

We may be sure that when, as sometimes happens in *Così fan tutte*, we find his sense of comedy in music not at its finest, or are unable to see much difference between an idiom which he apparently means to be comic and the idiom he employs elsewhere in connection with perfectly serious characters or situations, he was doing his musical best according to his lights and those of his epoch; and he would have been amazed, and probably annoyed, at the suggestion that he had allowed, even unconsciously, his dramatic sense of what was due to his subject to be over-ridden by "loftier" considerations. To regard his handling of Dorabella and Fiordiligi, Ferrando and Guglielmo as his special "contribution to the problem of sex" is to go beyond the limit of solemn absurdity permissible even to a German critic philosophising about Mozart. And even when one of these critics sensibly protests that it is unreasonable of us to play "the schoolmaster and moralist" towards Mozart, "the most sensuous of all German composers," he cannot refrain from adding that in forgetting sometimes the "idea of the whole" and losing himself in "the situation of the moment" — which is perfectly true — Mozart "forgot that he was making music for the impure souls of two seducers, who transform their loves into wenches (Dirnen)."

2

It is not to be wondered at that in a country predisposed to take this hyper-serious, not to say solemn, view of the nature of comedy, the most frantic attempts should have been made to rid the libretto of *Così fan tutte* of its " improbabilities " and purge it of its " frivolities." Da Ponte's story is of two army officers who, stung by the remark of their cynical friend Don Alfonso that all women are alike, consent to put their fiancées to the acid test. They depart, ostensibly, to join their regiment, but return disguised. Each of them now makes love to the fiancée of the other, with complete ultimate success, the ladies' servant, Despina, a minx who is obviously not a paragon of propriety herself, co-operating with Don Alfonso to throw the two couples together and break down the

27

women's resistance; finally, disguised as a notary, she celebrates a double mock-marriage between the re-shuffled pairs. Mozart had not been in his grave many years before the German theatre began to rationalise and moralise the action of the opera in its own virtuous way. In one version, some sort of exculpation was devised for the two erring ladies by making Don Alfonso a magician; not even the most eternally-feminine of women, of course, could be blamed for straying from the strait path of virtue when the ordinary wiles of male seduction are reinforced by necromancy. In this version Despina became Celerio, the ministering spirit of the magician doctor. In another version the ladies' fidelity is assailed not by the original pair of lovers in disguise but by two other characters created by the librettist solely for that purpose. Another arranger, also desperately anxious to prove that the sisters are not as black as Da Ponte has painted them, makes the servant betray the plot to them, so that in the final scene they are able to disconcert their peccant lovers by maintaining that their surrender was merely feigned. Another way of making the intrigue less offensive to " morality " was to have each of the ladies courted by her own lover in disguise, instead of by the lover of her sister; apparently the racy humour of the original version in this respect was far too frivolous for an ethically-minded German audience.

In most of these well-intentioned versions and perversions, Mozart's music, of course, was curtailed and mutilated in shocking fashion. In 1909 Karl Scheidemantel, a baritone famous in his own day, reverted to a plan that had been adopted in Paris a generation or so earlier. He scrapped Da Ponte entirely, concocting a new text of his own out of a play by Calderon, and adapting this as best he could to Mozart's score. The construction of the Spanish comedy enabled him to preserve, in the new milieu, the formal dualism that is so characteristic a feature of Da Ponte's text — once more we have two male and two female lovers, while Despina has her parallel in Dona Angela's maid Isabella, and Cosme, Don Manuel's servant, takes over the music of Mozart's Don Alfonso. The action, of course, is transferred to Spain, and the period is the mid-sixteenth century. Scheidemantel's version, which, under the title of *Die Dame Kobold*, was produced for the first time in Dresden on the 6th June 1909, had a certain success; but his libretto is of a naïveté that makes Da Ponte's text, flimsy as it is, seem in comparison almost oppressively intellectual. The final result of all these attempts to revive Così fan tutte by murdering it has been to convince the modern world that, with all its little faults, the opera is best given today as Da Ponte wrote it, or as near thereto as may be possible.

The parts of the sisters Dorabella and Fiordiligi, who are described in the opera as " two ladies from Ferrara," derived an additional mild piquancy for the Vienna audience of 1790 from the fact that Luisa Villeneuve, who played Dorabella, was the sister of Adriana Gabrielli del Bene, who played Fiordiligi, the latter lady being professionally known as Ferrarese Del Bene, or Ferrarese for short. She was notorious for her gallantries, and at the time when Così fan tutte was produced she was the mistress of Da Ponte. It was more or less for this reason, one surmises, that she was entrusted with the part of Fiordiligi, for she was not popular, either in the opera house or in Vienna society; she received, indeed, a Court order to leave the town in 1791. Da Ponte, who devised for her the soprano parts in three or four other operas, could not, in his Memoirs, find her beautiful, even in distant retrospect: but he speaks of the charm of her voice and of her exceptional talent. Mozart, however, does not seem to have had an equally high opinion of her; writing to his wife in April 1789 he says that a new singer of the name of Allegrante is much better than the Ferrarese, " though that isn't saying much." It was for the latter that he had added to the score of Figaro the coloratura aria " Al desio di chi t'adora" when the opera was revived in Vienna in 1789 with the Ferrarese as Susanna.[2] The music of Fiordiligi indicates that the Ferrarese's voice, besides boasting considerable flexibility, was of unusual range: in one of her arias in Così fan tutte Mozart takes her from the A below the stave to the B flat above it; and it is evident that the high C was also in her voice. How Mozart made use in Così fan tutte of the lady's vocal range for the purposes of rough-and-ready comedy will appear later.

[2] The brilliant coloratura and the general character of the aria, which are inconsistent, of course, with the mentality of Susanna, are explained by the fact that in the scene for which this aria was planned the Countess and her maid are each impersonating the other. For the Ferrarese as Susanna Mozart wrote also the arietta " Un moto di gioja mi sento in petto." These two pieces are printed as supplements in some scores of Figaro.

3

The overture employs only one theme from the opera itself. This is the actual " Così fan tutte " as sung by Don Alfonso and the two lovers towards the end of the second act:

In the overture it comes at the end of the brief *andante* introduction, which runs to no more than fourteen bars. This is followed by one of those gay quick movements that bubbled so spontaneously from Mozart: noticeable in it are passages of lively orchestral give-and-take of this type:

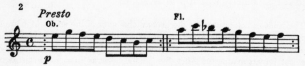

and this, which is always sandwiched between crashing orchestral tuttis:

Near the end the " Così fan tutte " motive returns.

The opera opens with a lively argument about the constancy of women between Don Alfonso, Ferrando and Guglielmo in a café in Naples. When the curtain rises the dispute has evidently been going on for some time, for the first thing we hear is Ferrando denying vehemently everything that the man-of-the-world Alfonso has been saying. His Dorabella is as good as she is beautiful, he maintains; and Guglielmo at once swears that that goes, so to speak, for his Fiordiligi also. Alfonso, for his part, is not going to be browbeaten by a couple of young greenhorns out of an opinion that is the product of a lifetime of experience. Woman's fidelity, he says, resembles the phoenix — everyone says it exists, but no one knows where to look for it. Swords come near being drawn; but in the end they agree to have a bet of a hundred sequins on the matter. The terms are agreed upon: for the next twenty-four hours the young officers are to do everything Alfonso tells them, but they are not to breathe a word about it all to " their Penelopes," as he cynically calls them. Already the lovers have decided how they will spend the money when they have won it: Ferrando will lay it out on a serenade for Dorabella, while Guglielmo will give " a dinner in honour of Cytherea" to which the discomforted Alfonso will be generously invited. They all raise their glasses on it. The music to the scene centres round a sequence of three trios, each of them striking a different vein of pure musical comedy.

The scene changes to the garden of the house, overlooking the Bay of Naples, of the two sisters who have been the unwitting cause of the dispute. Each has in her hand a medallion of her lover, which she is contemplating in sentimental rapture. They draw each other's attention to the many charms of the portraits: is there anything on earth to compare, for example, with Guglielmo's beautiful mouth or Ferrando's flame-throwing eyes? The comedy is mainly in the words and the miming, for the exquisite music would for the most part go with any of Mozart's serious operatic situations: from the opening bars of the orchestral prelude, with its clarinets in thirds softly cooing over string harmonies that rise and fall as gently as the Mediterranean itself in its most placid moments:

we are in the very land of romance. When the sisters sing together it is more often than not in thirds and sixths. Here and there is a touch of broad comedy, as when the women sigh their sentimental souls out in a cadenza in thirds on the word " amore."

They are behaving in a very kittenish kind of way, looking forward to speedy matrimony and wondering why their lovers are so late, when Don Alfonso enters in a great hurry. To an orchestral accompaniment that imitates his pantings for breath he pours out his agitated story. The ladies must steel themselves to receive bad news. The worst that could have happened to Ferrando and Guglielmo has happened — they have been ordered to join their regiment for active service. The officers follow almost on his heels. They are hardly able to speak for emotion, and the ladies are duly sympathetic, even going so far as to express a wish that their lovers will plunge their swords into their faithful, sorrowing hearts. The young men delightedly call Alfonso's attention to this striking proof of feminine fidelity; but he merely ejaculates " Finem lauda! " The voices then unite in a quintet on the subject of the shocking trials that destiny imposes on the hopes of poor humanity — a quintet of finely varied expression, sometimes obviously comic, sometimes coming as near entire seriousness as makes no matter. The little duet between Ferrando and Guglielmo that follows, in which they express the hope that soon they will be restored to their ladies, is hardly worthy of Da Ponte and not at all worthy of Mozart. It is therefore generally omitted in performance.

At the conclusion of the quintet, then, we hear a stirring drum-roll " off." It is the summons to depart for the wars. A ship has arrived at the foot of the garden: a regiment marches across the stage to embark, and the townspeople run to cheer the soldiers, singing a charming little chorus in praise of the military life, which is all pipes and trumpets and guns and glory. The music here is of a type that only Mozart has ever been able to achieve: it is completely unlike anything that could have been anticipated from the situation and the text, yet in some unexplainable way infallibly right.

Dorabella and Fiordiligi are in tears, and their lovers seemingly not in much better condition, now that the time has come to say farewell. One of the many difficulties in connection with the score of *Così fan tutte* is that of deciding whether Mozart is serious or not at this moment or that. His humour in its broader aspects, of course, admits of no misunderstanding; but in these aspects neither his humour nor the musical means by which he expresses it are invariably above criticism. At times both his humour and his wit are of the finest kind. There are times also when we can only say to him frankly, " Master, if you are asking us to believe that these are the accents of comedy, please tell us in what lines and colours you would paint a serious situation." The quintet that follows the first chorus of the townspeople is a case in point. On the stage the situation can always be counted on to extract a laugh from the audience; but the lovely music, in and by itself, breathes, surely, the very pathos of parting. These, we feel compelled to say as we listen, are not the wire-worked puppets of the preceding comic scenes, jerked this way and that by librettist and composer to wring an easy laugh out of us: if we listen to the music alone they are human beings touched to the heart by the pain of farewell. But Mozart's perfect tact enables him to work even Don Alfonso into this expression of truly romantic feeling without the smallest suspicion of incongruity: the cynic's dry laughter never strikes a jarring note.

After the boat has gone we get a trio in which the two ladies and Don Alfonso pray for gentle winds and a calm sea for the voyagers: and once again we feel that, so far as the music is concerned, we have left far behind us the atmosphere of broad comedy in which some of the preceding episodes have been set.

The ladies having left, Don Alfonso has a recitative and aria in which he expounds to his own satisfaction his philosophy of women — the man who puts his trust in them is ploughing the sea and sowing in the sand.

The scene changes to a room in the sisters' house. Their maid Despina enters: she is one of the stock figures of the older comedy, clever, self-assured, impudent and likable, the female counterpart of the valet who has more brains than his master and knows how to express his contempt for him without overstepping the bounds of prudence and decorum. She introduces herself with a tirade against domestic service, and samples the mid-day chocolate she has prepared for her mistresses. When Fiordiligi and Dorabella come in we are once more in the field of frank farce. Da Ponte lays on the colours with the heaviest brush he can find, and there is nothing for the composer to do but to follow him. The ladies indulge in the most exaggerated protestations of grief at the departure of their lovers. They rave about the Eumenides; they demand dagger and poison; they order Despina to close the windows, for light and air are hateful to them now.

Mozart gives Dorabella a recitative and aria in the grand style: much of the music we should take quite seriously did we not know that we are meant to be amused at the contradiction between these grand-opera heroics and the absurd figure that is enacting a farce in full view of us. It has often been remarked that not a single aria from *Così fan tutte* has established itself really firmly in the concert room, as arias from so many other Mozart operas have done. It is safe to say that were this fine aria of Dorabella's — " Smanie implacabili," with its recitative, " Ah, scostati! " sung at a concert today by a competent dramatic soprano who had no idea whence the thing came, and so had no suspicion that in its original environment it was sung by a comic character, an audience also ignorant of the Italian language, and therefore of the occasional rant in the text, would listen to it all with complete gravity.

Despina evidently does not take this outburst seriously. Her

advice to the languishing ladies is that instead of dedicating themselves to a life of misery until their lovers return they should take
advantage of their absence to have a good time — as the men are
doing, no doubt, in camp. Her philosophy, which she sets forth in
an aria " In uomini, in soldati," is the feminine equivalent of that
of Don Alfonso — men were deceivers ever, and should be paid
back in their own coin. She is still preaching this doctrine when the
indignant Fiordiligi and Dorabella flounce out of the room in a
state which a Victorian lady in a similar situation would have described as high dudgeon.

Don Alfonso now enters, and, having bribed Despina to help
him in his plans, introduces Ferrando and Guglielmo disguised as
gentlemen from Albania, sporting the national costume and their
false beards with grotesque exaggeration. Despina is most disre-
spectfully amused by the sight of them; but the men console themselves with the reflection that if *she* does not recognise them her
mistresses are not likely to do so. As the ladies are heard approaching, Despina pushes Don Alfonso into a place of hiding. Fiordiligi
and Dorabella are of course very angry with their maid for allowing these two strangers into the house, and still angrier when the
strangers begin to make love to them. In due course Don Alfonso
makes a formal entry and asks what all the fuss is about. " Just
look!" says Dorabella; " men in our house! " Alfonso is surprised,
when his attention is thus drawn to the Albanians, to find that they
are old and valued friends of his whom he is delighted to see again.
Ferrando and Guglielmo play up as they are told to do, making
love to the ladies in terms of the wildest hyperbole.

Dorabella having had her big aria a little while before, it is now
Fiordiligi's turn. She rounds on the two men in a recitative of the
approved high-dramatic type, bidding them depart and not profane this chaste abode with their infamous words: no power on
earth can make them unfaithful to the men they love. The recitative is followed by the famous aria " Come scoglio " (" Like a rock
stands my heart, unmoved by wind or sea "). The aria is burlesque
of the broadest kind, and at the same time a coloratura piece for
the glory of the singer. In the theatre we laugh at the great leaps
the voice has to take now and then — in the opening bars, for instance:

and again later:

The wit of this is not precisely of the finest, and one sometimes wonders to what extent Mozart was deliberately guying not only Fiordiligi but the first singer of the part. Everybody who has heard one of these female voices with an exceptional range knows how difficult it is, even when the voice and the art behind it are both first-rate, to repress a smile at some of the sudden changes from soprano to contralto and back again. As we have seen, Mozart was not particularly fond of the Ferrarese; and it is fairly probable that while flattering her vanity by providing her with the kind of vocal line that would enable her to display the particular virtuosity on which she prided herself, he slyly raised a horse-laugh in the theatre at her expense. Be that as it may, the aria is the broadest of musical farce.

Guglielmo ripostes with one of the most charming numbers of the score, the little aria " Non siate ritrosi ":

which is as fine-fingered, in both the vocal and the orchestral part, as "Come scoglio" is thick-thumbed. But Guglielmo's appeal to the ladies to be kind to two such fine young fellows as these new lovers of theirs has no effect on Fiordiligi and Dorabella, who go out with their heads in the air even before Guglielmo has finished his song. He and Ferrando throw themselves into chairs and have a hearty laugh at the expense of Don Alfonso, whom they imagine to have as good as lost his bet already. They offer to let him off with twenty-five sequins. He laughs at them in turn for their juvenile simplicity, and reminds them that they are still under his orders. With that he leaves them.

One of the defects of the construction of the libretto of *Così fan tutte* is its very symmetry. Everything goes in pairs, and whatever is entered at one moment on one side of the account must be balanced by an entry a little later on the other side. The baritone having had *his* aria, operatic justice insists that the tenor shall have his. Accordingly we now have Ferrando immobilising the action in order that he may sing a long aria — "Un' aura amorosa" — setting forth the regulation operatic thesis that a breath of affection from the one we love restores the heart of the lover, an admirable sentiment, no doubt, but perhaps one that does not bear repetition quite so many times as Ferrando and Mozart seem to think. Following Otto Jahn, it is the custom to regard this rather sickly-sentimental aria as a particularly delicate piece of witty characterisation on Mozart's part. We might perhaps be inclined to grant that contention, even against our critical judgment, if the aria were not so excessively long, and, if the truth must be told, sometimes not merely conventional but commonplace. There were occasions when even Mozart's almost infinitely adaptable genius could not find anything vital to put into the mouth of a character in whom he himself, seemingly, found it a little difficult to believe.

The exit of Ferrando and Guglielmo is succeeded by a dialogue between Alfonso and Despina, in which the plan for the undermining of the constancy of the latter's mistresses is further elaborated. Then the scene changes to the garden of the house, where, in the loveliest surroundings of land, sea and sky, the ladies are indulging themselves in romantic reflections upon life with its fleeting joys. Here we say good-bye to burlesque once more: the music is Mozart at his most enchanting. The sisters have barely

finished their duet when Ferrando and Guglielmo rush in, followed by Alfonso. Each of the lovers has in his hand a bottle containing, we are soon given to understand, arsenic. They swallow
the poison, and the place is soon in an uproar. It is supposed to be
a particularly humorous touch on Mozart's part to make the sisters
say "Heavens! it was poison?" in the most casual way imaginable.
But perhaps this is just another instance of our reading into Mozart's scores significances and subtleties of which he himself was
quite unconscious. This little ejaculation of Fiordiligi and Dorabella amounts to no more than five words in the flood of words that
is being poured out. Mozart is fully set for his grand ensemble;
and it is impossible for him to interrupt the continuity of the orchestral line merely to make Fiordiligi and Dorabella say their
five words in a more emphatic or more pseudo-tragic way. He just
lets the words flow with the stream and leaves it at that. It was not,
indeed, the first occasion on which he had acted in that very way
in his operas, putting a musical sentence of the most matter-of-fact
kind into the mouth of some character or other in the course of an
ensemble the totality of which was of far more importance to him,
and to his audience, than this or that part. It may be praiseworthy
piety, but it is hardly sound criticism, to try to persuade ourselves
that even Mozart's occasional little lapses are not really lapses at
all but subtleties beyond the range of any other composer — making him an accredited wit who, as Sydney Smith said of himself,
has only to ask someone to pass the salt to set the table in a roar.

Mozart is always happy when he can get the action moving and
let the players toss the ball from one to another in quick succession;
and he is at the top of his form in this long ensemble. The fun is
fast and furious, notwithstanding the fact that every now and then
the comic posturings and sentimentalisings are expressed in what
would be in any other Mozartian situation a musical language of
undoubted seriousness. Despina and Alfonso go off to fetch a doctor. While they are away the ladies, in spite of themselves, begin to
find the unhappy suicides rather interesting. The music takes on a
new character when Alfonso returns with Despina, the latter
amusingly transformed into a doctor of what was in 1790, no doubt,
the most advanced kind, one who put into practice the latest scientific discovery — the "mesmerism" that took its name from that
same Dr. Mesmer whom Mozart himself had known as a child.

After a lot of delightful nonsense in the best vein of medical pomposity the physician applies the infallible cure — a big magnet which makes the suicides heave and writhe to the accompaniment of similarly descriptive writhings in the orchestra, but which eventually restores them to life.

They raise their heads, and, naturally a bit weak at first, after all they have been through in the way of poison and antidote, try to take their bearings. Their first thought, it appears, is that they have died and wakened up in some paradise or other. Is this Pallas they see before them, they ask, or perhaps Cytherea? No, on closer inspection they turn out to be the beauteous ladies for whom they had wanted to die. They beg for a kiss; but though the doctor recommends the treatment on medical grounds, and is backed by Don Alfonso, the sisters mount their high horse again at this bold suggestion, and the curtain comes down on another big ensemble into which Mozart puts all he knows in the way of opera buffa excitement. While the ladies are protesting volubly that, poison or no poison, the strangers have no right to be so "forward," Mozart seems to remember that it is some time since he gave the Ferrarese an opportunity to make a bit of a donkey of herself with her stunt of a shift from soprano to contralto and back again. He accordingly lets her play fast and loose with the general texture of the sextet with a couple of passages of this sort:

We cannot help laughing, nor does it matter very much whether it is at Fiordiligi or the singer of the part.

4

Da Ponte's invention was always better in the first half of an opera than in the second, and in *Così fan tutte* he runs true to form in this respect. The mechanical symmetry of the characters, for one thing — two women and two lovers who have at one and the same time to run in pairs and be to some extent individualised, plus two intriguers of whom much the same is true — begins, in the second act, to hinder not only his own freedom of movement but Mozart's.

At the commencement of the second act, which opens in a room in the sisters' house, we have Despina once more telling her mistresses how silly they are to refuse a good thing when it comes their way; even a girl of fifteen, she assures them in a long aria of the sprightly buffa type, ought to know by instinct how to flirt and not be caught. Left to themselves, the sisters begin to wonder whether, after all, Despina may not be right. They decide that there can be no harm in amusing themselves with these two attractive strangers, so long as they are careful. Dorabella chooses the dark one (Guglielmo), because he is so merry; Fiordiligi's preference is for the blond. They settle this important question of the division of the spoils in a charming duet:

9 *Andante*

Pren-de - rò quel bru - net - ti - no,

Don Alfonso enters hurriedly, bidding them come down at once to the garden, where they will see and hear something worth their while.[3] They do so, and find the two new lovers there in a boat, with a number of singers and players of instruments. Ferrando and Guglielmo sing in duet a short serenade to the ladies. The orchestral colouring of this (flutes, clarinets, bassoons and horns) has a strongly rustic tang:

10 *Andante*

it suggests the divertimenti which eighteenth century composers were so fond of writing for some local occasion or other. Perhaps

[3] In one of the silliest of the many silly attempts to improve on Da Ponte — that of Eduard Devrient, made for the Karlsruhe theatre in 1860, and the textbook of which is still sold in Germany — a scene is interpolated here in which Despina, suddenly succumbing to an attack of virtue, discloses to Fiordiligi and Dorabella that the " Albanians " are their own actual lovers, and that the whole thing has been from the beginning a scheme on Don Alfonso's part to test their fidelity. From this point to the end of the opera, therefore, the ladies are only pretending to be duped! Thus was virtue triumphant, vice vanquished in the German operatic world of the latter half of the nineteenth century.

what was in Mozart's mind at this point of the opera was to suggest something which, if not authentically "Albanian," would stand out from the rest of the score as "foreign."

As there is at first a certain shyness on both sides, Alfonso and Despina give the two couples a lesson in the art of wooing and coyly accepting. Then they leave them together, remarking *sotto voce*, as they go, that if the ladies don't succumb now they must be superhuman. The lovers begin the great assault. After a little while Ferrando and Fiordiligi disappear, and Guglielmo takes up the attack on Dorabella in earnest. In spite of her putting up a fairly good resistance he has little trouble in hanging round her neck a heart that is meant to be symbolical of his respectful but ardent affection, while her own necklace, with the miniature of Ferrando attached to it, he removes from her neck to his, murmuring as he does so, " Poor Ferrando! I wouldn't have believed it! " The little duet strikes the happy medium between comedy and sentimental seriousness:

11   *Andante*

Il co-re vi do-no, bell' i - do - lo mi-o,

especially delightful are the realistic touches when a reference comes in the text to the pit-a-pat of their hearts.

The pair then pass down an avenue, their place on the stage being taken by Ferrando and Fiordiligi. Fiordiligi has been putting up a better fight than her sister. At once we are in the domain of farce again: she rants about his having behaved like "a snake, a hydra, a basilisk." She begs to be left alone: Ferrando at once obliges — or almost at once, for of course he has to stay long enough to sing an elaborate aria in which he fluctuates between confidence as to his ultimate victory and doubts about it:

12   *Allegretto*

Ah! io veg - gio, quell'a - ni-ma bel - la

When at last Fiordiligi really is alone she launches out into a detailed exposition of her state of mind. She is on " fire," it seems, but no longer with the fire of "virtuous love": "frenzy, grief, remorse, repentance, levity, perfidy, betrayal" are contending for mastery within her breast. All this in a highly dramatic recitative, with appropriate effects in the orchestra. The aria that follows is one with which even the Ferrarese must have been satisfied, so many opportunities does it give Fiordiligi to play the high-stepping opera heroine and at the same time display her vocal range and her coloratura technique. The aria is a rondo with a good deal of obbligato work for the horns: it commences with a pseudo-pathetic *adagio*:

which is succeeded by an imposing *allegro*:

When she has trilled her way off the stage, Ferrando and Guglielmo meet to report progress. Ferrando is sincerely delighted to be able to give his friend so comforting an account of Fiordiligi's resistance. Guglielmo, on the other hand, finds it far from easy to tell Ferrando all that has happened between himself and Dorabella, but cannot refrain from showing him the miniature. Thereupon Ferrando comes as near seeing red as is possible to a light tenor in an opera buffa. At first he talks about tearing the faithless one's heart out; but very soon he is asking his friend's advice as to what he ought to do. Perhaps Guglielmo's success has slightly turned his head; anyhow we find him now apostrophising women in a genuine opera buffa aria the thesis of which is the favourite one of Don Alfonso — that the sex is frail and cannot be trusted.

But Ferrando is not to be consoled in that way; and as he is entitled to an aria of his own after that of Guglielmo, he lets us know
at proper length that in spite of Dorabella's treatment of him she
still possesses his too fond heart. He is not at all consoled by Don
Alfonso's admission later that he has lost half his bet, for one of the
ladies at least has been faithful to her lover. And the old philosopher proposes yet another experiment, which will prove even to
the cock-a-whoop Guglielmo that it is foolish to count your chick-
ens before they are hatched.

The next scene is set in a room in the ladies' house. Despina congratulates Dorabella on having at last behaved like a sensible
woman; while Dorabella's excuses for her recent conduct run on
much the same lines as those of Polly Peachum in *The Beggar's
Opera:*

> *But he so teaz'd me,*
> *And he so pleas'd me,*
> *What I did, you must have done.*

When Fiordiligi enters she is obviously not in the best of tempers;
apparently while disapproving of her sister's capacity for fickle-
ness she cannot help envying it. Dorabella, in yet another aria,
which is so uninteresting that it is generally omitted, argues with
her very much as Despina herself might do.

Fiordiligi, when she is alone, thinks the matter over. A brilliant
idea strikes her: she rings for Despina and orders her to bring from
the wardrobe two uniforms of Ferrando and Guglielmo respectively. (It is a sign of the helplessness that Da Ponte was by now
beginning to feel with regard to the untying of his knots that he
should not make the slightest attempt to explain to us how these
uniforms come to be where they are. At this stage of a long libretto
almost anything was good enough for Da Ponte, who, as a dramatist, was first-rate at the hundred-and-twenty yards, so to speak,
but lacked the wind for the mile). Fiordiligi, we are given to understand, has arrived at the desperate conclusion that the only way
for the sisters to preserve their innocence is to don these uniforms
and go to the seat of war themselves, she in Ferrando's, Dorabella
in Guglielmo's, there to rejoin their legitimate lovers as soldiers
and die by their sides if necessary. She is regaling herself with the
thought of a reunion with her lover under these romantic condi-

tions when Ferrando himself, who has been watching the proceedings through the open door, comes in, still in the guise of an Albanian, and entreats her not to make him die of despair: if he really must perish, let it be by the sword she has in her hand. The struggle within Fiordiligi does not last long this time. " Yield, dearest! " cries Ferrando; and Fiordiligi sinks into a chair with no more than a feeble " Dei, consiglio! " Ferrando swears eternal fidelity to her, as lover, then as spouse; she falls on his breast, completely vanquished, and they go out of the room in an embrace that is not at all to the liking of Guglielmo, who, with Alfonso, has been watching it all from outside the door.

Alfonso has hard work to restrain Guglielmo, who, forgetting his own complacency when, a little while before, he had won over Dorabella, goes into something like the male equivalent of hysterics at the perfidy of his Fiordiligi. When Ferrando returns, looking most objectionably pleased with himself at having turned the tables on his friend, there is a moment or two of slight unpleasantness: then they both listen to the sage counsel of Don Alfonso. What are they making such a fuss about? he asks them. True, they could easily find any number of women to take the place of a Dorabella and a Fiordiligi. But will the others behave any better than these have done? If not, what's the use of changing? They still love the frail ones, don't they? Very well, let them take them as they are, for they cannot be otherwise; and meanwhile let the young men listen to a little song he will sing them. The burden of it is: " Everyone speaks ill of women, and I'm not surprised. If they change their lovers a thousand times a day, well, some people may call it a vice, others a habit, but in my view it is a necessity for them. If a lover is tricked he should blame not the lady but himself; for young or old, pretty or plain — come now, repeat it with me — they all do it! " And the young men dutifully repeat it with him, to the strain of No. 1.

But the joke is not yet played out, the imbroglio not yet cleared up. The ladies having consented to marry the fascinating strangers and to migrate to Albania with them, we next find ourselves watching the servants preparing the table for the wedding feast, under the supervision of Don Alfonso and Despina. Soon the betrothed couples come in, followed by a numerous company who sing a chorus of congratulations and good wishes. The two pairs of lovers unite in a quartet in which they thank the good Despina as the first cause of all their happiness; and the chorus having departed, the happy couples drink to themselves and to each other. Fiordiligi starts a melody which Ferrando and Dorabella take up in turn in a charming canon: Guglielmo, however, who has still not recovered from the shock of Fiordiligi's infidelity, only mutters in his beard a wish that what the others are drinking may poison them.

Don Alfonso had left with the chorus. He now returns with the notary, who, needless to say, is Despina in yet another of her disguises. The notary reads out in a professional nasal voice the contract of marriage between Sempronio and Fiordiligi and between Tizio and Dorabella — between, in fact, as he puts it, " these noble Albanians and these Ferrarese ladies "; the latter point was one which the Vienna audience of 1790 would not be likely to miss. He is just launching into the subject of dowries and settlements when the four of them declare that they will leave it all to him, and clamour for the contract and a pen. But the two ladies have no sooner signed than a distant drum roll is heard, followed by the " military " chorus from the first act. The sisters are terrified. Don Alfonso runs to the window, looks out, and confirms their worst fears — the regiment has indeed returned, and Ferrando and Guglielmo with it.

The agitated brides push their Albanian spouses into an adjoining room, wondering what is going to happen to themselves now, and putting up a prayer to heaven for help. Heaven does not answer them, but Don Alfonso does: they have only to leave it to him and all will be well. The lovers, meanwhile, who have slipped out of the room into which they were bundled, re-enter by the main door, not as the Albanians, of course, but as Ferrando and Guglielmo. The King, it seems, has countermanded the order to the regiment, so here they are again, safe and sound, and happy to be once more with their loving and faithful fiancées. But why are the ladies so pale, so speechless? they ask. Because, says the gallant and resourceful Don Alfonso, they are paralysed with pleasure at seeing their dear ones again.

The remaining heads of the intrigue are soon untied. Guglielmo, under the excuse of depositing his knapsack in the next room, opens the door and discovers a man hiding there — a notary! What is the meaning of this? Despina explains that it is no notary, but she herself, changing her costume after having been to a fancy dress ball. The ladies are a bit puzzled by this, but at the same time relieved. But they are dumbfounded when Ferrando picks up and reads the marriage contract, which Don Alfonso has rather ostentatiously dropped in front of him. The lovers bitterly upbraid Fiordiligi and Dorabella, who are now thoroughly beaten: they can only confess their fault and beg to be slain there and then. Their last faint hope is that Don Alfonso will do something for them. But apparently the traitor is against them, for he suggests to the lovers that they shall take a look in the next room, where they will find the proof they want of their fiancées' infidelity. They do so, and return once more in Albanian guise. Guglielmo hands over to Dorabella the miniature she had given him; and he and Ferrando praise "the magnetic doctor" who had been so clever.

The game is entirely up so far as Fiordiligi and Dorabella are concerned. They throw the blame for their lapse, of course, on Don Alfonso, who takes it in quite good part. It is true he has fooled them, he says, but it was for the education of their lovers, who will be wiser in future. He advises them to make it up and forget it all: he has had his laugh, let them now have theirs. "You are betrothed," he tells them: "now embrace and say no more about it." This they do. But do the couples now pair off as they were at the beginning of the opera, or as we found them at the signing of the marriage contract? We are not told: perhaps Da Ponte and Mozart themselves did not know and did not care. The lively finale ends with an ensemble to the text of "Happy is the man who takes everything as it comes, and in all the vicissitudes of life lets himself be guided by reason; who laughs when others weep, and remains unmoved when the whirlwind blows."

The Marriage of Figaro

WOLFGANG AMADEUS MOZART [1756–1791]

PRINCIPAL CHARACTERS

FIGARO	*Bass*
COUNT ALMAVIVA	*Baritone*
COUNTESS ALMAVIVA	*Soprano*
SUSANNA	*Soprano*
CHERUBINO	*Soprano*
DOCTOR BARTOLO	*Bass*
MARCELLINA	*Soprano*
DON CURZIO	*Tenor*
DON BASILIO	*Tenor*
ANTONIO	*Bass*
BARBARINA	*Mezzo-soprano*

1

OR some years after the production of *The Seraglio* (in July 1782) Mozart, so far as opera was concerned, could make no headway in Vienna. The Austrian empire of those days was a far-spread conglomerate of states and races, and Vienna was the meeting place of them all, the one town in which fame could be won and money made. The taste of the Court and most of the public being mainly for the facile, sparkling Italian opera, the town was overrun by Italian adventurers of all sorts. Mozart himself, though he would have preferred to do something in the German opera line, had in the end to swim with the current or go under. "Every nation has its own opera," he wrote to his father on the 5th February 1783; "why then should we Germans not have ours? Is not the German language as singable as the French or the English, and more so than the Russian? I am engaged now on a German opera on my own account.[1] I have chosen a comedy by Goldoni, *Il Servitore di Due Padroni*, and the text of the first act has already been translated by Baron Binder. All this is a secret, however, for the present."

But this plan came to nothing, and the struggling German opera in Vienna steadily went from bad to worse: not only were the native composers mostly second-raters but the Italian performances had a skill and a polish with which the Germans could hardly compete. In March of that same year the German company was disbanded, the best of the singers being absorbed into the Italian troupe that had been formed by command of the Emperor. Mozart was reduced to composing "numbers" for insertion in works by composers such as Anfossi and Bianchi to keep himself before the operatic public. By the spring of 1783, being bent on writing an Italian opera, he asked his father to get in touch with the Salzburg Abbé Varesco—who had made the *Idomeneo* text for him in 1780—and find out if he could be induced to co-operate with him again. He would like a libretto with seven characters, he said, among them two soprano parts of equal importance, the one "seria," the other "mezzo carattere"; a third soprano and, if necessary, all the men, were to be "entirely buffa."

In June 1783 he was in Salzburg, where he found that Varesco had prepared for him an involved and rather ponderously humorous libretto entitled *L'Oca del Cairo*, in which a goose with a human being concealed inside it played an important part. Mozart's views on libretto writing in general and his present collaborator in particular are expressed in a letter to his father of the 21st June. Varesco seems to have been attributing an exaggerated importance to his own share in the work, and Mozart had to tell him very frankly, through Leopold, that in an opera it is not the text but the music that mostly decides success or failure. Moreover Varesco would have to make whatever and as many alterations as he, Mozart, might demand, for the Abbé's own stage sense could not be trusted. Mozart got as far as writing eight musical numbers for the first act of the Varesco text, but eventually lost interest in it and let the plan drop. He still kept edging himself into the Vienna theatre whenever he got the chance by means of ad-

[1] i.e. without a commission from any theatre.

48

ditions to other composers' operas. But he was evidently getting rather desperate: "I have looked through a good hundred libretti, and probably more," he had written to Leopold on the 17th May 1783, "and have come upon hardly one that appeals to me." They would have to be altered a good deal, and no doubt the poet who would consent to do this would find it easier to write an entirely new text. Then he mentions "a certain Abbé Da Ponte" who seems to be coming to the fore in Viennese operatic circles. At the moment he is writing a libretto (*Il Ricco d'un Giorno*) for Salieri; this will take him about two months, and then he will do something for Mozart. But Wolfgang does not put much faith in the Abbé's promises: "you know as well as I do how pleasant these Italians can be to your face," he says. It is probable, however, that the shrewd Da Ponte was already quite as much interested in Mozart as the latter was in him.

2

This "Abbé Da Ponte" was an Italian Jew, originally of the name of Emanuele Conegliano, who had come into the world on the 10th March 1749 at Ceneda, a small town near Venice. His quickness of apprehension as a boy attracted the attention of a certain Bishop Lorenzo Da Ponte, who not only provided for his education and baptised him but permitted him to assume his own name. Having been admitted into the lower priestly order the young man became the Abbé Da Ponte, by which engaging title he chose to be known for the remainder of his life. After various wanderings he settled in Vienna in 1781, where he became the protégé of Salieri, and, through him, of the Emperor Joseph II. He was less in favour with Joseph's brother, who succeeded him, as Leopold II, in 1790, and soon his wanderings began again. He ended his days on the 17th August 1838 in the United States. His *Memoirs*, in which, with characteristic self-esteem, he tells us rather too much about himself and far too little about Mozart, had appeared in New York in 1823.

In Vienna he had soon wormed his way into influential circles, having all the qualities of self-assertion and capacity for intrigue that were necessary to keep one's head above water in the turbulent sea of Italian literary and musical life in the capital at that time. But he had also certain qualifications as a librettist which his competitors did not possess in anything like the same degree —comparatively little originality of invention, it is true, but a decided gift for adapting the work of more creative minds than his own to dramatic and musical ends, and a verbal dexterity that generally improved, for practical operatic purposes, on whatever he had appropriated. Mozart certainly owed a good deal to him in the long run.

In the summer and autumn of 1783 Mozart had worked for a time at an opera buffa with the title of *Lo Sposo Deluso*, of which he finished or sketched only the overture, a quartet, a trio, and a couple of arias. In July of the preceding year he had written to his father that an Italian librettist had shown him a text which he might accept if it were altered to his liking. It is conjectured that this librettist was Da Ponte and the work *Lo Sposo Deluso;* and though proof of this is lacking, it seems probable. There is evidence in plenty that he was merciless in his demands on his poets. His letters to his father are highly illuminative on this point: we seem to be reading the story of Puccini and his poets again when we see how imperiously Mozart insisted on dictating the handling of an action and the details of a text; his sense of the stage was evidently keener than that of the majority of opera composers. There must have been times when Varesco in particular felt like a toad under the harrow; and we may take it for granted that Mozart was equally exacting with Da Ponte, though contemporary records of their collaboration are necessarily lacking, as the pair did not correspond but simply talked together.

In all these years the only commission Mozart received was for a "festival" in honour of the Governor-General of the Netherlands. To a text by Stephanie the Younger (who had provided the libretto of *The Seraglio*) he wrote the short *Der Schauspieldirektor* (*The Impresario*), which was produced in the orangery at Schönbrunn on the 7th February 1786 and repeated on the 18th and 25th.

3

Meanwhile, however, he and Da Ponte had been drawing closer together. The latter's recent works had not all been successful, which naturally led to recriminations between him and his composers, each laying the blame on the other. It ended with his quarrelling with Salieri—without, however, losing the support of the Emperor, which was much more important. By this time Mozart, for all his longing to write a German opera, had realised that the only passport to the patronage of the Court and the favour of the public was an Italian opera buffa; Da Ponte, for his part, seems to have been well aware that as a composer Mozart stood head and shoulders above his competitors. A collaboration, therefore, would be to their mutual advantage; as to a new production, Da Ponte thought he would have influence enough with the Emperor for that.

The idea of an opera based on Beaumarchais's *Le Mariage de Figaro* seems to have been in the first place Mozart's; but Da Ponte must have seen at once the scope it offered for the display of his own talents. Beaumarchais alleged that his second Figaro comedy was written not long after the first, but that statement is not taken too seriously by his biographers. Certainly it was not produced in Paris until some nine years after *The Barber of Seville* —on the 27th April 1784. It is one of the commonplaces of literary history that the new work played a not inconsiderable part in producing the ferment of ideas that culminated in the Revolution of some five years later. Certainly the unfortunate Louis XVI was quick to perceive the danger to the old régime inherent in this unflattering picture of a grandee with none of the virtues and all the vices of his order being persistently put in the wrong dialectically and outmanœuvred by the superior intelligence of his lackey; and for a whole four years the French King had refused to licence a performance of the play. Not that there was anything really "revolutionary" in it. As André Hallays has pointed out, there was nothing of the revolutionary in Beaumarchais's make-up. He did no specific thinking about governments and constitutions, put forward no doctrinaire solutions of the political and social problems of the time. He had not the slightest *a priori* objection to things being as they were, and as bad as they were; all he wanted was a wider field for the exercise of his own talents and a larger share of the pickings. He disliked the aristocracy not because it was privileged but because it made too energetic use of its privileges to keep cleverer but less well-born people like himself in their place; and his objection to the French legal system was not the basic one that it was sometimes corrupt and unjust but the more opportunist one that *he* frequently had difficulty in achieving his own ends through it.

As Hallays says, it was not that the *Barber* and the *Marriage* were revolutionary in themselves but that a Parisian public in whom revolutionary ideas had long been germinating read what it wanted into the two plays: "the author proposes, the public disposes." What was really under fire, in the *Marriage* particularly, was not the monarchy or the political and social set-up in general but the arrogance and insolence of the aristocracy; and the audiences revelled in the spectacle of their being duped and outwitted by a barber-valet who had more brains in his little finger than they had in their little noddles. The aristocracy, more appreciative of finesse and wit in the author than apprehensive as to their own security, laughed as heartily as the man in the street at Beaumarchais's audacious sallies.[1] It was only a few of the more intelligent among them who could look ahead and imagine what all this was likely to end in. One of them, Baroness d'Oberkirch, noted that "the *grands seigneurs* laughed at their own expense, and, what was worse, made others laugh. *They will be sorry for it one day*." She was right.

The impact of the work on European public opinion in general can be gauged by the fact that no fewer than twelve translations of it soon appeared in Germany alone; and it was performed in several German theatres. It was read and quoted with the keenest delight in advanced Viennese circles; and its dangerous tendency was sensed by the Emperor Joseph II, who vetoed its production in the National Theatre. It occurred to the shrewd Da Ponte, however, that an opera on the subject might succeed in side-stepping the censorship.

4

Various reasons probably operated to make Mozart prefer the *Marriage* comedy to that of the *Barber*. For one thing, Paisiello's

---

[1] We have already seen Figaro, in the *Barber*, asking Count Almaviva with cool insolence, "Ah, Monseigneur, with your high ideal of the virtues necessary to a servant, how many masters, would you say, are fit to be valets?" In the *Marriage* he caps this with a stinging rejoinder to the Count's irritated query, "How is it that the servants in this house take longer to dress than their masters?"—"It's because they have no valets to help them."

opera on the latter subject had been given in Vienna in August 1783, and there would be little point in Mozart entering into almost immediate competition with that, even if he could have found a librettist of the quality he desired. For another, the *Barber* could hardly have fitted in with his general notions of a full operatic ensemble; it lacked, for one thing, a second soprano part of any importance. A mere glance at the dramatis personae of the *Marriage* would show him that the new comedy had the number and diversity of characters suitable to his own lively genius, that loved movement for its own precious sake. He would be as well aware as Da Ponte or anyone else of what in these days we would call the publicity value of the Figaro subject; moreover, he himself had suffered so many humiliations at the hands of those in power that it was bound to be a joy to him to write a work in which a typical representative of the ruling class was continually being outwitted and frustrated by his valet. But Mozart looked at the theme through eyes of his own. He saw it as a series of opportunities for the display of his own surpassing genius as a composer; but in order to permit of that display the characters had to be transmuted out of Beaumarchais into Mozart. His Figaro is a masterpiece of musical characterisation, but it is not the Figaro of Beaumarchais as Rossini was to paint him later; the Italian genius had more of what we may call, for convenience' sake, the Latin volatility and gay insouciance of the French original. Mozart's Figaro has more of Germanic seriousness in his make-up. The character of the Countess, again, Mozart deepens in his own way; she feels the pathos of her situation more profoundly than Rossini would have shown her doing. We may sum it all up, perhaps, by saying that while in the Rossini opera we feel that we are always in the company of Beaumarchais, in *The Marriage of Figaro* it is more of Mozart that we are kept thinking than of the French dramatist.

What Mozart does, in fact, is to give a more serious turn to each of the characters. His Countess becomes one of the great wronged characters of opera, a woman who has felt deeply and been deeply hurt. His Susanna has moments of romantic ardour that are not in the pert Susanna of Beaumarchais. Above all, there broods over the whole of the opera a sensuousness that is indeed latent in the original play but is found in nothing like the same profusion there. Consciously or unconsciously love and sex are everywhere present to some degree in the original drama. Figaro and his Susanna are sincerely, though not very romantically, in love with each other. The Count is shown as an inveterate pursuer of women. The Countess, we are subtly made to feel, has a more-than-motherly interest in the little Cherubino. And the page himself is a unique piece of characterisation; this boy somewhere between naïve puberty and artful adolescence in the creation of whom Beaumarchais, as we know, had drawn upon his memories of a precocious romantic adventure of his own at the age of thirteen. As Taine has pointed out, sex in some form or other is everywhere present in *Le Mariage*; even Marceline, approaching middle age, still feels something of its urge, while in Fanchette,[1] the little daughter of the gardener, we have a delicately drawn feminine foil to the not yet fully masculine "Cherubino d'amore." And at every point Mozart has graved more deeply the lines of Beaumarchais and given them a warmer infusion of colour.

5

The first problem that confronted the librettist and the composer was how to overcome the objection of the Emperor to the comedy appearing on the stage at all, in any form. Although Da Ponte's account of the affair was not committed to paper until nearly half a century later we may probably regard it as substantially accurate. The Emperor, to begin with, was inclined to doubt the operatic sufficiency of Mozart, who, he said, though admittedly good at instrumental music, had written only one opera and that not a particularly good one.[2] Da Ponte countered with a skilful piece of flattery: "without your Majesty's gracious protection *I* would have written only one drama for Vienna." Reverting to *The Marriage of Figaro,* the Emperor reminded Da Ponte that he had already refused his German actors permission to perform that work. To this Da Ponte replied that in converting the spoken play into an opera he had omitted several scenes and

[1] Barbarina in the opera.
[2] He was referring to the *Seraglio* of 1782. *Idomeneo* (1781) had been produced in Munich and was as yet unknown in Vienna. Of Mozart's earlier operas the Emperor would of course know nothing.

curtailed others, his virtuous intention throughout having been to eliminate everything that might offend against decency and good taste. He was sure he had created out of the original play a work that would not be unworthy of a theatre honoured by his Majesty's protection. As for the music, in his humble opinion it was masterly. Thereupon the Emperor graciously assured him he would rely on his suppliant's taste and discretion. When Mozart took a copy of the score, or as much of it as he had completed, to the palace, he was allowed to play some selections from it that earned the imperial approval: what they were we are not informed, but no doubt the composer saw to it that they were adapted to his and the librettist's artful strategic purpose. According to Da Ponte Mozart worked at the music step by step with him and finished the opera in six weeks. The overture was written last; it was entered by him in the Catalogue of his works on the 29th April 1786. It may be noted, however, that a letter of Leopold Mozart's of the 11th November 1785 to his daughter indicates that the composition was already well in hand even at that time. (In a letter eight days earlier he had casually mentioned that Wolfgang had "said something [in a recent letter] about a new opera.") On the 11th we get more detailed news: "At last, on the 2nd of this month, I had a letter of no more than a dozen lines from your brother, in which he asks for indulgence as he is up to his eyes in work at his new opera, *Le Nozze di Figaro*. . . . I know the original piece; it is very difficult, and to make it effective as an opera it must have been a good deal altered in translation. God grant that it comes out well dramatically; as regards the music I have no fears. He is in for a lot of trotting about and disputation before he gets the libretto exactly to his liking. . . ."

"On the 28th," Leopold writes again to his daughter on the 18th April 1786, "the *Nozze di Figaro* will have its first performance. A success will mean something, as I know that it will have terrific cabals to contend against: Salieri and his whole gang will once more set heaven and earth in motion. Duschek told me recently that your brother has so many cabals against him because he is so highly esteemed for his exceptional talent and skill." As a matter of fact the first performance did not take place until the 1st May. Perhaps, as the date of the entry in Mozart's Catalogue suggests, the overture was not quite ready by the 28th April.

The new work was highly successful; Leopold, who had gone to Vienna to hear it, told his daughter on the 18th May that at the second performance five numbers, and at the third seven, had to be repeated; and we know now that the Emperor—to the annoyance of the singers—had to forbid encores on the ground that they made the performance excessively long. The work was given nine times in Vienna during the year 1786; after that it dropped out of the local repertory, and did not reappear there until the 29th August 1789. In this revival Adriana Ferrarese del Bene, who was afterwards the first Fiordiligi in *Così fan tutte*, replaced Anna Storace as Susanna, and there was a new Countess—Caterina Cavalieri, who had been the Constanze in *The Seraglio* and the Mademoiselle Silberklang in the *Schauspieldirektor*, and in 1787 became the first Elvira in *Don Giovanni*. For the Ferrarese Mozart wrote in July 1789 a rondo, "Al desio di chi t'adora," to take the place of "Deh vieni, non tardar," and another new aria for Susanna, "Un moto di gioia mi sento." Neither of these numbers is sufficiently interesting to deserve a place in modern performances.

In a letter to his father of the 7th May 1785, in which he told him of the opening of a new and brilliant Italian season in Vienna, Mozart had singled out for special commendation the principal bass-baritone buffo singer, Francesco Benucci. Him he now chose to play Figaro.[1] Stefano Mandini was the Almaviva, Signora Laschi the Countess, Nancy (Anna Selina) Storace—a London-born girl of Italian parentage who had a great vogue just then as a singer of soubrette parts—was the Susanna, and Nannina Gottlieb (in later years the Pamina of the *Magic Flute*) the Barbarina. The parts of Bartolo and Antonio were doubled by Bassani, whose wife played Cherubino. The Marcellina was Signora Mandini. There is no first-rank tenor part in *The Marriage of Figaro*; the two minor rôles for that voice, Basilio and Don Curzio, were taken by the Irish singer Michael Kelly, to whose *Reminiscences* of forty years later (written by Theodore Hook) we owe some interesting sidelights on Mozart, the *Marriage*, and

---

[1] A contemporary engraving of him shows him as a man of spare build, with a face expressive of shrewdness and a decidedly sardonic humour. He looks the sort of man of whom Beaumarchais himself would have approved as the mercurial, ironic, resourceful Figaro.

the period. In the Catalogue of his own works Mozart enters him as "Occhely," which is explained by the fact that the Irishman was known in Italian operatic circles as O'Kelly. In December 1786 the opera was given in Prague with a success so tremendous that Mozart was commissioned to write a new opera for the local theatre. Thus it was that *Don Giovanni* came into being.

6

Ostensibly Beaumarchais's *Marriage of Figaro* is a sequel to his *Barber of Seville,* but to read the later play immediately after the earlier one is to find ourselves asking a few questions and not getting satisfactory replies to any of them. The setting of the *Marriage* is Count Almaviva's château of Aguas-Frescas, a few miles from Seville, where he had obviously settled down as a feudal grandee after his union with Rosina. But how soon or how late after? It is impossible to say. The interval has obviously been long enough for the Count to have got a little tired of his Rosina and taken to the pursuit of other women, while she, on her part, has had time enough to lose all kittenish high spirits and develop into a dignified *grande dame* with a knowledge of the world that is tinged with the melancholy of lost illusions. We learn, too, that the King of Spain has recently appointed Almaviva his ambassador in London—which suggests that he is no longer the irresponsible young harum-scarum of the *Barber* but a man who counts for something in the larger world.

On the other hand, there are indications that the period of the first act of the second comedy is not much later than the last act of the first. Basile is still Rosina's music teacher, domiciled in the château, where the Count finds his talent for intrigue useful to him. Doctor Bartolo is still practising his profession in Seville, and in his dialogue with Figaro in the second scene of the first act there are unmistakeable signs that his defeat in the *Barber* was so recent as still to be rankling in him. Although he is obviously the accredited physician of the household—one gathers that his summons to Aguas-Frescas is due to the Count having had an accident or the Countess being ill—it is clear that he knows little or nothing of what has been going on in the château recently; it is even news to him that Almaviva has been neglecting his own

lady and running after other people's. When **Marceline mentions
Basile's** name Bartolo ejaculates, "What! that other rascal also
lives here? The place is a rogues' den! What does he do here?",
which suggests that no appreciable interval of time has elapsed
between the end of the first play and the beginning of the second.
Figaro, again, chaffs Bartolo about the failure of his scheme to
marry his ward, in terms which suggest that the incident had been
recent enough for the subject to be still a sore one with the
Doctor. Figaro's ironic enquiry about the health of Bartolo's
mule—which unfortunate animal had had a cataplasm put on its
eyes by the barber in the course of his gay medical experiments on
the Doctor's household—again seems to indicate that not much
time has elapsed between the two plays. The general impression
given us by this second scene of the *Marriage* is that Bartolo and
Figaro are now meeting for the first, or near-first, time since the
last act of the *Barber*; and it is difficult for us to reconcile this
time-table with the impression derived from other quarters that a
fairly considerable time must be supposed to have elapsed between the two comedies.

7

The Marceline of the *Mariage* is a quite new character, now the
housekeeper at Aguas-Frescas, but at some time or other in the
distant past, we are given to understand, a flame of Bartolo's more
passionate youth, by whom she had a son who had mysteriously
disappeared in childhood—a motif that becomes of decisive importance later in the play and in the opera. For the purposes of
the imbroglio Beaumarchais has to show Figaro pledged either
to marry this housekeeper—who, of course, cannot be in her first
youth now—or to pay back some money he had borrowed from
her. The motif is really the nodal one of the *Mariage:* it is upon
this dilemma of Figaro's that the Count is relying in his machina-
tions to bend Susanna to his will, for Figaro can pay his debt
only by the financial assistance of his master, who will come to
his rescue only on his own terms. The knot, so awkward for
Figaro and Susanna, is cut by a bold stroke on the dramatist's
part: it turns out that Figaro is the long-lost child of Bartolo and
Marceline. There is comedy of the richest kind in the flabber-

gasted Doctor's discovery that the young ne'er-do-well who had cheated him out of Rosina and on whom he had hoped to revenge himself by marrying him off to his former mistress, is actually his own son.

At this point a word must be said about the current English misconception of Marcellina as "Dr. Bartolo's housekeeper," an error arising, perhaps, from her being so described in the list of dramatis personae prefixed to the best-known English vocal score of the opera. Nothing could be clearer, one would have thought, than that she is not Bartolo's but Almaviva's housekeeper. Beaumarchais designates her "femme de charge" at the château. In the Italian imprint of the libretto she is called "governante," which has two meanings, that of "preceptress," and that of "housekeeper"; and Marcellina happens to be both of these at Aguas-Frescas. The German commentators have not fallen into the English error in their analyses of the French play and the opera. Hermann Abert, for example, describes her as Rosina's duenna, whom, together with Figaro and Basilio, the Count had taken into his service when he married Rosina: Schurig speaks of her as Dr. Bartolo's "former housekeeper."

All this is as clear as daylight to anyone who has read Beaumarchais with any care. Though there is no acting character of the name of Marcellina in the *Barber*, there are some references there to someone of that name in Bartolo's household. We are told of a Marcellina whom Figaro has put out of action along with the other servants, by bleeding her foot. Towards the end of the *Barber* Doctor Bartolo, to make sure that none of the conspirators shall gain access to Rosina, orders her to go to Marcellina's room and lock and bolt the door. This invisible Marcellina, in fact, is in the *Barber* Bartolo's housekeeper and the young Rosina's governess.

It is obviously in Almaviva's household, not Bartolo's, that Marcellina figures in the *Marriage* as housekeeper and preceptress to the still young Countess. She is not an occasional visitor to the château but a resident there; she moves about freely in it. At the time when the play opens she has sent to Seville for Doctor Bartolo, to whom she explains the whole complicated situation in the château as regards Almaviva, Susanna, Figaro and herself.

The Doctor does not even know that Basilio is also located there until Marcellina tells him; and his impatient comment after hearing her story is, "Do I understand, then, that it was to listen to rubbish of this sort that you summoned me from Seville?"

It is unnecessary to pile up any further the evidence that Marcellina is domiciled in the château, not in Seville with Bartolo. Da Ponte follows the French play in all essentials. It is quite clear in the first act of the opera that she knows everything that goes on in the house above and below stairs, while he knows nothing: "Tell me everything," he says. That she has the run of the château is manifest: she walks in and out of Susanna's bedroom as a matter of course, and in the imbroglio in the second act the Count, playing for time, keeps hoping for her appearance. It is made perfectly evident that she was at one time Rosina's governess in Bartolo's household and is now her preceptress and *femme de charge* in Almaviva's. Susanna's parting shot at her after she has left the stage after the quarrel scene is, in Beaumarchais, this: "Goodbye, madame, you pedant! . . . This ancient sibyl! Just because she has a bit of learning and made the Countess's life a burden to her when she was a child she wants now to run the whole château." In the opera we get the same idea in a slightly different phrasing. "Decrepit sibyl!" is how Susanna describes her to her face; and after she has left the scene of combat Susanna calls after her, "Take yourself off, you old pedant, you arrogant Doctoress. You think that because you have read a book or two and plagued the life out of her ladyship when she was young" . . . which is as near Beaumarchais as makes no matter.

Marcellina, then, is *not* Dr. Bartolo's housekeeper but Almaviva's and Rosina's, a point which both audiences and producers would do well to bear in mind.

8

But let us now turn to the opera.

The overture is in no sense "programmatic": the full title of the original play had been *La Folle Journée, ou Le Mariage de Figaro*, and it is upon the "folle journée" in general, rather than the individuals or the incidents of the drama, that Mozart wisely concentrates. Gaiety reigns throughout the overture, from the racy opening theme:

1

through its fanfare-like supplement:

2

and their developments, to the contrasting second subject and beyond:

3

Mozart appears to have coquetted for a moment with the idea of delaying the final return of the opening theme (No. 1) in order to insert an andante con moto section in 6/8 time, based on a lilting melody in the oboe with an accompaniment of plucked strings, the general procedure thus being analogous to that in the overture to *The Seraglio*. The autograph score shows, however, that the page that presumably followed the first bare suggestion of this slower section has been torn out. We feel that Mozart's instinct was sound: it was best to keep the merry atmosphere of the "folle journée" one and indivisible in the overture from sudden start to quick finish.

The time of the commencement of the opera is the morning of the day on which Figaro, who is now the Count's factotum, and Susanna, the Countess's maid, hope to be married. The setting of the first scene is a relatively unfurnished room in the château, the only notable object in it, indeed, being an armchair in the centre; Figaro and Susanna, we cannot help commenting, seem to have delayed for an unconscionable time the full furnishing of what is obviously to be the nuptial chamber. Figaro is busy with a footrule, measuring the length and breadth and height of the room and calling out the figures; while Susanna, looking at herself in a mirror, is wholly absorbed in the ecstasy of trying on a new hat which apparently she has at last shaped and adorned to her satisfaction. It is some little time before the busy Figaro can be induced to take any interest in this masterpiece, but when he does so it meets with his approval.

After a delightful duet the pair discuss the situation in recitative. Figaro explains that he has been busy trying to decide on the best place for the handsome bed the Count has given them. Susanna makes it clear at once that her fiancé's choice of a bedroom is not hers, but she mysteriously refuses for a time to explain her objection to it. It is the most convenient room in the whole château, he tells her, for all concerned, master and mistress, valet and maid:

4

On one side of them is the Countess; if she wants Susanna in the night, all she has to do is to ring, and the maid will be with her in a trice. With equal celerity Figaro can answer the call of the Count, whose bedroom happens to be on the other side. Figaro is obviously not as quick-witted as we would have expected him to be after his exploits in the *Barber*, and the more wideawake Susanna has to teach him some of the facts of life. Suppose all this bell-ringing on the one part and prompt service on the other should turn out to be not quite so simple a routine matter as Figaro, in his innocence, imagines? Suppose the Count rings one night for his valet and sends him off three miles away on some errand or other, and—well, it is only a skip and a jump from the Count's bedroom to Susanna's. Exacting a promise from him that he will not entertain any suspicions on her account, she lays the whole situation before him in recitative. The Count, it appears, wearying a little of amorous hunts in the fashionable world, is now turning his attention to the home coverts; and the game he is planning to bring down is no other than Figaro's Susanna. How can her lover have been so blind as not to see for himself how things have been shaping for some time in the château? The nice dowry the Count has promised her and the fine bedroom he has placed at their disposal have not been disinterested benevolences on his part, as Figaro naïvely imagines, but have been designed to pave the way for the exercise of the feudal *droit du seigneur*. "But," Figaro protests, "he has renounced that right in his domains." No doubt, replies Susanna; but now he repents having done so and proposes to exercise the right where Susanna is concerned, and the insidious Basilio, the Count's crafty tool, whenever he gives her a singing lesson never fails to remind her of her duty to her feudal lord.

At first Figaro is inclined to be incredulous, but in the end he sees that Susanna is right. Now he understands why his master the Count intends to promote him to the rank of courier in the London embassy, for the better pursuit of his designs on Susanna. So far Figaro has undoubtedly been a little obtuse; but now that he sees everything clearly the old spirit of combat and intrigue revives in him. Susanna having run off to answer the Countess's bell, he declares, in the famous cavatina "Se vuol ballare, signor Contino":

5

Allegretto

Se vuol bal-la——re, Si-gnor Con-ti-no,

his intention to beat his master at his own game: "Do you want to dance, my little Count? Very well; but it shall be to my guitar. Join my school and I will teach you your capers." From now onwards the Count shall be involved in a net of counter-intrigues in which he will be helpless: he, Figaro, the master tactician, who had twisted Bartolo round his little finger in the *Barber*, is going into action.

9

Full of the joy of combat and confident of success he goes out, and as he does so Doctor Bartolo and Marcellina enter, the latter holding a document in her hand which turns out to be Figaro's

contract to marry her. Bartolo asks her testily why she had for-
borne to consult him on this matter until the very morning of the
valet's union with Susanna. She opines that it is still not too late
to frustrate the marriage; her plan is to confirm Susanna in her
refusal of the Count, who, in his anger, will then insist on Figaro
carrying out his contract either to wed Marcellina or pay off his
debt to her, which the valet cannot do without his lordship's
assistance. Bartolo, having read the contract, promises to do all
he can to help her: it will certainly be a good joke, he says, to get
the cunning rascal who cheated him out of Rosina married to his
old servant! He launches into a vigorous aria in praise of vengeance. Fools and slaves, he says, accept insults and humiliations;
the man of spirit avenges them. And in an affair of this kind,
which calls for secrecy and craft, no one can surpass Doctor
Bartolo, whose talents all Seville knows: so let this rogue of an
ex-barber beware! This time he will lose the game! The character
and the situation are stock ones in opera buffa, and there existed
for it a stock musical apparatus which Mozart employs with his
usual mastery. But, as so often happens with him, he puts so much
of himself and of the resources of music into the aria that much of
it could figure equally well in an episode as serious as the present
one is humorous. We have had much the same experience once
or twice with the Osmin of *The Seraglio*.

Bartolo leaves the stage, rather inconclusively, at the end of
his aria, for no better reason than that Da Ponte has no further
use for him at the moment.[1] Susanna now enters, carrying one
of her mistress's dresses, a cap and a ribbon; and there follows a
bantering duet between her and Marcellina in which, with youth
and a nimbler wit to help her, Susanna finally has the advantage
in the exchange of double-edged compliments. The older lady
felicitates the younger one on being a bride who has the good luck

---

[1] It is all managed much better in Beaumarchais, where the audience is
placed in possession of more of the essential facts leading up to the imbroglio,
and Bartolo remains on the stage, an amused spectator of the battle of wits
that follows between Marcellina and Susanna. In a performance of the opera
in Paris in 1793 the dialogue of Beaumarchais was substituted for the Da
Ponte recitatives throughout the opera. There is a good deal to be said both
for and against a procedure of this sort: Da Ponte has rejected or condensed
much that we would prefer to be set forth in more detail.

to be the apple of her master's eye: Susanna counters with an ironic tribute to her antagonist's years, which have earned her the respect of all Spain. So it goes on, in true feminine bargee fashion, until Marcellina, compelled to admit defeat, flounces off in a towering rage.

10

Susanna has only just time to preen her feathers and rejoice in her victory over the "sibilla decrepita," the "dottoressa arrogante," the "vecchia pedante" who, because she had a smattering of education, had managed to become Rosina's governess,[1] when the page Cherubino enters. The sensitive little fellow is bursting with self-pity: yesterday the Count, having caught him alone with the gardener's little daughter Barbarina, had dismissed him from his service; and had not the Countess, his kind godmother, interceded for him he would by now be on his travels with never a hope of seeing his dear Susanna again! This last touch amuses her vastly; she had understood, she tells him, that it was the Countess to whom he had secretly given his heart. Ah, the Countess! he sighs: how he envies Susanna, who can see her whenever she likes, who dresses her in the morning and disrobes her at night, pins and unpins her, and adjusts her lace. Learning that the ribbon in Susanna's hand is from the Countess's nightwear he snatches the sanctified object from her and refuses to give it up, swearing he would not surrender it to save his life. In Beaumarchais he indulges at this point in a significant piece of auto-psychoanalysis: he does not know why it is, but for some time the mere sight of a woman is enough to set his heart beating wildly; the words "love" and "pleasure" tremble constantly on his lips, and he roams the park murmuring "I love you!" to the trees, the clouds, the winds, his noble mistress, Susanna and Fanchette; even Marcellina—who, after all, as he explains, is a woman and therefore "interesting"—sets his too susceptible heart on fire. And little Fanchette is kinder to him than the ironic, worldly-wise Susanna, for at least the child listens seriously to the important things he has to say. In the opera Da Ponte gives him an aria to sing that is a skilful rendering of all this in verse:

[1] This was obviously when Rosina was Bartolo's ward and Marcellina his innamorata; but there is no mention of it in the *Barber*.

6

Allegro vivace

Non so più co-sa son, co-sa fac-cio, Or di fo-co,o-ra so-no di ghiac-cio

and Mozart has turned it all into music that is the very soul of juvenile love, ardent, troubled, self-doubting yet ineffably happy. (In the opera the immediate pretext for the aria is that Cherubino has written a canzone which Susanna can sing to the Countess, to herself, to Barbarina, to Marcellina, to every woman in the château; for it is a confession that all womankind ought to hear. This masterpiece he will give to Susanna in return for the ribbon. Mozart postpones the singing of the canzone to the second act of the opera).

Someone is heard approaching from outside; presumably it is the Count, and Cherubino, scared out of his wits, crouches down behind the big armchair, in which the Count, very much at his ease, seats himself when he enters. He has come to take the first decisive step in the siege of the Susanna fortress. He explains the situation in a long scene in recitative. The King has appointed him his ambassador in London, and he proposes to take Figaro —and of course Susanna—there with him. She must know already how much he loves her, for his agent Basilio will have told her all that. What he wants at the moment is that she shall give him an assignation at dusk this evening in the garden. Susanna, doubly embarrassed—by the suggestion, that is virtually a command, and by the awkward problem set her by the presence of Cherubino— can only stammer out a request to be left in peace. But while the Count is assuring her that in return for such a favour he will pay Figaro's debt to Marcellina the voice of Basilio is heard without. Having no desire for the music master's company just then and there the Count tells Susanna to get rid of him quickly, and makes to hide behind the chair. By standing between the pair for a moment Susanna gives the page, who is certainly not lacking in resource, time to slip unobserved into the chair, where she covers him with the dress she had brought with her on her entry. The situation is not without its attraction for the Count, who looks forward now to overhearing, unseen, how his hireling will plead

his cause for him. Basilio begins by telling Susanna how foolish
she is to reject the advances of an admirer so rich and influential
as the Count Almaviva and accept those of a mere page, "Cherubino d'amore," who has been seen hanging round the place that
very morning. And that canzone, continues Basilio—who seems
to know everything that goes on in and around the château—for
whom was that composed, for the Countess's maid or the great
lady herself? Anyhow, Susanna will be doing the page a service
to warn him not to look so amorously at the Countess when he
is serving her at table, for if the Count gets wind of it he will be
furious, and Susanna knows what he can be capable of when
roused.

11

She turns on him angrily, but he tells her smoothly there is
nothing he knows about all this that is not already the talk of the
whole château. This is too much for the Count, who now reveals
himself, and, in a towering temper, orders Basilio to see that the
seducer, as he calls the page, is expelled from the house at once.
Mozart now has his actors well set for a fine trio in which, as
usual with him, each of the personages speaks true to character
while all combine into an enchanting musical whole. The Count
storms and threatens; Susanna can only wail confusedly. Only
the practised intriguer Basilio remains calm, enjoying himself
immensely: this is a situation after his own malicious heart. He
addresses the Count in a phrase that is a masterpiece of oily
hypocrisy—"I seem to have arrived here at an unfortunate moment; pardon me, my lord":

7

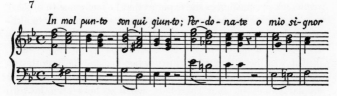

At last Susanna's nerves give way; and as she seems to be about to
faint the two men gallantly come to her assistance. Solicitously
they lead her towards the armchair; this restores her like magic,
and she violently repulses them both.

Basilio, once more to the unctuous strain of No. 7, protests that what he had said about the page was mere suspicion on his part; but the Count will not hear a word in excuse of Cherubino, who is to be expelled from the château immediately. The precocious boy is manifestly a menace to the morals of the estate; only yesterday, it appears, the Count, having occasion to speak to little Barbarina, the gardener's daughter and Susanna's cousin, had found the door of the cottage locked. At last it had been opened by the girl, who seemed somewhat embarrassed. Looking round for a possible reason for her confusion, the Count—turning for a moment Basilio's sly No. 7 to his own ironic purposes—had perceived the table-cloth; dexterously raising this, whom should he find cowering beneath it but the young Cherubino! He illustrates the situation graphically by lifting the dress from the armchair, thus disclosing the trembling page. He turns on Susanna: now, he says sarcastically, he understands everything. She loses her nerve completely; Basilio alone, as hitherto, is maliciously delighted with the latest turn of events. "Better and better" he ejaculates; "women are all alike," he assures the Count, "they always run true to form." What he had said about the page, he again remarks sardonically, was of course no more than mere suspicion. In the face of all the evidence against her poor Susanna can only raise her hands and implore the protection of heaven.

The delightful trio over, the working out of the drama is resumed in recitative. The Count orders Basilio to bring Figaro before him at once, so that his valet may see for himself the sort of creature his Susanna is. This rouses her to action. Asked by Almaviva to account for the page being there under such highly suspicious circumstances she explains that he had come to beg her to intercede for him with the Countess in the matter of his banishment: the entry of the Count had thrown them both into confusion, and in his terror the boy had taken cover in the chair. "But it was there that I sat down when I came in," retorts the Count. "Yes," says Cherubino timidly, "but when you did so I slipped behind the chair"; and later, when his lordship in his turn had retreated behind it for concealment, he had popped into it once more. The Count is now uncomfortably conscious that the page must have heard the whole of his compromising conversation with Susanna. This deflates him; he finds it difficult now to play the stern moralist, and he is not at all placated by Cherubino's innocent-artful assurance that he had done his best *not* to hear anything that was said.

12

Calling him a viper, Almaviva yanks him out of the chair [1] as a confused noise is heard without and Figaro enters, bearing a bridal veil in his hand, and accompanied by a number of servants and peasants, arrayed in white, who strew flowers before the Count. All this is Figaro's first crafty shot in his campaign against his master: he aims to embarrass him by an organised tribute on the part of his vassals to his benevolence and virtue. The Count, however, is on the alert. "What is the meaning of this comedy?", he asks. Figaro whispers to Susanna, "Now the dance begins; play up to me, my treasure!", to which she replies—rather despairingly after all she has recently gone through—"There's no hope for us!" Turning obsequiously to the Count, Figaro begs him to accept this tribute to the regard he has shown for virtue by abolishing the detested *droit du seigneur*. Almaviva loftily brushes that theme aside: what is it that the valet really wants? Figaro's answer is that he is anxious to be the first to benefit by his lordship's magnanimity: this is why he has arranged his marriage for today, and he asks the Count to make an impressive gesture by placing the white bridal wreath, the symbol of purity, on the head of the bride. "Diabolical cunning!" the Count mutters under his breath: "but I shall be a match for them." He confirms the abolition of the *droit*, modestly disclaiming any special virtue on his part in doing so. "Oh, what goodness!" exclaims Susanna admiringly; "oh, what justice!" echoes Figaro; and the vassals shout "Long life to our lord!" He will perform the ceremony, he

---

[1] Da Ponte's handling of this scene is one of many arguments in favour of the use of Beaumarchais's original text whenever possible in the recitatives of the opera. In the play the Count's fury with both Susanna and Cherubino and his resolve to frustrate Figaro's marriage are more fully and effectively brought out; and when he is checkmated by the page's artful hint that he had heard every word of Almaviva's attempted seduction of Susanna he whispers in her ear, "Perfidious one! Now you shall not marry Figaro!" This declaration gives the necessary point to the scene that follows; the Count may be baffled for the moment, but for all that the battle of wits is now joined between him and his valet.

assures them, at the first convenient moment, but suggests post-poning it a little while till he can do so on a more imposing scale; and under his breath he invokes Marcellina. The vassals repeat their chorus of praise, and he dismisses them.

The principal characters now have the stage to themselves. Figaro, Susanna and Basilio pay a final compliment to their gracious overlord, but Cherubino is silent, grieving, as Susanna explains to Figaro, over his banishment from the château. The Count at first disregards their appeal to his clemency; but when the page throws out another hint about his lips being sealed Almaviva sees the wisdom of temporising. He will do more than pardon Cherubino, he says; there is a commission vacant in his regiment and this he grants him—on condition that he leaves at once. The Count and Basilio go out, and Figaro, by way of consoling the boy for not seeing Susanna again for some time, sings the famous "Non più andrai":

8

Allegro

Non più an-drai, far-fal-lo-ne a-mo-ro-so, Not-te e gior-no d'in-tor-no gi-ran-do,

The young amorist must say goodbye to all this love-making and turn his attention to the stern realities of the barrack-room and the battlefield, sacrifice his flowing locks and plumed hats; "Narcissus-Adonis" must play a new part as a true son of Mars, sport long moustaches, shoulder a gun and rattle a sabre; dance no more fandangos but march in mud and snow over the hills and through the valleys to the music of trumpets and fifes and cannon. The chaff is all in good part, and it ends with them all marching off in formation to the strains of a military march. So ends the first act of the opera.

From the dramatic point of view Da Ponte's handling of this final scene leaves something to be desired. He does not bring out in his recitatives as Beaumarchais does in his dialogue the fact that already the Count and Figaro are at daggers drawn, the former being piqued beyond endurance by his frustration with Susanna and his suspicions of Cherubino and the Countess, the valet, quite sure of himself now that the talent for intrigue on which he prides himself can have free play, indulging in all sorts of polite insolences to his master. Secondly, Beaumarchais makes it clear that Bartolo and Marcellina have been seen making their way to the town—obviously to take legal action in the matter of Figaro's bond: the Count realises at once the importance of this to his own strategy, for it is through Marcellina that he has been hoping all along to put a spoke in Figaro's wheel. Thirdly, in Beaumarchais, after the Count has departed, Figaro tells Cherubino not to take his banishment too literally: he is to pretend to be resigned to it, put on his travelling clothes, ride away in presence of everyone, gallop as far as the farm, and then return to the château on foot by another route; after that, all he will have to do is to keep out of sight of the Count and trust to Figaro to arrange everything in his favour after that night's fête. Clearly Figaro's grand scheme for fooling and trapping the Count is already fully formed in his mind—which accounts for his self-assured gaiety and hardly veiled insolence throughout the scene. Fourthly, Beaumarchais brings the Countess on in the final moments of the scene, where her motherly—is it entirely motherly, though?—solicitude for poor little Cherubino fans the rising flame of Almaviva's suspicious jealousy of the page. As regards the omission of the Countess from the episode, however, there is something to be said operatically for Da Ponte: he would have weakened the effect of our first introduction to her in the next act had he brought her on for a few minutes at the end of the first. As often happens in opera, he is paying the penalty for being a librettist in the first place and a dramatist only in the second. The music always has a first mortgage on his purely dramatic interests: and to find time and space for the musical expansions insisted on by the composer he has often to omit something that is of the very essence of the action. We shall see a signal instance of this eternal liability of the librettist when we come to examine the structure of the first act of Puccini's *Tosca*.[1]

[1] Da Ponte himself was evidently well aware of the problem. A copy of the *Figaro* text has survived in a foreword to which he accounts for the length of the work by "the multiplicity and variety of the musical numbers" he had to introduce, which "had to be worked in (a) so as not to leave the actors immobilised, (b) to remedy the tedium of the long recitatives, (c) to give a more lively colour to the passions sometimes indicated there . . ." We

13

In the second act we see Figaro putting into operation a plan
of campaign that is superb in its audacity. He is evidently one of
those who believe that the best defence is attack; to paraphrase
his own words, the best way to keep a man from interfering with
other people's property is to make him doubtful about the security
of his own. The Count has designs on his valet's wife. Very well,
the valet will put it into his head that some one has designs on
the Countess and is about to proceed to action; this suspicion
should keep Almaviva too busy to have much time to devote to
Figaro's matrimonial affairs. Furthermore, he hopes to manœuvre
his lordship into a compromising situation in which he will be
the biter bit, the would-be seducer become the victim of his own
wiles. To bring all this about Figaro means to make a quite
impudent use of his noble lady; but the strength of his personality
and his reputation for skill in intrigue should be enough to overcome her feeble objections. Besides, he knows that the Countess
has *her* vulnerable spot—her tenderness for the pretty, amorous
page; and on this weakness of hers he works artfully, as we shall
see.

The curtain rises on a handsome room in the château.[1] On the
left is a window giving on the garden, on the right a door leading
to a dressing-room; further left, towards the back of the stage,
is an entrance door, while quite at the back is another door leading
to the service quarters. The Countess, a noble, dignified figure—
one of Mozart's rarest creations—sits musing sadly upon her unhappy lot as a loving wife whose husband, out of sheer frivolity,
has begun to neglect her. The key to her elegiac mood is given us
in a short orchestral introduction in which Mozart makes liberal
use of the twining thirds which he oftens draws upon for moments
of great tenderness:

---

shall probably not go far wrong in seeing in this the constant pressure put
on him by Mozart to keep the action always filled with musical interest.
There is also a long passage in Da Ponte's *Memoirs* in which he speaks
feelingly of the difficulties the poor poet often has in providing all the verbal
matter the composer needs for the elaborate musical structure of a finale.

[1] In Beaumarchais a bedroom.

9

Later there comes another orchestral passage:

10

in which sighing thirds again play their significant part: the phrase has a marked family resemblance to the lovely strain in Donna Anna's final aria, "Non mi dir," in *Don Giovanni*, in which, before the words "Calma, calma il tuo tormento," she pours out the vials of her tenderness and compassion upon Don Ottavio. The burden of the present exquisite aria is the Countess's grief over lost illusions: "Oh love, bring some comfort to my suffering heart: restore to me my lover, or let me die!"

At the conclusion of it Susanna enters, and, at the Countess's bidding, finishes (in recitative) the story she has been telling her of Almaviva's attempted seduction—or rather purchase, as she puts it—of her. While the Countess is once more lamenting the loss of her husband's affection Figaro enters in the highest spirits, trilling a gay "La, la, la." He tells his lady of the Count's desire to resume his ancient feudal right where Susanna is concerned, of the plan to attach him to the London embassy, and of the Count's resolve, after his frustration, to espouse the cause of Marcellina. The others are astonished that with such a load of care on him Figaro can be so gay. But he is gay, he explains to them, because of the certain success of the grand scheme he has already set on foot for the discomfiture of his lordship. He has sent the Count, through Basilio, an anonymous letter warning him that an admirer of the Countess has made an assignation with her at that night's festivities. The Countess is horrified at the audacity of this; surely Figaro knows what his master is capable of under the spur of jealousy? The angrier the Count gets, Figaro rejoins, the more blunders he will make in his strategy: the valet's plan is to give him so much to think about during the next few hours that he will have no time to bother about Figaro's marriage, which will then come about by itself, as it were.

14

But what about Marcellina? asks Susanna. They need not worry about her, replies Figaro: the Count is their target. Susanna is to grant Almaviva an assignation for that evening, at which she will be impersonated by little Cherubino, whom he has already taken the precaution to retain in the château; the Count and the supposed Susanna will be surprised at the right moment by the Countess, who will then have her husband in the hollow of her hand and will be able to dictate her own terms of peace. Rosina begins to like the idea; perhaps the prospect of seeing the charming page again has some influence on her judgment. The Count, Figaro explains, has gone hunting; so they have ample time in which to dress Cherubino up in Susanna's clothes and coach him in his part. Figaro goes off mightily pleased with himself, singing a gay snatch from his little aria in the first act—"If you are bent on dancing, my little Count, well and good; but it will be to my guitar accompaniment."

The Countess and Susanna resume their conversation. The former regrets that the page had been listening during the attempted seduction in the first act. But why has he not come to sing her the canzone he has written for her? The words are hardly out of her mouth when Cherubino enters, full of sighs and tears, as usual, at the thought of leaving his adored mistress. The incident is rather weakly handled by both Beaumarchais and Da Ponte: the former's prime object was plainly to provide a pre-determined charming stage picture of Cherubino singing his romance to Susanna's accompaniment, with the Countess following the words from the manuscript [1]; for Da Ponte the incident is simply useful as providing Mozart with a "cue for song." The result is the delightful "Voi che sapete"—"Ye ladies who know what love is,

[1] In a footnote in the play Beaumarchais lays it down that the tableau is to be a copy of Vanloo's engraving of *La Conversation espagnole*.

behold the turmoil of my heart, possessed with a desire that is now a delight, now a torment. I freeze and burn by turns: I am in quest of something, but I know not quite what it is. There is no peace for me night or day, yet even my torment is delight"; and so on:

11

Andante con moto

Voi che sa - pe - te   che co - sa è a - mor

Da Ponte is always a particularly dexterous artist in words in set situations of this kind, and Mozart finds by instinct the right musical vein for the little song, an atmosphere curiously compounded of naïveté and ardour.

The song and the singer having been duly praised by the two listeners they address themselves to the business of robing Cherubino for the girl part he is to play in the comedy ahead of them. Fortunately he is of the same height and build as Susanna, so that her clothes should fit him to a nicety. For a moment the Countess has her doubts and fears about the wisdom of all this disrobing: what if someone were to come in? Susanna settles that matter by locking the main door. The page's short hair is a bit of a problem, which the Countess solves by sending Susanna into the adjoining cabinet in search of one of her caps. Cherubino's military commission now comes to light—it had been handed him by Basilio, he says—and the Countess observes that in their indecent hurry to get the youngster out of the château they had forgotten to seal it. Then, to the accompaniment of a light-hearted aria, Susanna proceeds with the dismantling and reconstruction of the page, finding a little difficulty in doing so now and then because his head keeps turning in the direction of the Countess; and in any case he remains too much of a boy to make a credible girl without a good deal of coaching.

15

The critical eye of the Countess detects a flaw in his costume: his sleeves should be rolled up further above the elbow if he is to pass as a girl of Susanna's station. As the maid raises the sleeve the stolen ribbon comes to light. It has a spot of blood on it, which the page, in great confusion, explains by his having had a slight accident that morning. Sending Susanna off for some sticking-plaster the Countess takes possession of the ribbon, despite the poor boy's tearful plea that no plaster in the world could have anything like the same healing property. This moves the Countess deeply; but while she is gently reproving him for his infatuation they are startled by a knocking at the door, and the Count's voice is heard asking impatiently why it is locked.

The Countess loses her head: what will this quick-tempered husband of hers, already absurdly jealous of the page, say and do when he discovers him there in partial deshabille—and this after the Count has presumably received a "letter from a friend" palmed off on him by Figaro? Cherubino runs in terror into the adjoining cabinet; the Countess turns the key of it and hides it on her person, after which she unlocks the door to admit the Count. Her evident embarrassment, and her lame explanation that she had been trying on some dresses with Susanna, who had just gone to her own room, make him more suspicious than ever. He produces the letter and invites her to read it; but before she can do so his attention is distracted by a noise in the other room, where the agitated Cherubino has apparently overturned a chair. Almost fainting with fright, the Countess keeps making matters worse for herself by her attempted explanations. The person within, she stammers, is Susanna; whereupon Almaviva reminds her that a minute ago she had told him that Susanna had gone to her own room.

While he is insisting that the dressing-room be opened at once Susanna appears at the door by which she had gone out; catching sight of the Count, who luckily has his back towards her, she slips into an alcove and awaits further developments. A lively trio follows, in which Almaviva, now in a towering rage, demands that the cabinet door shall be opened, the Countess insists that it shall not, and Susanna, guessing from the absence of the page what has happened, wonders how they are to escape now the consequences of Figaro's faith in the perfection of his strategy. In a short ensuing recitative Almaviva declares that he will summon the servants to break the door down; but Rosina dissuades him from doing what will make them both the talk of the whole château.

He decides to do the breaking down himself, and goes off to fetch the necessary implements; but to make sure that there will be no trickery behind his back he makes her accompany him; he locks the door leading to Susanna's quarters and then makes his exit with the Countess by the main door, which we hear him locking behind him.

This makes the quick-witted Susanna mistress of the situation. Emerging from the alcove she runs to the door of the dressing-room and calls on the terrified Cherubino to open it:

12

Allegro assai

A-pri-te, pre-sto a-pri-te, A-pri-te, è la Su-san-na, sor-ti-te, sor-ti-te,

What are they to do? If the Count finds the boy there on his return he will kill him; yet all the exits from the room are now locked. The only way out is by the window on the left: it is a perilous jump, but the page makes it, and Susanna is relieved to find that he has landed safely in the garden and is now running away like a hare. There being no more danger from that quarter her further course of action is clear: she slips into the dressing-room and closes the door behind her just as the Count and his lady return, the former armed with the necessary implements for forcing the door. By now the Countess's nerve has given way completely. She surrenders unconditionally. The occupant of the room, she confesses, is not her maid but someone of whom it is really absurd of her husband to harbour any suspicions; they had merely been engaged in arranging an innocent little joke.

16

The more she pleads for mercy for the page, the more convinced is the Count of her guilt: now he understands why she had been so moved that morning when he had banished the boy from the château, and why she had assured him earlier in the present scene—a telling point in the play, of which, however, Da Ponte makes no use—that she intended to spend the whole afternoon and evening in her own apartment. She only adds fuel to the flames by protesting how innocent was the little masquerade she had planned, in which they had been so suddenly interrupted that at the present moment the boy is in the dressing-room only half-clothed. She is willing now to give up the key to the Count, but her last-minute plea for mercy for Cherubino, in the name of the love her husband had once felt for her, is the final faggot on the flames. Blind with rage he takes the key and rushes to the door. The whole scene is dramatically more tense in Beaumarchais and moves more swiftly there to its conclusion; but the opera has the advantage over the play of a final duet in which Mozart hits off admirably the agitation of the Countess and the implacable fury of Almaviva.

But his triumph is a short-lived one: his swift deflation is depicted in a single phrase given out by the orchestra as he opens the door of the dressing-room and draws his avenging sword: as will be seen, the phrase comes in like a lion and goes out like a lamb:

13

It is followed by a dazed ejaculation of "Susanna!" by the Count as he sees in the doorway the smiling maid, not the quaking Cherubino he had expected. She at once takes command of the situation: to a demure little phrase in the orchestra:

14

she expresses ironic sympathy with the Count in the little mistake that has turned out so unfortunately for him. The Count and the Countess are equally dismayed: and never in opera has a comic situation been better painted in music of mock-gravity than in the short andante trio that follows.

The Countess, who has been near fainting, is the first of the pair to recover something of her poise, though she is well aware that

her difficulties are by no means over yet. She takes advantage of
the momentary absence of her husband—who has gone into the
dressing-room to investigate for himself—to appeal in agitated
tones:

15

to Susanna for moral support: the orchestral figure that accompanies the maid's assurance that the page is safely away:

16

bubbles over with gay confidence. It is mainly to this strain that
the pair proceed to bait the unfortunate Count on his return. He
is now abjectly penitent, full of apologies for his behaviour and
prayers for forgiveness. The Countess plays magnificently up to
her new rôle of the loving wife unjustly suspected by her jealous
husband, and yields only gradually to Susanna's hypocritical pleas
to her to forgive and forget. But there is still a tiny remnant of
fight left in the Count. He is bound to believe that it was not
Cherubino who had been in the cabinet, and he confesses he had
been misled by the Countess's air of anxiety under his recent
interrogation, which she now makes him believe was only a clever
bit of acting on her part. But what about the letter? he asks.
Thinking there is no more necessity for concealment, the women
tell him that Figaro was the writer of it, and that he had fobbed it
off on the Count *via* Basilio. In his first flush of anger at this news
he launches into new threats of vengeance on his impudent valet;
but in the end he yields to their sly argument that he who wants
to be forgiven should be the first to set others an example of
forgiveness.

17

Everything appears now to be happily settled; and the lively
ensemble ends with a fermata that cannot be too scrupulously

observed in performance; the longer the silence after so much tension the more effective is the unexpected appearance of Figaro, brimful, as usual, of gay assurance. He has news for his lordship, whom he tells (allegro con spirito) that the vassals and the musicians are all ready and straining at the leash to celebrate his marriage. He takes Susanna by the hand and is whirling her off when the Count intervenes. He is not to be rushed like this: there is a little point, he says, that is troubling him, as regards which perhaps the valet can give him some information. The three conspirators at once scent danger; for of course Figaro does not know that they have already revealed him to the Count as the writer of the letter. A new and more dangerous imbroglio is now blowing up, in which the reins of direction seem to be passing again into Almaviva's hands. Dramatically and musically this is the greatest scene in the opera: from now until the end of the act, indeed, we are in the presence of one of the miracles of operatic music. The moods and the motives of the characters change from moment to moment: for each of them Mozart finds the perfect expression, while the texture is a single piece of smooth weaving from start to finish.

Figaro soon finds himself in difficulties. To a melody that is a masterpiece of polite irony:

17

Andante

Co-no-sce-te, Si-gnor Fi-ga-ro, que-sto fo-glio chi ver-gò?

the Count shows him the letter and wonders if he can tell him who wrote it. Unaware of the recent run of the scenario, the master intriguer makes a cardinal blunder: after pretending to examine the letter critically he denies all knowledge of it or of the writer. From now onwards his better-informed fellow-conspirators have to keep prompting him. Susanna leads off. "Why," she asks him, with an air of merely reminding him of a little thing that has escaped his memory for the moment, "wasn't it you who gave it to Basilio?" "To take it—," the Countess adds; but before she can complete the sentence the Count interposes a curt "Well, what about it?" Susanna resumes the rôle of prompter: "Don't you remember? the little dandy?". . . "Who was to be in the garden this evening?" supplements the Countess; and once more the Count asks him sternly if his memory is any better now. When the puzzled Figaro still denies all knowledge of the letter the Count tells him bluntly and rudely that he can see in his ugly face that he is lying. In repartee Figaro is always at home: he counters with "It is my face that is lying, then, not I," to a delightful snatch of melody:

18

upon which Mozart proceeds to ring, in conjunction with No. 17, the most exquisite serio-comic changes in one voice after another.

The women try desperately to get command of the situation again. They tell the floundering Figaro to cease his stupid denials, for they are no longer necessary, the harmless little comedy he had intended having come to its natural end. Particularly delightful is the little snatch of counterpoint to No. 18 in which, while Figaro repeats his assurance that "It is my face that is lying, then, not I," Susanna and the Countess try to knock it into him that there is no need for him to keep up the pretence any longer, as they have already told the Count all about the mysterious letter:

19

To gain time he suggests that his prompt marriage to Susanna will clear everything up to everyone's satisfaction. The women renew their entreaties to the Count to let the matter drop and bring about the happy ending: but he shakes them off and wildly calls for Marcellina to come to his rescue; for it is she, he feels, who holds the winning card.

18

Suddenly the tempo whips up as a new personage appears on the scene; it is the half-tipsy gardener Antonio—another stock comic figure into whom Mozart breathes a new life of his own. Antonio has in his hand a pot of dilapidated carnations, and is in the homicidal mood that takes possession of every professional gardener when his flowers have been maltreated. He had become resigned, he gabbles, to all sorts of rubbish being flung every day from the balcony of this room; but when it comes to throwing human beings out on to his frames—well, that's more than he can be expected to put up with. The Count at once pricks up his ears and asks for further details; but Antonio can add nothing more to his story than that a man had been thrown from the balcony, had picked himself up, and had made off with the speed of the wind.

Susanna, as usual, is the first to reassemble her wits. "It was the page!" she manages to say *sotto voce* to Figaro, who, not quite knowing as yet what line to take, plays for time by bursting into fits of helpless laughter, to the great annoyance of both the Count and the gardener. This lout of an Antonio, says Figaro, is in his usual condition—pickled [1] from morning to night; and Susanna and the Countess repeat the indictment. But Almaviva is not to be so easily hoodwinked. He again tells the gardener to get on with his story; whereupon Figaro, having realised that the flying man had got away too quickly for Antonio to be able to identify him, now brazenly declares that it was he. The orchestra seems to comment ironically on this audacious tarradiddle. Susanna and the Countess remark in admiring undertones, "What a brain! What ingenuity!" But the Count is not convinced, while Antonio puts what looks like a poser to Figaro: "Then how have you managed to grow so much taller since then?" Figaro's bland explanation that a man always crouches during a jump makes no impression on the stolid gardener. "It looked to me more like the page," he says; and a wild cry of "Cherubino!" comes from the Count. "Of course!" says Figaro ironically, "having galloped from Seville."

[1] In the libretto "cotto"—"cooked," or, as we would say in the vernacular, "stewed."

The gardener's naïve assurance that the man who had descended from the balcony wasn't on horseback tries the Count's patience severely. He tells the valet to get on with his story. It was really he who had jumped, Figaro explains blithely. He had been in the service quarters, waiting for his adored Susanna, when he heard the Count's voice raised in anger: remembering the anonymous letter he had been scared out of his wits and had taken a flying leap through the window, spraining his ankle in the process; and to prove it he puts on a most convincing limp. "If it was you," continues Antonio, "then I ought to give you this paper that fell from your jacket when you landed." Here is the beginning of a fresh imbroglio: new despair on the part of the Countess and Susanna, a new attempt by the baffled Figaro to gain time until his fellow-conspirators can come to his rescue again.

19

The next section of the ensemble is dominated by a demure little figure in the orchestra:

20

to which everything that the characters have to say accommodates itself. The Count takes possession of the document, reads it, and folds it up again: then he blandly invites Figaro to tell him what is in it. Antonio suggests sarcastically that it may be a list of the valet's debts, a remark that results in his being summarily shooed off the stage. He goes away muttering, to the strain of No. 20, threats of what he will do to Figaro if ever he catches him at his tricks again. The others now address themselves to the question of the mysterious paper. The Count, having glanced at it once more, again asks the valet what he has to say on the subject. Figaro is grounded; but the Countess, who has managed to get a closer glimpse of it, recognises it as the page's regimental commission. Bit by bit she and Susanna manage to relay the information to Figaro, who at last explains to the Count that it is the page's commission, which the latter had left with him. "Why?" is the next awkward question. More *sotto voce* relaying enables Figaro to reply "Because it hadn't been sealed"; whereupon the Count, losing his temper, tears the document up, and the four characters express their various reactions to this new turn of events to the ever-present strain of No. 20.

The action takes yet another turn with the entry of Marcellina, Bartolo and Basilio. The tempo of the music quickens as the foundations are laid for the regulation final ensemble. Everybody has his say, and what they say individually is fused into a perfect musical unity. Marcellina and her friends excitedly demand that the Count, as the law incarnate, shall see that justice is done her. She states her own case—this bankrupt valet is under contract to marry her, and he must do so forthwith: Bartolo is there as her legal representative, Basilio as the most respectable of witnesses.[1] They chatter on and on to the great annoyance of the Count, who from time to time tries to impose silence on them, protesting that he is there expressly to judge the case according to law:

21

Allegro assai

O-là! si-len-zio! si-len-zio! si-len-zio!   Io son qui per giu-di-car!

The strife of opinions and voices culminates in a lively buffo septet; and when the curtain falls everything is precisely as it was at the beginning, the Count no wiser, the conspirators no further.

20

Figaro, as we have said, is always Beaumarchais, Beaumarchais always Figaro. The impudent, adroit, resourceful, none too scrupulous or truthful adventurer that was Beaumarchais is drawn to the life in the Figaro who plans the intrigue and fights his way through the unexpected difficulties attendant on this in the second act, becoming the more dangerous, the more indomitable, the harder he is pressed. In the third act of the French play we

---

[1] In Beaumarchais he himself aspires to Marcellina's hand.

see the other Beaumarchais, the practised litigant, the gay derider of the portentous farce of "justice." A room in the château is fitted out faithfully as a court of law, with desks or seats for the judge, the counsel, the witnesses, the lawyers, the ushers, the reporters and the spectators; and the case of Marcellina *versus* Figaro is tried by the Count in gravely ironic style. But we have now arrived at the point in the play where the mass of detail and the intricacies of the intrigue become more than the librettist can cope with, compelled as he is to set aside so much space for musical numbers. As always happens when he loses the support, or much of the support, of his predecessor, Da Ponte's dramatic structure becomes loose and occasionally incoherent, so much has he to omit or to condense. From this point onward, then, the play is transformed into opera pure and simple; and it is to the opera that we now have to address ourselves again.

We are to understand that between the second and the third acts it has been settled between the Countess and Susanna that the latter is to give the Count an assignation in the garden that night, but with an amendment, suggested by the Countess, of Figaro's original plan—she will herself go disguised as the maid and impersonate her. By this means she will be able to test the extent of her husband's fidelity, and if she can catch him *in flagrante delicto* she can not only consolidate her own domestic position with him but impose her own terms in the matter of Susanna's marriage to Figaro.

The setting of the third act is a large salon in the château. The Count is soliloquising (in recitative) on the perplexities that envelop him. He runs over the events that have roused his suspicions: an anonymous letter; Susanna hiding in the dressing-room; the Countess's obvious embarrassment; a man seen jumping from the balcony into the garden, and Figaro impudently claiming that it was he. It may be that one of his lordship's vassals is amusing himself at his expense, for the rabble is inclined to get a bit above itself nowadays; but the serious character of the Countess makes him reluctant to suspect her. And yet—are not all women fundamentally alike? The more he turns it all over in his mind the less sense is he able to make of it, and the more uneasy he is about it. He has sent Basilio off to Seville to discover if the page is really there, and he should be back with his report before the time for the wedding in the evening. Susanna is a further perplexity to him. Has she betrayed his secret to the Countess? If so, he will see to it that Figaro marries Marcellina.

He has been partly overheard by Susanna and the Countess, and the latter having slipped away the maid comes forward to play the next card in the risky game. Ostensibly she has intruded on Almaviva because she wants the Countess's vinaigrette, her ladyship having an attack of the vapours; but this, it becomes evident later, was only a pretext. He is a little surly with her at first, but soon becomes his former ardent self. A bride who loses her groom at the last moment, he hints meaningly, may herself be glad of such feminine consolation as smelling salts can afford. "But I can pay off Marcellina with the dowry you promised me," she objects. "When did I promise a dowry?" he asks. "That was what I understood," Susanna continues; to which his dry reply is, "Yes, but that was when I thought you had made up your mind to understand *me*." Demurely she hints that at last she has seen the light; her duty to his lordship and her own inclinations now draw her in the same direction.

This sets him off on an ardent declaration of his passion: "Cruel one! why all this time have you been kindling my hopes only to extinguish them?":

22

She plays coquettishly with him, simulating an ardour equal to his own. She promises him that she will meet him in the garden when night falls; and the Count expresses his contentment in a lovely phrase into which he evidently puts all his amorous heart:

23

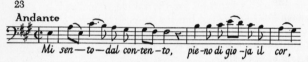

They pursue the delightful subject in a duet that is one of Mozart's little masterpieces, each speaking strictly in character, the Count being all passion, Susanna obviously only flirting with him, but with a serious background to her coquetry when she thinks of her Figaro.

She is departing without the vinaigrette. When the Count reminds her of it she archly confesses that she had invented her ladyship's indisposition as a pretext for a little private talk with him; this pleases him beyond measure. As she goes out he says to himself delightedly, "She's mine now, beyond a doubt!" But Susanna has a final little aside of her own: his lordship may think himself clever, but he will find out his mistake before long. Then, as usual, Beaumarchais springs a new complication on his characters and on us. In the doorway Susanna runs into Figaro, to whom she whispers excitedly, "Don't speak! I have won our cause without a lawyer!"

21

The pair go off exultantly. But the Count has overheard Susanna's incautious remark, and now the fat is all in the fire again. Not only has his passion been frustrated but his pride as a grand seigneur has been outraged by the discovery that his audacious vassals have been playing with him all this time. In an angry accompanied recitative he declares that he will punish Susanna for her treachery. The decision in the lawsuit still rests with him. True, but what if Figaro pays off the debt? Yet how can he? And there is in reserve the half-witted Antonio, who, with proper handling, can be persuaded to refuse his niece to this valet about whom he knows nothing and whom he does not like. Revenge will be sweet: the die is cast; and the Count launches his great aria, the burden of which is that he will not submit to seeing the object of his desire pass into the hands of his valet, that "vile creature," as he calls him. No; the lackey shall not triumph over the grandee; and the thought of his coming revenge fills him with joy. The vigorous aria is one of Mozart's finest; as always in circumstances of this kind, he takes his character for the time being out of the buffo atmosphere in which the drama as a whole is set: Almaviva is here as serious a character as any in the most serious of operas.

But we are soon back to comedy pure and simple. Marcellina, Bartolo and Figaro enter along with Don Curzio, a lawyer, who, by some process of operatic legerdemain which we try in vain to understand—for there has been nothing in the action to suggest that a trial has taken place—announces the decision of the court [1] —either Figaro must pay off his debt to Marcellina or marry her. She is in the seventh heaven of happiness, for she adores the sprightly young valet; while he is in the depths of despair. He appeals to the angry Count, who refuses to upset the judgment: Figaro must either pay up or marry; and he pointedly compliments Don Curzio on his verdict. So does Bartolo, on the grounds that now he too is revenged on his old enemy the barber. But Figaro is still the crafty fox with a thousand twists and turns. He now staggers them all by pleading that he is a gentleman by birth, and this being so he cannot marry without the consent of his noble parents. The Count, vastly amused, asks him who these notabilities may be and where they are. Figaro unfortunately does not know: he has been seeking them in vain, it appears, for the last ten years. He was not a foundling, as Bartolo had sarcastically suggested; he had been stolen by brigands when an infant, for the jewels and the gold and the richly embroidered clothes his exalted parents had lavished on him. And if all these do not constitute a proof of his illustrious origin, he says, what about the mysterious figure impressed on his arm?

"Not a spatula on your right arm?" Marcellina interjects excitedly; and learning that it is just that, she becomes quite incoherent with joy, for who can this be but her long-lost little Raffaello. "Behold your mother!" says Bartolo. "Do you mean my wet-nurse?" asks the incredulous Figaro. "No, your mother." "Behold your father!" says Marcellina, pointing to Bartolo; and the great recognition scene is complete. While Bartolo and Marcellina are embracing their offspring Susanna rushes in with a purse; she has received from the Countess the money to ransom her Figaro, and she appeals to the Count to reverse the verdict of the court. There comes a cloud over her sky for a moment when she sees Figaro embracing Marcellina; but after she has boxed his ears the necessary explanations are given her, Marcellina leading

---

[1] In Beaumarchais, as we have seen, there is a long trial scene. Mahler evidently felt that there was a lacuna in the opera at the point we have now reached, for in his Vienna performances he inserted Beaumarchais's trial scene, with recitatives of his own composition.

off by introducing herself in a delightful little phrase as her new
mother-to-be:

which Figaro caps with a melody still more charming:

as he presents Susanna formally to his long-lost father. The whole
lively action is enclosed within the frame of a sextet, in which
the only jarring note is that of the Count, who cannot conceal his
mortification at this latest unexpected blow to his plans.

At the end of the ensemble the Count and Curzio quit the stage.
Among the others all is gas and gaiters. Bartolo nobly decides to
marry Marcellina forthwith. She, in her turn, makes Figaro a
present of his promissory note for a thousand pieces of silver, by
way of a dowry. Susanna gives him the money she had intended
for his ransom; even Bartolo adds a cash contribution of his own.
Figaro feels like an Israelite in the desert who has unexpectedly
received several extra rations of manna; but while he is hinting
that if anyone has anything more to contribute to his privy purse
he will not hurt their feelings by refusing it, the happy Susanna
hurries him off with her to take the good news to the Countess
and her uncle Antonio. The recitative ends with the two happy
couples declaring in a brief passage in four-part harmony that if
the Count should now feel like bursting that will be all right so
far as they are concerned. Then they leave the stage arm in arm.

22

One of the most engaging features of this opera is the free-and-
easy way in which everyone seems to stroll into other people's
quarters; so we are not unduly surprised to find Cherubino and
little Barbarina now coming into the drawing-room, this being
the most likely place on the Almaviva estate, apparently, for the

gardener's daughter to tell the page that it has been arranged for him that he shall attend Figaro's wedding festivity disguised as a girl! He dreads, he protests, the anger of the Count, who believes him to be in Seville—which apprehension on his part makes it still more difficult for us to believe that he is now strolling about the château. However, there was no other place or time in the libretto in which Da Ponte could make us acquainted with this little piece of stage carpentry, which will become a vital part of the final dénouement; so here it had to come.

The little couple having left the stage after their very brief dialogue in recitative the Countess comes into the salon. In a recitativo accompagnato she tells us that she is anxiously awaiting news from Susanna as to the Count's reception of the promise of an assignation in the garden, of the wisdom of which she has her doubts. Still, she muses, there is nothing very wrong about her impersonating Susanna, and *vice versa;* and anyhow she has been drawn into all this by the frivolous conduct of her husband, who, by all appearances, no longer loves her; and she breaks into a pensive aria in which, for the second time in the opera—for Mozart manifestly has a special fondness for her—she pours out her sorrow over the days that are no more:

26

In the allegro section that follows, however, she indulges herself in the hope that her own constancy will have its reward in the return of the Count's affection.

As she leaves the stage Almaviva and Antonio enter. The gardener has some news that his master finds rather upsetting: the page supposed to be in Seville is in hiding somewhere on the estate; in proof of which he produces Cherubino's hat, which, with his clothes, the boy had left at the gardener's cottage. A minute or so suffices to convey this information to the Count and to us: then the pair go out and the Countess returns, accompanied by Susanna. The maid, it appears, has told her mistress by now of the Count's acceptance of the assignation at nightfall; the only thing necessary now is to fix up the details of the affair. This is done by the maid taking down from the Countess's dictation a canzonetta the opening words of which allude vaguely to the evening zephyrs playing about the pine-wood: as the Countess remarks after the charming little duet has run its course, the Count will be able to infer the rest. A pin from the Countess's dress has to be used to "seal" the letter, to which a postscript is added asking the recipient of it to return this "seal," as a token that he understands and agrees.

The room now fills with a bevy of young peasant maidens who have come to offer their homage and present bouquets to their gracious lady; among them are Barbarina and Cherubino, the latter dressed like the girls. They pipe an appropriately naïve little chorus, after which the action is carried on for a considerable time in recitative. The Countess has been particularly struck by the good looks and modest bearing of one of the girls—our friend Cherubino; and Barbarina explains that this is her little cousin, who had arrived last night to be present at the wedding. When the Countess accepts a bouquet from the "little cousin" the latter blushes painfully, and the Countess is struck by the resemblance of the child's features to those of the page. Susanna has only time for the ironical remark that this is quite natural when Antonio slips in, pulls off Cherubino's bonnet, and substitutes for it his regimental hat. The Countess is covered with confusion. The Count, who happens to be among those present, looks meaningly at both of them for an explanation. The Countess can do no more than stammer out a confession that it was precisely a little masquerade of this harmless sort that she and Susanna had been rehearsing when her husband had broken in on her that morning. Almaviva is sternly informing Cherubino that his disobedience shall be severely punished when the innocent Barbarina takes the wind out of his sails: "Oh, your Excellency always used to say, when you were kissing me, 'If you will only love me, Barbarina, I will grant you anything you may ask.' Now please let me marry Cherubino, and I will love you like my kitten." Well may poor Almaviva mutter to himself, "How is it that some one, some demon, some deity or other always steps in to frustrate me?"

A diversion is caused by Figaro, who enters protesting that if
his lordship keeps all these maidens here much longer there will
be no dancing. The Count, who of course knows something now
which Figaro does not yet know he knows, has spirit enough left
in him to wonder sardonically how the man can dream of dancing
with a sprained ankle; but the valet explains that that is better
now. How fortunate, the Count continues blandly, that the flower-
pots he had landed among were clay; and the unsuspecting valet
agrees that it was very fortunate. Antonio, who is not really such
a half-wit as he looks, puts him further posers about the page
having galloped to Seville and his commission being somehow
in Figaro's pocket all the time; and the schemer is completely
flabbergasted for a moment when the gardener tells him that the
page—whom he now drags forward—has confessed that it was·
he who had jumped from the balcony. But soon Figaro is his foxy
self again, as fertile in resource as ever. There is no law against
jumping from balconies, he points out, and no particular difficulty
about it; if he could do it, why not a page or anyone else? And
he defies Antonio to produce any proof that it was not so in
this instance.

A march is heard in the orchestra:

27

the after-strain of which:

28

has a faintly exotic tang that is very captivating. The Count and
Countess having seated themselves the stage fills up with a joyous
throng, among whom are the girls carrying bridal hats and veils

for the two brides. Bartolo presents Susanna to the Count; she kneels before him, and he hands her the hat and veil; then the Countess performs the same office for Marcellina, who is presented by Figaro; and at the conclusion of the march the company sing a chorus of felicitation to the two happy couples, joined with praise of their noble master. This is succeeded by a fandango:

29

While this is being danced, Susanna, on her knees before the Count, plucks him by the sleeve, surreptitiously draws his attention to the note, and keeps it in her hand while she adjusts her hair; pretending to put her veil straight he takes the note from her, conceals it, and then hands her over to Figaro; after which Marcellina is similarly given to Bartolo by the Countess. As the Count—still to the strains of the fandango—goes aside and furtively opens the note, he pricks his finger with the pin; this annoys him at first, but he philosophically reflects that it is the way of women to use a pin on all kinds of occasions: anyhow he understands the situation now and is greatly amused by it.

He has been observed by Figaro, who is also amused: some innamorata or other, he remarks to Susanna, has slipped his lordship a letter sealed with a pin; this has pricked his finger; he has let it fall, and he appears now to be searching for it. Well content with himself now, the Count dismisses the company until the evening, when they will all celebrate the dual nuptials in regal style, with music, feasting and dancing. They repeat their little chorus of homage, and the curtain falls.

24

Da Ponte makes a sorry mess of this episode. He follows Beaumarchais only as far as the moment when Figaro sees Almaviva reading the note and pricking his finger with the pin. Everything that ensues in the play immediately after that comes in perfect logical sequence. Beaumarchais's stage directions run: "The dance is resumed. The Count, after reading the billet, is folding it up again when he catches sight of the instruction on the reverse side to return the 'seal' to the writer by way of answer. [Obviously anything in the way of a reply either by letter or through an intermediary would be out of the question, the stage situation being what it is]. He looks round him on the ground, at last finds the pin, and fastens it to his sleeve." [Where it will be available for use as soon as circumstances permit]. This action of his also amuses Figaro: to the lover, he remarks indulgently to Marceline, the smallest object that once belonged to the loved one is dear.

A longish scene then follows in the play in which Basilio comes in and makes trouble over the marriage of Marceline, whom, as we have seen, he himself would like to marry. Still later, when Marceline and Figaro are left together on the stage, the former apologises to him for her earlier behaviour towards Susanna, to whom, she now admits, she had done wrong in believing that she was encouraging the advances of the Count. Figaro laughs to scorn the notion that he could ever entertain any suspicions of his wonderful Susanna. Just then little Fanchette (Barbarina) enters. She is looking for someone, she confides to them in her artless fashion—for her cousin Susanna, in fact, to whom she has been directed to return a pin. At once Figaro is on the alert. He leads Fanchette on by telling her he knows more about the matter than she imagines: it is the Count, is it not, who has sent her to Susanna with the pin that had fastened a little piece of paper he had had in his hand? Ah! the child counters, but there is something more that Figaro doesn't know—that the Count has given her a message for Susanna: "Deliver this pin to your lovely cousin, my little Fanchette," he had said, "and tell her that this is the seal of the big chestnut alley. Take care that no one sees you." (The chestnut alley had been named by Susanna as the place of the assignation: in the opera it becomes a pine-wood.)

Checking his rising rage, Figaro sends Fanchette on her way with the pin and the message; then he unburdens himself of his woes to Marceline, who, like a wise woman of the world, advises him not to jump to conclusions and condemn Susanna out of hand without a trial; after all, it may be the Count whom she is plotting to deceive. Figaro takes her advice; but he too, he says grimly, will be in the chestnut alley that night!

All this, in the play, occurs in its proper place, in logical connection, at the end of the third act, where it makes a first-rate curtain; and Da Ponte must have been fully aware of this. But the poor man was an opera librettist, not a dramatist, and so he had not a free hand. For one thing, convention suggested a choral ensemble, however short, as an "effective" ending for the act. For another, there are still four characters each of whom, by the rules of the game, is entitled to a solo piece of his or her own— Barbarina, Marcellina, Susanna and Basilio; and the only places Da Ponte can find for these solos are in the next act. So he most absurdly closes down, during the fandango, on Beaumarchais's well-constructed sequence of events before it has developed beyond its very first stage. We see only Figaro observing the Count reading the *billet-doux*, pricking his finger, dropping the pin and looking around for it. All that should follow straight upon this Da Ponte holds over to the next act; and when he does decide to use it there he makes a lamentable mess of it. And when he falls, as fall he does, he drags Mozart down with him—unless, as was by no means improbable, it was the composer who, for musical reasons of his own, insisted on the third act ending and the fourth opening in the way they do. Dictation or indolent acquiescence on the part of one or other or both of them? Who can say? But whether Mozart here acquiesced or dictated, he wrought his own undoing: from this point onwards the opera declines sadly for a time, not only in dramatic vigour but in musical interest. Nowhere else in the operatic output of his maturity has Mozart been so consistently mediocre for so long a stretch as in the first half of the fourth act of *The Marriage of Figaro*.

25

When the curtain rises for the final act we have passed on from late afternoon to night. The setting shows a garden, with a pavilion on the right and another on the left. It is as dark as is consistent with our just making out the characters and following the action: too dark, indeed, for the average spectator with no previous knowledge of the opera to grasp at a first seeing and hearing all the details of this final scene. Da Ponte begins where he had arbitrarily left off in the third act. Barbarina comes in, scrutinising the ground with a lantern for a pin she has lost, and, to a soft string accompaniment, sings an appropriately childish little cavatina as she does so: "Unhappy me! I have lost it! Where can it be? I can't find it. What will my cousin Susanna and his lordship say?" We are asked to believe, then, that all these hours, practically up to the very time of the assignation, the Count's message, *via* the "seal" of the note, has not yet reached Susanna!

Figaro enters with Marcellina, and the dialogue runs, in recitative, mainly on the lines of the corresponding situation in Beaumarchais's third act. Barbarina confides to Figaro that she is looking for a pin which the Count had ordered her to convey to Susanna, with the added injunction that no one else was to know anything about it. He palms off on her a pin he has taken from Marcellina's dress, and the child goes off on her errand to Susanna—and, what is more important to Barbarina, to her own secret assignation with Cherubino in one of the pavilions. When she has gone, Figaro breaks out in lamentations over Susanna's treachery. Marcellina, who, as we have seen, is now all pro-Susanna, advises her son not to condemn his bride too hastily; but he goes off fuming, swearing that now he knows where the assignation is—in the pine-wood —he will be there and will avenge himself and all other husbands. Marcellina, left alone, muses for a while on the situation: she will go and warn Susanna, whom she cannot bring herself to believe guilty; for fight as women may among themselves, when it is a question of dealing with the common enemy, peccant man, they fight as one. With this little soliloquy she goes off in the play; but Da Ponte makes it a "cue for song"—a long aria, with a liberal sprinkling of coloratura, on the universality of love in the innocent animal world and the reprehensible perfidy and cruelty of man towards woman. Unfortunately the aria is musically so banal that it is an act of piety towards the memory of Mozart to omit it from modern performances of the opera.

When Marcellina departs Barbarina makes another brief appearance, carrying a little basket containing some provisions she has managed to collect for Cherubino. As Figaro, Basilio and Bartolo enter she runs into the pavilion on the left, where she has arranged to meet the page. Figaro, now in savage mood, explains to the other two why he has summoned them here to meet him: on the very night of his wedding, he says, the Count and Susanna have come to an agreement behind his back, and he wants his friends' assistance in surprising them; [1] they are to wait until he whistles and then rush out on the criminals. With that he leaves them. The others discuss the eternal triangle problem for a moment, and Basilio seizes the opportunity to expound his own prudent philosophy in these matters in a long aria which we could quite well have dispensed with, for it is nothing more than a string of the musical commonplaces of the period. However, Bartolo had had *his* aria in the first act, and Basilio, with Da Ponte aiding and abetting him, feels that it is time to insist on his.

When at last he has made his exit Figaro comes into view again, and, with the end of all this fumbling in sight, the opera can begin to get into its musical stride again. Figaro, half-concealed in a long cloak and turned-down hat, indulges himself in an accompanied recitative and aria in which he rails against Susanna, himself, and the whole race of husbands, who, seemingly, will never learn what women really are. The aria is not Mozart at his very best, but at all events it is an improvement on what he has been ladling out to us recently:

30

26

As Figaro almost disappears from our view Susanna and the Countess enter, each disguised in the other's clothes: with them is Marcellina, who is now wholly on their side in the intrigue; [2]

---

[1] In Beaumarchais he summons all and sundry, Antonio, valets, peasants, etc.

[2] It should be pointed out that Beaumarchais's Marceline is quite a different character from Da Ponte's: in the play, after the touch of comedy given her in the early wrangling-match with Susanna and later in the recognition scene, she is a very sensible wordly-wise woman, wholly pro-Susanna and giving excellent calm advice to Figaro, of whom she is very fond. Beaumarchais has put some lofty remarks into her mouth on the subject of the grievances of women. In the opera she becomes mostly a figure of the broadest fun. There is no need, however, for laying on the burlesque with the thick brush employed by the ordinary player of the part. Crude farce is always the last refuge of the actor or actress who cannot play comedy.

Figaro must be taught a lesson, and there could be no better preceptress than Susanna, who gleefully undertakes the rôle. To see and hear without being seen or heard Marcellina retires into the pavilion on the left into which Barbarina has gone. The Countess's nerve is inclined to fail her now that the hour of danger is approaching, and Susanna has to breathe something of her own courage into her. Knowing, through what Marcellina has said, that the lurking Figaro is listening to everything, Susanna asks her ladyship's permission to stroll off for a while into the wood to enjoy the fresh air. Having obtained it, she launches a lovely aria "Deh vieni, non tardar, o gioja bella":

31

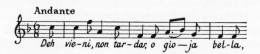

that shows Mozart in his best vein again; a tender romantic night-piece in which Susanna, serious for once, pours out all the love of her heart for some one unnamed.

We are to suppose that Figaro hears but does not see her very clearly, for of course she is dressed as the Countess: he accepts the amorous song as Susanna's, and is more perturbed and angry than ever at what he takes to be her perfidy. (Beaumarchais clarifies the situation for us by telling us, in a stage direction, that Susanna is now on one side of the stage, Figaro on the other.) While he is thus musing Cherubino appears. He is in high spirits, on his way to the pavilion where Barbarina and food are waiting him. But he catches sight of a woman, a spectacle always calculated to halt him dead in his tracks. It happens to be the Countess; but as she is in Susanna's clothes he takes her to be the maid, and at once proceeds to make love to her. A delightful duet follows: the ardent page cannot understand why the generally sprightly Susanna is so cold and coy, while the Countess is torn between fear of what will happen if the Count should arrive and annoyance at the boy's audacity.

Almaviva enters, very pleased with himself at having, as he thinks, found his Susanna at last; and everything is now set for the kind of ensemble in which Mozart revels. They are all in it, and all at cross-purposes. From opposite sides of the stage Figaro and Susanna comment on the present situation in their several ways. It is something the latter had not entirely foreseen. At last she recognises the page's voice, and feels that this unexpected turn of events has thrown a spanner into the works. Cherubino goes on with his eager wooing of the supposed Susanna, impudently reminding her that she need not put on virtuous airs with him, for was he not listening in the chair that morning when the Count had been making advances to her? The Countess tries in vain to get rid of him. Figaro and Almaviva are puzzled and enraged, in their individual ways, at the intrusion of this unknown person into the action. When at last Cherubino tries to kiss the supposed Susanna, the Count, unable to stand any more, steps between them and, to his vast annoyance, receives the kiss. The page, recognising him, runs off in terror. Figaro, who has come forward cautiously to see better what is happening, receives the cuff on the side of the head which his lordship had intended for the page, at which Susanna and the Countess break into laughter; everyone, in fact, is amused except Figaro, who, regretting his ill-timed curiosity, retires into the background again.

27

The imbroglio thickens. To a new strain in the orchestra:

32

the Count begins his wooing of the fictitious Susanna; the Countess plays up to him admirably, while the amused real Susanna and the angered Figaro comment on the situation in their various ways from their several hiding-places. The Count gives the pseudo-Susanna a ring as a supplementary dowry, which makes Figaro boil over: "Everything's going marvellously," he mutters, "but the best is yet to come!" The Count directs his adored one's steps towards the pavilion on the right; and when she coyly comments on the darkness of it he assures her that it isn't to read that he has come there. As he himself is following her, Figaro confronts them: the Countess goes into the pavilion, and the Count slips away and hides among the trees, promising to see her again shortly. "Venus has taken cover," Figaro comments sardonically, "to meet her charming Mars; but I, the modern Vulcan, will catch them in my net."

The pace and colour of the music change once more as Susanna, in a feigned voice, calls on him to be silent. Taking her, of course, for the Countess, he explains that his lordship has gone off with Susanna, and now *he* is in command of the situation. She intends to play up to him; but when she says "Speak more softly; I won't stir from here, but trust me, I will be avenged," she forgets to change her voice, which he recognises at once as Susanna's. Now, he thinks, he sees his way clear before him: pretending to believe still that this is the Countess dying to be revenged on her faithless husband he will make love to her until the time for exposure shall come: Susanna, for her part, sees through him and decides to amuse herself with him for as long as may be necessary.

He stages a comic love scene, throwing himself at the pseudo-Countess's feet and exhorting her to lose no time in co-operating with him in giving Almaviva a dose of his own medicine. The humorous point of this latest situation is that while Figaro knows that she is Susanna, she does not know that he knows, and is accordingly irritated at the passion he puts into the wooing of the Countess. Her hand is itching to punish him: at last she can control herself no longer and boxes his ears heartily again and again, resuming her proper voice and making it quite clear that she is not the Countess but Susanna: this will teach him, she says, to play the seducer. He is in the seventh heaven of delight at the lesson; now he knows his Susanna's virtue is impregnable.

In a charming phrase:

33

Andante

Pa-ce, pa-ce mio dol-ce te—so-ro! Io co—nob-bi la vo-ce che a-do-ro.

he asks her to make peace with him; he had known all along, he tells her, by her adored voice, who she is, in spite of her costume. Their voices blend in the happiest of duets.

Then the Count re-enters, calling "Eh, Susanna! Are you deaf?

Are you dumb?", and he goes into the pavilion where the Countess is. Susanna is relieved: she knows now that he had not recognised her ladyship in her disguise. She tells Figaro that it is time now to end the comedy, but they must first do something to "console" this "queer lover," with whom they have played long enough; this resolve they express to the heart-easing strain of No. 33. Delighted to co-operate with her, Figaro throws himself at the feet of the supposed Countess and makes love to her with exaggerated ardour: Susanna meets him halfway in this, and they go arm-in-arm in the direction of the pavilion on the left. But the Count has overheard them; he jumps to the conclusion that his wife is betraying him, and, seizing the presumptuous valet lover, shouts for his vassals, for he is unarmed. "My master!" ejaculates Figaro in mock terror as the Count seizes him, "I am lost!" Susanna slips into the pavilion. Basilio, Curzio, Antonio, Bartolo and a number of servants and peasants with lighted torches rush in. The Count tells them that the criminal he is holding has betrayed and dishonoured him: his depraved female accomplice they shall soon see for themselves. They register appropriate horror, while Figaro chuckles to himself. Retaining his grip on him, and telling him that resistance is in vain, Almaviva bids the supposed Countess come forth and meet the just punishment for her offence.

Receiving no reply he goes into the pavilion, and is very surprised by what he finds there. He hands out first Cherubino, who tries unavailingly to conceal his identity, then Barbarina, then Marcellina, and last of all the pseudo-Countess. The spectators are as astounded as he, as is evident from their turn-by-turn ejaculations:

The Count: "The Page!"
Antonio: "My daughter!"
Figaro: "My mother!"
Basilio, Antonio and Bartolo: "The Countess!"

The feigned Countess begs for mercy, which the infuriated Almaviva refuses, even when the others add their supplications to hers. The climax comes when the veritable Countess emerges from the other pavilion and remarks with gentle malice, "At least you won't refuse *me* when I ask you to pardon them."

The Count, recognising that this is really his wife disguised as the Susanna whom he has been trying to seduce, collapses like a deflated balloon. Humbly he implores pardon:

34

Con — tes—sa, per—do—no! per — do—no, per—do—no!

She answers the poor repentant, outwitted sinner with magnanimous tenderness; and in a lively final ensemble the whole company express their delight at this happy ending to a "day of torments, caprices, follies":

35

In con—ten—ti ein al—le —gri-a, So-lo a—mor può ter—mi — nar,

28

The equivalent in Beaumarchais of the aria (No. 30) in which Figaro laments his lot as a deceived husband is an eloquent three-pages-long soliloquy of the most serious and savage kind: it was this, more than anything else in the whole work, that gave the play its absorbing social interest for contemporary spectators. Apart from his railings against women, Figaro—here, more than anywhere else, speaking directly as Beaumarchais—poured out his gall upon the social structure of his period, in which mere birth counted for so much and ability for so little. In words that stab and sear he runs over his own chequered career, the straits to which he had been reduced time after time to keep his end up in such a world. He makes a vicious frontal attack on the French aristocracy, as symbolised by Almaviva, who enjoyed every advantage in life without ever having done anything to deserve one of them: "No, my lord the Count, you shall not have her [Susanna]; I say you shall not have her! Simply because you are a grand seigneur you flatter yourself that you are a great genius: nobility, fortune, rank, offices, these things make a man so proud! What have you done to deserve such a wealth of good things?

You have given yourself the trouble to be born, nothing more: for the rest, you are a very ordinary creature; while I, lost in the obscure crowd, have had to employ more knowledge and ingenuity merely to subsist than have gone to the governing of all the Spains in the last hundred years. And you dare to pit yourself against me!"

Two modern French authors, Jean Jacques Brousson and Raymond Escholier, have made this speech of Figaro's, that has more than a touch of prophecy in it, the starting-point for a play, *La Conversion de Figaro*, the setting of which is the Paris of a few years later than the *Marriage*. The Revolution has broken out: the Terror stalks through Paris. Figaro, in virtue of his brains, his courage, his gift for handling men, has become a person of some importance in the councils of the revolutionists, while Almaviva is now a mere cork on the swirling currents of events which he and his like cannot control and have barely managed to understand. The Count and Rosina are heading, as "aristos," straight for the guillotine, and it is Figaro who saves them from that fate, out of the affection and respect he has always had for Rosina, for the character and the intellect of the Count he still despises as of old. It has always seemed to me that *La Conversion de Figaro* might be made into a very effective opera by some librettist and composer of genius. There is no good reason why this amazingly vital character should remain for all time where Da Ponte and Mozart have left him.

The Magic Flute

WOLFGANG AMADEUS MOZART [1756–1791]

PRINCIPAL CHARACTERS

TAMINO	*Tenor*
PAMINA	*Soprano*
PAPAGENO	*Baritone*
PAPAGENA	*Soprano*
THE QUEEN OF NIGHT	*Soprano*
SARASTRO	*Bass*
THE SPEAKER OF THE TEMPLE	*Bass*
TWO PRIESTS	*Tenor and Bass*
TWO MEN IN ARMOUR	*Tenor and Bass*
THREE GENII OF THE TEMPLE	*Soprano, Mezzo-soprano and Contralto*
THREE LADIES OF THE QUEEN OF NIGHT	*Two Sopranos and Mezzo-soprano*
MONOSTATOS	*Tenor*

1

As Hermann Abert remarks in his monumental work on Mozart, the text of *The Magic Flute* has come in for more disparagement than all the rest of Mozart's libretti put together. It has frequently been described as the silliest of all opera libretti. On the other hand Goethe—who, by the way, began, without finishing, a continuation of the theme—declared that "it takes more culture to perceive the virtues of *The Magic Flute* text than to point out its defects," and laid it down that while for the generality the stage spectacle was the great

thing, it was the "higher meaning" of the work that would be
fastened on by "initiates." Writing in much the same vein in 1849,
Joseph Cornet—the Hamburg impresario to whom reference has
been made in our chapter on *Don Giovanni*—laid it down that
"*The Magic Flute* is the central point of German opera, towards
which for centuries to come the eyes of all will turn who want
to study the basic elements of the German opera style."

When opinions upon a work are as sharply contradictory as
this, the inference is that neither camp is talking at the same time
about quite the same thing; each is seeing only what it wants to
see in order to establish a thesis of its own and turning a blind eye
on the remainder. It can hardly be denied that if by some accident
or other nothing of Mozart's score had survived to be published
beyond the first of the two acts, the eulogies of Goethe and
Cornet and many others in the first half of the nineteenth century
would seem very wide of the mark today. If later the second act
had come to light, it would have been evident that the enthusiasm
of all these people had been evoked only by that act, to the discreet ignoring of the first; while the upholders of the thesis that
nothing so inane as the plot of *The Magic Flute* had ever been
seen or ever will be seen again on the operatic stage would obviously be judged to have underrated the second act out of sheer
exasperation with the first. Mozart's opera is manifestly not one
work, but two. How then did a musical dramatist of his quality
manage to persuade himself that the two halves constituted a
single valid whole? To that century-old question no satisfactory
answer has yet been given.

2

The circumstances of the origin of the opera are too familiar to
every student of musical history for it to be necessary to do more
than outline them here. About 1790 the old yearning to write a
"German" opera seems to have taken possession of Mozart once
more. The decisive moment came when, about that time, he
renewed an old acquaintance with Emanuel Schikaneder (1748–
1812)—a remarkable character in many ways. He had been in
turns or simultaneously actor, singer, stage manager, impresario
and heaven knows what else. In our time he would have drifted
as a matter of course to Hollywood, where he would soon have

become the leading purveyor of easy amusement for the simple-minded populace. He specialised in gorgeous and expensive stage and open-air spectacles—and generally made them pay. By 1791 he had established himself in Vienna, in a theatre of his own "auf der Wieden." At that time perhaps the most popular of all stage genres in Vienna was that of the fairy play or fairy opera, which gave the crowd its fill of marvellous happenings and romantic sentiments. The leading literary figure in this development had been Wieland, upon whose fantastic stories the playwrights and opera poets drew liberally. The most successful provider of this kind of theatrical fare in Vienna just then was one Marinelli, with whom Schikaneder boldly entered into competition.

It was Schikaneder, apparently, who first thought of the concoction that was ultimately to become the plot of *The Magic Flute*. He succeeded in interesting Mozart in it, though the composer, significantly enough, seems not to have been over enthusiastic about it at first, judging from his remark to Schikaneder in March 1791, which was in effect this—"All right! but if we come a cropper over it don't blame me, for I have never written a *Zauberoper* [magic opera] before." However, each needed the other at that time, Schikaneder because he was in one of his usual economic fixes, Mozart because he was desperately anxious, for both artistic and financial reasons, to get into the German theatre again. The fact that both the musician and the impresario were freemasons seems also to have influenced him to some extent, for he took his masonic obligations very seriously.

3

In the text book and on the theatre bills Schikaneder was named as the author of the libretto. In 1849 Cornet, in his book *Die Oper in Deutschland*, described how, some thirty years before then, he had met in Vienna a middle-aged gentleman, of the name (it was an assumed one) of Giesecke, who declared that *he* was the main author of *The Magic Flute* text, Schikaneder having contributed only "the figures of Papageno and his wife." The Mozart biographers have wrangled over this statement ever since. This Giesecke was a delver into mineralogy, geology and some kindred sciences who, after many years of capable work, ended his days, in 1833, as the much respected Professor of Mineralogy in Dublin.

Too much ink has perhaps been expended on the subject of this claim of his to the authorship of the libretto of *The Magic Flute*, but there seems to be no valid reason for disputing it. He had been on Schikaneder's staff in Vienna in various capacities round about 1790, and he is known to have written the whole or part text of more than one "fairy opera" or "magic opera." (He was a student in Vienna at that time, and possibly eked out a slender living, as Berlioz and others were to do later, by singing in the chorus and doing odd jobs about the theatre.) We need not assume that he was the author of every line of the *Magic Flute* text; things of that sort are usually pies in which more than one chef or scullion can have a finger. But on the main point there is no reason for doubting his veracity and Cornet's.

Mozart made good progress with the music of the opera in June and July 1791, and in the latter month began the orchestration of the first act; in that month too, apparently, although the work was far from finished, he entered it, in a handwriting that betrays haste, in his Catalogue—the *Verzeichnis aller meiner Werke*.[1] For some time after that he was occupied with other plans, in particular the Requiem Mass that had been so mysteriously commissioned from him, and the opera *La Clemenza di Tito*, for the production of which—on the 6th September—he had to spend some time in Prague. On his return to Vienna he took up *The Magic Flute* again, and on the 28th September completed the work with the composition of the March of the Priests (No. 9 of the printed score), and the overture. Both of these he entered in the *Verzeichnis*, together with the customary quotation of the opening bars of each. Two days later the opera was produced, with Mozart conducting, in Schikaneder's Theater auf de Wieden: Schikaneder was the Papageno, Schack the Tamino, Nannina Gottlieb (the Barbarina of *Figaro*) the Pamina, Josepha Hofer the Queen of Night, Gerl the Sarastro, and Nouseul the Monostatos. The opera soon became enormously popular, and remained so for many years, to Schikaneder's great profit. Its success, however, mattered little to poor Mozart, who died in poverty and misery

[1] As usual, he jotted down in the *Verzeichnis* the opening bars of the work —in this case the first four bars of the orchestral introduction to the aria of Tamino, "Zu Hülfe! Zu Hülfe! sonst bin ich verloren," with which the stage action opens.

ten weeks after the first performance of the work—on the 5th
December 1791.

4

Let us now glance at the curious farrago that was *The Magic
Flute* as first conceived. The overture does not concern us in the
least at this point of our study, for it lacks the smallest relevance
to the action that is now to be put before us. The setting is one
of trees and rocks plus a circular temple—where, we are not told.
There enters what is described as a Japanese (why Japanese?)
Prince, Tamino, carrying a bow. He is in a state of abject terror,
as well he may be, for he is being pursued by a great serpent, and
he has run out of arrows. He gives anguished expression to his
fears and calls desperately for help in a short quasi-aria, whereupon the doors of the temple most opportunely fly open and
three veiled Ladies appear, each armed with a silver spear, who
proceed to slay the serpent, congratulating themselves volubly on
having arrived in the nick of time to rescue the young man by
what they call their "heroic deed." It is their duty now, they
continue, to carry the news to their Queen; perhaps this handsome
youth will bring back her lost peace of mind. But each has been
favourably impressed by the comeliness of the youth who still
lies unconscious before them, and coquettishly each of them tries
to persuade the others to leave *her* to attend to him while *they* go
off to take the good tidings to the Queen. At last they depart in
company, each swearing fidelity to the young stranger until they
and he shall meet again. Their repetitive chatter occupies some
ten pages of the score. It is difficult to believe that Mozart could
have taken much interest in them; but his sound craftsmanship
enabled him to spin out their talk plausibly enough in the accepted
musical formulae of the period.

When they have left the stage, Tamino, having regained consciousness, is greatly astonished to find the terrible serpent dead
at his feet. Hearing sounds in the distance, he takes cover among
the trees as he perceives a man approaching across the valley. It
is the bird-catcher Papageno, a simple child of nature, for whom
Mozart, who dearly loved a character of this type, has written a
quantity of enchanting music. He is heralded by a light-hearted

strain, in the purest folk vein, in the strings, the horns joining in with gravely comical effect at the end of each line:

1

Strapped to his back is a large bird-cage, containing several little captives, and every now and then he puts a Pan's pipe to his mouth on which he blows an artless half-scale:

2

In a delicious little ditty to the tune of No. 1 he informs the universe that he is the care-free bird-catcher, known to young and old throughout the land; if he could only capture pretty girls by the same means and in the same numbers his happiness would be complete!

5

He and Tamino converse for a time in spoken dialogue. Tamino tells him he is a prince with large possessions. This astonishes Papageno, who did not know that there were any lands or people beyond the mountains. About himself he can tell Tamino little except that he was born some time or other, has a little hut of his own, exists, like other people, by eating and drinking, and makes a living by providing the Queen of Night and her maidens with captured birds. "Have you been so happy, then," asks Tamino, "as to have seen the Queen of Night?" No mortal has had that good fortune, Papageno replies. "Surely," Tamino muses, "this must be the great Queen of whom my father has so often told me." His brooding air rather frightens Papageno, who warns him to stand back, for when he fights, he boasts tremulously, he has a giant's strength. Then no doubt it was he, the Prince surmises, who had fought the serpent. Papageno, having first made sure that the monster is dead, modestly admits that his was the great deed, accomplished, too, without a weapon of any kind.

Thereupon the Ladies re-enter; he recognises them as the three who give him his daily bread, figs and wine in payment for his birds. Being the servants of the virtuous Queen of Night they are naturally all for truth; so they censure him for his fibs and teach him a lesson. Today he gets from them, instead of wine, cold water, instead of bread, a stone, and instead of sweet figs a golden padlock on his mouth. Then the Ladies inform Tamino that it was they, not the mendacious bird-catcher, who had killed the serpent, and hand him a medallion that is a gift from the great Queen herself; it contains the likeness of her daughter.

With an "Auf Wiedersehen" they leave the astonished young man to contemplate the portrait with wonder and delight, and to sing, in an expressive aria, of his love at first sight for the beautiful original, whom he longs to make his.

The Three Ladies return to assure him that that felicity shall be his, the Queen having promised that if the youth turns out to have as much courage as, according to them, he has tenderness of heart, he will be able to rescue her daughter, who has been stolen from her by an evil magician. Tamino has time only to ejaculate "Lead me to her!" when there is a sound of thunder in the distance; the rocks divide and the Queen herself appears. In a dignified recitative and aria, laid out on the grandest scale, she confides to him the task of "bringing solace to her sorely tried mother's heart"; for with the loss of her daughter—abducted by a miscreant—all joy in life had left her. But if the Prince can rescue the maiden then her hand shall be his reward; and to leave him in no doubt that she means what she says she performs the most wonderful feats of vocal agility through fourteen bars (60 notes in all) on the single word "then" ("Dann"), ending up with a staggering F *in alt.* ("Dann" was no doubt selected for this purpose because its vowel is the easiest of all on which to sing coloratura).

She leaves the stage with the Three Ladies, and Tamino is about to follow them when he is intercepted by Papageno, who, because of his padlock, is now incapable of articulate speech; in reply to Tamino's expressions of sympathy all he can do is to mumble "Hm!", mocked at the unison by a humorous bassoon:

The Three Ladies, however, soon come to his rescue; the Queen has relented, it appears, and the padlock is removed. The real business of the Ladies, however, is with Tamino. They hand him a magic flute, a gift from the Queen, which will protect him in danger and give him power to subdue human passions and increase the sum of happiness on earth. As for Papageno, he is horrified to learn that he must now, by order of the Queen, accompany the Prince to the castle of the terrible Sarastro; but to hearten him the Ladies give him a chime of silver bells. The music of this scene has so far been, on the whole, of only average quality; but we get a touch of the greater Mozart in a trio in which the Ladies promise Tamino that three young genii shall attend him on his quest; to their counsel alone must he give any heed. And so, after a charming quintet, the Prince and the bird-catcher set out on their mission.

6

The scene changes to a splendidly furnished room. We see the Moor Monostatos dragging Pamina in, who declares that she has no fear of death but is concerned about her mother, who must be dying of grief on her account. Breathing fire and slaughter, Monostatos summons his fellow-minions, who put fetters on her hands; whereupon she falls senseless on a couch. The slaves having been sent away, Monostatos, left alone with the unconscious Pamina, seems to be contemplating some further villainy when Papageno enters, after having observed the beautiful damsel admiringly from the window. There follows a humorous scene between him and Monostatos: each takes the other for the devil and is mightily afraid; and the comical situation ends with them running off in opposite directions, having meanwhile drawn from Mozart some naïvely diverting music.

Papageno soon returns, and Pamina having awakened and called piteously for her mother, the two have an explanation scene in recitative. He tells her who he is, and of the noble young Prince whom her mother, having given him Pamina's portrait, has sent out to rescue her. There is not a moment to be lost, she replies, for the sun is high in the heavens, and at noon Sarastro will return as usual from the chase. The conversation somehow turns upon love, and Papageno regrets that he himself, poor simple soul, is without a sweetheart; whereupon, regardless of the fact that time is now of the essence, the pair indulge themselves in a delicious duet on the theme of love as the greatest blessing mankind can know:

4

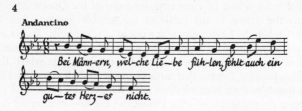

7

They depart in company, and the scene changes for the finale to the first act. The setting shows a grove, with a temple at the back, over the portal of which are inscribed the words "Temple of Wisdom." Rows of pillars lead to two other temples at the side, one the "Temple of Reason," the other the "Temple of Nature." And with this change of scene comes a great change in the spirit of the drama and in the mood and quality and colour of the music; three trombones and muted trumpets lend solemnity to the texture, while the strings are without double-basses. To a solemn melody three Genii, each carrying a silver palm branch, lead Tamino in. They inform him that he is at last near the goal appointed him, but if he is to win through to the end he must be "steadfast, obedient and silent." He asks them if it will fall to him to rescue Pamina, but they reply that it is beyond their powers to tell him that.

When they have left him he muses on his present condition. The words of his mysterious conductors seem to him to have been words of wisdom, and the place in which he finds himself appears to be the seat of the gods, for the very gates and pillars bear witness that here are the fruits of "industry and art." He will save Pamina from the tyrant, he vows, or die. He approaches the temple gates on the right and the left in turn, and from each is bidden sternly to "Stand back!" by a voice within. But his knock on the gate of the third temple brings out an aged Priest to whose question "What would you here?" he replies that he seeks the reward of love and virtue. How can he hope for that, answers the Priest, when he has been driven thither not by virtue and love but by the mere craving for revenge and death? Told that the ruler of the holy place is Sarastro he bursts into a denunciation of the evil magician, as he believes him to be on the strength of the word of an unhappy woman, crushed by a great wrong done her—the abduction of her daughter. The old Priest, calmly advising him never to pay too much attention to the chatter of women, assures him that while Sarastro had indeed conveyed the daughter away it was for no wicked end, though what his purpose was the Priest cannot at the moment disclose, for duty and his oath bind his tongue.

8

To a grave strain in the orchestra:

5

he tells Tamino that he shall learn the full truth when, led by friendship's hand, he is made one of the eternal brotherhood. A chorus of priests within assures him, however, to the music of the solemn No. 5, that Pamina still lives; and in wild enthusiasm he thanks the almighty ones in the medium that seems to him the most appropriate. He plays a charming melody on his flute, whereupon wild animals come forward and listen entranced, subdued. To the same melody he sings a song of praise to his flute, the giver of a joy that even the savage creation shares. But Pamina he has not yet found, and, still accompanied by gracious phrases in the magic flute, he pours out his anxious heart to her. Where shall he find her? he asks despairingly.

A cheery, companionable sound falls on his ear; it is that of Papageno blowing the only melody possible to him on his pipes (No. 2). The Prince has no sooner gone off in search of his birdcatching friend than Papageno himself enters with Pamina, both in quest of the promised rescuer. Papageno again essays his little melody (No. 2) and is answered from afar by the same figure on Tamino's flute. After a simple little duet they are both of them about to set off on the Prince's tracks when they are intercepted by Monostatos and a number of slaves, who are about to put fetters on them when Papageno opportunely bethinks him of his magic chime of bells; their pretty tinkle has an astonishing effect on the Moor and his minions, all of whom dance off singing a delightfully naïve little chorus, to which Pamina and Papageno add a comment in the same simple vein: "Would that every good man could find some such chimes; then would enmity disappear and he would live in the harmony of friendship, which alone can lift from him his load of care and give him happiness on earth."

From within comes a choral cry of "Long live Sarastro!" The name strikes terror into the hearts of Pamina and Papageno; the latter wishes he were a mouse or a snail that could creep away and hide. "What shall we say?" he asks. "The truth!" cries Pamina ecstatically; "the truth, even if it were judged a crime!" Just then, to solemn music, Sarastro enters in a splendid triumphal chariot drawn by lions (a genuine Schikaneder touch, this!), followed by a train of priests and attendants, all singing his praises as the giver of peace and joy and wisdom. Pamina throws herself at his feet and confesses her fault in trying to escape, to which she had been driven by the unwelcome attentions of the Moor. With dignity and gentleness he bids her rise; he knows her heart is given up to love:

6

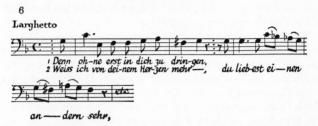

Larghetto

1 Denn oh-ne erst in dich zu drin-gen,
2 Weiss ich von dei-nem Her-zen mehr—,   du lieb-est ei—nen

an — dern sehr,

but as yet he cannot set her free. She speaks of the mother she
loves; but he tells her that her only hope of salvation lies in escape
from her mother's power: "Proud is she. A *man* must guide your
heart, for without the guidance of a man a woman steps out of
her proper sphere."

Monostatos enters, bringing with him the captured Tamino,
and the Prince and Pamina recognise each other as predestined
rescuer and rescued. Monostatos claims Sarastro's favour for having frustrated their plan for flight, and is very sorry for himself
when his master sends him off to be bastinadoed. At Sarastro's
command the Priests veil the heads of Tamino and Pamina and
lead them away to the temple, there to undergo the necessary
spiritual probation, and the act ends with a chorus in praise of
Sarastro: "When Virtue and Justice hold sway, then earth will
become heaven, and mortals the equals of the gods."

9

As the reader will have observed, in this last scene of the first
act (No. 8 of the score), the whole dramatic scheme has suddenly
been turned upside down. The virtuous Queen of Night, filled
with a most sincere mother love, has in the twinkling of an eye
become an evil principle from which her daughter must somehow
be saved, while the wicked magician is transformed into the best
and wisest of beings, the analogue of that Zoroaster from whom
his operatic name seems to have been derived. In general terms,
the work is no longer a naïve *Zauberoper* but an exposition of
freemasonry, the supposed Egyptian mysteries of long ago, and
the noble sentiments of "freedom," "truth," "human brotherhood" and all the rest of it that had long been circulating more
or less underground among men of intelligence and goodwill

and had recently come into the full light of day as the first result of the French Revolution of 1789.

What was the occasion and what were the real causes of this sudden right-about-face on Schikaneder's and Mozart's part? It has been conjectured that it came about primarily through the production by Schikaneder's rival Marinelli of a Singspiel entitled *Kaspar der Fagottist, oder die Zauberzither*, which ran on much the same general lines as *The Magic Flute* had done so far, the hero being endowed with a magic zither, and Kaspar, the simple child of nature, with a bassoon, an instrument capable of a good deal of rough rustic humour. This may have been a contributory cause of the Schikaneder-Mozart right-about-face, but surely not the whole cause, or perhaps not even the vital one. Granted that a change of direction now seemed advisable, why should the new course have been set with full sail for freemasonry and humanitarianism and all the attendant solemnities?

Schikaneder, Mozart and Giesecke were all masons, and it is probably the last-named, as the only literate of the triumvirate, who must be credited with an acquaintance with the Abbé Terrasson's novel *Sethos*, in which the ancient "Egyptian mysteries" and the mode of initiation into them were ostensibly set forth; this work was undoubtedly drawn upon for the business of recasting the opera. But when all the external facts are sorted out and put together again, so far as that is possible today, we are still no nearer a satisfactory answer to the question why the new *Magic Flute* should have taken so decidedly the line that it did.

There are, of course, traces even in the original scheme of a leaning in that direction from the beginning. Insufficient attention, perhaps, has been paid to the masonic and humanitarian slogans in the text *before* the change of course was decided upon. It is the Queen of Night whom we find, in No. 4 of the opera, spouting, through the medium of her Ladies, the best Sarastrian sentiments: the magic flute, the Ladies inform Tamino, will not only protect him in his wanderings but enable him to purify the passions of mankind, to turn tears into joy, to move even the unmarried man to submit to the bonds of love: "Such a flute is worth more than gold and crowns, for it will increase the sum of human happiness and content." Neither Sarastro nor his Priests could have phrased the aspirations of the epoch in general and of freemasonry in particular more precisely; yet it is the Queen of Night who is speaking! In the later duet between Pamina and Papageno— "Bei Mannern, welche Liebe fühlen, fehlt auch ein gutes Herze nicht" (No. 7 of the score)—the praises are sung of pure love, through which beneficent nature subdues all the creatures of earth. Once more we seem to hear the all-good and all-wise Sarastro and his Priests declaiming.

10

What with one thing and another we have the feeling that it was the basic intention of Schikaneder and Mozart from the first to make the drama one of humanitarianism and ethics (with comic and romantic elements liberally thrown in), the centre of which should be the virtuous Queen of Night, and that all the later change amounted to, in fact, was the substitution of a newly-conceived Sarastro for the Queen as the mouthpiece of the most enlightened views of the period on the ideals of brotherhood, industry and art towards which humanity should now strive. To give full value to this conception a Sarastro would obviously be more serviceable than a Queen—a man rather than a woman, and a man surrounded by a grave ritual, ostensibly derived from the "Egyptian mysteries," from which woman, by the very misfortune of her sex, was excluded.

The new "pull," in fact, seems to have been towards freemasonry in one guise or another. But how did that pull come to be so strong and so decisive as it was? Shall we be wrong in ascribing it primarily to Mozart? Had there been something in him, between his first work at the text in July 1791 and his return to Vienna in September, that was calling out more and more imperiously for expression and for which *The Magic Flute*, as it had originally been, provided only an imperfect outlet? Though he did not know it, he was already a doomed man, and something in the very depths of him was calling, as it did also in the Requiem, for realisation in music—a sense of the seriousness of life and the gravity of death. In the second act of *The Magic Flute* there is manifestly a great *approfondissement* of the spirit, resulting in what we should now be calling an elderly man's music had Mozart been one who had lived out the normal span of humanity—his *Parsifal*, his *Lied von der Erde*. He attained to ethical

117

illumination in his art so much earlier than most men because he was doomed to die so early. Now freemasonry was a channel to which his spirit had instinctively turned for a long time for the outpouring of his profounder broodings. His masonic music, in particular the impressive *Maurerische Trauermusik* ("Masonic Funeral Music," K. 477),[1] has a peculiar gravity not found anywhere else in his work except in *The Magic Flute*.[2]

11

Is the suggestion too far-fetched, then, that it was from Mozart himself that the idea emanated to change the action of the opera and from the end of the first act onward to make its central motive the exposition of certain "mysteries" and "initiations"? He had perhaps already become a little weary of the dramatically thin fantastic element in the work, and doubted whether he could sustain his interest in it much further. He clearly had no desire to turn back on what he had already written, no intention of scrapping this and beginning afresh on a completely rewritten text. Into what he had composed between Nos. 1 to 7 and No. 8 he had put much of the best of himself as he then was; and he saw no reason to sacrifice this music. Overall dramatic consistency mattered little to him so long as he could now throw himself heart and soul into masonic and other "mysteries."

It would help us a good deal in our enquiry if we could discover the dates of composition of the various numbers (9 to 21) of the second act. Mozart had returned to Vienna from Prague, deeply disappointed by the failure of *La Clemenza di Tito*, about the middle of September 1791. The first performance of *The Magic Flute* took place on the 30th. On the 28th of that month he noted in his *Verzeichnis* the composition of two pieces "for the opera *Die Zauberflöte*," a March of the Priests and the overture.

[1] It was written in September 1785 on the occasion of the death of two "brothers" the Duke of Mecklenburg and Count Esterhazy.

[2] It is noteworthy, too, that the last work of his to be entered in the *Verzeichnis*, the last of his completed works, indeed, was a masonic cantata (K. 623) to words by Schikaneder. This he wrote on the 15th November 1791, for the inauguration of the second temple of the lodge *Zur neugekrönten Hoffnung*; and he himself conducted the performance of it on the 18th. Two days later he took to his bed for the last time; on the 5th December he died.

Plainly these were the last to be written, yet it is in these two that for the first time the work becomes frankly "masonic" by the insertion at the end of the March of the three solemn long-held chords, given out with the full weight of the orchestra, that are so prominent a feature of the overture. It would be interesting to know when this motif was first decided upon, for presumably Mozart must have had it in his mind, in some form or other, for a little time before committing it to paper. But we know that it was his general practice to write his overture last of all, sometimes on the eve of the first performance, and the coupling in the *Verzeichnis* of the Priests' March with the overture seems to suggest that the former also was definitely decided upon at almost the last moment. Did the second act, one wonders, begin originally with the spoken dialogue between Sarastro and the Priests that follows the March in the score, the March itself being a later thought? That is a possibility, and it might account for the March not having come into being till practically the last moment. But let us now look at the second act in more detail.

12

It opens with this "March of the Priests"—so designated in the score—a strain of the utmost dignity and solemnity:

7

Then Sarastro informs the assembly of "servers of the temple of Wisdom of the great gods Isis and Osiris" that it has been called together to take part in the initiation of a royal youth, Tamino, who "desires to rend his veil of darkness and see into the sanctuary of the great light." Sarastro assures them that the Prince is virtuous, silent and well-wishing, whereupon they signify their approval of the proposed initiation by sounding the three solemn B flat chords referred to above. Sarastro, having thanked them "in the name of humanity," now tells them that for this worthy youth the gods have destined a virtuous maiden, for which reason he had taken her away from her haughty mother, who, in her

pride, "hopes to destroy our mighty temple." In this she will not
be allowed to succeed; for Tamino shall join with them in
strengthening it, and, as an initiate of it, become the upholder of
virtue and the scourge of evildoers. He orders the pair to be
brought in, and bids the Speaker instruct them, out of his wisdom,
in their duty to mankind and to the gods. After that he sings his
great invocation to Isis and Osiris, commending the pair to their
divine protection:

8

Adagio

O I-sis und O-si-ris, schen-ket der Weis-heit Geist dem
neu-en Paar!

then he and the Priests depart.

13

Tamino and Papageno are now led to the porch of the temple by
some of the Priests, Papageno providing an expected humorous
touch by his craven fears. He is no hero, and has no desire to
become one; to the Speaker he confesses that his modest desires
run to nothing beyond food, drink and sleep, with a nice little wife
thrown in if possible. Wisdom he can perfectly well do without;
he is the Natural Man pure and simple. The Speaker half-promises
him a pretty maiden named Papagena, on the condition that he
exercises sufficient control of himself not to speak to her. Henceforth Tamino's manly virtues and Papageno's little human weaknesses will be shown in humorous apposition.

On Tamino, too, the Speaker lays the injunction that when
he sees Pamina he shall not speak to her: this is to be the first stage
of his probation, the first injunction of Wisdom, for, as two of the
Priests assure him in duet, the basic law of the brotherhood is that
man shall see through women's falsity and escape the ruin that
invariably befalls those who trust in them. As if precisely to give
point to this sage masculine advice the Three Ladies now enter
to warn the young pair that they are doomed if they do not fly

from this evil place at once; and Mozart builds up an admirable quintet, in easy conversational style, in which the Ladies repeat their warning, Papageno would fain back out of the adventure, and Tamino has to remind him of the virtues of silence.

As the Ladies turn to depart they are consigned to Hades by a chorus of Priests within the temple, and they sink into the earth, to the great terror of poor Papageno. Tamino, however, is congratulated by the Speaker on his steadfastness; now, he is told, he can continue his pilgrimage. The Speaker throws a veil over the Prince's head and leads him out; Papageno too is veiled and taken away, much against his will, by some of the Priests.

14

We now lose sight of the pair for a time, for Mozart has at the moment two pressing operatic tasks on his hands—to provide first Monostatos and then the Queen with an aria. The occasion for the first of these is given by a change of scene to a garden, where the Moor finds Pamina sleeping and is overcome by passion for her, the passion, he explains in a lively aria:

that holds the whole world in its sway. Is he not also of flesh and blood? he asks; why then should he be condemned to go unloved? But if so it must be, he continues, still to the comically naïve strain of No. 9, he himself will love and bill and coo all the harder while life is in him; and he begs the moon to deny her light to the universe for a moment while he kisses the captive Pamina.

But before he can accomplish his fell design the Queen of Night appears, accompanied by a clap of thunder, and he makes an ignominious exit. Naturally the thunder has awakened Pamina. In reply to her mother's questions she discloses that the young Prince has become a devotee of the temple. "Then you have lost him forever!" cries the Queen, "for with your father's death my power came to an end; he gave of his own free will the sevenfold

shield of the sun to the brotherhood, and Sarastro now wears it
on his breast. But there is still a way out for us. Take this dagger—
I had it specially sharpened for Sarastro—slay him, and the
mighty shield is ours." Pamina is too shocked to do more than
ejaculate "But, my dear mother!"; and brushing her aside the
Queen launches the mighty aria of hatred and revenge that is to
this day the mingled delight and terror of dramatic sopranos who
pride themselves on their coloratura, or, to put it in another way,
of coloratura sopranos who imagine they can be dramatic. The
number of singers, however, who can reel off the difficult coloratura and at the same time convey a sense of the tornado of anger
and hatred that rages at the core of it is very small.

The exit of the Queen brings Monostatos once more on the
scene, and we are back for a moment to the simple humours of
the first act again. The Moor would persuade Pamina that there
is only one way out of her difficulties—to love him; and when she
refuses he tries to stab her with the dagger left behind by her
mother. In this nefarious design he is frustrated by the opportune
reappearance of Sarastro, who, telling him that his soul is as black
as his face, bids him depart. Monostatos' philosophical line as he
goes out is one of the surest laughter-makers in the opera—"Well,
if I can't have the daughter I must see what I can do with the
mother."

15

It is time now for an aria for Sarastro. He speaks comfortingly
to Pamina, telling her that he is well aware how her mother haunts
the subterranean vaults of the temple, breathing fire and slaughter
against him and all mankind. In due course he will take the right
revenge on her; but for the present the great thing is to endow the
Prince with courage and steadfastness in his pious purpose. For
that the Prince, it appears, has come to the right place, for, as he
explains in a noble aria:

10

In die-sen heil'-gen Hal—len kennt man die Ra-che nicht,

within these hallowed halls revenge has no place; [1] if a man has fallen, he must be raised up again by friendship and love.

They both go off, and with another change of scene we find ourselves in a large hall, into which the Speaker and the Priests conduct Tamino and Papageno, leaving them to themselves immediately, however, with the injunction that they are to maintain silence or be punished by the gods with thunder and lightning. The Prince obeys this command as well as Papageno will allow him to do, for soon there enters an old woman who brings Papageno a welcome cup of water, declares that she is only eighteen years and two minutes old, and tells him that she has a lover ten years older—whose name happens to be Papageno. But when he asks her own name there comes a clap of thunder, the old woman disappears, and Three Genii enter with a table (spread with food), Tamino's flute and Papageno's chime of bells. In a pleasant little trio they speak some words of comfort to the two men, exhorting the one to have courage, the other to keep silence; then they disappear. No sooner have they gone, and Papageno is beginning to compliment his absent host Sarastro on the quality of his viands and his wine, than Pamina comes in. Mortified to find that Tamino will not respond to anything she says, and seems indeed, anxious to get rid of her, she pours out her grief over a lost illusion in an expressive air in G minor:

11

Andante

Ach, ich fühl's, es ist ver–schwun–den, e—wig hin der Lie–be Glück!

If he no longer loves her she will be content to die.

[1] At first sight this may seem inconsistent with what he has said a moment before about "revenge" on the Queen; but there is really no contradiction. His "revenge" on her will be to nullify her attempt to "revenge herself" on Sarastro and all mankind, by rescuing the young Prince from her coils and making him an instrument for the highest good.

As she leaves them a peal of trumpets is heard—evidently the summons to the tribunal—and the two go out after the usual little witticisms from Papageno, for Schikaneder has taken good care that whatever may happen to the drama of noble sentiments, *he* will always be within call to get an easy laugh. With another change of scene we are transported to a vault beneath the temple, where Sarastro and the Priests are assembled. In a chorus of grave beauty the Priests commend the noble youth on trial to the favour of Isis and Osiris, for his heart is pure, his soul is brave, and he will prove himself worthy of admittance to their company. First Tamino is brought in, then Pamina—to receive, so Sarastro informs her, Tamino's last farewell. This leads to an expressive trio in which Pamina laments her sad lot, Tamino protests his undying love, and Sarastro exhorts them both to be brave and bow to the decree of the brotherhood, for the separation will not last forever.

The three go out, leaving Papageno alone, and it is now Schikaneder's turn once more. The Speaker enters to tell Papageno that owing to the incurable earthiness of his nature he can never be admitted to the company of the blessed, but that the gratification of such common appetites as his will not be denied him. He asks for a cup of wine, and one rises from the ground. But that is not enough for him; accompanying himself with his chime of bells he sings, in his simple, charming fashion, of his desire for a nice little wife after his own heart:

12

Andante

Ein Mäd-chen o-der Weib — chen wünscht Pa-pa-ge-no — sich,

The song over, the old woman presents herself again, transforms herself into a young girl, tells him her name is Papagena, and gives him her hand. But just as he is about to embrace her the spoil-sport of a Speaker enters, tells the maiden that Papageno is not worthy of her yet, and sends them both away.

16

We now meet again with the Three Genii, who sing a dignified little trio in praise of the rising sun, before which superstition shall vanish from the earth and Wisdom and Peace come into their own. We have now entered on the finale. This is by far the most extended and the most unified of all the "numbers" of the work: at last Mozart is free to develop his musical-dramatic plan organically according to his heart's desire, with only a few irrelevances from outside.

Pamina enters, half-crazed and carrying a dagger; soon, she declares, she will be united with her loved and lost Tamino in death. As she raises the dagger the Three Genii stay her arm, assuring her that what Tamino is doing is all for love for her, though the secret meaning of his apparent indifference they cannot as yet disclose.

With a change of tempo to adagio, and with trombones lending a solemnity of their own to the situation, the music now attains its profoundest depth of feeling. Wailing figures of this type:

13

repeat themselves in one mutation after another in the orchestra, while through the texture Two Men in Armour steadily intone an old German chorale: the whole episode is a masterly reversion to the chorale prelude form in which Bach achieved such wonders.

From within comes the sound of Pamina's voice calling to Tamino, and now the Two Men in Armour grant him permission to speak to her. The temple gates open, Pamina appears, and the lovers greet each other ecstatically. She bids him place his trust in the flute, which, we now learn, had been carved by her father in a magic hour out of a centuries-old oak tree; and their voices and those of the Two Men in Armour unite in a quartet in praise of the marvellous instrument. With Tamino playing a long melody on it the lovers survive the ordeal of passing first through fire, then through water: then the gates of the temple are thrown open, the scene is flooded with light, and a chorus within hails the triumph of the virtuous pair and bids them enter the shrine of Isis.

But there is still the irrepressible Schikaneder to be reckoned with. The scene changes to a garden, in which Papageno, playing on his pipes (No. 2), calls piteously on his Papagena to appear and make him happy. He is on the point of hanging himself, with much comic by-play, when the Three Genii arrive in the nick of time to frustrate that dire intent. On their advice he sets his chimes pealing; and soon Papagena appears, and the two children of nature express their joy in a duet that is one of Mozart's most delightful creations.

Even after this the road is not quite open to Mozart to end the drama. There comes a short serio-comic episode in which Monostatos ushers in the Queen and her Three Ladies: they have come to destroy the temple, the hand of Pamina being Monostatos' reward for his participation in the scheme. But a great upheaval of the elements—thunder, lightning and tempest—fills them with terror, and they sink impotently into the depths. The stage is flooded with light, and we see Sarastro in all his glory with Tamino, Pamina and the Priests. Sarastro hails the victory of moral light over darkness, and the chorus gives thanks to Isis and Osiris, who have brought the steadfast pair of lovers to the successful end of their trials. "Beauty and Wisdom and Strength and Constancy of spirit have triumphed over the forces of evil," they continue; and the opera ends in general jubilation.

17

The score of *The Magic Flute* is of great importance in the history of the development of German opera; but in the foregoing pages we have had to confine ourselves mainly to exposition pure and simple of the course of the action. The work has perhaps been rather over-written during the last century and a half, especially in Germany, where undue stress has been laid on its "ethical" virtues—its laudation of Virtue, Justice, Humanity, Universal Brotherhood, and all the rest of it. These academic expressions

seem a little fly-blown today, and we have got past the stage when
we can take a work of art to our bosoms merely because it spouts
lofty sentiments: in a work of art it is only the art that finally
matters. Still, these sentiments played a large part in making the
music of such works as *The Magic Flute* and the choral finale of
the Ninth Symphony what it is, and so we must be content, for
the time being, and for purely artistic reasons, to accept them
at the valuation Mozart and Beethoven placed on them, just as
when watching *Hamlet* we do not admit that ghosts exist, but
merely suspend temporarily, for the sole purpose of playing the
game along the lines laid down by the poet, our disbelief in them.

The familiar overture hardly calls for detailed analysis. It opens:

14

with the threefold "masonic" chords (now in the key of E flat
major instead of in B flat as in the opera) which, as we have seen,
had played so impressive a part in the action after the March of
the Priests at the beginning of the second act. The grave adagio
introduction to the overture (lasting only fifteen bars) leads into
an allegro section based on a subject:

15

that looks at first as if it were going to be the basis of a fugue, but
is actually treated later in a free sonata style, with a great deal of
contrapuntal device. Half-way through this development of it
the three *tutti* chords strike in again with arresting effect. Much

has been written, especially in Germany, of the profoundly "symbolic" nature of the overture. Without being able to subscribe to all this, we are at any rate conscious that in some strange way Mozart's imagination was playing strongly on the dramatic and psychological framework of the action, without even as much thematic quotation from the opera itself as he had permitted himself in the *Don Giovanni* overture.

Don Giovanni

WOLFGANG AMADEUS MOZART [1756–1791]

CHARACTERS

DON GIOVANNI, "an extremely licentious young nobleman"	*Baritone*
DONNA ANNA	*Soprano*
DONNA ELVIRA	*Soprano*
ZERLINA	*Soprano*
DON OTTAVIO	*Tenor*
LEPORELLO	*Bass*
THE COMMANDER	*Bass*
MASETTO	*Bass*

1

THE PROBABLE sources of the Don Juan saga have been investigated with great thoroughness by many scholars. Though the elements of the story are found in the folk lore of more than one country, including Iceland, there may have been an ancient tradition in Seville of a young rapscallion of noble birth whose career of crime came somehow to a violent end in a church; while folk stories are fairly abundant of a grisly supping of living people with the dead. It is possible that in the Spain of the sixteenth or seventeenth century these two cardinal dramatic factors had begun to coalesce in the imagination of either the people or the playwrights. With matters so purely antiquarian as these we need not trouble ourselves here; our concern is simply with the first literary results of that coalescence, the forms the story took in the hands of later dramatists, and the bearing of it all on the Mozart-Da Ponte opera *Don Giovanni*.

The original shaper of the complete tale as we now have it

seems to have been a Spanish monk named Gabriel Tellez (1571–1648), who wrote under the name of Tirso de Molina. Later reports as to his scandalous way of living seem to have no foundation in fact; he ended his days as Prior at Soria, "renowned as a preacher of most tranquil, virtuous life." The legend of his immorality no doubt sprang from the intimate acquaintance his plays show him to have had with the seamier and more adventurous side of human nature; but "it appears to be forgotten," as a historian of Spanish literature remarks, "that Tirso spent years in the confessional—no bad position for the study of frailty." [1]

The first part of his "theatre" was published in 1634, the fifth in 1637. His *El Burlador de Sevilla* appeared in Barcelona in 1630 as the seventh of *Twelve New Plays by Lope de Vega Carpio and Other Authors*, where it is described as a "famous comedy" by "the Maestro Tirso de Molina." The "famous" suggests that by 1630 the play had already been before the public for some time. Its popularity is shown by the number of editions it went through in the seventeenth and eighteenth centuries. Tirso's authorship has been questioned in some quarters, but it is now generally accepted. In 1878 a copy was discovered of a drama, dating from the first half of the seventeenth century, entitled *Tan largo me lo fiáis*, and stated on the title page to be the work of "Don Pedro Calderón." [2] No doubt the vogue of the subject led to more than one contemporary imitation of Tirso; and today his right to be regarded as the true creator of the long-lived saga is generally admitted. But even this might have gone the way of the rest of his large output, surviving to be read now only by specialists in Spanish literature, had it not been for one remarkable feature of *El Burlador de Sevilla, y Convidado de Piedra* [3]—the terrifying and edifying part played in the punishment of the hero-villain by the statue of a murdered man. It was this that quickly captured

[1] James Fitzmaurice-Kelly, *A History of Spanish Literature*, p. 308.

[2] This is now accessible to students in the complete annotated edition of Tirso's plays by Emilio Lotarelo (two vols., Madrid 1906–7). "Tan largo me lo fiáis" is an expression frequently in the mouth of Tirso's Don Juan; it seems to have been a catch-phrase of the period.

[3] "Burlador" means "scoffer," "jester," "mocker," "trickster," and other things of that sort. Perhaps the best colloquial rendering of it in the Don Juan connection today would be "playboy." "Convidado de piedra" means "the stone guest" (at a meal).

the interest of the Spanish, French and Italian world. Without some knowledge of Tirso's play it is impossible to understand how Da Ponte's libretto came to have not only the virtues but the faults we are now conscious of in it. It will be as well, therefore, to tell the story of the Spanish drama in some detail.

2

It opens not in Seville but in Naples. The scene is the interior of the royal palace; the time, night. A door opens, and we see Don Juan, his face carefully concealed in his cloak, being ushered out stealthily by one of the great ladies of the court, the Duchess Isabela. "Come this way, Duke Octavio," she whispers; "it will be safer." She would like an assurance that the favours she has just bestowed on him will find their legitimation in marriage. This the cloaked man promises fervently, but when she talks of bringing a light to facilitate his exit he protests vehemently that if she does so he will extinguish it. Her suspicions are now aroused; and discovering that he is not, as she had thought, her fiancé the Duke Octavio, she cries out for help. The clamour brings on the scene the King of Naples—with a lighted candle— the royal guard, and Don Pedro Tenorio, the Spanish Ambassador to the Neapolitan court. In the obscurity of the room the King cannot recognise either the man or the woman, for Isabela, like Don Juan, prudently keeps her face covered; but he orders the guards to arrest both culprits, consigns them to the custody of Don Pedro, and departs. Having sent Isabela away with the guard, Don Pedro turns for an explanation to the audacious young cavalier, who has sworn he would kill anyone who dared lay a hand on him. He claims, in a manner of speaking, diplomatic immunity; he is a gentleman, he says, attached to the Spanish embassy. To Don Pedro, however, when they two are left alone, he discloses his identity—he is Don Juan, Don Pedro's nephew. Asked by his startled uncle what he has to say in excuse for his conduct he brazenly declares that his youth and his ardours justify him in everything he does, including his recent triumph, disguised as the Duke Octavio, over the virtue of the highly respected Duchess Isabela. His uncle upbraids him for his crimes and his impious pride in them, but for family reasons feels bound to save him from punishment and disgrace; so he lets him escape *via* the balcony, bidding him fly to Milan or Sicily and there go into hiding.

When the King returns, Don Pedro tells him that his intrepid prisoner has managed to escape; though badly injured, he says, the man had fought off the soldiers who would have arrested him and had leaped from the balcony. Don Pedro gives the astonished King the further information that the lady in the case is the Duchess Isabela, and that her ravisher, according to her own story, was the Duke Octavio. The King orders her to be brought before him; she is either too confused or too crafty to disclose the whole simple truth of the affair, so the King orders her to be imprisoned; Duke Octavio also is to be arrested, brought before him, and made to put things right by marrying Isabela, who now consoles herself with the sage feminine reflection that, after all, if the Duke marries her not much harm will have been done.

The scene changes to a room in Octavio's house in Naples, where we find him rhapsodising to his servant Ripio over the charms and virtues of his adored Isabela. He is interrupted by the entry of Don Pedro, who tells him he has been sent by the King to arrest him. A seducer, it appears, had been found that night in the chamber of the Duchess Isabela. The libertine had escaped, but the lady herself had assured the King that he was none other than her betrothed, Duke Octavio. The Duke's grieved and angry protestations at the lady's perfidy are of no avail. Don Pedro kindly offers to connive at his escape; so the Duke goes off to Spain, there to rail at fate and the inconstancy and unveracity of woman.

3

The next scene is the beach at Tarragona, where the beautiful and chaste Tisbea, who lives in a nearby cottage, is congratulating herself at great length on her freedom from the ordinary weaknesses of her sex; her love is sought by all, but to their sighs and pleas she is indifferent. Just then two men are cast up on the beach by a storm that has wrecked their boat: they are Don Juan and his servant Catalinón. It all ends, of course, with the accomplished seducer triumphing over the virtue of the proud country maiden under the customary promise of marriage, and the soon-forsaken one registering the furies and despairs traditionally regarded by the poets as appropriate to such occasions. When the valet remonstrates with his master, as he often does, for living so evilly, and warns him that he will pay for his crimes after his death, Juan replies with a jaunty phrase that he employs throughout the play on such occasions, like a kind of leitmotif, and which we may render colloquially, for our purposes, as "Time enough for that." Before the climax of the Tisbea affair is reached, however, we have been taken to the Alcazar at Seville, where King Alonzo of Castille is congratulating a worthy gentleman, Don Gonzalo de Ulloa, on his recent loyal services as ambassador at the Lisbon court. Anxious to reward him for these, the King, having learned that he has a beautiful daughter, Doña Ana, declares that he will bestow her in marriage on a certain gentleman of his court, one Don Juan Tenorio.

In a later scene in the Alcazar we find the King receiving Don Diego Tenorio, the father of our hero, who gives him the latest news he has received from his brother Don Pedro, the Spanish ambassador in Naples—that the young Juan had been found at night in the apartment of one of the beauties of the court, the Duchess Isabela. The seducer and his valet, it appears, are now in Seville. The King is shocked, but out of regard for Don Diego consents to pardon Don Juan if he marries Isabela; meanwhile the young man must leave at once for Lebrija. As for the unfortunate Duke Octavio, he shall be properly indemnified for his prematrimonial misfortune. Then the King remembers that he has already promised Don Gonzalo that Juan shall marry Doña Ana. The situation looks like becoming a trifle awkward, but the keen royal intellect perceives a way out: the King will compensate Don Gonzalo by making him Grand Majordomo.

Just then a servant announces the arrival of Don Octavio. The alarmed Diego implores the King to forbid the duel that must inevitably follow a meeting between Octavio and his dear son Juan, whose peccadilloes, he pleads, are merely the product of his youth and high spirits. Octavio having entered and begged the King's support in his quest for vengeance on the author of his wrongs, Alonzo assures him that while he fully sympathises with him he has made a false step in leaving Naples. However, he will urge the King of Naples to restore him to his former condition, while he, Alonzo, will marry him to a lady far superior in beauty

133

to Isabela, none other than the pearl of Castille, the virtuous Doña Ana, daughter of Don Gonzalo de Ulloa, Commander of Calatrava. Octavio leaves the royal presence overwhelmed with joy. In the street he runs into Don Juan and Catalinón. (He does not know, of course, that it is to his friend Don Juan that he owes all his troubles in Naples.) Each of them courteously assures the other that he is wholly at his service on all occasions; and the dupe and the rogue part on the best of terms.

Octavio and his man Ripio having left the scene, a new character is introduced—Don Juan's boon companion in Seville debauchery, the Marquis de la Mota. We are concerned with him here only in so far as he contributes unconsciously to the downfall of Juan. Accident places in the latter's hands a letter from Doña Ana to her lover the Marquis: "My faithless father has secretly disposed of my hand without giving me any choice. . . . If you value my love and my volition as they deserve, and if your love for me is sincere, now is the time to prove it. Tonight at eleven my door will be left open for you. Come to me; your hopes shall be fulfilled and your love receive its recompense. To ensure that my duennas will let you pass, wear a coloured cape. . . .[1] Adieu, my unfortunate lover!" Thereupon Juan, perfidious as usual even towards his closest friends, goes to the Marquis, tells him that he has been entrusted with a message for him, and gives him the purport of the letter, making the hour of assignation, however, not eleven but midnight.

4

There follows another scene between Don Diego and Don Juan, in which the distressed father tells his son that all Seville knows now of his evil behaviour in Naples, and warns him that God will one day exact an account from him. The young man's reply is his usual one: "Time enough for that! Life is long!" Don Diego gives him the King's message—he is to go at once to Lerija and remain there until Octavio has received due satisfaction and the scandal has died down. Juan merely laughs at the distressed old man. Soon we find him encountering the Marquis again

[1] "In former times," we are told, "the cape was a military distinction worn by noblemen." Thus clothed, Mota's rank would be manifest, and the servants of the household presumably would not dare to bar his way.

(whom he recognizes in the darkness by his cape). Mota is waiting for midnight outside Don Gonzalo's house with a body of musicians for the serenading of Doña Ana. To help Juan in an alleged amorous adventure of his own, Mota lends him his cape; thus all the winning cards come, as usual, into Juan's hands. He steals into Don Gonzalo's house, whence there soon come frenzied cries from Ana: "Traitor, you are not the Marquis! I have been duped!" The venerable Gonzalo, coming to the rescue of his daughter, is killed by Juan. There follows a brief colloquy with the still unsuspecting Mota, after which Don Juan, having returned the cape, and told him of the fatal end to the adventure of which he had spoken, seeks safety in flight with Catalinón.

Lights and cries from the direction of the Alcazar attract Mota's attention. He is taken for the murderer of Gonzalo and arrested by Don Diego: then the King arrives, who promises him execution on the morrow. "As for the Commander," says the King, "bury him with royal splendour and solemnity; make a tomb for him of bronze and stone, surmounted by his statue, and engrave on it the story of his murder and the chastisement of the crime. Obsequies, statue, tomb," his Majesty adds grandly, "all at my expense." Doña Ana, it appears, has placed herself under the protection of the Queen.

5

The scene changes to Dos-Hermanas, where the still unrepentant Juan has the good luck to stumble on the wedding feast of a simple country couple named Aminta and Batricio, and in due course, under the usual promise of marriage, he seduces the bride. Then, highly pleased with himself and in defiance of danger, he makes his way back with Catalinón to Seville.

Next we meet with Isabela and Fabio (her servant) at Tarragona, on their way to Seville. Isabela, while regretting the Naples incident, is on the whole not displeased with the turn in her fortunes—to be the wife of "the noble Don Juan," whom the King has made a Count—but anxious that her "honour" shall be in no way publicly compromised. She falls in with a young woman bewailing her fate in flowery seventeenth century style. It is Tisbea once more, who tells the great lady of her deception and ruin by a villain who had been cast up on the shore by a tempest—a certain Don Juan Tenorio. It ends with the horrified Isabela taking Tisbea with her to Seville, in the hope that justice may be done to both of them.

Meanwhile Don Juan and Catalinón are back in Seville again. They find themselves in a church, in the chapel of which is a tomb surmounted by a statue. The valet warns his master, as he had often done before, of the perils in which he has managed to involve himself: Octavio, it appears, has at last learned the truth about the Naples affair and is hot upon the traitor's track; Mota has discovered the ruse of the letter and the cape; Isabela has arrived for her wedding to Juan; and so on. Juan cuts him short with threats and blows; what harm can come to one so bold and resourceful as he, especially here, on the sacred ground of the church? While he is chuckling over his exploit at Dos-Hermanas a curtain glides aside, revealing the tomb of Don Gonzalo. Juan gaily compliments the defunct gentleman on the magnificence of his present habitation, and reads the epitaph placed on it by order of the King: "Here, awaiting the vengeance of heaven on a traitor, lies the most loyal of gentlemen." This excites Don Juan's hilarity: "how can you," he gaily asks the statue, "an old man with a beard of stone, avenge yourself?"; and he lays an irreverent hand on the beard. Pursuing his jest, he addresses the statue: "this evening I will await you at dinner in my house; then, if it is vengeance you want, you can defy me. But what sort of a fight could you put up with your stone sword? If you are to have your revenge, curtail your sleep, for if you wait till I too am dead you may say goodbye to hope. You will have to nurse your anger a long while! Time enough yet for all that!"

Catalinón hurries him away, and the scene changes to a room in which servants are laying the table for Don Juan's supper. He forces Catalinón to sit down with him. Suddenly knocking is heard without. The trembling valet opines that it is the ministers of the law; but Don Juan angrily bids him go to the door and see who or what is there. Catalinón does so and staggers back in terror; what he has seen he cannot bring himself to say, for he dares not believe his eyes: "I saw him, I swear it!" he stammers, "He spoke to me. I answered him. I saw him . . . " But who it was he had seen he cannot or will not say. Don Juan, in a rage, himself takes a candle and goes to the door. It flies open, and he sees Don Gonzalo in the shape he had borne in the chapel. Juan mechanically draws his sword, but recoils. The statue advances slowly towards him, and, forcing him back to the middle of the stage, announces that he has come in response to his invitation. With much bravado on Juan's part and craven buffoonery on Catalinón's, and to the accompaniment of music from behind the scenes, the grisly meal goes on, till at last Juan orders Catalinón and the servants to leave him alone with his guest. "Now then," he says: "the door is closed and I await your will. Shade, vision or phantom, what do you desire of me? If your soul is in torment and demands satisfaction of me, speak, for I give you my word to do whatever you wish." The statue, "slowly, in a voice that seems to come from another world," bids him give him his hand as pledge of the word of a gentleman. Defiantly Don Juan does so: "you should have my hand if you came from hell itself!" Grasping the hand, the statue makes him swear to be his guest at ten the next evening in the church: "and see you keep your word as I have kept mine."

6

It goes out slowly, leaving Juan, for the first time in his life, troubled and a little afraid, for strangely enough the stone hand had seemed to burn his flesh. Then, with a great effort, he masters himself: "Bah! all this is pure imagination. Fear of the dead is the worst, the most craven of all fears. Tomorrow I will go to supper in the church, for all Seville admires and marvels at my courage."

There follows a short scene in the palace, where the King and Juan's father, Don Diego, are awaiting Isabela. Diego has heard that she has arrived in Seville in an ill humour: the King, still ignorant of the real character of Don Juan, commands him to be sent for; if he shows any signs of a good disposition he will make him a Count and endow him with a fief. Isabela, says the King, should be satisfied with the way things have turned out: true, she has lost a Duke, but she has won a Count. This day Doña Ana too shall be married, though not to Octavio: that would perhaps be asking too much of that honourable gentleman. Ana has begged the Queen to obtain a pardon for the Marquis de la Mota, whom she wishes to marry. This pardon the King now grants. Everything seems, especially to Don Diego, for the best in the best of all possible worlds, when Octavio enters and demands the royal permission to execute personal vengeance on Don Juan. There is a brief quarrel and a threat of a duel between Diego and Octavio, but the King intervenes: after he is married, he tells the Duke, he will be able to talk at greater length. "As for Don Juan, he is a gentleman of my household, my liegeman, and the son of Don Diego here: respect him!" And so Octavio resigns himself to having a bride provided for him by the King on the morrow.

The King having left, the forsaken Aminta and her father Gaseno enter and innocently ask Don Octavio, who is evidently a gentleman of the court, where they can find a certain Don Juan Tenorio, of whom they are in search, for the young cavalier is Aminta's husband. They have come to Seville to complain to the King if justice is not done her. The light dawns on Octavio at last; now, he is convinced, he holds Juan in the hollow of his hand and can have his revenge on him; and he takes Gaseno and Aminta with him to see the King.

7

But vengeance from quite another quarter overtakes Juan. The scene changes to a street outside the church in which Don Gonzalo is buried. Juan and Catalinón enter. The former tells the valet with glee how excellently his recent audience with the King has gone off: he is in full favour, and that very evening he is to be married to Isabela. But first of all he has another engagement to fulfil—his promised supper with the statue. Catalinón tries to dissuade him, but Juan insists: has he not pledged the word of a gentleman? They go into the dark church, where they are greeted by Gonzalo (in statue form). He rouses Juan's ire by taunting him with cowardice in having run away the night he had murdered him. "I fled," Juan replies, "only for fear of being recognised. Now I face you here. Tell me what you would have of me." "I would have you sup with me," says Gonzalo. The intrepid Juan raises the cover of the tomb, and a black table set for a feast is disclosed. Two black-robed figures draw up chairs for the statue's guests, and the meats and wines are served—scorpions and vipers, vinegar and gall. Juan, for all his bravado, is secretly ill at ease. The meal over, the statue says to him, "Have no fear: give me your hand." Scorning the suggestion that anything can make him afraid, Juan does so. Once more, at the touch of that hand, he feels he is being consumed by fire—a faint foretaste, the statue tells him, of what is in store for him. "Such is the divine law; what a man sows, that he reaps." Juan cries out in impotent and incoherent rage: "I am burning! Do not stifle me! I will drive my dagger through you! My blows pierce only the air! I did not outrage your daughter: she saw at once through my guile." "That avails you nothing," is the reply: "you made the attempt." Then Juan's spirit breaks. He calls wildly for a confessor to absolve him of his sins. But it is too late: still crying out that he is on fire, he falls dead. The tomb sinks into the earth, taking with it Juan and the Commander: there is a noise like thunder, and the terrified Catalinón crawls out, calling incoherently on God and all the saints to save him: "I will take the news to his father! St. George! St. Agnus Dei! See me to the street!"

There follows a scene in the palace in which Batricio, Gaseno, Tisbea and Isabela tell the story of Don Juan's perfidies and demand reparation; then the Marquis de la Mota denounces Juan as the real murderer of Don Gonzalo, and even Don Diego turns against his criminal son. The horrified King orders Juan's arrest. But just then Catalinón rushes in with a strange story of how his master had impiously plucked the beard of the statue and otherwise insulted the murdered Gonzalo, invited the statue to supper, confessed that he had failed in his attempt on Ana, and been duly punished by heaven for all his crimes. Octavio, who is one of the company, now demands the hand of his injured Isabela, Mota claims that of Ana, Batricio that of Aminta; and the King orders the sepulchre of Don Gonzalo to be moved to Madrid and given a place of honour in the church of St. Francisco.[1]

---

[1] There is a modern French version of Tirso's *El Burlador de Sevilla* by Jean Cassou and Jean Camp that is reasonably representative, for the most part, of the original, though occasionally a speech is allotted to a wrong character, which is a trifle confusing. The translation ends, however, with the flight of the terrified Catalinón from the church. There is no justification for this. Tirso's final scene in the palace is a dramatic necessity, for naturally we want to know how matters are finally arranged between the various lovers, while it is equally necessary for all the characters to learn how the vengeance of heaven had overtaken the libertine at last.

8

As the reader will see, here are all the basic constituents of the Don Juan story as it was to be reproduced in many forms in European literature before it came into the hands of Da Ponte and Mozart—a reckless, impious adventurer among women, a half-assenting, half-protesting valet who is a mixture of servility and impudence, the seduction of two great ladies under the cover of darkness, the murder of the father of one of them when he comes to her rescue, comic relief of a sort in the adventure of the hero among maidens and their lovers of a lower degree than his own, the vengeful pursuit of him by the gentleman whom he has most wronged, the insult to a statue, the acceptance of an invitation to supper, and the final judgment of heaven on the villain. Reshape the characters and select and rearrange the episodes as future dramatists might according to their fancy, the essential pattern remained the same: Tirso de Molina had created a genuine saga, a story that could take on as many forms as future dramatists might choose, and into which each epoch, each culture, could read itself afresh over a period of some three hundred years. Molière, in his *Don Juan, ou Le Festin de Pierre* (1665), gave a turn and a complexion of his own to the saga. Shadwell, in his play *The Libertine* (1676), endowed Don Juan liberally with new and worse debaucheries and impieties. Goldoni, in his *Don Giovanni Tenorio, o sia Il Dissoluto*, upon which Da Ponte drew to some extent, as he did upon everyone and everything that could be useful to him, aimed at ridding the story of some of the buffooneries that had become part and parcel of its very being by this time, and to that end dispensed with the character of the valet. Two French seventeenth century plays on the subject, each entitled *Le Festin de Pierre, ou le Fils Criminel*, by Dorimon (1659) and de Villiers (1660) respectively, have been made accessible to modern students in a reprint by Gendarme de Bévotte.[1]

---

[1] G. Gendarme de Bévotte, *Le Festin de Pierre avant Molière . . . textes publiés avec introduction, lexique et notes*. Paris, 1907. He reprinted also the Italian text of Cicognini's seventeenth century play *Il Convitato di Pietra*.

During the seventeenth and eighteenth centuries the story of the "Dissoluto punito" was highly popular also not only with the actors of the Italian impromptu comedy—the commedia dell' arte—but the German puppet booths, where, as might have been expected, it suffered a progressive degradation. For the gaping mob everywhere the two great things in the story came to be the farcical antics of the valet and the vengeance of the statue on the young criminal. We are fortunate in the possession of a document that gives as a close-up view of what the part of the valet had already become as early as the middle of the seventeenth century. In 1658 an Italian company of commedia dell'arte players drew all Paris with a version of their own of *Le Festin de Pierre*; it was this production, indeed, that moved de Villiers to write his five-act play.[1] The part of the valet (Trivelin) seems to have been played in Paris originally by the manager of the troupe, Locatelli, but he was replaced in 1662 by a certain Biancolelli, who wrote out with great complacency a full account of his buffooneries in the part. (The original Italian manuscript has been lost, but there survives a French translation of it made in the eighteenth century, by one Thomas Gueullette, that is now in the Paris Bibliothèque Nationale.)[2] From this we get an excellent idea of the devices to which the valet had recourse to extort the tribute of a guffaw from the groundlings; and evidently some of the buffooneries of the part had become traditional by Mozart's time. Goldoni protested against this and other degradations of the subject: he tells us in his memoirs that audiences were accustomed, in the scene of the shipwreck of Don Juan and his valet, to see the latter save his life by floating ashore on a couple of bladders, while the aristocratic hero somehow made his way through the sea without so much as his coiffure being disarranged or his fine clothes getting wet.

By Mozart's time the saga had crystallised into an excellent working formula for opera purposes—the hero-villain and his

[1] In the commedia dell' arte the actors improvised their dialogue and their miming within the framework of a dramatic action the main lines of which were already agreed upon.

[2] It is printed in the book of Gendarme de Bévotte already mentioned.

rascally buffoon of a servant; a dignified victim of Don Juan's
sensuality; her aristocratic lover; a lady of somewhat lower social
rank who had previously been seduced and deserted by Juan and
who follows him about with her heart equally divided between
love for him and the desire to be revenged on him; a group of
peasants, with a bride and bridegroom at their head, to provide
a lighter *décor* for Juan's amorous exploits; and, of course, a
murdered father who reappears, as the avenging instrument of
heaven, in the form of a statue in the closing scenes. So conceived,
an opera would have everything that an audience of all degrees
of taste and intelligence could require for its delectation—gaiety,
gravity, tragedy, psychological variety, action, humour, farce,
religion. Tirso de Molina had builded more wisely than he knew.
And, on the whole, he had builded better than many of those who
succeeded him. "Of these later artists," says Fitzmaurice-Kelly,
"not one has succeeded in matching the patrician dignity, the
infernal, iniquitous valour of the original. To have created a
universal type, to have imposed a character on the world, to have
outlived all rivalry, to have achieved in words what Mozart alone
has expressed in music, is to rank among the great creators of all
time."

10

Parallel to some extent with the story of Don Juan Tenorio,
though apparently later in origin, there ran a Spanish story of a
Don Juan de Marana, at the end of which the hero found not hell
fire but heavenly grace. This other legend seems to have travelled
to France early in the nineteenth century. It was the theme of an
excellent short story—*Les Âmes du Purgatoire*—by Prosper
Mérimée (1834), and it was turned by the elder Dumas into a
drama, little known today, that is one of the curiosities of the
French romantic stage—*Don Juan de Marana, or the Fall of an
Angel, a Mystery in five acts, in nine tableaux*, produced at the
Porte-Saint-Martin Theatre, Paris, on the 30th April 1836. The
lively action takes too long to be set forth in detail here; it can
only be said that it concerns the struggle, with God's permission,
between a Good and a Bad Angel for control of the soul of the
depraved young Don Juan de Marana. "One of my ancestors, if
not one of my race," the hero boasts, "descended alive into hell,

where he supped with a Commander whom he had killed after dishonouring his daughter. I have always been jealous of this man's reputation; and I want to surpass him, so that the Devil himself will not know which of the two to prefer, Don Juan de Tenorio or Don Juan de Marana." In a fit of terrified repentance he becomes a Trappist for a while: then, having killed his brother José, he muses, "upon my word, it looks as if the Devil doesn't want me to become a hermit"; and he takes to debauchery and crime again.

In the ruins of an old castle the phantoms of his victims appear to him and dance a ballet "in the style of the nuns in *Robert the Devil*." The finale of the drama is one of Dumas' most magnificent flights into the very stratosphere of the prodigious. To his rival Sandoval, whom he has wronged, Don Juan says, "Listen! God has given me one hour in which to repent: I give Him a quarter of an hour in which to strike me with His thunderbolt!" There follows a duel with Sandoval, whose sword, as it crosses that of Juan, darts flame. Juan is dismayed. A shade rises out of the ground: it is Juan's former love Caroline; she is followed by a Vittoria, a Teresina and an Ines. At the back of the stage is a great fiery clock, with flames for hours and minute fingers; the pendulum swings slowly between two points, one of which is marked "Never!" the other "For ever!" The time is five minutes before midnight: our nerves are now on edge. Caroline ascends the steps leading to the clock, and, to Juan's horror, advances the minute hand one degree. Then come Vittoria, Teresina and Ines, each of whom inexorably registers another minute on the clock. Juan, terrified at last, falls on one knee. But now comes a certain Martha, with angel's wings and a star on her forehead, and accompanied by angels; she had loved the wicked Juan, she says, when she was alive, and still loves him now she is dead; and in the name of that love she exhorts him three times, with increasing urgency, to repent. He cries out despairingly, "It is too late! Midnight is about to strike!" But Martha arrests the hand of the clock and once more cries "Repent!" This gives Juan a second's grace. With a last great effort he raises himself and then falls at her feet. "O Lord, thou has heard him!" she ejaculates. A song of angels is heard: the background opens, showing heaven in all its splendour. Juan is convinced that he is dying, but Martha assures him that this is a delusion on his part, and that his eyes will reopen to eternal life.

Thus did Don Juan de Marana, according to Dumas, by a grand last-second spurt win the Eternity Stakes by the shortest of short heads. He probably developed into heaven's champion bore, telling the story again and again to each new arrival and to as many of the older club members as he could buttonhole, no doubt finishing in the style of the Duke of Wellington's classical description of the battle of Waterloo to Mr. Creevey—"It was a damned near thing, sir, the nearest thing you ever saw in your life!"

Out of this Dumasian farrago, however, Arnold Bennett, by concentrating on the saner elements of the play, succeeded in constructing the libretto for Eugene Goossens' opera *Don Juan de Mañara*, which was given at Covent Garden in 1935.[1]

11

The Don Juan saga as established by Tirso has been a favourite subject with the poets, dramatists and novelists in many countries for something like three centuries.[2] Christian Dietrich Grabbe (1804–1836) made a characteristically German attempt, in his tragedy *Don Juan und Faust* (1824), to run the two sagas in harness; but the venture was more praiseworthy than successful. In our own day Edmond Rostand has treated the theme in quite a new way in his play *La dernière Nuit de Don Juan*, which might be turned into an excellent opera by a librettist and a composer of genius; and Suzanne Lilar, in her drama *Le Burlador*,[3] has shown once more how adaptable the great drama is to all the psychological changes that humanity undergoes in the course of the centuries. Mme Lilar's original and searching reading of the soul of Juan is perhaps one that only a woman could have accomplished. One thing is very significant in the modern literary his-

[1] The libretto was adapted by Bennett from a play of his own on the subject written in 1913, but never performed. It was published in a limited private edition in 1923. He had followed Dumas in his spelling of "Marana": in the opera the more correct "Mañara" is restored.

[2] The most comprehensive survey of the various treatments of the theme is Gendarme de Bévotte's *La Légende de Don Juan, son évolution dans la littérature des origines au romantisme* (1906).

[3] Produced in Paris in December 1946; published in Brussels in 1947.

tory of the saga—the gradual disappearance from it, as it were
by tacit consent, of the two features that accounted for most of
its popularity in the beginning and as late as the eighteenth century—the comic character of the valet and the moral ending in
hell fire. With these primitive elements the story can now quite
well dispense; it is the psychology of Don Juan and of some of
the women into whose orbit the Fates throw him that is now the
really important thing, and the possibilities in this field seem
infinite.[1]

12

The stupendous popularity of *The Marriage of Figaro* in Prague
in 1786 had made the impresario of the local theatre, Bondini,
eager to have another opera from Mozart's pen; and naturally
the composer turned for his text to the collaborator who had
served him so well already. The Prague commission was particularly acceptable to Mozart just then, for his operatic stock did not
stand very high in Vienna at that time, both the Court and the
public preferring the simpler art of the Spaniard Martin y Solar's
Una cosa rara and Dittersdorf's *Doktor und Apotheker* to what
were regarded as the complexities of *The Seraglio*. Da Ponte, for
his part, was eager to add to his growing reputation in Vienna
as a writer for the theatre. He has left us his account of how he
set to work on receiving the new commission in the early part of
1787. So great was his vogue just then that three text-books were
commissioned from him at the same time. For Mozart, he says, he
chose the subject of Don Giovanni, and for Martin y Solar that of
L'Arbore di Diana; while for Salieri he had only to make an Italian adaptation of the *Tarare* that had already proved a success in
Paris. (It was based on Beaumarchais's play of the same name.)
The total task was certainly a formidable one, having regard to the
short time at his disposal and the very different natures of the
three subjects; but Da Ponte managed to pull through, he tells us,
with the assistance of some bottles of excellent Tokay, a good

[1] I need hardly remind the reader of Shaw's brilliant *Man and Superman*,
nor, in the operatic sphere, of the Pushkin-Dargomizhsky *Stone Guest*. The
Don Giovanni of Bertati and Gazzaniga, which alone bears directly on our
present study of Da Ponte and Mozart, will come up frequently for discussion later.

supply of Seville snuff, and the company of a charming young girl
of sixteen, living in the same house, who brought him, whenever
he rang for her, a cup of coffee, a biscuit, or a loving disposition,
according to his requirements at the moment. To the Emperor
he said, according to his own story written many years later, "I
shall write for Mozart at night, regarding it as reading Dante's
Inferno; in the mornings for Martin, which will be like reading
Petrarch; and in the evenings for Salieri, which will be my Tasso."

If we are to take his word for it, his first night's labour produced the first two scenes of *Don Giovanni*, two scenes of *L'Arbore
di Diana*, and more than half of the first act of *Tarare*, the title of
which he changed to *Assur*. "The next morning I took these three
texts to the respective composers, who could hardly believe their
eyes; and in sixty-three days I had finished the Mozart and Martin
texts and nearly two-thirds of *Assur*." But even a genius of
the first order, as Da Ponte frankly admitted himself to
be, could hardly have turned out three masterpieces in two
months; and the libretto of *Don Giovanni* in particular is far
from perfect.

As was his custom, he paid various predecessors in the same
field the compliment of borrowing from them whatever he found
useful to him in his work. He evidently knew the *Don Juan* of
Molière. But the work he principally laid under contribution was
one by Bertati,[1] with music by Gazzaniga, that had been given
in Venice in 1787 and had had a great success there and elsewhere.[2] This was constructed on a formula much in vogue in those
days—in the first part the manager of a travelling opera company
discusses with his personnel the necessity of finding something
new to attract the public, while the second part consists of a
performance of the work finally decided upon, in this case a
version of the Don Juan story in one act (twenty-five short
"scenes").

The Bertati opera opens, as that of Mozart does, with the valet
(Pasquariello) awaiting the return of his master from the noc-
turnal adventure with Donna Anna and the duel in which the

[1] Who later wrote the text of *Il Matrimonio Segreto* for Cimarosa (1792).
[2] It seems to have been originally produced in 1782, and to have undergone
various modifications in various revivals between then and 1787, and again
later.

Commander has been killed. There follows the regulation episode of the seduction of a country maiden (Maturina, whose betrothed is Biagio), while Bertati adds a second lady of higher degree, Ximena, to the traditional Elvira. As far as its limited time-scale allows the opera follows for a while the familiar course, till in the nineteenth scene we find Anna's lover, Ottavio, of whom we have seen and heard nothing since the opening episode, giving a stonecutter instructions as to the carving of an inscription on the base of the equestrian statue of Anna's father. After he has left the stage the drama runs its expected course—Don Giovanni's encounter with the statue, the fateful supper, and the descent of Giovanni into hell—after which Ottavio, Lanterna (another of Giovanni's servants), Maturina, Elvira, Ximena and Pasquariello (but not Anna) pour into the room to take part in a buffo ensemble.

13

Even where he stole from Bertati, Da Ponte often improved on him. He wisely dispensed with Donna Ximena, and fused Pasquariello and Lanterna into one. But in one instance he blundered badly. That his and Mozart's Ottavio is a woeful "stick," dramatically considered, few would question today. Even when he is convinced that Giovanni was Anna's assailant he does nothing about it. It is true that here and there a critic has racked his brains to discover some profound psychoanalytical reason for this irresolution and inactivity; some of them have even managed to persuade themselves that poor colourless spineless Ottavio is another Hamlet. Others have surmised that, like the good law-abiding citizen he is, he feels that it is not *his* task to execute vengeance on the reprobate, whose punishment should be left to the officers of the law. But it is always a waste of time and intellectual energy to go about beating the bush for a subtle explanation of a simple fact when an equally simple commonsense explanation of it stares us in the face. Obviously the reason why Da Ponte can never bring matters to a head as between Giovanni and Ottavio is that if a duel were to take place between them either Ottavio would be killed—in which case the opera would from that point onward be without a tenor and the drama without its virtuous counterpart to the wicked baritone, all which is operatically unthinkable—or Don Giovanni would be killed—in which case the performance would come to a summary end, and the audience would be cheated of its prescriptive right to the dreadful ethical joy of witnessing the Statue's vengeance on the murderer of Anna's father.

All the dramatists had been aware of this dilemma, and consequently had seen to it that the two male protagonists did not arrive at the decisive moment of meeting too soon. In Molière, for example, Don Alonso, a brother of Elvira, tracks Juan down in the third act and is about to take vengeance on him there and then. He is restrained, however, by his brother Don Carlos, whom, as it happens, Juan has just saved from being robbed and murdered by some brigands. (Carlos has never seen Juan before, but Alonso has.) As Carlos' Spanish sense of honour will not permit him to consent to Alonso's slaying his benefactor out of hand, he persuades his brother to postpone vengeance for one day. Before the trio can meet again, however, Juan has his first encounter with the Statue (in the mausoleum), invites it to supper, and so starts the train of events that leads swiftly to his end. Carlos comes upon him in the cemetery and insists on his marrying Elvira. Juan refuses, hypocritically pretending that he cannot do so as he has seen the error of his ways and is resolved to adopt the religious life, and therefore cannot fight a duel. The furious Carlos swears he will have vengeance, but recognises that to kill his man on consecrated ground would be sacrilegious. Juan leads him to believe that he will soon be passing through a small street leading to a convent, where they can settle their differences. Carlos departs, but before the two can meet again the Statue has avenged him on the betrayer of his sister. It is only Da Ponte who has been maladroit enough to give Ottavio too soon not only the justification but the opportunity for vengeance on Don Juan, so making it dramatically impossible for him to act decisively—to do anything, in fact, but be the mellifluous tenor of the production.

Da Ponte was partly forced into this awkward situation by the necessity imposed on him of finishing the libretto in the shortest possible time. In his initial hurry he took over Bertati's first four scenes very much as they stood—Leporello waiting for his master, the emergence of Giovanni and Anna from the house, the latter's frenzied expostulations, the arrival of her father, the duel, the opportune entry of Ottavio, Anna's grief for her father's fate, Ottavio's affectionate attempts to console her, and his vow that he will discover and punish the criminal. Had Bertati's opera been a longer one he too would at some point or other have been confronted with the difficulty that ultimately floored Da Ponte— that of keeping Ottavio inactive and yet interesting after Anna had revealed the name of her assailant. But Bertati was saved from this by the fact that his opera—mainly a buffa one at that—was in one act only. By the time he had regaled the audience with the conventional humorous scenes between Don Giovanni on the one hand and Elvira, Ximena, Maturina and Biagio on the other it was necessary for him to go without more ado to the hungrily expected closing scenes—Giovanni's parley with the Statue, the supper, and heaven's punishment of the young rake. As we have seen, Ottavio does not appear anywhere in Bertati's text between that introductory scene between himself and Anna and the near-final scene in which he is found telling the stonecutter what to carve on the Commander's tomb. Donna Anna too disappears completely from the action after that early scene: she would go into a retreat, she had told Ottavio, until the villain had been tracked down and punished; and so stoutly does she adhere to this resolution that Bertati does not even bring her on with the others, as Da Ponte does, for the buffo ensemble that ends the opera.

14

Mozart must already have been as well acquainted as Da Ponte was with the popular Don Juan story and Bertati's handling of it, and possibly he knew something also of Gluck's *Don Juan* ballet, which had been produced in Vienna in 1761. If we are to take literally Da Ponte's chronology (of a much later date), Mozart must have been engaged from about the middle of May to the end of August (1787) on the composition of *Don Giovanni*. In the early days of September he went to Prague to study the local conditions on the spot, as was generally necessary in the operatic world of that day, when the extent of the resources of a company and the capacities or limitations of individual singers had always to be taken into consideration. Da Ponte followed him shortly afterwards, but had to return to Vienna before the first performance. Mozart, who was an excellent producer of his own works, must have done a good deal of coaching of the Bondini troupe in collaboration with the gifted regisseur of the Prague theatre, Guardasoni. Apparently the only sections of the score remaining to be composed in Prague were the overture, Masetto's aria "Ho capito, Signor, sì!", an expansion of the recitative that had originally opened the second act into the present duet ("Eh via buffone") between Giovanni and Leporello, and the closing ensemble of the opera. Many minor details in the action would of course be modified in rehearsal.

It had been Bondini's intention to produce the new opera on the occasion of the visit to Prague, on the 14th October 1787, of the newly married couple the Archduchess Maria Theresa and Prince Anton of Saxony; but that plan fell through owing to the slow progress made with the rehearsals for one reason or another. Possibly, for one thing, the work confronted the singers with difficulties of a kind rather new to them; for another, Bondini's company seems to have been so small that he had to work on a narrow margin of safety.[1] On the 21st October Mozart wrote thus to his Vienna friend Gottfried von Jacquin: "Yet another delay has been caused by the indisposition of one of the female singers. As the company is a small one the impresario is in a constant state of worry; he has to take the greatest care of his people for fear of some sudden ailment or other that may mean no performance at all! Consequently everything here moves by slow stages, since the actors, out of sheer laziness, won't do any work on days when there is a performance at night, and the impresario is too scared to put any pressure on them." It was not until the 29th that the opera could be produced, with the following cast: Don Giovanni, Luigi Bassi;[2] Anna, Teresa Saporiti;[3]

[1] The Masetto had to double the part of the Commander.
[2] He had just turned twenty-one. He had joined the Bondini company in 1784. A legend has sprung up that he was not very intelligent and gave Mozart some trouble, causing him in particular to rewrite the duet with Zerlina—"Là ci darem la mano"—no less than five times. Proof is lacking for all this: Mozart's manuscript shows the duet to have had its present form before he left Vienna. In 1816 Bassi became regisseur of the Dresden Opera. Eight years later we find Beethoven speaking of him as a "fiery Italian." He died in 1825.
[3] Apparently she survived her trying experiences as Donna Anna rather

Ottavio, Antonio Baglioni; Elvira, Catarina Micelli; [1] Zerlina, Catarina Bondini (the impresario's wife); the Commander and Masetto, Giuseppe Lolli; Leporello, Felice Ponziani. Mozart conducted. The opera was an instantaneous success: "Evviva Da Ponte! Evviva Mozart!" Guardasoni wrote exultantly to the librettist in Vienna; "every impresario, every artist must extol you to the skies, for as long as we have such men among us there will be no more talk about the theatre being in a bad way!" Mozart, in the seventh heaven of happiness among his good friends and admirers in Prague, delayed for some weeks his return to Vienna.

A new crop of difficulties sprang up for him in connection with a production in the capital. The new singers made fresh demands on him, which Mozart had to meet; the result being a series of changes that have meant a headache for producers and audiences ever since. The new Ottavio, Francesco Morella, felt himself unequal to the exacting "Il mio tesoro," so Mozart wrote a new aria, the less difficult "Dalla sua pace," in substitution for it; and as both are included in modern productions the right places for their insertion are to some extent a matter for conjecture and caprice. The Elvira (Catarina Cavalieri) demanded an extra show piece, and was gratified with the great recitative and aria "Mi tradì quell'alma ingrata," which is today placed either near the beginning of the opera—after Leporello's Catalogue aria—or near the end—just before the churchyard scene. In the place of "Il mio tesoro" there was inserted a grossly farcical scene between Zerlina and Leporello ending with a duet, "Per queste tue manine"; all this is omitted in present-day performances, out of respect for Mozart's reputation and for the intelligence of the audience. One result of these changes being to prolong the opera unduly, the final sextet was omitted. The opera was given in its new form on the 7th May 1788. It was too much in advance of Viennese taste to have much success; and after fifteen performances it disappeared from the repertory for the remainder of Mozart's lifetime. [2]

more than eighty-one years, dying in March 1869 at the age of a hundred and six—nine days before Berlioz!

[1] The contemporary view of her voice seems to have been that it was "flexible but not agreeable": she appears to have been best in soubrette rôles.

[2] Owing to the haste in which the libretto was put together, and the vague-

15

Little importance attaches to the fact that the overture was not
written until the night before the final rehearsal of the opera; for
Mozart must have had it completely worked out in his mind long
before then, and putting it on paper would be a mere act of
penmanship.

The orchestra seems, by modern standards, a small one for the
tremendous dramatic effect obtained at the very commencement—
strings, two flutes, two oboes, two clarinets, two bassoons, two
horns, two trumpets and kettledrums. The overture, which is in
the so-called "French" form—a slow movement followed by a
fast one—begins with an andante introduction the thematic material of which is drawn from the final supper scene. The full
orchestra first of all gives out a suggestion of the impressive
chords (see No. 44) that seem to strike the startled Giovanni full
in the face when he flings open the door and sees confronting him
the statue he has rashly bidden to supper:

It is rather curious that Mozart's marking for the chords in the
overture is simply forte, whereas in the opera fortissimo is prescribed; strange, too, that when he came to enter the motifs in the
"Catalogue of my Works" in which it was his habit to record the
completion of a work and quote the opening bars of it, he should

---

ness of some of the scenic indications, the staging of the work bristles with
problems for the modern producer. Already there is quite a literature dealing
with this subject. It would carry us too far afield to attempt to deal with all
the ramifications of it: we must content ourselves with an analysis of the
opera as it stands in the score. Nor need we waste any time debating whether
Don Giovanni is an "opera buffa" or not. We can afford to take the simple
common sense view that for comic purposes Mozart wrote comic music, and
for serious purposes serious music, and leave it at that.

have failed to remember that in the score the bass D in the second bar and the C sharp in the fourth, in the bassoons, violas, 'cellos and double basses, being of minim length, continue to sound after the crotchets of the upper chords have ceased to be heard. (We meet with the same procedure in the opera itself.) Quoting the passage in his "Catalogue" on the 28th October 1787 he cuts the bass D and C sharp down to crotchets.[1]

There follows, in quieter tones, a six-bars repetition of the impressive rhythmic figure:

to the accompaniment of which the Statue declaims the words, "Don Giovanni! You have invited me to sup with you. I have come!"

There has been much futile debate as to whether the overture to the opera is "programmatic" or not. What is certain is that the andante introduction follows so closely the pattern of the corresponding scene in the drama that we are compelled to read into it the various significances the music has there. A vacillating syncopated figure in the first violins:

that follows immediately upon our No. 2, depicts unmistakably the agitation and self-doubt into which Giovanni is thrown by the appearance of the supernatural guest. For a moment he loses

[1] A facsimile of the precious little *Verzeichnis aller meiner Werke* was published in a limited edition a few years ago.

his normal arrogant self-poise. "Never would I have believed it!" he stammers; "but I will do what I can. Leporello, have another table laid at once!"

Next come, in the overture as in the opera, a few bars connected with the half-serious, half-farcical tremors of the valet, and the rejection by the Statue of the idea of serving earthly food to beings who have passed beyond all that. "I come here on a graver matter," it says; and a grisly gliding figure in flutes and violins in octaves, with alternating crescendi and diminuendi:

4

surrounds the words with a sinister meaning.

But now Mozart departs from the procedure of the opera and enters upon a feverish symphonic development (molto allegro) of new motifs, beginning with one in sixths in the violins:

5

which is capped by a fanfare in the whole orchestra except the strings:

6

Though there is no longer any following of a dramatic "programme," the general psychological implications of the themes that follow are obvious—Don Giovanni is posed before us in all his youthful levity and audacity. In the following example we seem to see him answering a threat with his usual gay mockery:

7

Mozart dwells with particular insistence on this antithesis, and, towards the end of the overture especially, on the "threat" portion of it:

8

Our quotation, taken from almost the closing bars of the overture, shows him settling down into the key of F major; there is no "recapitulatory" return, such as we would have expected him to make if he had been writing an overture for its own formal sake, to the prime key of the allegro, D Major.

16

The modulation to F major was foreordained by the fact that he had already begun the stage action with Leporello's monologue in that key (see musical example No. 9). Evidently, then, he wanted the action to follow the overture without a break; and that being so, it behoves the conductors to make the transition from the one to the other as natural as the composer intended it to be. But few of them do this. They mostly fall into two errors. In the first place they try to impose a more or less self-existent formal structure on the overture by introducing a rallentando in the last half-dozen bars or so, oblivious of the fact that, as will be seen from our example No. 8, Mozart has already achieved all the rallentando *he* desired by the simple process of changing his time-values from crotchets to minims: an additional slowing down on the part of the conductor is not only superfluous but harmful, suggesting, as it does, a sort of concert close to the overture never intended by the composer. In the second place the conductors and singers, with rare exceptions, take Leporello's opening solo too slowly. Mozart, who knew perfectly well what he was about, had marked that molto allegro—the same tempo as he prescribes for the allegro of the overture.[1] The over-slow tempo mostly adopted for the solo today is due to the irresistible inclination of a long line of basses to angle for the public guffaw.[2] In that process something of the real character of Mozart's Leporello is lost. Only a rapid tempo can bring out the impatience and bad temper of this ill-conditioned underling whom, when the curtain rises, we dimly see keeping watch by night in the garden of the Commander's house; his only objection to his master's villainies is that the gentleman regales himself with all the fruits of debauchery while the valet does no more than keep an eye on the tree. "Wearing myself out night and day, in wind and rain," he grumbles:

9

Molto allegro

[1] The marking for the *Nozze di Figaro* overture in the score is presto; but when Mozart entered it in the thematic Catalogue of his works on the eve of the first performance he marked it allegro assai. The latter is the marking for the *Don Giovanni* overture in the Catalogue, while in the score it is molto allegro. So again with the overture to *Der Schauspieldirektor*: in the score presto, in the Catalogue allegro assai. It is evident that for Mozart the terms allegro assai, allegro molto and presto meant the same thing, a point which conductors and singers of his operas would do well constantly to bear in mind. If they did, we might be spared some of the nonsensical tempi under which we suffer during performances of *Don Giovanni* in particular.
[2] It is perhaps a small point, but one worth taking into consideration that when Beethoven uses the Leporello theme (our No. 9) as the basis of the 22nd of his Diabelli Variations he not only marks it "Alla 'Notte e giorno faticar' di Mozart" but reproduces the "molto allegro" direction of the score. That variation is always, and rightly, taken at a great pace by pianists, not at the leisurely tempo adopted by our present-day Leporellos for their solo, which is untrue both to the *molto allegro* marking and to the psychological atmosphere of the episode in the opera.

"eating badly and sleeping badly, and for what? I too would like to play the gentleman, not the lackey. A nice gentleman indeed! he inside there with the lovely lady, while I just act the watch-dog"—"the watch-dog!" he repeats three times with surly sarcasm.[1]

But soon he hears confused sounds proceeding from the house, and at once he smothers his envy and resentment and becomes the craven lackey anxious before all else for his own safety. As he hides himself Donna Anna rushes from the house, holding Don Giovanni firmly by the arm; he is concealing his face in his cloak. In an agitated trio, for which a pelting *molto allegro* is a *sine qua non*, Anna swears she will discover who her assailant has been, even if it costs her her life:

10

Non spe—rar, se non m'uc—ci—di, ch'io ti la—sci fug—gir mai!

Giovanni swears that she shall not; and from his hiding place Leporello comments, "What a tumult! My master in another scrape!" As the distracted and furious Anna becomes more trouble-some Giovanni becomes angrier and more threatening: he bids her be silent or take the consequences. (This episode again is taken from Bertati, but Da Ponte has given both greater dramatic energy to the action and more point to the words. In Bertati, Don Giovanni tries to score a debating point by saying, "If it had been the Duke Ottavio you would not have had a word to say";[2] to which Anna replies, "Never has the Duke done anything base." This little verbal interchange has been omitted by Da Ponte—on the whole, we feel, wisely. He has been dramatically right, again, in expanding the scared comments of Leporello, whose sole fear is that this latest escapade of the libertine master whom he serves so unwillingly may get *him* into trouble.)

[1] Da Ponte took the general idea of the monologue from Bertati; but there is a more malicious bite in his own lines, and Mozart's skilful phrases give them an extra curl of the lip. Note particularly the fermata over the first syllable of the final repetition of "sentinella"; Leporello seems to dwell on it to get the last drop of acid comment out of it.

[2] Here we get a distant echo of Tirso's play, in which the woman who figures in the opening scene is not Ana but Isabela.

17

At last Anna's father, the Commander, enters, bidding the unknown interloper draw his sword and give him satisfaction. Giovanni, about whom there is always a certain aura of cavalier *grandezza*, will not deign to fight a man so much older than himself. It is only when the Commander taunts him with cowardice that he loses his self-control and says gravely, *mezza voce*, "Wretched man! So be it, if you are bent on dying!"

A few orchestral bars suggest the crossing of the swords, the thrust and parry. As the Commander falls, mortally wounded, Mozart for the first time changes the tempo. In a short andante trio in F minor, of the most impressive quality, the old man gasps out his farewell to the world; Giovanni, still with a certain nobility about him, laments the tragic turn events have taken; and even Leporello is moved to a seriousness not hitherto observable in him. Was it by chance or by design, by the way, that Mozart used the phrase to which, in her furious dialogue with Giovanni, Anna had sung "I will pursue you like a desperate fury":

11

for the *sotto voce* comment of Don Giovanni with which the tragic trio opens, now, of course, in the minor—"Ah! unhappy man! Already his agonising soul is leaving his miserable body"?

12

As the Commander breathes his last a wailing chromatic descending phrase in the orchestra sings his elegy: [1]

[1] Most conductors, desirous of an easy "effect," turn these few orchestral bars into a languishing adagio. This is quite wrong: the tempo of the trio should be andante from beginning to end, as Mozart has marked it; and "andante" in that epoch had its literal meaning of "walking"—"going" at an easy, natural pace, as Leopold Mozart puts it in his *Violinschule*.

Giovanni and Leporello are now alone, for Anna had fled into the house on her father's entry. The two take their new bearings in a brief recitative. "Bravo!" says the valet ironically; "two pretty deeds accomplished—a girl ravished and a father killed!" "He willed it so," replies Giovanni sombrely; "his the blame." "And Donna Anna?" asks Leporello slyly; "did she will it too?" But Giovanni quickly checks his insolence, for which he is in no mood just now: "Keep your mouth shut and come with me, unless you want something to happen to you as well"; and the valet, cowed as usual when his imperious master asserts himself, follows him off the stage, muttering "I want nothing, Sir; I will not say another word."

As they disappear in the darkness Anna enters with Ottavio. Her object in running into the house had evidently been to find him, though how and why he happened to be there at that time of night is something Da Ponte does not pause to explain. Anna, not having seen the duel, believes her father merely to be in some peril. Ottavio, of course, assures her that he will shed the last drop of his blood to help the old man. "But where is the villain?" he asks her. "I left him just here," she replies; and then, to her horror, she sees the body on the ground.

Once more the tempo whips up—or should do—to allegro assai as Mozart plunges into one of the finest scenes of the opera. Stabbing phrases in the orchestra accompany Anna as she laments her loss, followed by wailing figures as she points to the old man's wounds. It is in this episode that the conductors are generally seen at their worst. They slow down the time to adagio at this point and that, making Anna dwell pathetically on her loss, whereas she should be in a frenzy of despair that allows her no time, just then, for indulgence in the luxury of self-pity. Such slowing down as is required is once more amply provided for by Mozart by a change from crotchet to minim time-units.

Some servants with torches have come in, and these Ottavio, always fertile in good advice, sends back into the house for smelling-salts and cordials to revive the fainting Anna, over whose drooping body he bends with gestures of tender compassion. He bids the servants carry the body away, and exhorts her to take heart again. She abandons herself (*allegro*) to a passion of grief: "Leave me!" she cries; "let me die!":

14

Ottavio and the orchestra vie with each other in tendernesses and solicitudes; "put away these sad memories," he exhorts her; "in me you have father and spouse in one":

15

but she is inconsolable. The tempo slows down as she solemnly exacts from him an oath to avenge her father's murder: this he swears by her dear eyes and by their love. With a return to the previous rapid tempo they reaffirm, in duet, their oath, and go into the house.

18

This scene had run differently in Bertati. After the exit of Giovanni and his valet, Ottavio, Anna and some servants come upon the stage. In a few short lines the body of the Commander is discovered and taken away, and then Bertati feels that some explanations are due for the benefit of the audience. "Duke," says Anna, "my father is dead, and I do not know who the dastard was who has slain him." Naturally Ottavio asks, "But how did the villain get into your apartments?" She reminds him that, in virtue of their being betrothed lovers, she had given Ottavio an assignation in her room.[1] Her waiting-woman having left her, a

[1] Bertati is at pains to make it clear to his audience that the assignation was quite open and innocent:

"A voi, Duca, stringendomi
La promessa di sposa, io me ne stava

man enveloped in a cloak had entered, whom she had taken to be the Duke. Without saying a word he had embraced her passionately. Covered with confusion she had shaken him off and said, "How dare you, Duke? What are you doing?" But the man had only renewed his assault, calling her his dear one and protesting his love. This naturally induced something like paralysis in her; and taking advantage of her weakness the vile intruder had resumed the assault. She defended herself as best she could and called out to her maid; whereupon the villain had turned to flee. She tried to unmask him, at any rate, and called for her father, immediately on whose appearance she had fled from the dreadful scene; and then the assassin had run the old man through.

Her story told, Ottavio (in Bertati) protests that he is absolutely on fire with rage: it will not be long, he assures her, before the miscreant is discovered, and then his punishment will fit the crime. However, he goes on to say, Anna can surely console herself with the reflection that if she has lost her father she still has her lover and the sure prospect of a happy union. She tells him, however, that for the present there can be no more talk of marriage: until the murderer of her father is found and punished she means to go into a retreat. With that she leaves him and disappears from the opera—for good. Ottavio, left alone, bewails, tenor-like, his hard lot in an aria, hopes for the dawn of a better day, and disappears, in his turn, until the cemetery scene.

One of Da Ponte's most effective strokes was to substitute a construction of his own for this of Bertati's. He saw that what was required at the moment was not cold explanation but passionate emotion; so—perhaps at the urging of Mozart, whose imagination the scene had evidently captured—he allowed Anna full scope for the expression of her grief. Her explanation to Ottavio he brought in in a later scene, with excellent dramatic effect.[1] But he

---

Ad aspettarvi nel mio appartamento
Pe' l nostro concertato abboccamento":
(in virtue of their being betrothed, she had arranged with Ottavio for a "colloquy" with him in her room). Here the distant affiliation with the opening scene of Tirso is obvious; but Tirso's Isabela and the Anna of the opera are quite different characters.

[1] And of course, with three-fourths of the first act and a long second act before him, Da Ponte could not make *his* Anna go into a retreat there and then!

overlooked one point when laying out that scene. Bertati does at
least give us, for what it is worth, some sort of explanation why,
in the first place, Anna was not surprised at the appearance of a
man in her room at that hour of the night, and, in the second
place, why Ottavio should so conveniently be on the premises
just then. Anna had actually given her lover an assignation in her
room, regarding his promise of marriage as justification for doing
so. But in the later scene in Da Ponte in which she tells Ottavio
what had happened that night, her story is that when sitting
alone in her room she saw a man enter, wrapped in a cloak, whom
at first she took to be the Duke. But just *why* the mild Ottavio,
whose morals are beyond reproach and whose behaviour is always
scrupulously correct, should have been calling on a virtuous Donna
Anna at that hour of the night, unknown to her father, is something that remains quite unexplained. Da Ponte seems to have
no better reason for making him be on the spot than the fact that
he is necessary for Anna's great scene after the discovery of the
body of her father.

19

The setting now changes to "a street": the time is "early morning"—possibly the morning of the following day, for Leporello
speaks at one point of it "now being full dawn"; and already, at
the first change of scene, we find Da Ponte burdening himself
and us with some awkward problems of time and place. According to dramatic tradition the valet takes it on himself on one
occasion and another to reprove his master for living so dissolute
a life; and Da Ponte chooses this point at which to introduce the
theme. From their colloquy (carried on in recitative) we learn
that, far from repenting and reforming, Giovanni has a new adventure in prospect. He has captivated, and been captivated by,
a young beauty who has promised to come to his country house—
or so it seems—that night. He breaks off abruptly as his trained
senses detect what he calls an "odour of femininity" in the air.
Just then a woman enters, and Giovanni, taking Leporello with
him, retires into the background the better to spy out the land.

The newcomer is Donna Elvira, who has just arrived in the
neighbourhood, hot on the traces of the deceiver who has triumphed over her in Burgos under the usual assurance of marriage

and then basely abandoned her. She gives vent to her outraged feelings in a passionate aria, the substance of which is that if she can only come upon the scoundrel again she will be satisfied with nothing less than cutting out his heart. It is a distinguishing feature of the score of *Don Giovanni* that often the main burden of psychological expression is borne not by the voice but by the orchestral texture, in which Mozart revels in felicity after felicity of characterisation.[1] Elvira's present aria ("Ah! chi mi dice mai quel barbaro dov' è"), for example, derives its driving and cutting power less from the vocal line than from pelting and stabbing orchestral figures such as this:

16

and this:

17

Giovanni and Leporello eavesdrop on her for some time before they recognise her, and, in a trio that is one of Mozart's little masterpieces in the way of fusing the serious with the humorous, they comment on the lady's tantrums with mock pity. "Poor little thing!" says Giovanni; "we must try to console her"—"As you have 'consoled' some eighteen hundred already," Leporello comments sardonically. Giovanni approaches the angry lady ingratiatingly, and the swift disconcerting recognition is mutual. The malicious valet is amused and delighted by this unexpected turn of events. Giovanni, soon recovering something of his normal aplomb, addresses Elvira with elaborate courtesy. She interrupts him with a lengthy and furious recital of the wrongs she has suffered at his hands: "she reels it off like a printed book!" interjects Leporello

[1] During the period of gestation of *Don Giovanni* his instrumental genius was functioning with rare ease and power, as witness in particular the great string quintet in G minor and the *Kleine Nachtmusik*.

admiringly, borrowing a phrase from Molière. Giovanni turns the awkward business of explanation over to his servant, disappears, and leaves the ground clear for Leporello and his Catalogue aria.

20

We may enlarge our view of this episode a little by going back to Bertati. He describes the scene as "in the country, with rustic dwellings and a fine country house, outside the walls of Villena" [1] (the general scene of the action in Bertati). From the dialogue between Giovanni and Pasquariello we learn that the former's new conquest—the "pretty lady" of Da Ponte—is a certain Donna Ximena, who had arrived "yesterday" at her country house— evidently the one shown on the stage—for the purpose of having secret meetings with Don Giovanni. While master and man are talking Elvira enters. She is a lady of quality attended by two servants, who has just arrived from Burgos in a splendid carriage: she decides to put up for the present at an inn in "this village" rather than in the town, the better to keep an eye on the comings and goings of the man who had deceived and abandoned her after a mere three days of sham wedlock. When, after their short colloquy, Giovanni, with apologies for having to leave her "on pressing business," deputes his valet to explain his past behaviour to her, he "goes into the casino" (the country house), manifestly to keep his assignation with Ximena. At the conclusion of the Catalogue aria Elvira simply "exits," presumably to make her way to the inn.

Bertati had all along a clear and consistent idea of the setting and the action: his next scene (following on the "Catalogue" episode between Pasquariello and Elvira), shows us Giovanni and Ximena in amorous communion inside the house, she trying to pin him down to a promise of wedlock, the consummate confidence trickster taking evasive action as usual. But Da Ponte was in too much of a hurry to think very hard about it all. He sensibly abolished Ximena, whom he could hardly have made use of now without having her on his hands for the rest of the evening. It was precisely Ximena, however, who, in Bertati, had accounted for the "casino," for Don Giovanni being stationed outside it, and for his running away so unceremoniously from Elvira. Bertati

[1] In Aragon.

makes it perfectly clear that Giovanni and Pasquariello are so early out of their beds—or not yet in them—because the assignation with Ximena in her country house is for that very hour. What Giovanni says to Leporello in Da Ponte, however, is this: "Know that I am in love with a beautiful lady who loves me; I have seen her, I have spoken to her, and she will come with me to the casino [whose? presumably his] *tonight*." The "tonight" makes sheer nonsense of it all. Truly Da Ponte could be the most slovenly of craftsmen at times: the best he can do now in the way of getting his hero off the stage is the direction "Don Giovanni escapes"!

21

Let us take up the dropped thread of the Da Ponte opera. Giovanni having been got out of the way by hook or by crook the stage is now set for one of the most famous show pieces of the work—the Catalogue aria, the subject of which has a place of its own in the history of the Don Juan drama.

There is nothing resembling it in Tirso's *El Burlador*: Tirso was too good a dramatist, and wrote for too cultivated an audience, to bring the minor character of the lackey too much to the forefront. But it was inevitable that in proportion as the Don Juan story descended to the smaller European theatres and the puppet shows and the chawbacon public it should drift more and more into common clowning in the places where the comic character could assert his traditional rights.[1] This process of degradation set in first in Italy, where the commedia dell' arte specialised in characters whose prime concern it was to lay the fun on with a trowel. It was in Italy, apparently, that the Catalogue of the Spanish hero's conquests first came into being. The motif appears to have made its first, or at all events an early, appearance in Cicognini's *Il Convitato di Pietra, opera esemplare in prosa*, produced shortly before 1650. (The first Venice imprint bears no date; but it is generally agreed that the author died about 1651.) This Cicognini was a prolific and highly popular writer for the Italian theatre in the first half of the seventeenth century. He obviously played to the gallery: a later historian of Italian litera-

---

[1] Think of the often dreadful buffoonery, for the delectation of the groundlings, in some of Shakespeare's and Marlowe's finest tragedies!

ture, Crescimbeni, regarded him as on the whole a degrading influence.

Cicognini's *Il Convitato di Pietra* is accessible to students today in the reprint of Gendarme de Bévotte. It is a very free handling of Tirso's story, often coarsened by the influence of the commedia dell' arte. In the eleventh scene of the first act Don Giovanni and his servant Passarino, having escaped from the wrecked ship, make the acquaintance of the fishermaiden Rosalba (Tirso's Tisbea at a considerable remove). As soon as he has recovered from the effects of his immersion Giovanni observes that Rosalba is uncommonly pretty. "Vedi che buon bocconcino" ("A nice little mouthful, this"), he remarks *sotto voce* to Passarino, who comments, "Another one for the list!" That is all, for the time being, in Cicognini; but in the thirteenth scene, when Giovanni is about to leave Rosalba and she is reminding him of his vows, Passarino remarks that if his master had kept all the promises of marriage he had made he would now find himself with four thousand wives. (We are already very far from Tirso, it will be seen, well on the way towards the broad farce of later days.) As Giovanni leaves Rosalba, the valet, according to the stage directions, throws the list *at the audience*, bidding them see for themselves how many hundreds of names there are in it; and with that he leaves Rosalba to bewail her lot alone. As yet, then, there is no actual reading from the list; the mere mention and exhibition of one was presumably enough to set the audience in a roar.

22

The treatment of the motif remains much the same in the Biancolelli scenario (1622) of which mention has already been made.[1] When, in this Italian production in Paris, Don Juan abandons the fishermaiden after having betrayed her under a promise of marriage, Arlequin (the valet) tells her, by way of consolation, that she is only one of more than a hundred damsels who have been similarly honoured. "I say to her," so Biancolelli's scenario runs, "'Look, here's the list of all the others in the same case as yourself; I'll add your name.' Then I throw the scroll into the pit, keeping hold of one end of it, and I say, 'Gentlemen, just see if the name of one or other of your own female relatives isn't down

[1] See p. 141.

here.'" The theme, it will be seen, was capable of all sorts of comic variations.

Dorimon and de Villiers make the valet reel off to the forsaken maidens the names of some others of the hero's victims, and show them the scroll. In Molière, where the valet is not the ordinary Italian buffoon but a shrewd, brainy fellow, coolly critical of his master and rather contemptuous of him, there is neither production nor mention of a "list." The play opens with a scene between the valet (Sganarelle) and Gusman (the majordomo of the abandoned Elvire), who has been commissioned to find out why Juan has behaved so callously to his mistress. Sganarelle assures Gusman that his master, about whom he has no illusions, simply does not know the meaning of the word honour. "It costs him nothing to contract a marriage; that's his usual trap for women. He marries right and left—high-born lady, young girl, bourgeoise, peasant, none is too warm or too cold for him. If I were to tell you the names of all the women he has married here, there and everywhere, it would keep me going till nightfall. You look surprised at this: you change colour; but it is a mere sketch of the man, and to complete the portrait would mean many more brush-strokes. Suffice it to say that one of these days the wrath of heaven will overtake him. I would rather belong to the Devil than to him. . . ."

But Molière was writing for a Paris audience with some claims to intelligence and taste. The Italian small town public was satisfied with lower standards: there a clowning servant was a well-established figure of fun, and it was in the Italian tradition that Bertati and Da Ponte were content to work.[1]

---

[1] The register of a lady-killer's operations was no doubt something of a stock comic apparatus even before the Don Juan saga acquired its vogue. In John Fletcher's play *The Wild-Goose Chase* (probably about 1621) the hero Mirabell (the "Wild-Goose") is described in the list of dramatis personae as "a Travell'd Monsieur, and great defyer of all Ladies in the way of Marriage, otherwise their much loose servant, at the last caught by the despis'd Oriana." He is, in truth, merely a harmless young poseur whom no one, and least of all the women, take very seriously; but he keeps a register of his alleged conquests and shows it confidentially to his friend De-Garde—"this book, this inventory," as De-Garde describes it, "the debt-book of your mistresses."

We have left Elvira alone with Leporello, who has been commissioned by his master, before he "escapes," to tell the lady just why she has been treated so scurvily. He takes this as his cue to reel off the expected Catalogue; Elvira is to console herself with the knowledge that she has had many forerunners, in proof of which Leporello holds out to her the "little book" of names and places, inviting her to read it with him—in Italy six hundred and forty, in Germany two hundred and thirty-one, a hundred in France, ninety-one in Turkey (it will be seen that Don Juan has travelled a good deal since Tirso's days), and here in Spain no fewer than a thousand and three, making a grand total of two thousand and sixty-five.[1] His master's tastes, Leporello assures Elvira, are catholic—from the princess and the marquise, the baroness and the countess to the lady's maid and the bourgeoise, blonde or brunette, old or young, the plump being more fancied in the winter, the slim in the summer; in fact, virtually anything in petticoats, but in general novices preferred. Da Ponte as a verbal artist has improved here on Bertati, and for every one of the many piquancies of the text Mozart finds the perfect musical characterisation, the ribald chuckle of the orchestra, for example, as Leporello reads out the score in Italy, Germany and elsewhere:

18

[1] Giovanni's record does not surpass that of Alphonse Daudet's Brichanteau, who confessed to having in some forty-five years seduced six hundred young girls, saved seven or eight hundred persecuted female orphans, married thousands of *jeunes premières*, and even violated ladies of quality. These exploits, however, were performed by him merely in his capacity as an actor, "between the footlights and the back curtain," as he explains. But even a stage character of this vital sort takes some sort of living up to. Has any of us ever seen a Don Giovanni who suggests the veracity of Leporello's laudatory account of him? Many of them put us in mind only of a good-looking barber's apprentice with a respectable score at purely local targets. A few are so frankly undemonic as to be incredible; they put us in mind of that Don Giovanni whom Berlioz saw in Paris, who ought to have been

The aria, thanks to Mozart, practically sings itself, so that most of the farcical by-play that the average bass over-zealously insists on in the delivery of it is superfluous.

Having finished his "consolation" Leporello goes off. It is almost incredible that Da Ponte keeps Elvira on the stage all through this long ordeal, enduring the lackey's suggestive insolences without saying a word; but that was what the librettist was reduced to through having departed from Bertati without taking due thought of all the consequences. In Bertati the Catalogue is shorter and less farcical in its exaggerations: Elvira cuts the rascal short, refusing to listen any more; she orders him away, and when she is alone she voices in a few lines of recitative her determination to find out if she has a rival, and, if so, to deal appropriately with her. In Da Ponte the equivalent recitative put into her mouth seems so feeble after the lengthy Catalogue aria that some producers dispense with it, sending her off the stage along with Leporello. Others feel that she ought to be allowed to make her exit with more dignity than this, so they tack on to her words the recitative ("In quali eccessi, O Numi") and aria ("Mi tradì quell' alma ingrata") which Mozart added to the score for the Vienna production of the opera. But there the recitative and aria had been rightly placed near the end of the work: they are the last expression of Elvira's feelings, fluctuating between anger with Giovanni and pity for the doom she is now sure will overtake him, after the further proofs she had experienced of his perfidy and levity since the opera opened. To remove this aria from its proper place to the few minutes following on the Catalogue aria is to drift into sheer nonsense. For the difficult situation now created, however, only Da Ponte can be held responsible.

24

Towards the end of the present scene, when he is promising to marry Zerlina, Giovanni says to her, "This casinetto is mine. There we will be alone, and there, my jewel, we will be made one"; and again, at the commencement of the duet "Là ci darem la mano," "See, it is quite near: let us go there." Now in an earlier scene, as the reader will remember, Giovanni had spoken of the

given, he said, the *prix Montyon* (a prize awarded to the most outstandingly virtuous Paris schoolboy of the academic year).

country house in which his unnamed latest conquest had arranged to meet him that night. All this had made better sense in Bertati, where there really is a new conquest—Donna Ximena—and it is in *her* house, shown on the stage, that the meeting is to take place. But in *Don Giovanni* we hear no more of that assignation, for Da Ponte dispenses entirely with Donna Ximena. Having taken over from his predecessor the notion of a "casino," yet having failed to make use of it in circumstances that would have been appropriate to it, he now decides to work it into the Zerlina episode. In this there was certainly a touch of ingenuity. But Bertati had throughout a better construction in mind. He makes the entry of Giovanni and Ximena into the latter's house, and their exit from it a little later, not only dramatically credible but suggestively operative as regards time. All this goes for nothing in Da Ponte: he makes Giovanni "escape" at a critical moment, but where he escapes to we do not discover. Leporello "goes off" after reeling off the list to Elvira; but again we are not told, nor can we discover, where. In Bertati it had all been quite simple and logical, as well as scenically economical. Da Ponte requires two settings —first the "street" in which Giovanni and Elvira accidentally meet in the early morning, followed by the Catalogue aria and so on, and afterwards the "open country" near Giovanni's house, where the peasants are merry-making. In Bertati *one* scene suffices—"the open country, with rustic dwellings and a handsome villa, outside the walls of Villena." Giovanni is hanging about the house— Ximena's—because that lady had arrived there yesterday and would receive him today. There follow, in logical sequence, the chance meeting and mutual recognition of Giovanni and Elvira, the slipping of the former "into the villa," as we are expressly told, Leporello's detention of Elvira by means of the Catalogue aria,[1] the later emergence of Ximena and Giovanni from the house, and their brief dialogue. With the exit of Ximena, Bertati at once brings the peasants on the stage. There is no need, as in Da Ponte, for any change of scene. This is all provided for in the one setting: to celebrate with song and dance the nuptials of Maturina (Zerlina) and Biagio (Masetto) all that the villagers have to do is to

---

[1] What was meanwhile happening in the villa we can infer from Giovanni's closing remark, *sotto voce*, as he leaves Ximena: "I must be off and enter her in the list."

come out of their cottages into the "open country" near the patrician house. When Giovanni succeeds in wearing down Maturina's resistance the pair leave the others and, according to the stage directions, "go into Maturina's house"—obviously one of those "rustic dwellings" described by Bertati as forming part of the stage setting.

Moreover, Bertati's transition from the previous scene to the present one is much more logically and naturally managed than Da Ponte's, where we see Giovanni "escaping" from Elvira—whither and why? Next Leporello escapes from Elvira—where? Master and man reappear together after the opening ensemble of villagers, and from Giovanni's first words, "Good riddance! But see, what a number of pretty girls . . .", we gather that the pair have met again just after the exit of Elvira. Bertati has a better sense of timing. After the Catalogue aria Pasquariello obviously strolls around on his own account, waiting for the return of his master from Operation Ximena in the villa; and when Giovanni and Ximena leave the stage the former as obviously goes off trusting to come upon his valet sooner or later. Da Ponte makes the mistake, in terms of stage time, of bringing master and man on together in the villagers' scene. Bertati is defter: he brings Pasquariello in again almost as soon as Maturina and the peasants have burst upon the scene and begun their little song and dance; clearly he has not been far away since he turned his back on Elvira. At first he listens and watches in concealment; then, unable to repress the amorous ardours he shares with his master, he runs into their midst, takes Maturina by the hand, and makes her dance with him, until the hackles of the jealous Biagio rise and he packs the other villagers off and turns roughly on Pasquariello, who, attempting an imitation of his master's technique, tries to pass himself off as a gentleman of the name of Don Giovannino. It is while the two are quarrelling that Giovanni enters, contemptuously puts the lackey in his place, and then turns his attentions to Maturina. Bertati's Giovanni, then, we can assume to have been wandering about for a little while in search of Pasquariello after his exit from Ximena's house. Da Ponte's construction, in which master and man—the former ejaculating "That's a good riddance!"—meaning Elvira—enter together without any credible time-interval, is a lamentably feeble piece of work in comparison. Further, Bertati's more extended treatment of the scene, with the consequently more gradual breach of Maturina's defences, is dramatically superior to Da Ponte's, which hardly gives Zerlina any time to do more than say first "I want to and yet I don't" and then "Yes," before she goes off towards the house with Giovanni.

25

Let us return to the point in Mozart's opera in which Giovanni and Leporello find themselves in the midst of a number of villagers who are celebrating the espousals of two of their number, Zerlina and Masetto.

Giovanni, who knows every move in the game he has played so successfully for so long, soon insinuates himself into the favour of the pretty bride, whom he promises to take under his gentlemanly protection; while a little commotion among the other girls is explained by Leporello having suggested taking one or two of them under *his* protection. Poor Masetto tries to assert his rights, but the peasant is soon cowed by the veiled threats of the nobleman. He vents his rage in an aria (allegro di molto) that is one-third craven cringing, one-third rough irony and one-third surly threat: "Yes, I understand, Signor. A cavalier like you can wish a man like me nothing but well. But as for you, you slut [turning to Zerlina] my calamity, my ruin! . . . [Then to Leporello, who is shooing him out] Yes, yes, I'm going! [To Zerlina again, sarcastically] The fine gentleman here will make a fine lady of you, I'm sure!"

As soon as Masetto has been hustled off the stage Giovanni turns on little Zerlina the blend of charm and flattery that has always worked with her sex. She is too pretty, he assures her, to be the wife of a country bumpkin like Masetto: he, Don Giovanni, will make a lady of her forthwith: "so let us slip into my villa here, where we will be made one":

19

She takes very little persuading; her defences are soon down, and she becomes as ardent for the adventure as Giovanni himself.

As they are leaving for the villa, arm in arm, they are confronted by Elvira, who has overheard their colloquy and now intervenes to save "this poor innocent girl" from the cavalier's "cruel claws." At this Zerlina naturally hesitates, and for a moment or two Giovanni's craftsmanship is put to a severe test. To Elvira, whom he addresses cajolingly as "my idol," he explains in a rapid aside that he is merely amusing himself with a country maiden, which draws from her the acid comment that *she* knows only too well what "amusing himself" means. In another aside he tells the puzzled Zerlina that this poor excited lady is crazily enamoured of him, and to keep her quiet he has to pretend, out of the sheer kindness of his heart, to be in love with her.

But Elvira is not so easily fooled. In a vigorous aria, "Ah, fuggi il traditor":

she warns Zerlina that the plausible gallant is a rogue and a liar, and ends by hustling her away. Giovanni takes his frustration philosophically. "Everything seems to be going wrong with me today," he soliloquises; "the Devil seems to be amusing himself at my expense, opposing all my pleasant little plans." "But this is the last straw!", he ejaculates disgustedly as Ottavio and Donna Anna enter. Ottavio, as usual, is more heart than head; and as he comes into view we hear him bidding Anna not to give way to vain tears but to think about vengeance for her father. Before he can get even as far as talking about this, however, he and Anna catch sight of Giovanni. He is well known to both of them, it appears. Anna's opening words to him are, "My friend, we meet you in the nick of time. Have you courage, a noble soul?" ("Now I wonder," he mutters under his breath, "if the Devil has been putting ideas into her head!") He courteously places himself at her disposal, however, and, with a sigh of relief, discovers from her next words that he is in no danger of recognition. "Fair Donna Anna, why are you weeping?" he asks; "has any villain dared to grieve you?" He is hers to command, he protests; his relations, his friends, his possessions, his good right arm, his sword, all are at her service if she has been wronged.

26

But before she can satisfy his generous curiosity on this point Elvira breaks in upon them with the remark "Ah! do I find you again, perfidious monster?"—which, considering she had left him in that very place only a minute before, can hardly be regarded as a masterpiece of dramatic construction on Da Ponte's part. There seems to be no valid reason why she should return at this point except the fact that a quartet has now been called for by the composer. She begins by taking Anna under her protection as she had done Zerlina: "Wretched one, put not your trust in this ribald rogue: he has already betrayed me, and now he would betray you":

21

Anna and Ottavio are impressed by the nobility of her bearing and the signs of suffering in her face.

Giovanni resorts to a technique that has served him well before; the poor creature, he informs the others confidentially, is mentally deranged; if they will leave him alone with her he will see if he can calm her down. For a while Ottavio and Anna do not know which of the two to believe; but gradually Elvira's passionate reiterations of Giovanni's perfidy have their effect on them, and the masterly quartet, in which each personage is aptly characterised by Mozart, ends as it were on a note of interrogation. Don Giovanni has not lost his case; nor, on the other hand, has Elvira entirely won hers.

Da Ponte now wants to have the stage clear for the decisive

"explanation" scene between Ottavio and Anna, which opens with an agitated orchestral figure:

22

suggestive of Anna's horror at the realisation that the murderer of her father was Don Giovanni. He cannot be altogether congratulated as a dramatist, however, on the way he brings this about. He can think of nothing better than to make Elvira leave the stage—just at the point when the dramatic tension has reached its climax!—and send Giovanni hot-foot after her, with a lame explanation to Ottavio and Anna that he must see that the poor deluded creature does not do herself some injury. With polite apologies and a renewed assurance that if he can be of any service to Anna and Ottavio they will find him in his villa, Giovanni bids them goodbye and hastens after Elvira.

Da Ponte's handling of Elvira so far, and for some time later, is the great blot on the libretto; what should be the most *positive* female character in the work—for Anna is throughout more negative than positive—is apt to become in performance a mere figure of fun, popping in and out of the action like a jack-in-the-box as she does; in particular her sudden appearance in the present scene within a minute or so after she has bundled Zerlina off to safety has an effect of sheer farce that the most seriously disposed audience cannot resist. For this unfortunate result Da Ponte's reliance on Bertati in general outline and his departure from him in matters of detail are about equally responsible. Bertati, with only a few minutes now to fill in before coming to the decisive mausoleum scene for which his audience has been eagerly waiting, decides to pile on the fun thick and fast. After the exit of Giovanni and Maturina into the latter's cottage he has a comic scene in which Giovanni, on his reappearance, plays off Elvira and Ximena against each other, whispering to each of them in turn that the other is mentally deranged. Ximena having left the stage, he repeats the process with Elvira and Maturina. Then he goes off, leaving these two to indulge in a lively duet in which each of the supposed "wives" slangs the other in true Italian buffo style, and the great lady Elvira is brought down to the peasant girl's level. They go off, still exchanging insults, and the scene changes to the mausoleum and the episode with the Statue, for which, by this time, the audience can be presumed to be getting impatient.

Henceforth Da Ponte is left to his own resources: his opera being in two acts, he still has a large canvas to fill in before he can arrive at the climactic Statue scene. He will do so with some difficulty, as we shall see: meanwhile it is important to take note of the awkwardnesses in which he has already landed himself by playing the in-and-out game he has done with Bertati's construction, and especially by his having dispensed with the character of Ximena.

27

It does not seem to have been observed by the writers on the *Don Giovanni* subject that of all the Don Juans of literature and the drama that of Da Ponte is professionally the most futile. (We are not talking now of the Don Giovanni of Mozart.) He is the last poor ineffectual scion of an illustrious race of conquerors. Tirso's Don Juan would have refused to sit at the same table with anyone so inefficient; Shadwell's Libertine would have scorned to be seen raiding the same nunnery in his company. For when it comes to action Da Ponte's Giovanni accomplishes simply nothing to justify his reputation. Bertati's hero, in his short innings before he is given "Out!" by the Great Umpire, at least manages to run up almost before our eyes the respectable score of three. It is clear that he had been successful with Donna Anna: "Bravo!" says Pasquariello to him after the death of the Commander; "Two heroic deeds—Donna Anna violated and her father run through the body!", and the hero, be it noted, does not deny either impeachment; witness also his cynical remark to Anna when he was trying to escape from her—"If it had been Duke Ottavio you wouldn't have had anything to say about it." Later he retires into the villa of the enamoured Ximena, and does not reappear until after an interval long enough to allow the audience to draw its own conclusions as to how he had occupied his time there. So again when he goes off with the equally amorous Maturina into the latter's cottage, with a scene's convenient time-interval between that disappearance from our view and his next appearance on the stage.

But in Da Ponte his record is one of continuous frustration and failure. In the critical case of Anna he confronts us with two alternatives—either we are to come to the conclusion that her story to Ottavio of the merciful frustration of Giovanni's attempt is deliberately false, in which case what becomes of our conception of "the noble Donna Anna"?—or we must accept her story as unquestioningly as Ottavio does, with a similar sigh of relief, in which case Giovanni's first adventure in the opera must rank as his misadventure number one. It is true that there is some confusion, even among Mozart students, with regard to this. Alfred Einstein, for instance, confidently lays it down that "what is true is that she is one of the hero's victims, that Don Giovanni in the dark of the night, disguised as Don Ottavio, has reached the summit of his desires, and that the curtain rises at the moment when Donna Anna has come to the realisation of the terrible truth of her betrayal. In the eighteenth century no one misunderstood this." For all these *ex cathedra* assertions Einstein offers no evidence at all. There is nothing whatever *in the text* to lead us to believe that Anna is "one of the hero's victims." The "eighteenth century"—whatever, if anything, that may mean in this connection—would be aware that in Bertati it had been made tolerably clear that Anna had been outraged. But why should it collectively assume that in Da Ponte also she had been, when neither in the text of the opening scene of the opera nor in that of the "explanation" scene with Ottavio is there a single line to warrant that assumption? [1] To invoke the whole "eighteenth century" in this

[1] To this it may be objected that in the short dialogue in recitative that follows the murder of the Commander, Leporello says "Bravo! two pretty affairs; the daughter outraged, the father killed." To this Giovanni makes, in effect, the sombre reply, "What he got he asked for." Then, when the lackey asks insinuatingly, "And Donna Anna, did *she* ask for it?", his master checks his impertinent familiarity with a curt "Silence: do not annoy me: come away with me [drawing his sword] unless you want something to happen to *you*." All this is consistent with the view that Giovanni had *not* succeeded with Anna, but was for the moment sobered by the thought of the consequences of the killing of her father. The parallel dialogue in Bertati suggests

high-priori manner in support of a theory that is nothing but guesswork on Einstein's part is going a trifle too far.

Einstein seems to have worked on the vague notion that Da Ponte's Anna is the equivalent of Tirso's Isabela. But though Isabela confessedly succumbed to the seducer at the beginning of the drama, the daughter of the Commander whom *his* Don Juan slew was Doña Ana, with whom, as he himself admitted, he had failed. The fact that neither Da Ponte nor Bertati took the trouble to make a self-consistent unity out of the two women of the original saga is regrettable but beside the present point: what we are finally left with is the *Don Giovanni* libretto of Da Ponte, and this contains no warrant for Einstein's obiter dictum that Anna is lying to Ottavio when she gives him her account of what had happened in her chamber. "It goes without saying," he writes, "that in the famous recitativo accompagnato in which she designates Don Giovanni to her betrothed as the murderer of her father she cannot tell Don Ottavio the whole truth; and his 'Respiro' [his sigh of relief when he hears her story] has always had a tragi-comic flavour for every understanding listener." Einstein, in his confident invocation for his own purposes of "the eighteenth century" and "every understanding listener," and his question-begging "it goes without saying," is throughout merely taking for granted the very thing he has to prove. And the final result of his disquisition is not only to make Anna out to be a slut and a liar but to make the simple Ottavio look a positive fool in the eyes of the audience, in which "every understanding listener" can see at a glance what is hidden from him!

It cannot be emphasised too strongly that the Anna of the opening scene of Da Ponte's *Don Giovanni* is *not* the Isabela of Tirso's first scene, and that all the usual misunderstanding— Einstein's for example—of the character of the Anna of the opera is due to the librettist's clumsy attempt to fuse Tirso's Isabela and his Ana into one. In *El Burlador* Isabela is obviously no better than she should be: she is a woman of the world who has no

_____

no such psychological dilemma: when Leporello says "Bravo! two heroic deeds, Donna Anna violated and her father stabbed," Giovanni merely rejoins "I have told you before now that I don't want any criticisms of my conduct ["rimostranze"—"remonstrances"] from you. Follow me, and keep your mouth shut."

objection to being "seduced" so long as the "seducer" is her lover
Ottavio. In the later stages of Tirso's play Isabela is a coolly
calculating creature for whom our sympathies are never sought.
Tirso's Doña Ana, the daughter of the Commander, is another
character altogether, and Giovanni, as we have seen, admits that
he had failed with her. The confusion between the two on Da
Ponte's part landed him in another difficulty—one not of psychology but of dramatic structure. To open his opera with a
Donna Anna who was originally a Doña Isabela, then to make
her the daughter of the Commander, was to make the murder of
the latter the *first* and worst of Giovanni's crimes (in the opera),
whereas, as Tirso's surer dramatic instinct had told him, it should
be the last and worst, after which the laws of God and man
closed in inevitably and inexorably on the Burlador. And from
this cardinal blunder, as has been pointed out already, arose the
failure to make Ottavio anything more than the tenor windbag
of the opera.

Later we find Giovanni boasting to Leporello of an assignation
with some enamoured lady (unnamed) who is accompanying him
to the villa "tonight." Of this adventure, which appears, so far
as the opera is concerned, to exist only in the hero's imagination,
we hear no more. Later still all seems to be going well with him
in the Zerlina affair, till at the last moment the girl is snatched
from his clutches by Elvira. Much later, his attempt on Zerlina
in an inner room of his villa is frustrated by her shrieks for help.
Later still, it is true, he tells Leporello gleefully of a successful
adventure he has had on his way by night to their last rendezvous
—with a young woman (seemingly Leporello's wife) who at
first took him for the valet and discovered her mistake too late.
But for this, let us remember, we have only his word; and the
braggart's reputation for veracity has been proved to be none
of the best.

All in all then, what conclusion can the realistic spectator in a
modern opera house come to but that, judged by purely professional standards of achievement, Da Ponte's Don Giovanni is the
merest impostor? He owes his reputation with our trustful modern
audiences entirely to the questionable book-keeping of Leporello.
Pasquariello, in Bertati, while anxious to glorify his master and
annoy Elvira, had not let his imagination run away with him in

the Leporello fashion. He had contented himself with assuring
Elvira that the list ran to a hundred or so in Italy and Germany,
plus he did not know how many in France and Spain. Perhaps
Da Ponte's Leporello believed, like Hitler, that if you are going to
tell a lie at all you may as well make it a whopping one. Or perhaps, on the other hand, he was simply a bad secretary and his
list merely the irresponsible arithmetic of an amateur in account-
ancy. Anyhow, having regard to all the known facts of the case,
we are surely entitled now to ask for an independent audit.

28

As we have remarked, Da Ponte, after the "explanation" scene
between Anna and Ottavio, has still a long sail before him, un-
piloted now by Bertati or anyone else, before he can reach the
sure harbour of the Statue scene. Great as his ingenuity is, the
voyage will task it to the utmost. Obviously tragedy, or even,
on the whole, a high degree of seriousness, is ruled out for the
next stage hour or so, for the spectator's stronger emotions must
not be allowed to suffer any preliminary dissipation on smaller
matters before the falling of the terrific blow of the final scene.
So from now onwards, until shortly before the end of the work,
the prevailing element in the libretto is bound to be the buffo
one, or something near that. With this the genius of Mozart was
exceptionally competent to deal musically, with ample left over
for the interweaving of a serious thread in the humorous texture
when an opportunity for that should present itself.

By the laws of the operatic game Da Ponte's immediate object
must now be to manœuvre his characters in such a way that all
of them who matter will be in the same place at the same time for
the big finale to the first of the two acts; and he has decided that
the place of the assembly shall be in Don Giovanni's house. He
could easily have arranged for this to happen fairly quickly after
the recognition by Anna and Ottavio of Giovanni as the murderer
of the Commander; but he has rather more time on his hands
than he quite knows what to do with, so he falls back on safe
operatic routine. Anna, after her story to Ottavio, is given an
aria in which she tells her lover that now he knows who her assailant was she looks to him to avenge her on the dastard: "Remember the wound in my poor father's breast and the blood that

drenched the ground around him," she says, and let this lover of hers now nerve himself to avenge her wrongs. After saying this at considerable length and with much repetition she leaves him, whereupon, as usual, Ottavio becomes the man of sentiment rather than the man of action. "Is it believable," he asks the universe distractedly, "that a cavalier like Don Giovanni could be guilty of so black a crime?" He must take all steps, leave no stone unturned, explore every avenue, he continues, to bring the truth to light. Two voices are speaking to him, one of them that of the lover, the other that of the friend; his duty is clear before his eyes—he must either undeceive Donna Anna as to the identity of her assailant or avenge her father's murder on this monster of a Giovanni.

His first practical step towards one or other of these ends is to sing an aria, "Dalla sua pace," in which he sets out to explain (either to himself or to the audience, for he has no other listeners) that upon Anna's peace of mind depends his own—whatever pleases her gives him life, whatever grieves her means death for him; when she sighs or weeps so does he; in a word—though, owing to the exigencies of an eighteenth century opera aria, it is rather a long word—he knows peace of mind only when she does. This is the aria spatchcocked into the score for the Vienna performances as a sort of consolation prize to the local tenor who was unequal to the bravura of the great tenor show piece of the Prague production, "Il mio tesoro"; and a lovely piece of music it is—in the concert room. In the opera house it serves only to slow down the action and to confirm us in the suspicion that has been slowly stealing over us from the commencement that whatever else Ottavio may turn out to be it will not be one of history's leading men of action.

Ottavio having left the stage Leporello returns. He begins, in recitative, a new variation on his favourite theme—he will remain no longer in the service of this crazy master of his; but before he has got very far with it he is interrupted by Don Giovanni, who seems to the lackey to be even more debonair than usual, carrying himself as if he had nothing on his conscience and not a care in the world. Leporello reports progress—as his master had commanded, he had taken the villagers off to the house, where he had entertained them with small talk, cajoleries and lies *à la* Don

Giovanni; he had calmed the jealous Masetto down; and all of
them, men and women, had been drinking themselves tipsy, some
of them singing, others larking, when who should walk in but
Donna Elvira and Zerlina, discussing Don Giovanni and finding
nothing good to say about him. With much address Leporello
had enticed the great lady into and then out of the kitchen garden, and locked the gate on her. His master commends his ingenuity; with the troublesome interfering Elvira out of the way he
can now settle down to serious work among the country maidens;
and he launches his great aria—the only one he has in the whole
opera:

23

Fin ch'hon dal vi—no cal-da la tes—ta, u-na gran fe-sta
va pre-pa—rar.

a feverish, explosive canticle (presto), the burden of which is
that all his guests are to drink, dance and make merry while he
adds, before morning, another half-score or so names to his already bulging list.

29

Master and man go out, and the scene changes to the garden
of Giovanni's house, where a number of country folk are enjoying
themselves, while Zerlina is trying to get a very sulky and can-
tankerous Masetto to see reason. What does she mean, he growls,
by abandoning him for another man on the very day of their wedding? His fears are groundless, she blandly assures him; the fine
gentleman had not so much as touched her with the tips of his
fingers. To soothe and soften her angry spouse she sings him an
enchanting aria, "Batti, batti, o bel Masetto," in which she assures
him that he may beat his poor little Zerlina as he pleases, tear out
her hair, pluck out her eyes, and she will kiss the hand that mal-
treats her if only he will believe her innocent: why should they
not make peace and live in happiness together day and night for
ever and ever?

The little witch, as he calls her, succeeds in calming if not quite convincing him. There is sound stuff in this Masetto, country bumpkin though he be; he will keep his suspicious peasant's eyes open, we learn. His meditations are interrupted by the voices of Giovanni and Leporello without. Zerlina turns pale: if there were only some hole, she stammers, into which Masetto could creep! This confirms his suspicions: now he understands and will investigate. He sees a recess in which he can conceal himself yet see and hear all that goes on between Zerlina and the cavalier. There is an agitated duet (allegro assai) between him and his bride, in which she vainly tries to dissuade him from his plan; and as he slips into the recess Giovanni enters with a number of his servants, who, at his command, conduct the country folk into the house, where they are given every opportunity to enjoy themselves.

Giovanni and Zerlina are left alone on the stage, with Masetto in hiding; and Mozart proceeds to turn his full genius upon a situation in itself of the most ordinary kind. Wagner used to maintain that the art of composition is the art of transition—leading the listener on imperceptibly step by step, from one musical mood, one dramatic situation, to another. The ten pages or so that now follow in the score show us Mozart at the height of his musical-dramatic power; they are as remarkable in their quiet way as the terrific Statue scene is in another. The music keeps changing perpetually; yet we feel all the time that one great line encloses it all, psychologically as well as musically.

As the crowd had left the stage the trembling Zerlina had tried to take cover behind some trees, but Giovanni, who has never lost sight of his prey, now begins to weave his spells about her. A gracious, insinuating figure in the violins:

24

gives us a hint of the courtly charm he can exercise when he feels that to be the right technique for the occasion. Conscious of her danger, and mindful of the watching Masetto, Zerlina implores the cavalier, for pity's sake, to let her go to the others; but in soft cajoling terms he urges her towards an alcove where, he assures her, her good fortune shall be crowned. The alcove happens, however, to be the one in which Masetto is concealed; and at the unexpected appearance of the surly peasant the seducer, thrown off his guard, stands for a moment as if petrified. Here is the situation as Mozart has depicted it musically, with Giovanni's startled ejaculation "Masetto?" and the peasant's grim reply "Yes, Masetto!":

25

It will be observed that Mozart still keeps going in the orchestra the curious quiet tread of the quavers shown in the opening bar of our quotation No. 24; but what a different suggestion they carry now, especially with their changed harmonic basis! The tread is now as menacing as it had formerly been ingratiating: here, emphatically, is the unity in variety and the variety in unity which the aestheticians laud as the acme of art.

Giovanni, as usual, soon regains his poise. In the smoothest of tones, but with mocking laughter playing about them in the orchestra, he assures Masetto that his lovely Zerlina has been feeling quite lost without him. Masetto is not fooled: "I understand, Sir, I understand," he growls. But Giovanni cuts him short. Music is heard from inside the house: the musicians are tuning up, he says; should they not join the rest of the merry throng? Zerlina eagerly agrees, and Masetto also succumbs to the seductive lure—or appears to do so.

As they leave the stage Donna Anna, Elvira and Ottavio enter, all masked. They are nerving themselves and each other to expose Giovanni and deal sternly with him. The most resolute of the three is Elvira, who, true to her character from the beginning of the opera, cannot forget her own wrongs at his hands: Ottavio is trying to keep up the courage of Anna, who is apprehensive of what may befall her lover. Notable in the orchestral accompaniment are hurrying ascending figures in sixths:

Progressions of this kind seem to have had for the eighteenth century certain connotations which they have now lost: they have been a telling feature of the theme (No. 7) in which Giovanni is first introduced to us.

From within the house come the strains of a minuet:

and the sensitive listener will feel, in the rhythmic structure of this, the same pulse as in our Nos. 24 and 25. This minuet will dominate a great deal of the later texture of the scene; and we cannot sufficiently admire the art that with such simple technical means can give such psychological unity to the changeful action.

Leporello, opening a window from within, draws his master's attention to the maskers—evidently people of quality. Giovanni orders him to invite them in; and in his smooth, courteous tones the pursuers find fresh confirmation of their suspicions. Still to the dignified strains of the minuet Leporello invites the maskers to enter. They accept, and when Leporello has closed the window, thereby shutting out the music from within the house, the whole character of the music changes as Anna, Elvira and Ottavio unite in a grave trio in which they once more exhort each other to have courage and pray for the protection of heaven. The decisive moment of the action has arrived, we feel; the die is cast.

30

The scene changes to a brilliant ballroom, where a dance has evidently just been concluded. To the gayest of strains in the orchestra:

Giovanni is politely urging the women to rest for a moment, while Leporello is busy persuading the men to take some refreshment before beginning the revels again. Zerlina's simple mind is delighted by it all. Masetto thinks it well to warn her to be on her guard, but she only laughs at him, much to his annoyance. Both Giovanni and Leporello see that it will be necessary in the interests of the Catalogue to get the jealous peasant out of the way somehow or other; but while they are discussing this the three masks enter. They are greeted politely first by Leporello, then by Giovanni, who, on an occasion of this kind, he assures them, keeps open house. The general tempo of the music has now changed to maestoso. The maskers thank Giovanni gravely for his courtesy, and then join him in a paean to liberty.

He invites the company to another dance, and the minuet is resumed, Giovanni selecting Zerlina as his partner, while Ottavio dances with Anna. It is with dismay that she and Elvira have observed that Zerlina is among the company. Giovanni, seeing that Masetto is showing fresh signs of restiveness, orders Leporello to "take care" of him. Here a second stage orchestra begins a country dance, and a little later a third orchestra strikes in with a waltz. There is thus something in the way of music and dancing for all tastes, the formal courtly minuet for the gentry, more popular fare for the rustics; and Mozart weaves all three strains into a contrapuntal whole, though it is rightly the minuet that mainly engages our attention, for it is between Giovanni and the maskers that the dominant dramatic issue now lies.

Giovanni manages to edge Zerlina into an adjoining room against her will, and soon the storm breaks. Even Leporello, who, under Giovanni's instructions, has been forcing Masetto to dance with him, cannot help ejaculating "Now there's going to be a crash!" Anna, Elvira and Ottavio realise that the decisive moment has come; "Now the criminal has put the noose round his own neck!" they say. Suddenly the minuet ceases, there is a drastic change of key, and over a pounding figure in the orchestra (allegro assai) we hear from the inner room a frenzied cry from Zerlina: "Help, good people! Villain!" The musicians hurriedly leave the scene, the company breaks up in confusion, and the three maskers, headed by Masetto, declare, in true operatic fashion, that they must rush to the maiden's assistance, remaining, however, rooted to the spot the while. The tempo has been whipped up to the highest pitch of excitement; but it slows down again to an andante maestoso as the ever-resourceful Giovanni comes out of the inner room holding Leporello by the ear, stigmatising him as the ruffian who had assailed Zerlina, and vowing that he himself will be the first to punish him. The lackey plays his part well in the momentary tragi-comedy, whining for mercy as his master pretends to set about killing him.

But the game, it would appear, is now up, the fox cornered. Anna, Elvira and Ottavio unmask and deride Giovanni's clumsy attempt to impose on them: Ottavio even goes so far as to produce a pistol—an act no less impressive in its own way than Mr. Snodgrass's removal of his coat and his announcement to the company that he is about to go into action. But this is opera, and before the characters take whatever steps may be regarded as appropriate to the occasion they have to join in a big end-of-the-act ensemble; besides, it is foreordained that Giovanni shall get out of the net, tightly as it appears to be closing about him, or what will become of the second act? So Ottavio does nothing with his pistol but flourish it. In a massive finale Masetto, Anna, Elvira, Ottavio and Zerlina warn the villain that vengeance is now about to overtake him, while Giovanni—a trifle perturbed for a moment—and Leporello bow for a while before the storm. It is not long, however, before Giovanni regains full possession of himself, and, with the orchestra hammering away repeatedly at a figure of this type:

29

he and Leporello are heard through the turmoil declaring that they fear nothing, even though the heavens fall. Giovanni draws his sword and makes his escape with his lackey as the curtain descends.

31

Da Ponte has still another long act to fill up, and for some time after the rising of the curtain for the next scene his invention is not at its best, only the genius of Mozart keeping him afloat. The none too bright idea has occurred to the librettist of endowing Elvira with a serving-maid, and showing Giovanni in pursuit of her. (She plays no part in the action; we have only Da Ponte's word for her existence.) The setting shows a street, on one side of which stands Elvira's dwelling, which has a balcony. It is now night, and we find Giovanni and Leporello in conversation. The valet is once more swearing that he will stay no longer in the service of a master who gets the pair of them into such terrible scrapes; and Giovanni, in the gayest spirits, is telling him not to be a fool but to take all that has recently happened as just good clean fun. The recurrent theme of the lackey's revolt has begun to be a trifle tiresome by now—or would be, had not Mozart made it the subject of a racy colloquy in the purest buffo style. Leporello turns to go: Giovanni, taking out his purse, persuades him to reconsider his decision; and the remainder of the episode is played out in recitative. The valet hopes that his master's thoughts are not still running on women; but Giovanni assures him that he will not be satisfied until he has subdued the whole brood of them; they are more vital to him, he says, than the food he eats, the air he breathes.

Leporello, as usual, gives in, and Giovanni discloses to him the plan of a new adventure that has taken his fancy. He has discovered that Donna Elvira has a charming serving-maid; she has kindled his acquisitive appetite, and his scheme now is to woo her under the guise of Leporello—for, as he explains to the staggered lackey, young women of that class are rather apt to be on their guard when a well-dressed gentleman begins to tell them the old, old story. Leporello is still reluctant, and only a burst of anger on his master's part makes him consent to an exchange of cloaks and hats.

No sooner has this been effected than Elvira appears on the balcony, to breathe out the affliction of her soul over this deceiver of a gallant whom she hates for his perfidy but for whom she still cannot help feeling a certain tenderness and pity. As usual with him when there is something in an ostensibly humorous situation that is also capable of a serious interpretation, Mozart puts into Elvira's mouth music of the most heartfelt kind:

Even when Leporello and Giovanni, from their hiding-place, begin to comment *sotto voce* upon the unforeseen turn of events—"Softly!" whispers Leporello, "it's Donna Elvira; I recognise her voice":

—we are conscious of something in the music that goes rather deeper than the words and the buffo situation: Mozart, we feel, has too much interest in and compassion for his Elvira to involve her any more than he can help in the buffoonery of the lackey and his master.

Giovanni resolves to exploit the comic possibilities of the situation. Standing behind Leporello, who makes the gestures appropriate to a serenading lover, he sings of his love to Elvira, in phrases that are an echo of hers (No. 30); but it is upon No. 31 that Mozart draws to blend, in the way of which he has the secret, the serious with the humorous aspects of the scene. There is no need whatever for it to be so grossly clowned as it generally is on the stage by actors who know no mean between humour and thick-thumbed farce; the comedy is inherent in the situation, but curiously interfused with pathos, and to reduce it all to mere buffoonery is to pay a poor compliment to Mozart's consummate art of blending humour and seriousness so subtly that we cannot say where one ends and the other begins.

When Giovanni launches into a snatch of song that sounds—whether by accident or design it is impossible to say—rather like an anticipation of the serenade he will shortly sing (No. 32) to the invisible serving-maid, and Elvira replies that she can no longer believe him and Giovanni protests that he will kill himself if she does not, and Leporello, in low tones, swears that if the fun goes on much longer he must either laugh or burst, the comedy element in the scene necessarily comes more to the forefront, but even now it should not degenerate into yokel clowning. When at last the voices unite in a short trio, in which Giovanni chuckles over the success of his little stratagem and Leporello mockingly invokes the protection of heaven for this latest victim of his master's wiles, it is Elvira who commands almost the whole of our attention with lovely music, of the type of No. 30, that is wholly serious and heartfelt: the composer's sympathies are evidently with her, though he never loses sight of the comedy of the imbroglio.

Overcome, in spite of herself, by Giovanni's pleading, Elvira leaves the balcony to join him. There follows a brief recitative in which Giovanni gives Leporello his final instructions; when Elvira descends he is to overwhelm her (as the supposed Giovanni, of course) with caresses and cajoleries, mimicking his master's voice as best he can, and then lead her off somewhere so as to leave the course clear for his master. When she reappears, Giovanni recedes into the background to watch the fun. Elvira tells the supposed Giovanni that she now believes in the sincerity of the return of his heart to her, and forgives him for all the tears he has made her shed. The comedy thickens: the more pressing Elvira becomes for the renewal of her happiness the more Leporello, to Giovanni's quiet amusement, actually becomes interested in the part he is playing. But once more let it be said that the fun should not be laid on with the broad and rather soiled trowel that is the only comic tool of which the average Leporello has any command; anything of the nature of crude farce is always quite alien to Mozart, the subtle master of fine shades and borderline states of mind, always himself, even when the less delicate sensibility of his librettist is edging him towards the domain of the chawbacon grin and the loud guffaw. It occasionally happens with Mozart that, if not openly at variance with a librettist, he does not walk exactly in step with him.

32

The situation is broken up by Giovanni, who descends on them in the manner of a footpad; as they run away a light appears in the supposed maid's window, and Giovanni sings, to a mandoline accompaniment, the enchanting canzonetta, "Deh, vieni alla finestra, o mio tesoro" ("Come to the window, my treasure, come and take pity on my woe, or you will see me die before your eyes, o maiden with mouth sweeter than honey, with sugar at the centre of your heart"):

32

Allegretto

Deh, vie—ni al-la fi—nes-tra,   o   mio —— te—so——ro

and once more we see Mozart declining to go as far as his librettist in the way of facile exaggeration. The canzonetta is purely appropriate to the occasion, to the situation and to the mentality of the supposed serving-maid, and to nothing and no one else in the whole opera—for Mozart's dramatic instinct even in little things of this sort is well-nigh infallible: but for all that the song breathes the purest Mozartian atmosphere.

In what follows we get further and further away from the central current of the opera, and have little more to do than to accompany Da Ponte in his rather desperate efforts to fill up the space that still intervenes between where he is now and the climactic point that, foreordained for him as it is, still lies uncomfortably far ahead of him. It has apparently occurred to Masetto that whatever the others may think of doing next it is his business, and at last within his capacity, to bring the dissolute cavalier to book. He enters now, carrying a musket and a pistol and accompanied by some villagers, also armed after their fashion. They are searching for Don Giovanni. He and Masetto catch sight of each other in the dim light simultaneously. In a longish recitative Giovanni pretends that he is Leporello, tired beyond further endurance of his criminal master, and willing to co-operate with Masetto in his desire to track the miscreant down and murder him. In a long aria Giovanni-Leporello expounds to the others his plan of campaign: they are to hunt about until they come upon a man and a young woman in the piazza, or perhaps making love under a window. The man will be wearing a hat with white plumes, a great cloak over his shoulders, and a sword at his side. This is the villain they are in search of. The villagers are to disperse, some going in this direction, others in that; Masetto is to accompany the pseudo-Leporello, "and you will soon see what happens," the latter assures him with sinister humour. The aria is unduly spun out by repetition, but both Da Ponte and Mozart obviously have more stage time on their hands just now than they quite know what to do with.

The villagers having all departed, and Masetto having assured the pseudo-Leporello that nothing short of wallowing in the miscreant cavalier's blood will content him, Giovanni gets the musket and the pistol from him on the pretext of examining them, then turns on the poor fellow and beats him savagely before leaving him. Zerlina, who has heard his howls, enters with a lantern. In another long recitative Masetto tells her how he has been maltreated: she cannot resist the temptation to tell him that he has brought all this on himself by his jealousy, but having done that she invites him into the house, where, she says, if he will promise to reform she will apply a remedy that will make him forget his bruises; whereupon she sings her aria "Vedrai, carino, se sei buonino, che bel remedio ti voglio dar." Her words, water them down as the translators may, leave us in no doubt as to what her "remedy" is, and are intended to leave no doubt in Masetto's; it is "natural," "not to be obtained at the apothecary's," "far from unpleasant," "a sure balsam," his for the asking. "Would you know where I keep it? Place your hand on my heart and feel its beating." She has no difficulty in persuading him to try her sure specific; and as he limps off with her the orchestral accompaniment to the cajoling melody, which has been wonderfully soft and insinuating so far, develops into a sort of ironic paean with laughing trills rippling along the surface of it. Masetto has put up a good fight so far in the opera, but this is decidedly the artful Zerlina's round.

Da Ponte now feels it is time to return to Leporello and Elvira. We come upon them again in what the libretto informs us is "a dark courtyard before the house of Donna Anna." The lackey's one thought now is how to get away from this nuisance of a love-struck lady; and while Elvira, maintaining her own characteristic idiom, tries to tell the supposed Giovanni of her love and fears he keeps feeling along the wall for a door through which to slip. But before he can succeed in this they are joined in the darkness by Anna and Ottavio, both in mourning, and preceded by servants bearing torches. They bring, of course, a psychological atmosphere of their own with them, which Mozart suggests by the simplest of means—three bars of bold modulation in the orchestra from the key of B flat to that of D major:

33

and a dignified rhythm appropriate to the two patrician lovers.

As usual, Ottavio is heard exhorting Anna to dry her tears and have courage; her constant weeping, he says, can only bring more sorrow to the shade of her beloved father. (Throughout the opera it is obviously the murder of her father, rather than the assault on herself, that is Anna's grievance against Giovanni.) When she begs to be allowed at least the consolation of grief it is to a melody that carries on, in the minor, the strain launched by Ottavio; and in every bar of the brief duet Mozart plays "symphonically" and expressively upon orchestral mutations of this short figure:

34

which leads, by the most natural of transitions, into a descending chromatic figure of lament:

Bass C ——————— B♮ ———— C ———— F♯ ———— G

as Elvira (who is of course invisible to Anna and Ottavio in the darkness) bewails having lost sight of her supposed lover, and Leporello, his nerves now on edge, catches sight of a door in the wall through which he thinks he can escape. But before he can do so Zerlina and Masetto rush in on him. At the same time Anna and Ottavio perceive him, and of course assume from his costume that he is Giovanni. The phrase shown in our No. 35 comes into its full expressive rights as they all comment on the new situation, Elvira pleading with Masetto and Zerlina to spare her "husband," and all of them being as astonished as Anna and Ottavio are to find Elvira in their midst.

On one thing, however, all except Elvira are resolved, that the cornered criminal shall die. Sinking down upon his knees, Leporello, to descending orchestral phrases derived from No. 35, begs them to have mercy on him; and once more we light upon a distinguishing feature of Mozart's genius, his capacity for describing a scene in musical terms that are at the same time comic in relation to the episode and serious in themselves.

The discovery that the supposed Giovanni is really Leporello throws the minds of all of them for a moment into confusion, which they express in their various ways, while Leporello is full of self-pity in the tight fix in which he finds himself. With masterly hand Mozart weaves all the moods in a single whole, in a sextet that is one of the high-lights of the score.

Anna having gone away with her servants the others turn upon Leporello. Elvira is furious with him for having passed himself off as his master, Zerlina and Masetto for having, as they think, maltreated the latter, Ottavio for no stated reason: the one thing they are agreed upon is that the valet shall be punished. In a lively aria Leporello protests to each of them in turn his innocence, laying the blame for all that has happened on his tyrannic and unscrupulous master. At last he finds a door and runs out. The others would pursue him, but Ottavio stops them, for he has an important announcement from the chair to make to the shareholders' meeting: "My friends, after these unspeakable iniquities we can no longer have any doubt that the impious murderer of Donna Anna's father was Don Giovanni.[1] Remain you in the house for a few hours; I will have recourse to the proper authorities, and I can promise you that before very long you shall be avenged. . . ." That is in recitative; the aria that follows—the long and technically difficult "Il mio tesoro intanto"—is in the same vein: "Meanwhile go you and console my dear one and help her to dry her eyes. Tell her that I have gone to avenge her wrongs, and that I will return only as the messenger of death." With these brave words the heroic Ottavio goes out on his grim errand, taking Masetto and Zerlina with him.

34

Elvira remains behind, for she, able at last to shake herself free of the buffoonery that has surrounded her for so long, also has an aria to sing.[2] The recitative, in the grand eighteenth century manner, is held together by an arresting figure entrusted to the orchestra:

36

She is appalled at the further evidences Giovanni has given of his wickedness; for these, surely, retribution must fall on him, and

[1] Here Da Ponte becomes unintentionally but irresistibly funny: it apparently takes such "unspeakable iniquities" as the crude befooling of Elvira and the lambasting of Masetto to convince Ottavio finally that Giovanni was the murderer of his beloved's father! Ottavio seems to have anticipated De Quincey in his fine perception of the insensibly merging degrees of criminality. "For," says the author of *Murder as a fine Art,* "if once a man indulges himself in murder, very soon he comes to think little of robbing; and from robbing he comes to drinking and Sabbath-breaking, and from that to incivility and procrastination. Once begin upon this downward path and you never know where you are to stop. Many a man has dated his ruin from some murder or other that perhaps he thought little of at the time."

[2] Between Ottavio's aria and that of Elvira there comes, in the scores, a scene between Leporello and Zerlina that is always omitted in performance. On this matter see *infra,* pp. 207 ff.

already in imagination she sees the destroying thunderbolt from heaven and the abyss opening to receive him. But there is room in her tender breast for other sentiments than personal vengeance, as is shown by the expressive orchestral figures that accompany the final part of her recitative:

37

(It is the bad practice of many conductors to drag these passages out to an adagio. There is no warrant for this in the score: Mozart's general marking of allegro assai still holds good, and presumably he knew better what he wanted than any conductor can do.) The aria that follows—"Mi tradì quell' alma ingrata"— is on the same grand scale as that in which Mozart has indulged himself in Ottavio's aria and will shortly indulge himself again in one allotted to Donna Anna. The burden of the present aria is that in spite of all the wrongs done her by this one-time lover of hers Elvira feels for him, if no longer love, at least a great pity. True, when she remembers the pain he has inflicted on her something within her cries out for vengeance; but when she thinks of the dangers that now environ him her heart trembles. Yes, from now until the closing scene the dominant emotion in Elvira's breast is pity for her betrayer.

With her exit Da Ponte and Mozart have at last shaken themselves free of the low-comedy padding they had had to fall back on to fill out the big time-scale of their opera, and can set their course for the tragic dénouement. The next scene shows us a churchyard in which stands a Statue of the Commander. Giovanni, in excellent spirits, leaps over the wall; in this churchyard, he is sure, he will be safe from any pursuit by a woman (unnamed) whose problematic identity will be revealed to us later. It is a lovely moonlit night, as bright as day, an ideal night for the amorous hunt; and it is still only two o'clock. He would dearly love to know how Leporello had managed with Elvira and if he had been adroit enough to get out of the scrape. Just then Leporello himself appears on the wall, still sore in body and spirit from his recent experiences. His master makes light of his complaints and tells him that if he will join him in the cemetery he shall hear something that will interest him. Leporello jumps from the wall, and after the pair have exchanged cloaks and hats Giovanni tells him of one adventure that night that had particularly delighted him—the conquest of a very young and pretty girl he had encountered, who, mistaking him for her "caro Leporello," had loaded him with caresses. He had taken appropriate advantage of this mistaken identity, and then, somehow, the girl had discovered the facts of the case and screamed; so Giovanni, hearing footsteps, had given her the slip and jumped the cemetery wall. "And you tell me all this quite calmly?" protests the lackey. "What if it were my wife?" at which Giovanni laughs uproariously.

35

This ribald laugh of his, in such a place, at such an hour, sets the avalanche moving that will before long engulf him. A deep voice is heard addressing him in slow, solemn tones: "You will have finished with laughter before the dawn!"[1] "Who spoke there?" Giovanni asks sharply. "Some spirit from the other world," Leporello suggests ironically, "who knows you inside out." Giovanni silences him and again asks "Who spoke there?", this time slashing angrily with his sword at some of the tombs and monuments. The voice of the Commander sternly bids him respect the dead. Thereupon Giovanni orders Leporello to read the inscription on a certain tomb. The valet, who is beginning to be scared, protests that his education never got as far as reading by moonlight; but as his master insists he at last reads out the inscription: "Here I await vengeance on the impious one who dealt me death." Giovanni laughs at the "old prince of jokers," as he calls him, and at his command the trembling Leporello invites the Statue to supper with his master. The episode is one of Mozart's masterpieces of characterisation, the terrified stammerings of Leporello, the impressiveness of the Statue's curt "Yes!", and the comments, half genuine courage, half bravado, of Giovanni all being woven into a consummate musical whole.

[1] Here, for the first time, the trombones make their appearance in the score, with awe-inspiring effect.

It ends with Giovanni hurrying off to give orders for the festive meal, Leporello being only too glad to accompany him.

To fill up the necessary interval between this scene and that of the supper Da Ponte draws once more upon Anna and Ottavio. The new setting is a room in the house of the former. Ottavio enters to assure her once again that justice will soon be dealt out to the author of all her woes; meanwhile he suggests a marriage on the morrow as an aid to forgetfulness. To his astonishment she rejects the affectionate proposal, not because her heart is not his, but from the rather curious consideration of what the world will say: let him not doubt, however, her constancy. Into her recitative there has stolen a moving fragment of melody in the orchestra:

38

which, transposed into the key of F major, becomes the generator of her exquisite aria "Non mi dir" ("Say not, beloved, that I am cruel: you know how truly I love you; but no longer grieve unless you would have me too die of grief"). These last words are accompanied in the orchestra by one of the most searching expressions of tenderness that ever came from Mozart's pen:

39

to which conductors and orchestras rarely do anything like justice. But it is not long before Mozart realises that he has on his hands a coloratura soprano whose appetite for applause he must satisfy; so with a change of tempo to allegretto moderato he launches a bravura second section that has always been a source of pain to most of his admirers, who find it difficult to understand why the singer should suddenly cease to be the sympathetic and noble Donna Anna and become transformed into a mere Madame This or Madame That, angling for applause.

Berlioz, in his *Mémoires*, bewails this lapse into bad taste on his adored Mozart's part. The first section of the aria, he said, is "a song of profound sadness, in which all the poetry of love pours itself out in sorrow and tears"; but the roulades that follow are "of such shocking impropriety that one wonders how a composer like Mozart could have been guilty of them . . . Anna seems suddenly to have dried her eyes and broken out into indecent buffoonery. The words of this passage are 'Forse un giorno il cielo ancora sentirà-à-à-à'—here comes an incredible roulade in the worst style imaginable—'pietà di me.' Surely this is a strange way for the ill-used noble lady to express the hope that 'some day heaven will have pity on her'! I found it difficult [in his young days] to pardon Mozart for such an enormity. Today I feel that I would shed my blood to erase these shameful pages and certain others of the same kind found in his works." To this, in later years, Berlioz added a footnote: "Even the epithet 'shameful' seems to me hardly strong enough to blast this passage. Mozart has committed one of the most odious and senseless crimes in the whole history of art against passion, feeling, good taste and good sense." [1]

Having finished imploring heaven to take pity on her, in a concluding flourish on high A's and B flats, Anna departs, leaving Ottavio, before he too quits the stage, to assure us, in three lines

[1] The justice of the indictment cannot be gainsaid; one listens to this second section of the aria with a wry face. And no one seems to be aware that Mozart himself, were we able to tackle him now on the subject, would probably agree with Berlioz and the rest of us. In 1849 one Joseph Cornet, the director of the Hamburg theatre—who comes into Wagnerian biography by reason of his production of *Rienzi* in Hamburg in 1844,—published a book entitled *Die Oper in Deutschland und das Theater der Neuzeit (Opera in Germany and the Stage of the Present Day)*, in which he comments severely on the vogue of senseless coloratura in the first half of the nineteenth century and the bad effects it had on the genuine expression of feeling in opera; it was the singers who insisted on it, because it won them the applause of the unintelligent mob. Cornet had known Mozart's widow, and he assures us that she had told him more than once that the composer, while bowing to the spirit of his time in this connection, did so with his tongue in his cheek, so to speak, "and always had it in mind to alter these numbers later." We met with Cornet in our discussion of *The Magic Flute*.

of recitative, that it will be his privilege to ease her burden by
taking some of it on himself.

36

The scene now changes to a room in Don Giovanni's house,
where a table is laid for supper; there is also a small band of
musicians, for Giovanni, being a man of quality, likes music with
his meals. After a few bars of lively orchestral introduction he
enters with Leporello: some producers show him accompanied
also by a bevy of gay ladies, but there is no warrant in the text
for this. The music is throughout spirited and joyous; Mozart,
the lover of fun and movement, the inveterate dancer, is always
in his element in such situations as this. The tide of life is rising
high in Giovanni's veins; while there is breath in his body he will
drain the cup of pleasure to the dregs. He bids the musicians
strike up, seats himself at the table, and is served by Leporello.
The first tune he recognises, with delight, as one from Martini's
opera *Una Cosa Rara*, which had been produced with great success in Vienna a couple of years earlier. The second part of the
melody:

40

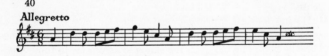

is particularly captivating; Mozart evidently knew a good thing
when he heard it, by whatever rival of the moment it may have
been written. He falls to with renewed appetite, and is equally
gratified by the next tune the musicians give him, one from Sarti's
opera *I due litiganti*:

41

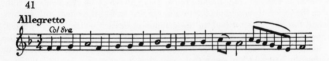

which goes well with the excellent marzimino wine and the
pheasant that Leporello has just served. The third tune the lackey

knows, he says, only too well: it is the "Non più andrai" from
Figaro, which all Prague had been singing, humming, and whis-
tling for the last eighteen months or so. This section of the supper
scene is primarily Leporello's; by long custom it was here that
the lackey, gormandising and guzzling surreptitiously on his own
account, had full licence to indulge in all the robust humours of
the commedia dell' arte and the buffo operatic stage.

37

The gay music, so full of the carefree joy of life, comes to a
sudden end as Elvira runs in distractedly. There is a change of
tempo to a feverish allegro assai as she tells Giovanni that she has
come to give him the last proof of her love: she has forgiven him
all the wrongs he has done her, and her one desire now is to save
him from justice. This episode derives ultimately from the impressive one in Molière's *Don Juan*—by way, of course, in Da
Ponte's case, of Bertati. In the latter's libretto Elvira begins by
announcing that she is "another Elvira" than the one we have
seen hitherto. Her former passion for Giovanni has now turned
to a protective pity: all his intrigues have been unmasked, she tells
him, everyone knows him to be the slayer of the Commander, and
outraged justice is about to exact the penalty from him; but before
that can happen she implores him to save himself by true repentance and a reformation of his ways: as for herself, she intends to
go into a retreat for the remainder of her life. Giovanni's mocking
reply to this appeal is an invitation to her to put up for the night
in his house.[1] She tells him with dignity that her carriage is
waiting outside for her, and goes out with a final passionate exhortation to him to think not of her but of himself—pausing only
long enough to deliver herself of an aria that begins with a
renewed assurance of her love if he will reform, and ends, after
further ribald caricature of her on the libertine's part, with an
exasperated revulsion of feeling: "Ah, miserable man, you still
laugh at me! I see now that you are a tiger at heart![2] But perhaps
the thunderbolt is not far away."

[1] In Da Ponte she receives a similar impertinent invitation.
[2] In the original, "Di tigre le viscere già che avete." In Molière it is
the valet Sganarelle who comments ironically that Giovanni must have a
"cœur de tigre." No doubt all expressions of this kind derive ultimately from

In Da Ponte the episode, though similar in sentiment and layout, is more condensed; his sense of the theatre told him that the action should now hasten on to its catastrophe without unnecessary delay; and Mozart seconds him nobly, weaving all the contending elements, the anxiety of Elvira, the reckless mockery of Giovanni and of his sycophantic echo Leporello, into one incomparable whole. There are two other strokes of genius on the part of the collaborators: first the entire hedonistic being of Don Giovanni is summed up in an immortal phrase (repeated several times), in praise of women as "the sustenance and glory of humanity":

42

So-ste-gno e glo-ri-a d'u-ma-ni-tà,   so-ste-gno e glo-ri-a d'u-ma-ni-tà.

and second, Elvira does not walk off, prima donna fashion, at the conclusion of her aria as she does in Bertati, but receives full in the face the first impact of the coming tragedy. As she turns from Giovanni with a final cry of "Remain, then, monster of iniquity!" and Leporello comments with indecent irony, "If all this grief of hers doesn't move him he must have a heart of stone!", the orchestra whips up the excitement with mounting phrases of this sort:

43

Allegro assai

Bass: Bb ——————————————————————— B♮

which culminate; as Elvira reaches the door by which she has entered, in a stabbing chord of the diminished seventh that seems

the "Hyrcanian tigresses" of the abandoned Dido's passionate reproach of Aeneas:

> Nec tibi diva parens generis nec Dardanus auctor,
> Perfide, sed duris genuit te cautibus horrens
> Caucasus Hyrcanaeque admorunt ubera tigres,

which had become a classical tag for situations of this sort.

to halt her in her tracks. She recoils with a wild cry and rushes out by a door on the opposite side. "Why does she scream like that?" asks the exasperated Giovanni; and he sends Leporello off to investigate.[1] Repetitions of the feverish No. 43 accompany the lackey on his way, with another culmination in a diminished seventh chord as he gives a wild cry from the other side of the door.

He returns in abject terror, closing the door behind him, with only enough breath left in him to stammer out that the "white man of stone" is outside; and he describes as best he can the pounding "ta! ta! ta!" of the Statue's footsteps. There is a heavy knocking at the door. No threat of the angry Giovanni can induce Leporello to go near it; instead he crawls under the table. So Giovanni, taking a light with him, flings open the door himself.

38

Then Mozart strikes like a thunderbolt. The whole orchestra, including the trombones, seems to blare out our example No. 1 in Giovanni's face as the Statue strides in with the words, "Don Giovanni! You invited me to sup with you. I have come!"

44

Andante

[1] Here Da Ponte's superior sense of the stage asserts itself. In Bertati, as we have seen, Elvira had flounced out prima donna fashion after her vain appeal, and there had followed a long buffo scene in which Giovanni and Leporello resume the banquet; the latter indulges in more and more of the buffooneries traditional at this point, and the gaiety of the pair culminates in a toast to Venice as *the* city of pleasure and to the Venetian ladies as the finest flower of womankind. (This would be appropriate enough in the Venice production of the Bertati-Gazzaniga opera.) Then comes a repeated knocking at the door, and, at long last, the entry of the Statue. Da Ponte and Mozart did wisely in cutting all this out and going straight from the failure of Elvira's exhortation to the dénouement.

Giovanni tries to brazen it out: "I would never have believed it," he says, "but I will do what I can"; his words are accompanied in the orchestra by the unsteady No. 2, the purport of which in the overture now becomes manifest. He bids Leporello have another cover laid for the guest, but the lackey is too terrified to move. The Statue bids master and man not to trouble about earthly food for one who has passed beyond the needs of the mortal body. It has come with a graver purpose, the solemn voice goes on, accompanied by the sequences, ascending and descending, alternately forte and piano, shown in our No. 4. The Statue's summons becomes more and more emphatic: "You invited me: I have come; now will *you* come and sup with *me*? Answer me! Decide! You will come?" Leporello manages to get in a word or two in character: he must be excused; he has no time: "tell him no, Sir." Giovanni's courage still holds: he accepts the grisly invitation. The Statue demands his hand in pledge; an icy cold creeps through Giovanni's veins at the touch, but his hand he cannot release, struggle as he will. "Your last moment is near: come: repent!" the voice thunders on, the ever-useful chord of the diminished seventh supplying the necessary touches of horror in the orchestra. "Never!" replies Giovanni, "never, old fool that you are!" They bandy their "Yes!" and "No!" for a while, till the Statue, as a solemn hush comes upon the orchestra, abandons the unrepentant sinner to his fate: "Your time has come!" it says, and disappears.

The tempo now whips up; flames shoot out in all directions, and the earth trembles. From below comes a chorus of invisible spirits, bidding Giovanni join them, and warning him in hollow tones of the eternal punishment awaiting him for his crimes. Now at last he breaks down, while Leporello comments gibberingly on his dismay. There is a final "Come!" from the spirits, followed by a tortured "Ah!" from Giovanni as he disappears in the depths.

This is the end preordained for him by the saga; but it is not the end of the opera. For the grand finale we are spirited off into the buffo, though a buffo with some serious moments. Anna, Ottavio, Elvira, Zerlina and Masetto enter, crying in unison, "Where is the villain? Vengeance on him!", Anna adding ferociously on her own account that only the sight of him in chains will compensate her for all she has suffered through him. Leporello advises them to give up hope of laying hands on him, for he has

gone far away. Bit by bit, and rather disconnectedly, he tells
them what had happened—the stone man had come and handed
his master over to the Devil, who had dragged him below. The
others can hardly believe it, though they realise now that this
must have been the apparition seen by Elvira when she opened
the door—a thought on which they dwell for some time. Then
the tempo slows down to a larghetto, and one by one they speak
of their future plans. Ottavio begins with an appeal to Anna: now
that heaven has avenged them all, he pleads, surely she will not
keep him waiting long for his happiness. Gravely she asks for a
year in which to forget her grief for her father, and the pair renew at some length their assurances of mutual devotion. Elvira, for
her part, vows that she will enter a convent and there end her
days. The more materially minded Zerlina and Masetto decide
to make for home and dine in style; while Leporello will go off to
the inn and try to find another and better master. The three subsidiary characters indulge in a brief trio in which, displaying more
classical learning than we would have expected of them, they
consign the villain of the piece to Proserpine and Pluto, and exhort
the others to join them—which Anna and Ottavio do—in repeating
the joyous ancient song, "See now the end of all bad people,
whose death befits their life":

45

Que-sto è il fin di chi fa mal, di chi fa mal, que-sto è il fin.

It was the fashion for a long time to omit this final scene in
performance, and modern British producers glow with pride
when they restore it. But more than a century ago Thomas Love
Peacock was protesting against the barbarous excision in the name
not only of Mozart but of good taste. The original ending to the
opera, he wrote, is "one of the finest things in dramatic music,
and the most appropriate possible termination of the subject; and
yet is this most noble composition, this most fitting and genuine
conclusion, sacrificed [in London] to a dance of devils flashing
torches of rosin, for no earthly reason but that so ended the
Drury Lane pantomime."

Two points in connection with the opera remain to be considered that could not have been dealt with in the text without interrupting the narrative unduly.

1. The first relates to what occurs in the second act between the escape of Leporello from his tormentors [1] and Elvira's recitative ("In quali eccessi, o Numi") and aria ("Mi tradì quell' alma ingrata"). In his score the reader will find the following sequence: (A) In a short aria after the sextet Leporello begs for mercy from the people who have cornered him (Elvira, Ottavio, Zerlina and Masetto; Anna has by now left the stage), protesting that he has been, as usual, the innocent victim of the wiles of his unscrupulous master. At the end of all this he finds a door and escapes. (B) A short comment of the others in recitative:

Elvira: Stop, wretch, stop!
Masetto: The rascal's feet have wings!
Zerlina: How artfully he has got away!
Ottavio: After misdeeds so enormous who can doubt, my friends, that the impious murderer of Donna Anna's father was Don Giovanni? Go now into this house for a while. I myself will go to the authorities concerned, and I promise you that you shall be avenged, as is demanded alike by duty, compassion and love.

(C) Ottavio's aria "Il mio tesoro intanto" ("Meanwhile go ye and console my dear one"). (D) A comic scene in which Zerlina, with a razor in her hand, drags Leporello in by the hair, manhandles him severely, threatens him with dire punishment, and finally, with the help of a peasant, ties his hands. (E) An excessively long duet, "Per queste tue manine," in which he begs her to have pity on him, which she refuses: he and his wicked master, she says, should both receive the punishment they deserve. At last she goes out, leaving him tied to a chair, and the chair to a window-frame.[2]

---

[1] See p. 194.

[2] Manifestly, then, episode (D) takes place inside a room; yet the setting of the scene so far had been "a dark courtyard, with three doors, before Donna Anna's house"! No doubt when (D) was spatchcocked into the opera in the Vienna production (1788) a change of scene was made here, regardless of the pre- and post-context. Nobody seems to have reflected then on the absurdity of the peasant girl's making free of the great lady Donna Anna's

Leporello appeals to the peasant for a glass of water—apparently hoping by this ruse to get his knots untied; but the man goes away without saying a word. Thereupon Leporello, by means of a great tug at the chair, manages to wrench out the window-frame to which it is fastened, and so makes his escape, dragging the chair and frame behind him. (F) Zerlina returns, bringing with her Elvira, and the following brief dialogue ensues:

> *Zerlina:* Come, my lady, and you shall see how I have fixed the rascal.
> *Elvira:* Ah, I will vent my rage on him.
> *Zerlina:* Heavens! How has the scoundrel managed to escape?
> *Elvira:* His wicked master must have got him away.
> *Zerlina:* He it was, without a doubt. We must inform Don Ottavio, and trust him to avenge us all.

(G) Zerlina having left the stage, Elvira sings her recitative and aria—"In quali eccessi, o Numi" and "Mi tradì quell' alma ingrata" ("In what excesses of crime the wretched man has involved himself . . . This ungrateful creature betrayed me . . ."). At the end of her aria she leaves the stage, and the scene changes to the churchyard, where Leporello and Giovanni find each other again.

The reader will already be aware that Ottavio's aria "Dalla sua pace" and the duet—"Per queste tue manine"—were additions to the score made by Mozart for the Vienna production of 1788. Surely nothing but dire theatrical necessity could have induced him to consent to Leporello being brought back after his escape, tied up by Zerlina and the peasant, and then made to escape for the second time. By common consent this miserable piece of clowning is omitted from modern performances. Dramatically the action goes to pieces at this point if we accept the present scores at their face value. After Leporello's first escape—which really coheres with the drama—the other characters comment briefly on the matter, as in our (B), and then dismiss it from their minds. Their thoughts are now concentrated on the punishment of Don Giovanni: Ottavio sings his "Il mio tesoro," and all leave the

---

house in this fashion. The great thing for the groundlings would be Leporello's comic exit with the chair and the window-frame trailing behind him; and for these stage properties a room was of course necessary.

stage, upon which, as we have seen (D), Zerlina drags Leporello in for the farcical scene of the razor, the tying up and the second escape.

There follow next our (F) and (G), and we naturally ask ourselves why Zerlina's discovery that the Leporello she had tied up is no longer there should lead to such grave ethical reflections on Elvira's part on the tragical iniquity of Don Giovanni; Elvira feels now that he is doomed irrevocably by his crimes and his constitution, yet her heart is filled with compassion and affection for him.

40

The mystery was solved for us in 1938 by a fine piece of research work on the part of Alfred Einstein. Various people had had their doubts for a long time as to the authenticity of the recitative in which Leporello asks the peasant to get him a drink of water: "for pity's sake, friend," he says, "a drop of fresh water or I shall die. Just see how tightly that murderess [Zerlina] has tied me up. . . ." ("Guarda un po' come stretto mi legò l'assassina"). In the recitative as we have always known it in the scores the word "legò" is accented musically on the first syllable instead of on the second, a blunder of which Mozart would have been incapable; the inference seems to be that the recitative is someone else's work, someone with no more than a passing acquaintance with Italian verb-tenses.

Einstein was able to prove that the recitative as it appears in our scores is not by Mozart at all; it was evidently a substitution for the original, inserted in some Prague performances of the opera after 1787. A manuscript of *Don Giovanni* discovered by Einstein in Florence is plainly a copy of Mozart's autograph score for the Vienna production of 1788; and there the recitative in question is given in an entirely different form—Mozart's own form—which Einstein printed in full for the first time in an article in *Music and Letters* for October 1938.

But that is not all. In the Vienna libretto of 1788 there occurs a little episode which is not to be found in our scores, but which is absolutely vital to our understanding of the situation. In the scores all we have is our (F), after which Elvira plunges without any apparent rhyme or reason into her intensely serious recitative and aria (G). But in the score as it left Mozart's hands there was more than this. After Zerlina's ejaculation "Heavens! how has the scoundrel managed to escape?", Masetto enters accompanied by two peasants. Zerlina impatiently asks him where he has been all this time, and Masetto's explanation supplies what has hitherto been lacking—the reason for the great emotional disturbance set up in Elvira's soul, and consequently the justification of the horror and pity expressed in her recitative and aria. The authentic Mozartian text runs thus:

Masetto, entering after Zerlina's "How has the scoundrel managed to escape?": Never has there been a soul so vile!

Zerlina: Ah Masetto, Masetto! Where have you been all this while?

Masetto: It was heaven's will that I should save an unfortunate young woman. Hardly had I left you when I heard cries from the opposite path. I ran there with the others, and found a woman weeping and a man in flight. I tried to overtake him, but he disappeared from my view. From what the girl said to me, however, from the behaviour of the man, from his appearance and his bearing, I concluded it was that rascal of a cavalier.

Zerlina: It was he without a doubt. This, too, let us report to Don Ottavio: to him we look to act for us all and exact vengeance.

What the author of the Prague forgery has done is to retain these last sentences of Zerlina—see our (F)—but to make them apply to Don Giovanni's conjectural participation in Leporello's (second) escape, whereas, as we have just seen, they refer, in the original, to the horror created by Masetto's story of yet another crime on Giovanni's part.[1] As Einstein rightly remarks, the episode with the Masetto narrative supplies what otherwise has been lacking to us—the reason for the serious sentiments expressed in Elvira's aria. The recitatives which appear in our present scores were forgeries made in Prague for some performance or other there and innocently included in the first edition of the full score (1801) in the belief on the publisher's part that they were Mozart's own.

It is fairly easy to see what must have happened in Vienna in 1788. Somebody or other steeped in the Italian buffo tradition must have decided that a bit of farcical relief was called for between Ottavio's aria and Elvira's, so Mozart, no doubt for peace' sake, consented to the addition of the episode of Zerlina dragging

---

[1] Mozart's musical setting of the scene in recitative is quoted in full in Einstein's *Music and Letters* article.

Leporello in by the hair of his head, the duet ("Per queste tue manine") in which he pleads for mercy, the tying of him up with the aid of a conveniently handy peasant, and his ultimate escape, dragging behind him the chair and the window-frame—which could be counted on to bring the house down. Mozart has noted in his "Catalogue of my Works" the exact dates of composition of "Per queste tue manine" and "Mi tradì quest' alma ingrata"— the 28th and 30th April 1788 respectively. (The first Vienna performance took place on the 7th May.) The Masetto recitative discovered by Einstein was obviously intended to supply the necessary motivation for the new "Mi tradì" aria which had been demanded of the composer by the player of the part of Elvira. The dramatic intention is better than the realisation of it: it strikes us as rather odd that in the moment or two beween Masetto's rushing to the aid of the girl and the escape of her assailant he should have been able to divine from the latter's appearance and bearing that he was Don Giovanni—for it will be remembered that the episode takes place in semi-darkness; besides, if the criminal were really Giovanni he would be in Leporello's clothing, which makes it all the more difficult for us to understand how Masetto could deduce from the man's appearance and his bearing that it was not a valet but a cavalier that was fleeing from him!

It will be remembered that in the scene that follows Elvira's aria, where Giovanni and Leporello meet again in the churchyard and each changes back into his own cloak and hat, Giovanni tells the valet of an adventure he claims to have just had with a young woman whom the startled Leporello surmises may have been his own wife. It would be interesting to know whether the Masetto recitative was designed to fulfil a double purpose—not only to afford Elvira a "cue" for her aria, but also to add a touch of verisimilitude to Giovanni's story of his alleged recent conquest.

41

2. The second point concerns a supposed participation of Casanova in the text of the Da Ponte-Mozart opera.

In 1784 the famous amorist had settled down, at the age of sixty-three, in the castle of Dux, in Bohemia, as librarian to Count Waldstein. He became friendly with the Prague impresario,

Bondini, and with various local notabilities in the circle that formed round Mozart during his stay in the town in 1787. A contemporary letter from a man in Brünn to one in Tschaslau, dated the 4th November, indicates that Casanova was in Prague at the time of the production of *Don Giovanni*: "Casanova is in Prague; his letter to me is dated the 25th October." He had gone there to arrange for the publication of a novel of his, *Icosameron*. In the list of subscribers to the book appears the name of Franz Duschek, the husband of the singer Josepha Duschek whose hospitality Mozart enjoyed during his stay in the town; and as the first performance of the new opera took place on the 29th October it is a fair presumption that Casanova attended it.

In 1937 Paul Nettl announced in the Alt-Prager Almanach the discovery at Schloss Hirschberg, in Bohemia, of a document undoubtedly in Casanova's writing, with a number of emendations in the same hand, that is obviously a sketch for what follows in the score of *Don Giovanni* immediately after the sextet in the second act. The few lines from the document printed by Herr Nettl on that occasion were sufficient to show that they formed part of an alternative version of the aria—"Ah, pietà, signori miei"— in which Leporello pleads with his captors for mercy, obviously playing for time until he can find a door through which to escape, as eventually he does.

The fragments quoted by Herr Nettl gave rise at the time to the conjecture that Casanova was helping Da Ponte and Mozart out of a little difficulty. Da Ponte, it will be remembered, being pressed for time, had had to return to Vienna some days before the first performance of *Don Giovanni*. The conjecture was that Mozart had come to the conclusion in Prague that some alteration in the libretto was necessary at this point, and, Da Ponte not being available and time being short, he had called Casanova in to supply the necessary words, the latter's contribution consisting of (*a*) the brief recitative that follows the sextet, (*b*) Leporello's aria "Ah pietà," (*c*) the recitative of the other characters that comes after his escape and before Ottavio begins his "Il mio tesoro."

Against this theory it has to be pointed out, in the first place, that the Leporello aria was composed before Mozart left Vienna

for Prague;[1] and in the second place that any collaboration of
Da Ponte with Casanova is extremely improbable. We know
comparatively little of the relations of the two adventurers, but
we have evidence that Casanova's failure to rate Da Ponte's
poetical efforts as highly as that gentleman did himself was always
a sore point with the latter. Casanova, one imagines, would be
the last person in Europe whose intervention in the matter of the
Don Giovanni libretto would have been agreeable to the vain and
touchy librettist; and in the absence of even the smallest direct
evidence as to Casanova's "collaboration" we shall perhaps do
wisely to rule it out.

42

In 1938 Herr Nettl printed the Casanova document in full, with
a facsimile of the manuscript, in his book *Mozart in Böhmen*. It
consists of a single sheet of paper, divided vertically into two
halves by either a line drawn down the middle of it or by it having
been folded from top to bottom. At the end of each half is the
word "Fugge," i.e. [Leporello] "Flees." This had given rise to the
conjecture in 1937 that the paper—of which, it will be remembered, Herr Nettl had at that time quoted only a few lines—contained two alternative sketches for the episode. Now that we have
the complete text it is more probable that there is only one sketch;
for Herr Nettl, I venture to suggest, may have transcribed them in
the wrong order in his book. He begins with the text on the right-
hand side of the paper and then continues without a break with
the text on the left-hand side; but if we reverse that order the
sketch, I think, makes something like complete dramatic sense.
The left-hand side obviously begins where we should expect the
episode to do after the completion of the sextet and the departure
of Donna Anna. Leporello confesses that he is cornered and confused and has no defence. He begs for pardon, which Elvira,
Ottavio, Zerlina and Masetto refuse. He makes another appeal,
which is also rejected; his captors telling him that they would like
to tear his insides out, or, as an alternative, see him dangling from
a gibbet. For a third time he appeals abjectly to them, only to be

---

[1] The numbers of the opera composed in Prague are written on a different-
sized paper, with a different ruling, from those Mozart brought with him
from Vienna.

greeted with the same contumely and threats; and for the third time he repeats his refrain, "My fate is in your hands alone: my beating heart asks for your clemency." That brings us to the foot of the left-hand page, and the terminal word "Fugge."

The right-hand half seems to follow naturally on this. It is allotted wholly to Leporello. He explains how he comes to be in the position he now occupies. His tyrannical master, he says, had forced him to exchange clothes with him, and is the *fons et origo* of the whole imbroglio. The basic trouble is Giovanni's passion for the female sex, that traditional root of all evil. Leporello addresses an *argumentum ad hominem* to each of them in turn—as he does in the opera—explaining, for instance, that it was his master, not he, who had thrashed Masetto and dictated the burlesque wooing of Elvira. "What I am telling you is the truth," he concludes. "It is with Don Giovanni alone that you should be furious. Let me go free." By this time, apparently— again as in the opera—he has managed to find the door he has been searching for, and he escapes, as is indicated by the final stage direction "Fugge." If the two halves of the sheet are taken in the order I have suggested, which happens also to be the order shown in the facsimile, it all constitutes a dramatic unity. Taken in the reverse order the two halves necessarily look like two alternative treatments of the episode. The *double* "Fugge," however, must be admitted to be inexplicable; only the second, agreeing as it does with the course of events in the opera, makes stage sense.

We may dismiss, I think, the theory that Da Ponte and Mozart were concerned in any way in the matter. We have evidence, as Herr Nettl shows, that in Prague it was the custom to insert broadly farcical improvised passages in buffo scenes for the amusement of the groundlings; and the discovery of Einstein to which reference has been made above is proof enough that after Mozart's death the local hacks took liberties of one kind and another with *Don Giovanni*. We shall perhaps be correct in assigning the Casanova document to that period. Casanova, by the way, died at Dux in 1803, at the age of seventy-eight.

Tosca

GIACOMO PUCCINI [1858–1924]

PRINCIPAL CHARACTERS

Floria Tosca	*Soprano*
Mario Cavaradossi	*Tenor*
Baron Scarpia	*Baritone*
Cesare Angelotti	*Bass*
The Sacristan	*Baritone*
Spoletta	*Tenor*

1

In order of composition *Tosca* follows the *La Bohème* of 1893–1896; but Puccini's attention seems to have been first drawn to the subject about 1889 (after the completion of his early opera *Edgar*), when he saw a performance of Sardou's play at the Teatro dei Filodrammatici in Milan. As he knew no more than a word or two of French he could have understood only vaguely what most of it was really "about"; but the main situations must have gripped him—especially the torture scene and the shooting of Cavaradossi—he could be in no doubt as to what Scarpia stood for, while the part of the impulsive, convulsive Tosca, played as Sarah Bernhardt played it, hardly needed words to explain it. Six years later, in a letter of the summer of 1895, we find Puccini telling his publisher Giulio Ricordi that he and his wife are "off to Florence, where they are giving [Sardou's] *Tosca* tonight." The next reference to the play in his published correspondence is on the 15th May 1898, when he writes to Ricordi from Paris, "I shall see Sardou in a few days and will settle definitely the question of that eternal Act I"; from which we gather that the opera was already on the stocks and that the first act, on the construction of which we shall have to turn a critical eye later, was even then a nut which neither he nor his librettists nor even the master-craftsman Sardou himself could crack.

In the years between *Edgar* (1889) and about 1897 a good deal happened. Verdi, whose sense of "theatre" was almost as lively as that of Sardou, had evidently had his eye on the French dramatist for many years; as far back as 1869, when rejecting a suggestion of his friend Camille Du Locle that he should write an opera based on Meilhac and Halévy's *Froufrou*, he had said that if he were going to write a work for Paris at all he would prefer something from Sardou with text by Du Locle. Some time in the mid-1890's the news reached Puccini's ears that another Italian composer, Alberto Franchetti, had had a *Tosca* libretto made for him by Luigi Illica, that this had been read to Sardou in Paris, and that Verdi, who was present, had bubbled over with enthusiasm for the subject, even, it was alleged, going so far as to say that if he were not too old for the task he would have written an opera on it himself. This was enough to convince Puccini that the subject must be his or no one's. Illica was his friend as well as Franchetti's; Ricordi was Franchetti's publisher as well as Puccini's— and Giulio saw more lire ahead of him with the composer of the successful *Manon Lescaut* and *La Bohème* than with the composer of *Asrael* and *Cristoforo Colombo*. So librettist and publisher got quietly to work on the innocent Franchetti, and by a piece of chicanery on which the moralist in us may frown but of which the opera-goer in us cordially approves, the good man was persuaded that Illica's book was a poor one and the theme quite unsuited to him—indeed, to the operatic stage. The day after the persuasion—some say the very same day—a contract for a *Tosca* was signed by Illica, Puccini, and the firm of Ricordi; and Giocosa was called in to collaborate in the making of the libretto.

2

Sardou seems to have played a considerable part in the enormously difficult business of boiling the play down for operatic purposes; otherwise, we may be sure, he would certainly not have said, as he is credibly alleged to have done, that the libretto was perhaps better than the original drama. Part of his enthusiasm, of course, may be accounted for by the fact that he had done so good a deal with Ricordi in the matter of royalties that he stood to profit handsomely by the success of Puccini's work. He certainly threw himself heart and soul into the first Paris production of the opera: and we are told that by that time the energetic old gentleman had almost managed to persuade himself that he had written the music also. But the final word all along in the many disputes with the librettists had rested with Puccini. Like Wagner and Richard Strauss, he would sometimes write the music for an episode before he had the text: we find him, for example, sending instructions to his librettists for a number of lines that *must* follow precisely the metrical scheme he indicates; even the alternations of Mario-Tosca must be observed. He always knew what he wanted, was determined to have it, and persisted till he got it. If he had set his heart on space for musical expansion at this point or that, space had somehow to be found; if he thought anything poor "theatre" it had to come out. The librettists had made Cavaradossi sing a sort of aria while he was being tortured; this may have been in the tradition of Italian opera, but Puccini would have none of it. In the original drama Tosca's death-leap from the parapet of the castle of Sant' Angelo had been simply "dans le vide." Sardou wanted the heroine of the opera to leap into the Tiber; and when Puccini pointed out to him that this meant a jump of some fifty feet horizontally on Tosca's part, seeing that the river does not flow, as the dramatist imagined, between St. Peter's and the Castello but on the other side, the great man, "calm as a fish," as Puccini said, merely remarked "Oh, that's nothing!"

Puccini had a keen sense of the difference in suggestiveness between two phrases that on the surface look practically alike. Thus for the "Tu mi odii?" ("You hate me?") which the librettists had put into the mouth of Scarpia in the scene with Tosca in the second act he insisted on substituting the cynically complacent "Come tu mi odii!" (How you hate me!"), which lends itself to a much more telling vocal inflection.

In Sardou's play the fourth act had ended thus after the stabbing of Scarpia: "She goes round the table to the glass," say the stage directions, "arranges her hair before it, then turns to the corpse of Scarpia. 'And it was before this that a whole town trembled!' A drum roll in the distance. Trumpets sound the morning call. She shudders: 'The call! Day has dawned!' She goes back to the space between the table and the dead man and blows out the lights on the table. 'And the safe-conduct? . . . What have I done with that?' " There follows the finding of the paper at last in the dead man's hand, the arranging of the lights on either side of the body, the laying of the crucifix on Scarpia's breast, and all the rest of the well-known effective "business" before her exit. Puccini was wiser. He saw, for one thing, that Tosca ought to say nothing at all after her remark about the one-time terror under which the city had groaned. Sardou's "And the safe-conduct? What have I done with that?" is something of an anti-climax; Puccini wisely left the feverish search for the document to be carried out in dumb show, knowing that with his orchestra he could convey a nervous tension far beyond the power of words. Moreover, it is to him that we owe the phrasing of Tosca's last words: "E avanti a lui tremava tutta Roma!" ("And before him trembled all Rome!"). The substitution of "all Rome" for "a whole town," with the cadential "Roma" as the final word, was a master-stroke on the composer's part. Incredible as it may appear, the librettists wanted to strike the line out, but Puccini insisted on its being restored; he knew better than they what would be the effect in the theatre of this line delivered in a low-pitched monotone that is virtually ordinary speech.

3

Over the big choral ensemble in the church at the end of the first act he took particular trouble. Apparently mistrusting his own knowledge of ecclesiastical usage he appealed to a friend of his, a Roman priest, Father Pietro Panichelli, to help him out. He outlined the scene for him—the abbot and the chapter emerging from the sacristy en route to the altar, the people watching the procession from either side of the stage, and the baritone "soliloquising independently, or nearly so," in the background. He wanted some prayers to be recited during the procession—whether by the chapter or the people did not matter much so long as the effect was obtained of a "murmuring of prayers in subdued and natural voices, without intoning, precisely as real prayers are said." The *Ecce sacerdos* he thought "too imposing to be murmured." He knew that it is not usual for anything to be said or sung before the Te Deum, which is given out when the high altar is reached; but whether it would be ecclesiastically right or wrong, he wanted something to be murmured during the passage from the sacristy to the altar, preferably by the people, because—a sound operatic reason, this!—"they are more numerous and therefore more effective musically." How his wishes were met will appear in our musical analysis of the scene. It may be added that for this church music Puccini drew to a small extent upon a Mass (still unpublished) written in 1880, in his twenty-second year.

The first performance of the opera was given in the Costanzi Theatre in Rome on the 14th January 1900, under Mugnone, with Ericlea Darclée as Tosca, Emilio De Marchi as Cavaradossi, Eugenio Giraldoni as Scarpia, Enrico Galli as Angelotti, and Ettore Borelli as the Sacristan. For one reason or another everyone's nerves were on edge, so that the performance as a whole was an indifferent one; but the work soon became a pronounced success, especially in London, where it was given in the summer season at Covent Garden in the same year, with Ternina as the first of a series of great Toscas and Scotti the first of several notable Scarpias.

4

The musical world pullulates with schools and instruction books for pianists, fiddlers, singers, conductors, composers and what not. It still lacks, however, a school for librettists. To recast a novel or a play as an opera text calls for a special technique; yet after three hundred years there is still nothing resembling a code for the guidance of a librettist in his fumbling hand-to-mouth practice. What generally happens is that the poet—to employ what in this connection is generally no more than a technical term—and the composer, after an infinity of discussion, correspondence, and from time to time heated recrimination, eventually settle down to a rough-and-ready compromise between the claims of the drama and those of music: despite the struggles of the poor librettist the composer always has the last word, and we know from history that it is not always the most rational word. So it pays us to compare now and then in some detail the text of an opera and that of the well-constructed novel or play from which it was derived, if only to get a rough idea of the difficulties attendant on this species of collaboration; and *Tosca* is about as instructive a subject for an enquiry of this sort as could be found.

Sardou's drama *La Tosca* had been produced in Paris on the 24th November 1887, with Sarah Bernhardt as the heroine. The play, with its five acts and twenty-three characters, had of course to be drastically condensed for the purposes of the opera, which is in three acts and has only nine characters in all, of whom four —Spoletta (the police agent), the gendarme Sciarrone, a gaoler and a shepherd—play only minor parts in the action. A fair amount of what happens in the play could be dispensed with in the opera without fatal dramatic loss; Sardou's effective second act, for instance, disappears *en bloc*. On the other hand, much of the Sardou drama that is vital to the spectator's understanding of the opera has been entirely eliminated or passed by with the most casual of hints.

Puccini had a consummate sense of "theatre," which, however, is not always quite the same thing as "drama." Moreover, his musical genius was on the whole a slow-moving one. His music seldom hurries; his strength lay to a great extent in unrelenting insistence on a motif once launched, the piling up of obsessional effect on effect in some episode or other that lent itself well to that kind of musical treatment. This psychological bias led him, now consciously, now unconsciously, to see a dramatic action as concentrated in a few peak-situations supercharged with musical emotion. If the dramatic layout as a whole lent itself to this sort of simplification, well and good. But if the action had been dependent, in the play or story on which Puccini founded his own work, on the dexterous piecing together of a number of small psychological motives or episodes, his own structure necessarily suffered to some extent by his sweeping all that aside in order to get more room for his music.[1]

[1] The general situation is summed up in a despairing passage in one of Giacosa's letters to Giulio Ricordi, written at the time when he was struggling with the far smaller difficulties of condensing the subject matter of *La Bohème:* "It is a terrible undertaking to reduce to the required proportions an act crammed full of events. I worked desperately hard, but on the one hand I have to make clearness my aim, and on the other I must not make the act longer than three hundred lines."

This is decidedly the case with the first act of *Tosca*: the critical spectator who sees it for the first time keeps wondering precisely who or what Cavaradossi, Tosca, Angelotti and "the Attavanti" are, how it comes about that Cavaradossi is painting in the church, why the Sacristan keeps mumbling serio-comic doubts about the artist's religion and morals, why Angelotti should be taking refuge in this particular church, why Cavaradossi should be so ready to assist him at the risk of his own liberty or even life, and so forth; and the full answers to these and many other questions are to be found only in Sardou's play, some knowledge of which should always be at the back of our minds when we are listening to the opera—as of course it was at the back of Puccini's mind when writing it.

5

The action of Puccini's first act is briefly as follows. Into the empty church of Sant' Andrea della Valle in Rome there steals, when the curtain rises, an agitated Angelotti; the stage directions tell us that he is "in prison garb," though how the spectator is to recognise the Italian prison garb of the year 1800 we do not know; all he sees is a panting man in rags. Angelotti proceeds to lock himself in one of the side chapels, the key of which he has found, after a little search, at the feet of a statue of the Madonna: for his sister, he obligingly informs the audience, has sent him—where? when? why? how? the spectator cannot help asking—a letter telling him that it is there he will find the key. The painter Mario Cavaradossi then enters, and, during and after a colloquy with the Sacristan, sets to work at a half-finished easel picture of a blonde and blue-eyed Magdalen. The garrulous old Sacristan recognises the face as that of an unknown lady he had seen in the church lately, praying to the Virgin; [1] and Cavaradossi informs him—though one fails to perceive why he should confide in him to this extent—that, fascinated by her features, he had begun

[1] That her identity should be a mystery to the Sacristan is incredible; the Marchesa Attavanti's face would be as well known in Rome as that of any other member of the local aristocracy. Moreover, no one can know better than the Sacristan that the chapel on the right of the stage is that of the lady's family: it is he, indeed, who points it out later in response to Scarpia's enquiry. This difficulty with regard to the recognition of the lady does not arise in Sardou.

painting her at her devotions without her having observed him; he has incorporated also in his picture something of the beauty of his mistress Floria Tosca, a miniature of whom he takes from his pocket and contemplates rapturously. Once more we are at a loss to understand why he should tell the Sacristan all this—and particularly that, unlike the original of the picture, his Tosca is a brunette and her eyes are black; the truth is, of course, that it is only in this way that the composer can convey the information to the audience. The Sacristan does a good deal of *sotto voce* grumbling about the artist's addiction to mundane things and his lack of pious interest in the saints, and mutters something about "these dogs of Voltaireans who are the enemies of the Holy Office"—a line to which the spectator cannot attach any meaning, and for the significance of which we have to go back to Sardou.

When the Sacristan leaves and all is quiet, Angelotti, believing the church to be empty now, turns from the inside the key of the chapel grille, apparently intending to make his escape. (Why he should have gone there in the first place, with the intention of leaving it so soon, has so far not been divulged to us.) Scared at the unexpected sight of a stranger, he is about to slip back into the chapel when, to his joy, he recognises in the painter an old friend of his, Mario Cavaradossi. At first the latter does not know him, for, as Angelotti explains, as much for our benefit as for Cavaradossi's, his imprisonment in the castle of Sant' Angelo has changed him greatly; but the painter eventually remembers him as "the Consul of the extinguished Roman republic"—a phrase incomprehensible to the audience—and hails him as such. Their very brief colloquy is interrupted by an off-stage call from Cavaradossi's mistress, Tosca: and giving the starving Angelotti his own basket of food and wine Mario hurries him back into the chapel and settles down to a long duet with Floria. Her suspicions have been aroused by his delay in unbolting the church door, and her jealousy by the picture, the original of which she recognises as a certain Marchesa Attavanti. However, Mario manages to placate her, and finally persuades her to depart and leave him to his work.

When she has gone Angelotti comes out of the chapel again, and Cavaradossi informs him that delightfully amorous as Tosca is she is very pious and given to telling her confessor everything;

for which reason he had had to be very guarded in his conversation with her. Angelotti now discloses his plan for flight. It appears that his sister the Marchesa had concealed a woman's clothes in the family chapel; he was to don these, slip out of the church at dusk, and so escape the clutches of the scoundrelly Chief of Police, Baron Scarpia. It is now arranged between the two men that Angelotti shall make his way over the fields to Cavaradossi's villa in the country, the key to which the painter gives him, promising to rejoin him there at night. There is no need to put on the female garments now, Cavaradossi explains; let him take them with him and make use of them later if need be. But just as Angelotti is going back to the chapel for the clothes the boom of a cannon is heard—the warning to the town that a prisoner has escaped. Cavaradossi and Angelotti leave the church hurriedly. The Sacristan and the populace come in, rejoicing over the news that has just reached Rome of the defeat of the French under Bonaparte. They are followed by Scarpia; and the remainder of the act follows on the purely operatic lines which will be familiar to the reader.

All this, however, leaves a great deal to be explained which it is necessary for us to know if we are to understand all that has happened before the rising of the curtain, and why Puccini had obviously earmarked the bulk of his space in the first act for two big musical show pieces—the duet between Cavaradossi and Tosca, and Scarpia's outburst of erotic frenzy, with the massive choral ensemble that accompanies this and brings the act to a sonorous close; he had consequently little space left for explanation of the core of the drama. For a fuller knowledge of the characters and the action we have to turn to Sardou.

6

The period of the spoken play is that of the invasion of Italy by the army of the French Republican Government. Puccini's score gives the date of the action as June 1800; Sardou, with his "17th June," is more explicit. His drama begins with a talk between the Sacristan (Eusèbe) and little Gennarino, Mario Cavaradossi's boy servant, who, when the curtain rises, is cleaning his master's brushes, preparing the palette, and so forth. It is the hour of the siesta, and Eusèbe is anxious to close the church and go home to his sleep; but he cannot do so until Cavaradossi arrives as usual, and the artist is late today. We gather from what the garrulous Eusèbe says that Cavaradossi has obtained permission from the authorities to work in the church at this hour each day, when he will be free from disturbance by worshippers, choir, organist and English tourists with their guides. Eusèbe, a pious plebeian of low intellectual development, has nothing against the artist personally, for he is liberal with his tips. But though the man comes of an old patrician family on his father's side, Mario's mother, Gennarino is informed, was French, which, for Eusèbe, accounts for everything that is morally wrong with the son. Cavaradossi, though he is decorating the church, never takes part in the services, never goes to confession; "a Jacobin, Gennarino, an out-and-out Jacobin." His father had lived a long time in Paris, where he associated with "the abominable Voltaire" and other reprobates of that kidney; and the son has imbibed the father's reprehensible opinions on religion and politics.

As for Eusèbe, he is looking forward gleefully to a festival at the Farnese Palace that evening in celebration of a great victory of the Austrian General Melas which has just been announced in the Roman news-sheets: Genoa has been captured, Masséna has barely escaped with a few thousand demoralised troops. And so her Neapolitan Majesty Queen Marie Caroline (daughter of the Empress Maria Theresa and sister of Queen Marie Antoinette of blessed memory), glorious and worthy spouse of his Majesty Ferdinand IV, being at the moment in Rome on her way to Vienna, has commanded a splendid concert and ball at the Palazzo Farnese and a public fête in the Piazza. Soon there will be an even greater victory to rejoice over. There is a lot of nonsensical street gossip about General Bonaparte being at Milan, but Eusèbe has it on the best authority that Bonaparte has died in Egypt, "drowned in the Red Sea like Pharaoh," and is now being impersonated by his imbecile brother Joseph, a farceur who is really trying to persuade people that he has crossed the Alps with all his cannon!

So we have gathered that this Mario Cavaradossi, while there is nothing definite against him on which the Church and the Government can fasten, is not in the best odour in Roman political and clerical circles. He enters the church now, dismisses

Eusèbe and Gennarino, and prepares to resume work at his easel. Absorbed in this he does not hear a key being turned from the inside in the grille of one of the chapels; but happening to turn round just then he sees a man making steathily for the door of the church, where he pauses and listens intently. (The reader will recall that in the opera Angelotti enters immediately on the rising of the curtain and slips into the chapel before anyone else arrives on the scene. In Sardou he has been there all the preceding night.) The stranger announces himself as a prisoner escaped from the castle of Sant' Angelo: he had been engaged, he says, in revolutionary activities in Naples, and on the failure of these he had fled to Rome, where once more his name—Cesare Angelotti—figures on the list of proscriptions. Having overheard Eusèbe's account of Cavaradossi and his "Jacobin" antecedents he is confident the painter will not betray him. Thus in Sardou Cavaradossi and Angelotti have no knowledge at all of each other before the action opens; the only link between them is that of a common detestation of tyranny and clericalism. This gives all the more point to Mario's resolve to save Angelotti even at the risk of his own life.

7

The painter assures Angelotti that they are secure from interruption for a good two hours; the church is closed, even the Sacristan being unable to enter except by a side door the bolt of which Cavaradossi has shot. How has Angelotti managed to escape from prison? he asks. Angelotti tells him in full detail. He has been helped by his devoted sister the Marquise Attavanti.[1] She had bribed one of his gaolers, a certain Trebelli, to unlock his fetters yesterday, and profiting by the confusion in the castle where they were busy repairing the damage done by the French during the occupation of it, he had made his escape in his prison clothes. But where was he to go first? From the evening to the morning Angelus the gates of the town would be closed as usual. He could not go to his sister's house, for her husband the Marquis is a fanatic for Church and throne and would assuredly deliver him up to the authorities. So his sister had concealed a woman's

---

[1] She herself does not appear either in the play or the opera, though her husband plays a part in the former.

costume, including a cloak, a veil and a fan—the purpose of this last, of course, being to hide his face if need be—together with scissors and a razor (Sardou thinks of everything!), in this family chapel, the key to which she had conveyed to him through Trebelli. The plan was that he should slip into the chapel before the church was closed, spend the night there, cut his hair and shave off his beard. In the morning Trebelli was to come for him at the hour of High Mass and accompany him—now made up as a woman—to a place where a carriage would be waiting for them; at Frascati, outside Roman territory, where he would be safe, his sister would join him. But this morning, Trebelli not having appeared, Angelotti had not known what to do, whether to wait or to make the dash for freedom alone; for it is possible that his escape from Sant' Angelo has been discovered by now, and Trebelli may have confessed everything under torture. The one encouraging feature of the situation is that so far the alarm cannon has not been fired from the castle.

Cavaradossi tries to reassure him; the delay in Trebelli's coming may be due to some trifling last-minute hitch that had not been foreseen. Angelotti had better wait until evening begins to fall before slipping out of the church disguised. If he does so now, as had obviously been his intention, he is certain to attract the notice of some of the women knitting at the doors, or of the children who are playing about; whereas after the church has reopened he can mingle with the crowd of comers and goers without fear of detection. He is anxious, however, he replies, about his devoted sister, with whom there is no way of communicating. Mario tells him that he understands now why the fair devotee whom he had surreptitiously painted had been so assiduous in her attendance at the church of late; and Angelotti tells him the full story of his sister and himself.

Some twenty years ago he had been living a life of pleasure in London. At Vauxhall one night he had made the acquaintance of one of the light-o'-loves who used to frequent the Gardens. The liaison had lasted only a week. Years passed, and on the death of his father he inherited considerable property in Naples. Dining one day at the house of Prince Pepoli he had been presented to the wife of Sir William Hamilton, the English ambassador in Naples; and to his stupefaction he realised that this famous Lady

Hamilton was none other than his casual Vauxhall pick-up of years ago, not yet the figure she became later by her association with Admiral Nelson, but already a power at the Neapolitan Court. Exasperated by the hostility she showed towards the revolutionists he had told the whole company what she had once been, and where and in what circumstances he had formerly met her. Two days later his house was searched and his papers seized. They contained nothing incriminating; but an agent provocateur had craftily slipped a copy of Voltaire among his books, and this was sufficient to send him to the galleys for three years.

After that, ruined, exiled, he had left Naples, to return only with Championnet. When the royal troops re-occupied the town he had fled to Rome, thus escaping the imprisonment and torture that were the fate of his fellow-libertarians. But when the French troops had to leave Rome he was arrested once more and thrown into Sant' Angelo, where he had spent a year. Thanks to his sister's social influence he had been shown a certain passive benevolence by the governor of the prison, who hoped that when a new Pope was elected Angelotti would receive an amnesty along with other prisoners. But the court of Naples had recently sent to Rome, as head of the police, a certain pitiless Baron Scarpia, whom Cavaradossi, who knows the man well, describes as a thorough-paced scoundrel who conceals his ambitions, his lechery and his lust for blood under a mask of religion and courtesy, "an artist in villainy, subtle in wickedness, delighting in cruelty, bloody even in his orgies, a foul unscrupulous satyr." Yes, says Angelotti, this scoundrel had pursued his sister the Marquise Attavanti, and having been repulsed, and sensing in advance a design on her part to rescue her brother, he had arranged for Angelotti to be sent three days hence to Naples, where Lady Hamilton would have the pleasure of hanging her one-time lover. In that, however, she will be disappointed, for in a ring given him by his sister he has poison enough to make an end of himself. At that moment there is a sound of battering at the church door. The two men's hearts go into their mouths; they listen in anxious silence for a while, but the noise proves to have been only that of the ball of some players in the street. This little episode is one of Sardou's most telling pieces of stage craftsmanship; the emotional tension gathers up into itself all that has so far happened, and when the real coup de théâtre comes later—the thunder of the Sant' Angelo cannon—it strikes us with double force.

8

The spasm of terror having spent itself, the two men resume their conversation. Mario now tells Angelotti all about himself. He is the son of a Roman gentleman who had spent the greater part of his life in France, where he had been intimate with such people as Voltaire and Diderot, and had married a great-niece of Helvétius. Mario himself had been brought up in circles that breathed revolt against the established political and clerical order. Family affairs had made it necessary for him to return to Rome, which he did at the very time when the French troops were leaving the city. Nothing kept him in the abhorred place now but his passion for Floria Tosca, the great singer, the idol of musicians and populace alike, who is at present performing at the Argentina Theatre. He is madly in love with her: she has only two faults—a tendency to crazy jealousy, and a religiosity which Cavaradossi finds excessive. So he remains in Rome. He takes no part in revolutionary activities; but his un-Roman way of behaviour and his former Paris associations go against him with the authorities. He would have come within reach of Scarpia's claws by now if it had not been for his ingenuity in getting permission from the chapter of Sant' Andrea to decorate gratuitously the walls of the church. Soon Tosca will be leaving Rome to fulfil a season's engagement in Venice, and he intends to slip away quietly with her. Till then, he believes, he is safe; anyhow he is prepared to take the risk. He and Tosca meet freely, either at his villa in the country or here in the church; she would have been here by now, indeed, were it not that she is rehearsing for this evening's concert.

Cavaradossi rejects the suggestion that he should let her into the secret of Angelotti's identity. For one thing, he does not believe in bringing women into serious affairs of this sort; for another, he could not rely on a woman so subject to nervous crises as Tosca is, and a fanatical royalist into the bargain. Moreover she is very pious and hides nothing from her confessor. So, all in all, the less she is told the better: "the only really discreet woman is the one who knows nothing."

9

Just then a knock at the church door is heard, and Tosca's voice impatiently calling "Mario!" He hustles Angelotti into the chapel, saying he will cut Floria's visit as short as possible; then he opens the church door. At once she begins to vent her jealous suspicions. Why is the bolt shot today? With whom was he talking? Some old flame of his, no doubt? She piously protests against his kissing her hand until she has offered placatory flowers to the Madonna, which she does kneeling at the feet of the statue. This done, she becomes her normal amorous feline self again. They cannot meet tonight as usual, she complains, because she has to sing at a fête at the Farnese Palace. After that there is to be a ball, at which the Queen of Naples has reserved a special place for her; so it will be mid-day tomorrow before she can see her lover again. Her suspicious eye catches a look of relief which he has been unable to conceal. In a flash she becomes the jealous, suspicious Tosca once more.[1] Who is that woman he is painting? Why has he made her so beautiful? It must be some former mistress of his, through whom he is now recalling his memories and realising his secret desires. Why is her hair golden, Tosca's being black? Why are her eyes so blue? Then she recognises her —the Attavanti! He admits it, but patiently tries to explain that he has seen the original of the picture only here in the church, and that by hazard, she having come in to pray before the statue of the Madonna while he was at work: she had seemed so truly the ideal Magdalen that he had at once committed her features to his canvas, without her having been aware of it, without his having spoken a single word to her.

Floria traduces the character of her supposed rival: why does she not try to reform that villainous brother of hers, "an enemy of God, of the King and of the Pope, a demagogue, an atheist?" Mario tries to laugh all this off, but only succeeds in angering her more. He must himself be as bad as Angelotti, she rants, or he would not be so complacent about him. Now she thinks of it, does not Mario himself read Voltaire? Has he not given her to read—

[1] We see at every point that it was Sarah Bernhardt, with her capacity for rapid changes of expression, whom Sardou had in his mind's eye all along as his Tosca.

her, the pious Floria Tosca!—Rousseau's *La Nouvelle Héloïse*, a
book so infamous that her good confessor had given her the
choice of either burning it or herself burning in hell! though it
soon appears that her private feminine grievance against the
people in the book is that they are untrue to life—they talk too
much about love and practise it too little. Her confessor has
warned her against this artist lover of hers, denounced her passion
as abominable, and adjured her to convert him if she can. As a
preliminary sign of conversion, says the good priest, she ought
to persuade him to get rid of that moustache of his; it is a revolutionary symbol, and he flaunts it in the street with such assurance!
Then, with another of her kittenish quick changes, Tosca declares
that she will not obey the priest in this, for Mario's moustache
becomes him. Altogether she lives in a constant state of mortal
sin on his account, and dreads dying suddenly, in which case,
she feels, her chance of salvation would be small. Her only consolation is that she stands well with the Madonna, thanks to her
pious attentions to her. Mario listens to all this feather-headed
gabble calmly and indulgently. He knows his Floria too well to
take her tantrums very seriously; all the same, it is inconvenient
to have her carrying on so long in this style just now.

10

The problem of how to get rid of her is solved for him by her
servant, who enters with a letter for Tosca from the composer
Paisiello. This being read aloud, we learn—as does Angelotti
also, listening in the chapel—that the Queen has just heard from
General Melas that on the 14th he had completely routed the
French army under General Bonaparte at Marengo. Public prayers
and thanks are to be offered in all the churches. As for Paisiello,
in his loyal enthusiasm he has dashed off a cantata for the fête in
the Farnese Palace that evening, and he begs Tosca to come to a
quick rehearsal of it before the supper. The Queen's wishes, she
recognises, will have to be complied with; so she quite resigns
herself to seeing no more of her lover that day. For his part, he
promises her, he will work as long as the light allows, then sup
and sleep at his villa, and they will meet again at mid-day on
the morrow.

She goes away, leaving the two men in the depths of despair

over the bad news of the Austrian victory; Tosca's last words
are a coquettish request to Mario to make the Magdalen's eyes
not blue but black, like hers. Angelotti comes out of the chapel,
and they hastily concoct a new plan. The church is now certain
to be opened before the usual time for the prayers and thanksgiving that have been commanded: a great crowd will be there,
and perhaps in the general excitement they will be able to get
out of Rome before the gates are closed, without waiting for
Trebelli. But at that moment the cannon of Sant' Angelo booms
out: the escape has been discovered. Yet another plan is hastily
improvised: Angelotti is to don his female disguise, slip out of
the chapel by a grille on the other side, steal through the dimly-lit
church, and join Cavaradossi at the great door. He goes back into
the chapel just as Eusèbe enters,[1] followed by a number of women
and children. Mario poses himself before the canvas, looking as
unconcerned as he can. The Sacristan is in high glee; a notorious
Jacobin, one Angelotti, he and Gennarino tell Cavaradossi, has
escaped from Sant' Angelo with the connivance of his gaoler,
who has confessed everything under torture. A price of a thousand
piastres is set on Angelotti's head, and the hue-and-cry is on.
While Eusèbe, with his back to the chapel, is gloating over the
defeat of the farceur Bonaparte, Angelotti is vaguely perceived
escaping by the other grille of which Cavaradossi had spoken
and disappearing in the dim depths of the church. With a sigh of
relief Cavaradossi makes his own exit, leaving Eusèbe still chattering. The church begins to fill, the choir is heard in the distance,
and Scarpia, in pursuit of Angelotti, enters with his two hench-
men, Spoletta and Schiarrone.

11

This detailed outline of Sardou's first act has been necessary to
show what an ill-made piece of work, dramatically speaking, the
first act of Puccini's opera is. The basis and essence of the original
drama are political; it is the community of feeling between the

[1] He has come in by the main entrance to the church; the first thing he
does is to draw the bolts of the side door from the inside. Sardou has not
forgotten that Cavaradossi had assured Angelotti during the first few moments of their meeting that "the church is empty and completely closed.
The sacristan himself cannot get in at that [side] door until I draw the bolts."

two men in that field that makes the painter ready to risk everything to save the life of a man whom he had never seen until that
day. In Sardou, not only has Eusèbe expressed to Gennarino his
disapproval of the moral character of this "Voltairean," this
"Jacobin," but Mario himself has told Angelotti at considerable
length the story of his early life and French associations and the
danger of his present position in Rome. In the opera all this
logical motivation disappears; the only attempt at a hint of it
(and it is so vague that the spectator who does not know Sardou's
play cannot possibly make anything of it) is in the Sacristan's
mumblings to himself about the painter being more taken up with
worldly than with religious things—a remark actually evoked by
the mere fact of Mario's rhapsody over the beauty of his mistress
Tosca.

The woman's-clothes motive, again, that is treated so plausibly
in Sardou, is clumsily handled in the opera, where the absence of
any mention of Trebelli results in a certain obscurity in the action
later. In Sardou, the moment we hear of the confession of the
gaoler we visualise everything that has happened at Sant' Angelo.
The full details of the plan to escape had been disclosed under
torture; that is why Scarpia has made straight for the church,
where he knows Angelotti had gone into hiding. His first words to
the Sacristan are "Listen to me. A criminal has escaped from Sant'
Angelo; he spent the night in this church; he may be here yet.
Where is the Angelotti chapel?" [1] Schiarrone is sent into the chapel

---

[1] In the opera this becomes the "Attavanti chapel." We may reasonably
wonder why the Marquise should be so imprudent as to deposit the female
disguise in the *Attavanti* chapel, which any member of that royalist family
might have visited! Sardou, who never leaves a loose thread of this kind
anywhere in a play, makes it quite clear from the outset, in the tale Angelotti
tells Cavaradossi, that no such danger could threaten the plan. "But where
was I to find shelter for the night? My sister had provided for that. The
Angelottis, whose ancestors had founded this church, have a chapel of their
own here to which they alone have the key: in this she placed the woman's
clothes. . . . She conveyed the key of it to me through Trebelli. I slipped in
before the church was closed. . . ."

In the play, almost Scarpia's first words to Eusèbe are "Where is the
Angelotti chapel?" A later remark of his, when the agent finds the fan, is
"This was part of the toilette." Obviously he has learned every detail of the
plot from Trebelli: that is why he has made at once for the church of Sant'

and returns with the news that there is no one there: all he has found that bears on his quest is "divers objets de toilette," a mirror, scissors, a razor, some hair on the ground—and a fan. Scarpia at once recognises the crest on the latter as that of the Attavanti family; Angelotti, he says, "must have forgotten it in his haste or decided he would have no use for it." This is consistent with what we have learned earlier in the play; the fan, Angelotti tells Cavaradossi, had been included by the Marquise in the bundle of woman's clothes in order that he might cover his face with it during his flight from the church. It is really upon the fan that the whole ingenious working-out of the action turns in Sardou; and it is a pity that operatic exigencies, particularly the need for compression in order to get plenty of space for the two big musical episodes of the first act, made Puccini and his librettists depart from Sardou's expert handling of the motive. On the general matter of music *versus* drama in the opera we shall have more to say later.

12

Let us now follow the dramatic and musical course of the first act of the opera in detail.

Three terrific chords, hurled at us by the orchestra without preamble:

1

Andante molto sostenuto

Andrea, and why he says to Schiarrone, "Nothing else? No woman's clothes? It is in that disguise, then, that he has fled."

Sardou makes it clear at the very opening of the play, in his stage directions, that the chapel was that of the Angelotti, not the Attavanti, family: ". . . the Angelotti chapel, with a grille . . . surmounted by the Angelotti arms." Puccini and his librettists missed or ignored the whole point—that the fugitive was safe for the night in that chapel because it was not accessible to anyone but a member of the Angelotti family. His sister was an Attavanti only by marriage.

first of all flash an image of the brutal, ruthless Scarpia upon our inner eye. Then, the curtain having risen, we see a section of the interior of the church of Sant' Andrea: on the right is the "Attavanti" chapel, as the stage directions describe it; on the left is a low platform with an easel on it, and on the easel a large canvas covered with a cloth; lying around are various implements of the painter's craft and a basket containing food and wine. Towards the centre of the stage is a statue of the Madonna, surmounting a font of holy water. To a series of hurrying, stumbling, syncopated chords of this type:

2

Angelotti staggers in by a side door—a broken, emaciated creature in rags, out of breath, trembling with fear. After a rapid glance round him he sees, to his relief, that he has taken the right direction; in his terror he had imagined that everyone in the streets who had looked at him was a police agent. Another nervous glance around confirms the fact that this is really the church of Sant' Andrea; and he gives a sigh of relief as he sees at last what have been staring him in the face all along—the statue and the font. "At the feet of the Madonna, so my sister wrote to me . . .," he ejaculates for our information; and we hear in the orchestra a motive obviously intended to be associated by us, in part, with the sister who has been working for his life and liberty:

3

He searches for a key that was to have been left at the foot of the column supporting the statue, fails to discover it at first, and for a moment gives way to despair. At last he finds it and runs with a cry of joy towards the chapel: "here is the key, and there is the chapel," he obligingly tells us. He looks round him, once more a prey to terror, then cautiously inserts the key in the lock of the grille, enters, and closes the gate carefully from the inside.

13

Hardly has he disappeared from our sight when the Sacristan enters from the back of the church with a bundle of paint-brushes in his hand. While he fusses about, seeing that everything is all right in the church, the orchestra gives out a couple of motives:

and

that suggest that he is the simplest of souls, easily pleased with his own little world and himself. To dispel any possible doubts we might have that he is intended to be a comic character Puccini tells us in his stage directions that he is afflicted with a nervous *tic,* a recurrent twitch of the neck and shoulders; and many a Sacristan with no voice to recommend him to us manages to get through the act quite successfully on the strength of that serio-comic twitch alone. The brushes are dirty, he tells us, dirtier, to use a professional simile that occurs to him, than a shabby priest's neckband. After a while it dawns on him, to his surprise, that the painter is not yet at his easel: "I could have sworn that the Cavaliere Cavaradossi would have been here by now." He peeps into the basket: the food and wine have not been touched. As the Angelus sounds he falls to his knees and mumbles a prayer: "Angelus Domini nuntiavit Mariae, et concepit de Spiritu Sancto. Ecce ancilla Domini; fiat mihi secundum verbum tuum. Et Verbum caro factum est et habitavit in nobis."

He rises to his feet as Cavaradossi comes in by the side door. The artist ascends the platform and removes the cloth from the picture; it is that of a Mary Magdalene with great blue eyes and a cascade of golden hair. He contemplates it for a while, the orchestra giving out a theme which we learn later to associate with the original of the picture, the Marchesa Attavanti: though some of Puccini's uses of it are rather puzzling:

6

towards the end, following the bent of Mario's thoughts, it glides into one afterwards representative of Tosca and her lover. (See No. 12.) The Sacristan stares at the picture in amazement: he has recognised the subject of it as "the unknown lady who has been coming here lately to pray devoutly to the Madonna." [1] "Quite right," agrees Cavaradossi; "and she was so absorbed in her devotions that I painted her without her being aware of it." The Sacristan is scandalised; "Get thee behind me, Satan!" he cries. Mario sets to work, painting rapidly, and now and then stepping back to study the result, while the Sacristan potters about, washing the brushes in a bowl, etc.

Cavaradossi's mind is beset by thoughts of his Tosca:

7

and, somewhat irrelevantly, he treats the Sacristan and us to a little professional discourse on the abstruse harmony that can exist between diverse kinds of beauty:

No. 8

Lento moderato

Re—con—di—ta ar—mo—ni—a   di bel—la-ze di—ver—se!

[1] As we have remarked already, it is incredible that the Sacristan should not have recognised the praying lady as the Marchesa Attavanti to whose family the "Attavanti" chapel belonged.

His ardent Tosca is dark and her eyes are black, while the unknown devotee he is painting is blonde, with eyes of the bluest
blue. "Yet Art, in its mysterious way," he muses to the accompaniment first of all of No. 7, "blends all kinds of beauty; while I am
painting this other it is still you, Tosca, who are the sole subject
of my thoughts." All through the soliloquy the shocked Sacristan
keeps mumbling *sotto voce* that "he amuses himself with puppets
and neglects the saints; these women of all sorts, rivals of the Madonna, emit a musty odour of hell. But with these dogs of Voltaireans, enemies of the Holy Office, it's best to have nothing to
do. All these fellows"—pointing to the artist though there is no
one to see or hear him but the audience—"are impenitents"; and
he makes the sign of the cross. This is the futile best that Puccini
and his librettists can do to cover the ground Sardou had been
over so fully in his account of Cavaradossi's antecedents and those
political and religious opinions of the painter that are so vital to
our understanding of his actions and motives in the Angelotti
drama.

14

It is time for the Sacristan, having played out most of his small
part in the construction of the drama, to leave us. But before he
does so there are one or two little bits of "business" he must go
through for our benefit. In the first place he has to make a final
assertion of himself as the comic relief of the piece; this he does
by hypocritical pretensions of regret, accompanied by some self-
satisfied hand-rubbing and snuff-taking, when Cavaradossi accounts for the fact that the basket of food is still untouched by
the further fact that he is not hungry. In the second place, the
Sacristan has to impress it on us that the basket is full when he
leaves the church, because, as we shall see later, this becomes, for
Scarpia, a link in the chain of evidence against Cavaradossi and
Angelotti; the whole episode, however, is managed more plausibly
in Sardou than in the opera.

With a final exhortation to Cavaradossi to close the church door
when he leaves, the Sacristan goes out, and the painter settles
down to work again, with his back, of course, turned towards the
chapel. "Angelotti," the stage directions inform us, "believing
the church to be empty now, appears behind the grille and inserts

the key, intending to open the gate." Why he should assume *both* speakers to have gone, seeing that he must have just heard the departing Sacristan tell the artist to make sure that he closes the church door when *he* goes, is an insoluble mystery to us. At a later stage of the same scene, after the colloquy between Cavaradossi and Tosca and the departure of the latter, Mario, according to the stage directions, runs at once to Angelotti, "who, of course, has heard the preceding conversation" of the lovers. If this overhearing occurs as a matter of course on that occasion, why should it not be just as much a matter of course in the earlier one? And, strange to say, when Angelotti now comes forward to open the gate his eyes serve him no better than his ears had done; he actually does not see Cavaradossi, who is right before his eyes only a few feet away. The truth is that for Puccini and his librettists the emergence of Angelotti from the chapel, and his recognition of Cavaradossi as an old friend, *had* to take place just at that point of the action and in just that way, whether plausible or not. Puccini, having in mind little beyond his lyrical expansions, troubles himself, for once, as little as need be with what he seems to have regarded as minor points of dramatic plausibility.

Cavaradossi, hearing the grating of the key in the lock, turns round with a startled cry of "Someone in there!" Angelotti, we are invited to believe, had inserted the key without seeing Cavaradossi painting within a few feet of him; it is only the noise made by Mario as he turns round on the platform that makes him aware that he is not alone in the church, as he had thought! The nervous No. 2 is now heard as he pauses in terror, and, for a moment, seems about to retreat into the recesses of the chapel. But "having raised his eyes," as the stage directions naïvely inform us, he "gives a cry of joy, which he immediately stifles in fear: he recognises the painter and stretches out his arms towards him, as if to an unexpected hope." "You, Cavaradossi!" he cries; "God has sent you!" It is a little while before Cavaradossi recognises his old friend, who has been greatly changed by his imprisonment. When he does so he ejaculates, "Angelotti! The Consul of the destroyed Roman Republic!" What meaning, if any, Puccini expected this to convey to the ordinary spectator we cannot imagine; but that he was anxious to force it on the attention of the audience is shown by his making the sentence stand out clearly without any accompaniment, and marking it "rapidly, declamatorily, loudly": manifestly he has an uneasy sense that somehow or other, somewhere or other, he must give at least a hint of that political background to the drama on which Sardou lays such stress.

15

But Angelotti has time to say no more than "I have just escaped from the Sant' Angelo castle," and Cavaradossi to reply "Count on me!", when the poor man has to make another hasty exit, for Tosca's voice is heard outside, impatiently crying "Mario!" The painter bids Angelotti get back into the chapel, telling him that the caller is "a jealous woman," and assuring him that he will get rid of her quickly. But Puccini's Angelotti is too well aware of the part the provisions basket is booked to play later in the opera to take cover there and then: instead, he staggers to the platform and says, "I am at the end of my strength; I can't hold out any longer"; whereupon Cavaradossi hands him the basket, telling him that it contains food and wine; and after a little interchange of "Hasten!" on the one side and "Thanks!" on the other, Angelotti re-enters the chapel, taking the basket with him, and Mario admits the fuming Tosca. Puccini has seen to it that that basket is forced on our attention.

Tosca, as soon as the bolt is drawn, sweeps in like the Italian prima donna she is, under full sail, with an armful of flowers:

9

She is very angry at having been kept waiting, and Mario has difficulty in allaying her suspicion that he has been entertaining a rival. Puccini does his best to present her to us as the changeful, capricious creature of Sardou's play, by turns amorous and religious. Cavaradossi makes to embrace her, but she piously reproves him: "Oh! in front of the Madonna!" And so, to the accompaniment of the insinuating No. 9 and its no less insinuating ending:

10

she arranges the flowers—"artistically," we are assured—at the feet of the statue, kneels, prays "with great devotion," crosses herself, and then turns to the painter, who artist-like, has been showing signs of wanting to get on with his work. She has come to tell him that she is singing that evening, but the opera is a short one; he is to wait for her at the stage door, and they will go straight to his villa in the country. A flash of the agitated No. 2 in the orchestra shows Mario wondering how all this is to be made to square with his plans for aiding Angelotti in his flight.[1] Whenever she speaks to him he answers her abstractedly. Abandoning herself to the luxury of her amorous imagination she paints for him the joys that await them in the villa, that hidden nest known only to them, full of mystery, warm with love:

11

Non la so—spi—ri la nos-tra ca—set—ta che tut-ta a-sco—sa nel ver—de ci a—spet-ta?

[1] Most conductors, being almost wholly intent on the music, to the neglect of the drama, dissipate much of the tension of this episode by failing to give its full value to one of Puccini's favourite devices for creating suspense—a sudden pause for both orchestra and voices. Puccini's handling of the present episode is admirably dramatic. After Tosca's "Wait for me after the performance and we will go off, just we two, to your villa," there is a quick reference to the Angelotti motive (No. 2) in the orchestra, and Cavaradossi interjects abstractedly "Tonight?!" The actor must convey to us this sudden sense on Mario's part of the difficulties that Tosca's plans bring into the arrangements made for Angelotti's flight. Tosca runs on thoughtlessly: "The moon will be full, the night scent of the flowers intoxicating." Then she senses a certain reserve on Mario's part. "Are you not pleased?" she asks him wonderingly, seating herself by him on the steps of the platform. It is at this point that the typical Puccinian pause occurs—a dead silence as Mario turns the situation over in his mind and then replies (according to the stage directions "absent-mindedly"), "Oh, of course!" That pause and its psychological implications cannot be too strongly impressed on the audience.

and we hear again the feline, caressing cadence that is so characteristic of her (No. 10).

Cavaradossi, while sharing her transports, cannot help adding, looking distractedly over her head, which is resting on his shoulder, towards the chapel, "And now leave me to my work!" She is hurt at being "dismissed," as it seems to her; and catching sight of the picture on the easel she asks who is this person with the blonde hair and blue eyes. "The Magdalen," he replies casually. After a closer scrutiny she recognises "the Attavanti," and by a misuse of the leitmotif principle—for there cannot be any possible association in Tosca's mind of the Marchesa with the prisoner who has escaped from Sant' Angelo—the orchestra gives out the Angelotti theme (No. 2). In many places in this first act Puccini uses motifs and fragments of motifs in a rather mechanical and meaningless way.

16

In vain Mario tries to calm her; now she is all jealousy. "It was she who was with you, the coquette!" she cries furiously. He patiently explains that it was by pure accident that he had lighted upon the unknown lady at her devotions. He assures her ardently that no eyes in the world can compare with Tosca's, and gradually gets her to see reason. Their voices unite in a passionate duet:

12

that is the highest musical light of the opera so far, Mario calling Tosca affectionately "My jealous one!", and she repentantly accepting the description and accepting his pardon gratefully. Towards the end of the duet she becomes kittenish again, breaking from his embrace and reproving him for having ruffled her hair —in church! At last he manages to persuade her to leave him, after she has made him promise—a point that will become of importance later in the drama—that he will go on working till the evening, will not admit any other woman to say her prayers, and will change the eyes of the Magdalen from blue to black.

She leaves behind her a thoughtful and troubled Cavaradossi.

There comes another of those musical pauses that are so frequent and so significant in Puccini, or would be if conductors in general observed them as they should. Having assured himself that there are no signs of her returning, Mario brings Angelotti out into the open: "My Tosca," he explains, "is a good soul, but so pious that she tells everything to her confessor": that is why he had thought it safest not to confide in her. While the orchestra rings the changes on the motif shown in our No. 3 Angelotti, in response to Cavaradossi's enquiries, at last reveals his plan—either to get out of Roman territory or hide in the city, according to the immediate run of events. "My sister"—"the Attavanti!" Mario interjects for our benefit—"had concealed a woman's costume there under the altar, a dress, a veil, a fan"; at dusk he was to slip out of the church disguised. The orchestra perhaps justifies our identification of No. 6 with the Marchesa when it accompanies Cavaradossi's praise of her: now he understands her visits to the church, he says; at first he had suspected some amorous intrigue on the part of the unknown lady; but it was evidently just a sister's love.

She had indeed done everything she could, says Angelotti, to save him from the scoundrelly Scarpia. (No. 1 raises itself menacingly in the orchestra, then repeats itself in softer tones and more insidious colours, like something evil lurking in the shadows.) "Scarpia!" cries Cavaradossi passionately; "a bigot, a satyr, who conceals his lusts under a mask of piety, confessor and executioner in one! I will save you if it costs me my own life!" But for Angelotti to wait until night falls is dangerous. (No reasons are given, as they are in Sardou.) Better for him to go now. The chapel opens on to an enclosed kitchen garden, from which a cornfield leads to a villa of Cavaradossi's, to which he gives Angelotti the key, telling him to take the female outfit with him. He will rejoin him there at night, he says, No. 10 in the orchestra reminding him and us of his promise to Tosca to work until it grows dark.

17

Angelotti is making for the chapel to get the clothes, when Cavaradossi stops him: "If danger threatens you at the villa," he says, "run to the well in the garden: at the bottom of it is water, but half-way down is an opening leading to a large cave, inaccessible and safe." The words are hardly out of his mouth when the usual warning to the town of a prisoner's escape from the castle booms out. Cavaradossi now decides to accompany Angelotti, and the two men leave the church hastily.

Even while they have been talking we have heard in the orchestra the merry theme of the Sacristan (No. 4)—another instance of Puccini's haphazard use of leading motifs, for the Sacristan does not enter until the others have gone. He has returned, out of breath with excitement, to give the painter, to the accompaniment of Nos. 4 and 5, a piece of news that fills him with joy but is calculated to annoy the Voltairean Cavaliere. "Your Excellency! Not here? A pity! Whoever brings grief to an unbeliever gets an indulgence."

The orchestra becomes all jubilation as a crowd of clerics, choristers, small boys and others pours into the church, to whom the Sacristan gives the glad tidings of the annihilation of Bonaparte, who has gone where he belongs—to the Devil. To a gay new melody:

13

everyone rejoices as the Sacristan tells them that in the evening there will be a grand torchlight procession, a fête at the Palazzo Farnese, a new cantata, expressly composed for the occasion and sung by Floria Tosca, and in the churches hymns to the Lord. There are loud cries of "Long live the King! Te Deum! Gloria!" But before they can complete the word "Vittoria!" they are hushed by the terrible No. 1 fortissimo in the orchestra and the appearance of the dreaded Chief of Police himself, followed by Spoletta and other minions of his. Scarpia upbraids the crowd for its scandalous uproar in the church. One by one they creep out silently. The terrified Sacristan would follow them, but Scarpia halts him. Sending the agents to search every nook and cranny of the church and chapel, he turns coldly on the Sacristan and bids him weigh his words carefully. A prisoner has escaped from Sant' Angelo and taken refuge here, he tells him, to the accompaniment of a sinister bass figure that runs through the whole of the ensuing dialogue:

14

Allegro moderato

Col 8va bassa

He may still be here. Which is the Attavanti chapel? "That is it!" replies the Sacristan. Going to the gate, he finds it, to his astonishment, open. "A good sign!" ejaculates Scarpia. He and the Sacristan go into the chapel; when they return, Scarpia is visibly annoyed at having found it practically empty except for a fan which he now dangles nervously.[1] There is a pause in the music prescribed at this point: it can hardly be too long for dramatic effect. Then Scarpia muses, "That cannon shot was a great blunder: the rascal has fled in haste. But he has left behind him a priceless clue—this fan! Who was his accomplice?" He stares long and thoughtfully at the fan: then his face brightens—"The Marchesa Attavanti's crest!" "Who painted that picture?" he suddenly asks. The trembling Sacristan replies "The Cavaliere Cavaradossi." (There is some irresponsibility, we cannot help thinking, in Puccini's use of leading motives during this episode.) "He?" says Scarpia, "Tosca's lover! A suspect! A Voltairean!"

---

[1] The librettists seem to have bungled here. In Sardou the female clothes are not in the chapel, because Angelotti has escaped in them. But in the opera they are, on the face of it, still there when Scarpia arrives. "Take the woman's clothing with you," Cavaradossi had told Angelotti (in the opera) when giving him his final instructions to make his way to the villa. Angelotti, according to the stage directions, "goes to get the clothes left by his sister." "Shall I put them on?" he asks. "No need at present," replies Mario, "for the road is deserted." As Angelotti is leaving the church Cavaradossi runs to him and tells him about the well in the garden. He has no sooner done this than the Sant' Angelo cannon booms out, and the startled pair make a hurried exit. Did the librettists intend to convey to us that Angelotti actually went into the chapel and returned with the bundle of clothes in his arms in the short space of time occupied by three bars of orchestral music, or are we to take it that his query to Mario, "Ought I to don them?", and the latter's reply, "No need at present, for the road is deserted," imply that he had only *made towards* the chapel without actually going inside? It is all very unclear.

18

Meanwhile the Sacristan has been examining the basket which one of the agents has brought out of the chapel. "Empty!" he exclaims. Scarpia, who has overheard him, quickly drags the facts out of him. The basket belongs to the painter, he stammers; it contained his usual repast, and the Sacristan can vouch that it was full when he last saw it. Cavaradossi himself could not have taken it into the chapel, for he had no key to that; and besides, he had assured the Sacristan that he had no intention of eating, as he was not hungry.

All is now becoming clear to Scarpia. But just as the solution of his problem is dawning on him, Tosca, accompanied—for no good reason that we can see—by the Angelotti motive (No. 2), enters in nervous haste. At the sight of her Scarpia conceals himself, making an imperious sign to the Sacristan to remain where he is, by the easel. Not finding Mario where she had expected him to be, Tosca goes to look for him in the nave of the church. "She must not see me," Scarpia mutters; "to bring jealousy to the brink of frenzy Iago had a handkerchief: I have a fan!"

Tosca returns, calling impatiently "Mario! Mario!" and the Sacristan approaches her. "The painter Cavaradossi?" he says; "who knows what has become of him? Vanished: spirited away by witchcraft." With that he takes to his heels—which rather makes nonsense of his terrified obedience to Scarpia's imperious order to remain where he is. His going, however, accomplishes the composer's musical purpose, which is to clear the stage for the big scene between Tosca and Scarpia which he has long since been impatient to get down to. Thoroughly in his element now, Puccini launches the theme that is to dominate the episode, one of those typically Puccinian motives that lend themselves so well to his fondness and his genius for insistent repetition:

15

(The church bells double the orchestral statement of the theme.)
To this colourful accompaniment Scarpia comes forward, offers
Tosca holy water, and, in his oiliest tones, tells her that while her
art of itself is a stimulus to piety, not content with her triumphs
on the stage she comes here to pray, very different in this respect
from some shameless creatures—he points meaningly to the
picture on the easel—who have the air and wear the robe of the
Magdalen and play at love! Her suspicions now thoroughly
aroused, Tosca demands proofs. Showing her the fan, he asks
suavely if that is a painter's implement. He had found it on the
platform, he tells her: someone must have entered and disturbed
the lovers, and in her hurried flight the lady had dropped her fan.
Tosca examines it and recognises the Attavanti crest: her forebodings have come true! To another of those repetitive phrases
which Puccini always handles with such mastery she sobs, "And
I who came here full of sorrow to tell him that in vain night
would spread its dark mantle over the earth, for Tosca, the loving
Tosca, is a prisoner of the royal jubilation"; i.e. she has been
commanded to sing at the palace that night. (It may seem curious
that she should confide all this, and in such flowery poetic terms,
to the Chief of Police; but our surprise is diminished by the knowledge that only in this way can the librettists convey this vital
information to us in the audience.) Her lament is punctuated by
melodramatic asides from Scarpia.

Undeterred by his dread presence, and regardless of the fact
that it is obviously intruding upon a private conversation, the
public infiltrates into the church again, singly, in pairs, in groups,
for of course it will be wanted very soon for the big choral ensemble that is to end the act in the best grand opera manner; but
Tosca and Scarpia continue their colloquy as if they were still
alone, with No. 15 pealing out again in the bells. Smoothly,
insinuatingly, he regrets that cheeks so beautiful as hers should
be bedewed with tears, and swears he would give his life to
bring her consolation. She hardly listens to him: "and I," she
moans, "consuming myself while he was laughing at my folly
in the arms of another!" ("My poison works!" Scarpia interjects
sotto voce; he has manifestly read *Othello.*) "If I could trap them!"
she goes on. "For a double love, no doubt, the villa serves!

Traitor! Traitor! My lovely nest soiled with mud!" (Here the fate-
laden No. 14 weaves its way through the depths of the orchestra,
which is intelligible enough; what one fails to see is just why the
Angelotti motif—No. 2—should also figure in the tissue as she
cries, "I will surprise them there! You shall not have her tonight!
I swear it!"). Scarpia piously reproves her for such a display of
mundane passion in the church. She begs God's pardon, weeps,
and goes towards the door, Scarpia accompanying her with feigned
expressions of sympathy, while the orchestra depicts her meditat-
ing on her lost happiness (No. 12).

19

Tosca having departed, Scarpia summons Spoletta to him with
a sign, the Angelotti motive (No. 2) showing us what is in his
mind. He orders his lieutenant to follow Tosca in a carriage with
three of his men and to meet him later at the Palazzo Farnese;
and, melodramatic to the last, he apostrophises his victim ironically: "Go, Tosca! Scarpia has wormed himself into your heart!"
From now onwards the psychological emphasis is on this satyr-
like passion for the singer—a motive that does not appear in
Sardou's handling of the action of this first act, and, indeed, in
the play is subordinate throughout to Scarpia's desire to save his
own head by the sacrifice of Angelotti's.

All this while the crowd has been growing in size. It is shep-
herded into two groups, one on each side of the stage, by the
Swiss soldiers who have entered with the cortège of the Cardinal.
The latter makes his way towards the high altar, blessing the
people; Scarpia inclines himself in prayer as the prelate passes.
To a broad theme that dominates the remainder of the act a
service of thanksgiving to God is begun by choir and organ, the
former murmuring their words, not singing them. The object of
this procedure is obviously to give Scarpia freer play in his
accompanying monologue; he is supposed to be communing
with himself, regardless of his surroundings. He begins by explaining for our benefit ("ferociously," say the stage directions), that
he has a double purpose in view—not merely to bring the escaped
prisoner to the scaffold but to see love for himself flaming in
Tosca's beautiful eyes as she satisfies his desire: (this "con pas-
sione erotica"), "the one" ("ferocemente") "to the halter, the

other to my arms." It is in order that he may say all this as it were *sotto voce* and still be heard by us that Puccini, in addition to keeping down the organ and the orchestra, restricts the choral co-operation to a toneless murmur.

By now the scene is fully set for the final tableau, with all heads turned towards the high altar. Choir, orchestra, and organ launch a Te Deum, with bells and cannon joining in for greater effect. Scarpia alone stands aloof, staring into the void, as if lost in a dream. Suddenly rousing himself he exclaims "Tosca, you make me forget God!"; then ("con entusiasmo religioso") he thunders "Te aeternum Patrem omnis terra veneratur!" with the rest and the best of them; and after three fortissimo reiterations of No. 1 in the orchestra the curtain falls.

On the whole this first act, dramatically speaking, is a poor piece of work. Things happen in it not because they develop naturally out of what has gone before but simply because they have to be inserted at just that point and handled in just that way purely for the enlightenment of the audience. The episode of Tosca's return to the church is a case in point. That return may be vital in the opera—the reader will remember that it does not occur in the play—but while it is understandable that the sight of the fan shall kindle her jealousy it is imposing too great a strain on our credulity to ask us to believe that she *must* confide to the Chief of Police straight away that she had come back to tell her lover that she would be unable to meet him that night as they had arranged. And Scarpia, with his sudden transitions from the cruel to the erotic and then to the religious, his often ludicrous asides, and his sudden reminder to himself at the end that Tosca has "made him forget God"—a feeble attempt to show him as the bigot and satyr in one that Cavaradossi had described to Angelotti—is the merest villain of melodrama. It may be replied that Sardou's play is melodrama in every fibre of its being. That is true; but it happens to be such consummate melodrama, so thoroughly competent at playing the game according to the rules of the game, that while we are watching it we put our critical faculty in our pocket, having no use for it; as indeed we shall do later in the case of Puccini, whose second and third acts are melodrama of the most unblushing kind, but, in virtue of the musical expression, melodrama *in excelsis*.

Sardou's cunningly constructed second act was not drawn upon by the librettists until near the end of it. It shows us a Scarpia not in the smallest degree interested amorously in Tosca but himself in danger of his life, and only gradually seeing a way out of his difficulties. In the final scene of Sardou's first act Tosca had not been brought on the scene at all, as she is in the opera. Scarpia had learned from the terrified Eusèbe that the name of the painter who had been working in the church before the escape of Angelotti was Cavaradossi. "Ah!" he ejaculated, "we are getting warm! The Chevalier Cavaradossi! A Liberal, like his father." Next it appeared that the painter had often had a visitor—Tosca; and judging from the flowers by the figure of the Madonna, Eusèbe had said, she was here today while he was absent. Scarpia has no reason to associate her in any way with the Angelotti affair: "she is faithful to the Church and the King; all the same we will keep an eye on her," since her name has been mentioned. Nothing more can be done for the present, he tells his minion Colometti, the fugitive having escaped him by a few moments; so they will join in the general thanks to the God of Armies who has given them victory over the French, and pray to the Madonna "to bless our further efforts in our war on impiety." With that the first act closes abruptly. The spoken play, of course, could not give us, as the composer can, an elaborate thanksgiving service with music; moreover, mass effects of that kind had no part in Sardou's dramatic technique. All we hear at this point in the play, according to the stage directions, is a faint suggestion of prayers and chanting in the distance. There is no one at all by the Angelotti chapel in the final moments except Scarpia, his men, and Eusèbe. It is a pity, in some ways, that the musician in Puccini thought it necessary to end the first act of the opera as he did; one feels, indeed, that by a general curtailment of his lyrical expansions he could have indulged himself in the luxury of four acts instead of three and made a better drama of his opera.

Let us now see what happens in the second and third acts of Sardou's play.

The scene of the second is the great salon in the Farnese Palace, later in the same day. The room is filled with a great crowd of talkers and card players. Among them is the Marquis Attavanti, who is throughout a fatuous figure. Also present is one Trivulce, the sigisbeo of the Marquise—the male companion permitted by Italian custom to a married lady of quality, who might or might not be her lover in the ordinary sense of the term, the beau monde not troubling itself about a detail of that kind so long as a convention that suited all the parties to the triangle was discreetly observed.

The subjects of the conversation of a group in the foreground are the two great events of that afternoon, the reported defeat of the French and the escape of the republican Angelotti. The Marquise Attavanti, it appears, is not present at the fête, or even in Rome; she has gone to Frascati. Scarpia enters, preoccupied with his own grave problem, for as yet he has not succeeded in discovering Angelotti's latest hiding-place; Cavaradossi's town house has been surrounded and the servants questioned, but the painter has not put in an appearance there. The fox no doubt has several holes, Scarpia remarks to Schiarrone; what is certain is that Cavaradossi and Angelotti are together somewhere. Tosca, the police agents have discovered, went to her own house after taking part in the rehearsal for the concert, supped alone, and is now in the Farnese palace. Scarpia does not know what to make of it all. Is Tosca an accomplice? What if Cavaradossi has been astute enough to take into his confidence a woman whom everyone knows to be of the royalist and clerical party?

21

Tosca enters, and in a brief conversation with Scarpia shows the better side of her nature: her womanly sympathies are with this prisoner who, she has heard, has escaped a horrible death, and Scarpia cannot decide whether all this is the calculated bravado of an accomplice or real ignorance. The Queen of Naples enters, and goes straight to the point with the fretted Scarpia. "Be careful lest this affair should turn out fatally for you," she warns him. "You have many enemies; unpleasant rumours circulate with regard to you; people are pointing out that this Angelotti, after being in prison for a whole year, escapes a mere week after your arrival in Rome." The criminal's sister, the Queen insinuates, is rich and beautiful. "You had better find Angelotti, tonight if possible, for if not I shall have difficulty in curbing the King's ill humour." With that she leaves Scarpia to his gloomy reflections, which are not brightened by the cries of "Death to Angelotti! Death to Scarpia!" that float up from the excited crowd in the piazza. He turns the situation over in his worried mind. If Angelotti escapes, he himself is ruined; the person he fears most is not the Queen but Lady Hamilton,[1] who will not spare him if Angelotti is not recaptured and hanged. What is he to do? Arrest Cavaradossi when he turns up at his villa? But by that time Angelotti will be far away: Scarpia must somehow get hold of both men before the city gates close that night. Is the key to the affair, he wonders again, in the hands of this singer Floria Tosca? Does she really know nothing, or is she only pretending not to know? Against the other woman, the Attavanti, he certainly has a weapon of a sort—her fan. An idea strikes him: the Attavanti being out of his reach, why not use that weapon against Tosca? Here is a notoriously amorous, explosive, jealous woman upon whom, perhaps, he can work for his own ends; "a jealous woman is more useful than any police agent." Either she knows all and he will get it out of her, or she knows nothing, in which case she will want to find out for herself the truth about the fan—and so find out for him. Now at last, he thinks, he sees his way clear: "Iago achieved his ends by means of a handkerchief";[2] he will do likewise with a fan. That fan, it is becoming ever clearer, is the tiny point upon which the whole fateful action has been poised from the first.

He engages Tosca in further conversation and gradually entangles the unsuspecting woman in his coils. He begins by sounding her on the subject of Cavaradossi. Why did she take him for her lover, this man Roman by birth but French in his opinions, this Voltairean, this revolutionary? Her reasons, which she deems sufficient, are that she loves him and he is devoted to her. Is she sure of that? he asks, casually producing the fan which, he tells her, he had found in Sant' Andrea just after the Chevalier had

---

[1] The reader will remember that, as Angelotti had informed Cavaradossi in the first act, this Baron Scarpia had just been sent to Rome, as chief of the police, by the court of Naples.

[2] As we have seen, Puccini's librettists transferred this line to Scarpia's erotic monologue in the church.

left the church—about the hour of compline. This little sentence is the explosive spark. "He told me he would remain there until night!" she ejaculates.[1] Scarpia assures her (falsely, as we know) that he had found the fan on the painter's stool while examining the picture, and, innocently assuming it to be Tosca's, had brought it away to return it to her. She denies that it is hers, examines it, and, recognising the Attavanti crest, at once succumbs to the suspicious jealousy that constitutes one half of her weathercock personality. Everything, she says, is crystal-clear now to her: the Marquise must have been concealed there when she arrived in the church, which explains why Cavaradossi had been so slow in opening the door to her and why he was so embarrassed and so anxious to get rid of her. She summons the Marquis Attavanti to identify the fan as that of his wife, which he, or rather the useful Trivulce, at once does. She becomes a raging fury, especially when she learns that the Marquise has gone to Frascati, where Cavaradossi has no doubt joined her by now. She swears she will go there and trap him, and crazily refuses to sing at the concert, Queen or no Queen, in spite of Scarpia's threat to arrest her if she disobeys the royal command. If she sings—a mere matter of a quarter of an hour, he reminds her—he promises he will assist her to find the guilty pair.

22

The Paisiello cantata is about to begin, Tosca raging madly all the time, and the company excusing her on the score of an attack of singer's nerves, when a courier enters and hands a message to the Queen from General Melas. Confident that it contains the news of another victory she reads it out to the company: but what Melas has to announce is the destruction of his army by Bonaparte at Marengo.[2] Tosca's only reaction is a glad cry that

[1] The reader will see at once how vastly superior Sardou's handling of this matter is to Puccini's. It is perfectly natural that in the spoken play Tosca should cry "He told me he would remain there until night" *after being told by Scarpia* that he had found the fan in the church after Cavaradossi had left; whereas it is mere theatrical mechanics for the opera Tosca to inform the Chief of Police that she had come back just to tell her lover that they could not meet that evening.

[2] The course of Sardou's action is quite in conformity with the historical facts and dates. Early on the morning of the 14th June the Austrians, under

now she need not sing in the victory cantata but can go straight to her vengeance: she rushes out, followed by Scarpia and his sleuths, Attavanti, much to his surprise, being ordered to go with them. That is the end of the second act.

Sardou's third act takes place at Cavaradossi's villa in the country, where Mario and Angelotti have at last arrived after a perilous crossing of Rome. The house, built by one of his ancestors, had passed later into the possession of an Englishman, from whom Mario now rents it, using it only for his secret meetings with Tosca. As no one in Rome has any reason to associate him with the place the police are not likely to look for them there; and when they further consider that no one has any cause to link his name with that of the fugitive from Sant' Angelo it is evident, he says, that they are perfectly safe. But if they should after all be traced, he tells Angelotti, they still have a trump card to play. The layout of the garden is as it had been when the house was first erected on the site in the days of ancient Rome. Someone, for safety's sake in the faraway days of barbarism, had constructed a sort of well from the shaft of which, twenty feet down, a small opening concealed by vegetation led to a chamber of some size. This had served as a hiding place for a former Cavaradossi who had got on the wrong side of the Medici through a trifling matter of an assassination: Mario had stored the chamber with all that would be required for his own retreat in case he ever got into trouble with the Roman authorities, and now it will serve to conceal Angelotti until it is safe for him to leave Rome, not by the gates but by swimming the adjacent Tiber. (We have learned already, by the way, from the conversation between the two men in the first act, that

General Melas, had attacked the French at Marengo, and, by virtue of superiority of artillery fire, had forced them to retire. Confident that his victory was final, Melas went back to his headquarters at Alessandria, leaving General Zach in command. The latter, instead of pursuing the French energetically, as he had been ordered to do, paused to consolidate his forces. Napoleon, who had arrived on the field just before a retreat became necessary, formed a new line of battle and advanced on and defeated the Austrians with heavy loss. The next morning Melas asked for an armistice. We may therefore suppose his first false report of the annihilation of the French to have reached Rome, as in Sardou, on the 16th or early 17th, and the counter-news of Napoleon's victory on the evening of the latter date.

Angelotti is provided with poison if the worst should come to the worst.)

While they talk, someone is heard approaching; it can be no one but Tosca, for she alone, besides Cavaradossi, has a key to the garden. She enters, and there follows a long scene between her and Mario in which he eventually succeeds in ridding her of her suspicions with regard to the Marchesa Attavanti, clears up the mystery of the fan, and lets her into the secret of Angelotti's escape. With one of her quick changes of mood she admires him for the nobility of his conduct, humbly begs his forgiveness, and gives him the welcome news of Bonaparte's victory. She wishes to remain with him, but he persuades her to return to the city, where he will join her on the morrow, after Angelotti has made his escape. He is rather disquieted by the thought that Scarpia's men have in all probability followed her; but even if they come now, he says, they will not discover Angelotti's hide-out. He presumes she had returned to the church after he had left and thus found the fan; when he learns that it was not so, but that Scarpia had discovered it and given it to her, they both realise the danger he is in now; it was to trap Cavaradossi, and through him Angelotti, that Scarpia had played upon Tosca's jealousy.

Cavaradossi's old servant runs in with the news that police agents are at the garden gate, and Mario calls out to Angelotti that they have been tracked down. Angelotti, in his panic, is making for some ruins in the fields; but Cavaradossi tells him it is too late for that, and sends him to the well. Scarpia, Attavanti and the police agents enter. Cavaradossi calmly assures Scarpia that Tosca is there simply because she had come to satisfy her suspicions with regard to his fidelity; this is a purely domestic affair with which the State has nothing to do. Scarpia, however, informs him coldly that he is present in the exercise of his moral duty to the community as head of the police; the Marquis Attavanti would like to know how his wife comes to be in Cavaradossi's house at this hour. Mario denies that she is there, and Tosca corroborates him. Scarpia throws off the mask; he sends Attavanti back to his Rome house, where, he says, he will no doubt find his wife, she having been too prudent to accompany her criminal brother here; and he is to inform the King that it is only a matter of minutes now before Angelotti is caught.

Having made sure that the house is surrounded, Scarpia has Mario removed to another room, where he is put to the torture, with the agonised Tosca aware of every turn of the screw, as in the second act of the opera. Bit by bit Scarpia wears Tosca down emotionally until she admits that Angelotti was there when she arrived; and in the end, to save her lover from further suffering, and in spite of his exhortations to her to stand firm, she discloses that the fugitive is in the well in the garden—again as in the opera. The exhausted Mario is brought in: he faintly asks for an assurance from her that neither of them has said anything; all she can do is to sob out an evasive "No! No! You have said nothing! Nothing!" Just then one of the agents returns with the news that Angelotti has been found in the well—but dead by poison. Mario curses Tosca for having betrayed him, heedless of her cry that she had done so to save him. As the curtain falls, Scarpia orders Cavaradossi to be taken away—"for the gallows." "And the woman?" asks Schiarrone. "The woman too!" is the reply.

23

It would have been impossible, of course, for Puccini's librettists to reproduce all the detail of Sardou's second and third acts. Music has always to work on broader and simpler lines than spoken drama, condensing and simplifying an action in order to secure room for its own more elaborate emotional expression. The librettists, to do them justice, have done some ingenious things in the way of condensation, transposing a telling dramatic point from one scene to another, and so on; and as we know that Sardou himself collaborated with Illica and Giacosa we may assume that some at any rate of these ingenious transpositions originated in the agile brain of that master craftsman of the theatre. But when all is said we are still left with the feeling that a better job might have been made of the adaptation of the play to operatic ends. We may smile as patronisingly as we like at Sardou today, but the fact remains that what he did not know about dramatic construction is not worth knowing. He foresees and provides for everything and forgets nothing: there is a reason for everything; piece fits perfectly into piece, and every one of them is indispensable. Throw all or most of this cunning dovetailing of details to the winds for a purpose other than his, and what remains of the coherence of the play?

One's grievance against Puccini and his collaborators is that they have retained enough of the original to furnish forth a few particularly striking episodes, but not preserved enough to make these always plausible or endow them with the effect they have in the play. The fan motif has been bungled. In Sardou the significance of it only slowly dawns on Scarpia; at first, at the end of the first act, it means nothing more to him than that it tallies with Trebelli's story of the plan for escape in female attire. It is only in the second act that he manages slowly to piece the facts and the broad inferences from them together. The Attavanti's complicity in the affair is proved by her fan, but she is safe in Frascati; Cavaradossi's is suggested by his flight from the church at the same time as Angelotti's, and proved by the discovery of the empty basket of provisions. To find one of the men will be to find the other. But it will have to be done before the city gates open again, otherwise Angelotti will have slipped away—which means disgrace and ruin for Scarpia—and there will remain no valid evidence against Cavaradossi. Then comes the illuminating idea. He has only been a week in Rome, but he knows—it is the business of the Chief of Police in times like these to know everything!—that Mario Cavaradossi's antecedents and behaviour have made him politically suspect, and that his mistress Tosca is notoriously a woman given to hysterical accesses of jealousy. What if the key to unlock the mystery can be found in this jealousy of hers? By playing on that, perhaps he can send her away from the palace in furious search of the elusive Cavaradossi—and have her followed. And so the first wheel of the tragic dénouement begins slowly to revolve.

How is all this handled in the opera? Very lamely. The librettists' hands were to some extent tied: the second act would obviously have to be devoted mainly to the torture scene and the murder of Scarpia, and the third act to Cavaradossi's last moments, before which, he being an operatic hero, and a tenor at that, he would necessarily have a good deal of singing to do, including an affecting farewell to Tosca. So the only place in the opera for confronting Tosca with the fan was the end of the first act; and for this purpose the librettists had to resort to the lame device of Tosca returning to the church the moment after the fan had been discovered in the chapel. She had gone away to rehearse for the evening performance in the theatre; and the only reason given us for her return now is her odd description of herself—to Scarpia —as "the prisoner of the royal rejoicings." She stalks in, calling impatiently "Mario! Mario!" The Sacristan comes forward: "You mean the painter Cavaradossi?" he asks. "Who knows where he is? Vanished, spirited away by a magician"; whereupon the old man decamps and we see no more of him for a while. Tosca has time only to say "Deceived? No, no! he could not betray me!" before Scarpia, who has been hiding behind the Madonna column, comes forward and insinuates himself into her company. Was ever a vital moment in any realistic opera so badly, so unconvincingly handled?

Without the political background of the action, again, being made clearer than it is in the opera, much of what happens, and why, is unintelligible to the spectator. In the following analysis of the remainder of the work attention will be drawn to the rather helpless efforts of the librettists to remind themselves and the audience now and then that there *is* such a background. It is a fair assumption, indeed, that they were only too painfully conscious that something would have to be done in connection with the matter. For some time, we are authoritatively told, they clung to the idea of making Cavaradossi's farewell to the world "an excessively tedious and pedantic 'Latin Hymn,' embracing, amongst a number of other topics, the whole range of politics and the arts." Puccini was both musically and dramatically right in rejecting this ending: it would have had a chilling effect on the audience to have Mario spend his last few minutes in this world spouting the political theories of 1800 instead of bidding a poignant farewell to his Tosca. But the mere fact that Illica and Giacosa wanted to do this dreadful thing at just that point seems to be proof enough that it was a last desperate attempt on their part to do what they had striven in vain to do until then—to give the fundamentally political motivation of the drama a final glimmer of a chance to assert itself.

Puccini's second act is set in Scarpia's apartment on the first floor of the Palazzo Farnese. On the left a large window looks out on to the courtyard. It is now night.

When the curtain rises we see Scarpia seated at a table laid for supper near the window, brooding on his problems and feverishly awaiting the return of Spoletta with his report:

16

Now and then he pauses in his eating and looks at his watch. Tosca is a good hawk, he muses: surely by this time his sleuths have the two men in their clutches? Tomorrow's dawn will see them both hanging from a halter; and at that comforting prospect the general quietude of the music is shattered for a moment by an upsurge of his motive (No. 1) in the orchestra.

Sciarrone (Spoletta's subordinate) enters with the news that Tosca has arrived at the palace. At a sign from Scarpia he throws the great window open, and from a room below, in which the Queen is giving a grand fête in honour of Melas, there float upwards the soft strains of a gracious gavotte:

17

Evidently the diva is not in the salon yet, says Scarpia to himself, or the cantata would have begun: then, to Sciarrone, "Wait for Tosca's arrival there, and tell her I shall expect her here when the cantata is finished; or, better still," he adds, going to a writing-desk and scribbling a few lines, "give her this note."

He resumes his brooding: "she will come," he says to himself after Sciarrone has gone, "for love of her Mario—and will give herself to my pleasure, for the deeper the love the greater the misery"; and when once again No. 1 rears itself in the orchestra it takes on a fresh psychological significance by appearing in new colours, beginning *mf* and tapering off into a sinister *ppp*. Then, to a broad melody, he surrenders himself in imagination to the blend of ferocity and eroticism that is characteristic of him: "there is more savour to a conquest by violence than to the most honeyed consent." No insipid wooings by moonlight for him, no songs to the guitar, no horoscope of flowers, no casting of sheep's eyes, no turtle-dove cooings. He is all brutal desire: "God has created every variety of beauty as of wine, and I would drain the divine work to the last drop."

Spoletta comes in, and Scarpia seats himself at the table again to interrogate him. The servile agent is trembling with fear: he and his men had followed Tosca, he says, to a rural villa hidden in a thicket. She had entered, but very soon came out again—alone. Then he had scaled the garden wall and searched the house from top to bottom—but found no Angelotti. Scarpia rises in a fury, curses him, and threatens him with the gallows. The terrified Spoletta stammers out the remainder of his story: he had come upon Cavaradossi, whose ironical manner with him was proof enough that he knew where the fugitive was hiding; so he arrested him, and now has him in the antechamber. "That's not so bad!" says Scarpia, and the orchestra gives out a sombre theme that will henceforth be associated with the sufferings of Mario under torture:

18

At that moment the choral cantata in honour of the Austrian victory is heard through the open window, and Scarpia realises that Tosca is there at last. The suave strains of the cantata:

19

contrast dramatically throughout with the increasing tension and ever-darkening colour of the stage action that accompanies it, in which No. 18 plays a cumulative part.[1]

25

An idea strikes Scarpia. Seating himself at the supper table again he orders Spoletta to bring in Cavaradossi, Roberti ("the executor of justice"), the Judge of the Fisc, Sciarrone and a scribe. Mario faces him boldly, demanding to be told why he has been brought there. Scarpia replies with elaborate courtesy, begging him, to the accompaniment of the fateful No. 18, to be seated in a chair facing the table. Mario has hardly done so when Tosca's voice is heard soaring above the chorus: "Her voice!" he ejaculates with profound emotion. Scarpia begins his interrogation quietly, smoothly. The Cavaliere no doubt knows that a prisoner escaped today from Sant' Angelo. "I did not know that," says Cavaradossi. "Yet it is said that you met him in the church of Sant' Andrea, provided him with food and wine, and took him to your villa in the country." Cavaradossi denies all knowledge of the affair and demands proofs: "your police searched the place and found nobody." Scarpia continues with the utmost suavity of tone and manner. "That merely proves how well he was concealed." Mario, too sure of himself, only laughs at him.

Scarpia rises in anger. "This is a matter rather for tears!" he says: "have a care!" The cantata, which has been steadily increasing in volume as it rises to its climax, gets on his nerves, and he closes the great window violently. Turning to Cavaradossi he thunders, "Where is Angelotti? Do you deny that you gave him food, clothes, and shelter in your villa, and that he is hiding there now?" Then, changing his tone to one of paternal solicitude, he says, "Come, Cavaliere, reflect. Your obstinacy is unwise; a confession will save you much suffering"; and a dolorous phrase in the orchestra:

20

[1] At one time Puccini thought of using some actual Paisiello music for the "cantata," but he wisely abandoned the idea.

gives a horrible emphasis to his warning. "For the last time, where is Angelotti?" Mario's replies to all his questions are simply "I deny," "I do not know."

Suddenly Tosca enters breathlessly, to a reminiscence of one of the fragments of melody associated with her; she has come, of course, in response to Scarpia's note. Surprised to find Cavaradossi there, she runs to him and embraces him. "Say nothing of what you saw at the villa, or you will be my death," he warns her *sotto voce*. She makes a sign of comprehension. To a thunderous enunciation of No. 18, which has been heard at intervals all through the scene, Scarpia warns Cavaradossi that the Judge is awaiting his confession, and Sciarrone, in response to a gesture from him, opens a door at the back that leads to the torture chamber. "Just the customary procedure at first," says Scarpia blandly to Roberti; "then as I shall direct." Roberti, the Judge and Sciarrone go into the inner room, taking Mario with them; Tosca remains behind, facing Scarpia, while Spoletta takes up a watchful position by the door.

26

Everything is now set for the tremendous scene in which Puccini rises to his greatest height as a master of the musical macabre. After some agonised phrases in the orchestra Scarpia addresses Tosca in the smoothest tones:

21

Ed or fra noi par-liam da buo-ni a—mi-ci

"And now let us have a little talk like good friends. Do not look so frightened. What about the fan?" he asks, leaning familiarly over the sofa on which Tosca is seated. "Mere foolish jealousy on my part," she replies with simulated indifference. "The Attavanti was not at the villa, then?" "No, he was there alone." "Alone? are you sure of that?" "Alone," she insists angrily. Scarpia turns towards the door and calls out to Sciarrone, "What does the Cavaliere say?" "He denies," says Sciarrone, appearing for a moment on the threshold. "Insist, then," says Scarpia; and Sciarrone goes back and closes the door. Tosca now tries irony: "Then to please you one must lie?" To a new theme:

22

the effect of which Puccini intensifies as usual by repetition, Scarpia slowly, inexorably, breaks down her poor defences. No, he replies, but the truth might shorten a very painful hour; the law must be vindicated, justice must be done. He becomes all tigerish ferocity again as he tells her, to the accompaniment of No. 22, the sinister effect of which is now increased by the writhing turns, like a serpent's coils, given to the bass line:

23

that her lover lies bound hand and foot, with an iron circlet pressing on his temples, from which blood gushes afresh at every denial on his part. Listening in nervous horror during a momentary silence in the room she hears a groan from the torture chamber. To her wild appeal for pity Scarpia replies that it rests with her to save her lover. Approaching the door he orders Sciarrone to unbind Cavaradossi. Tosca calls out Mario's name: he answers with a faint, dolorous "Tosca!": he assures her that the torture has ceased and bids her have courage and be silent.

The ever-resourceful Puccini finds music that surpasses in horror and frenzy all that has gone before as Scarpia approaches Tosca, and, disregarding her cries of "Monster! you are killing him!", first of all compliments her ironically on being more superbly tragic now than she ever has been on the stage, then suddenly reverts to the satyr and the beast of prey. He orders the door to be opened a little so that she may hear Cavaradossi's groans better as the torture is renewed. The climax comes with another reiteration of No. 23 as Scarpia asks her again and again, "Where is Angelotti? Speak! . . . Where is Angelotti?"

With the last refinement of cruelty he allows her a glance into the inner room. This comes near breaking down what remains of her power of resistance. "I can bear no more!" she moans, to a persistent sobbing figure in the orchestra:

24

Bass: D

and she begs Mario's permission to disclose the truth. In a faint voice he forbids her to speak: "What can you say? What do you know?" This exasperates Scarpia, who calls out angrily "Silence him!" Tosca falls prostrate on the sofa: Spoletta, in an attitude of prayer, murmurs some lines from the *Dies irae*. Tosca appeals for the last time to Scarpia, who stands before her silent and impassive: "it is I whom you are torturing, my soul that you are torturing." He sees that she is weakening and that the decisive moment has come: without saying another word he goes to the door and gives a sign for the torture to be resumed. A deathly quasi-silence in the orchestra, followed by one of Puccini's usual significant pauses, is broken by a harsh reminder of No. 1, at the end of which Tosca murmurs brokenly, "In the well in the garden."

His end gained at last, Scarpia orders the torture to cease. "He has fainted," says Sciarrone, appearing in the doorway. "I must see him," Tosca insists, and at a word of command from Scarpia the victim is brought in, to dolorous accompanying figures in the orchestra. The fainting man is laid by the police agents on the sofa: Tosca runs to him, but recoils and covers her eyes with her hands as she sees the blood on his temples. Then, ashamed of her weakness, she covers his face with tears and kisses, while the orchestra gives out a poignant reminiscence of a phrase from their duet in the first act, to which Cavaradossi had then sung the words "What eyes in the world can compare with yours, eyes tender with love?"

The myrmidons of justice leave the stage, only Spoletta and the police agents remaining behind at a sign from Scarpia. Cavaradossi and Tosca murmur a few tender words to each other: then he asks her faintly, "Did I speak?" "No," she assures him. "Truly?" Once more she replies "No." But as No. 1 projects itself in the orchestra again Scarpia says loudly, "In the well in the garden. Away, Spoletta!" Hearing this, Mario turns on Tosca and curses her for having betrayed him.

Then for the first time in this act there comes a piece of poor dramatic construction.

28

We have seen that in Sardou the news of Bonaparte's victory at Marengo is brought to the company—which includes Tosca and Scarpia—assembled in the Palazzo Farnese to celebrate the supposed triumph of Melas. The incident serves there a double purpose, to bring the party and the act to a quick and telling dramatic close, and to make it unnecessary now for the impatient Tosca to remain in the palace to sing in the cantata; she is free to go away at once to surprise Mario, as she hopes, with the Marquise, and Scarpia can set Spoletta on her traces. In the opera the battle of Marengo has no bearing whatever on the dramatic action. Why then is it introduced into the opera at the point at which we have now arrived?

For no other *dramatic* reason—the musical reason will appear later—than that the librettists, uneasily aware of the importance of the political background of Sardou's play, but having had no opportunity as yet to make us acquainted with it, suddenly decided to create, by hook or by crook, an opportunity here. The composer had rightly rejected their desperate plan to make Cavaradossi spout political and other theories in the tense final scene of the last act. The opportunities in the first act for sketching in the background against which Angelotti and Cavaradossi play their parts had been sacrificed to Puccini's determination to devote the major part of his space in that act to the lyrical endearments of Tosca and Mario and the imposing grand opera finale. The close construction of his second act as a whole provided no moment for a political manifesto on Cavaradossi's part, so one had to be made; and in the nature of the case it could not possibly be made anywhere but here.

The episode that now follows, dramatically considered, will not bear critical examination. Not the slightest hint has been given us previously of any passionate interest taken by Cavaradossi in the Franco-Italian events of the day; nor, indeed, is any light thrown for us on the activities that had brought Angelotti to Sant' Angelo, apart from that meaningless recognition of him by Cavaradossi as "the Consul of the destroyed Roman Republic." The bringing of the news of Marengo, at the point in the opera which we have now reached, has not the smallest bearing on either the past, the present or the future of the action. And how is the news brought? Cavaradossi has just cursed Tosca, and the latter has replied with an appealing "Mario!", when Sciarrone runs in out of breath, stammering "Your Excellency, such news!" Scarpia is naturally surprised at the intrusion of his hireling. "A despatch announcing a defeat," says Sciarrone, "at Marengo. . . . Bonaparte is victor. . . . Melas is retreating." Can we imagine this cowed hound of a police agent, who, like Spoletta, is always in mortal fear of his Chief, presuming to break in in this fashion on a colloquy between Scarpia, Cavaradossi and Tosca?

As to the dramatic incongruity of the exhausted Mario suddenly finding strength to deliver a long tirade in praise of the French victory and liberty we need say little. After all, operatic tenors in general, and Italian opera tenors in particular, often manage to display a remarkable vigour of lung and larynx even when at the point of death; and we must bear in mind that this is the only opportunity the tenor of *Tosca* has had during the whole long second act to impress it on us that he *is* the tenor. So far he has had only an acting part, making an interjection here and there in merely conversational tones. The hero cannot be expected to leave the stage without giving us at least one taste of his vocal quality, to which end the composer now kindly gives him a liberal allowance of high A flats. So Puccini bows the knee to operatic convention; and after all we forgive him, if not dramatically at any rate musically, for Mario's outburst is of itself excellent, electrifying stuff.

29

"Cavaradossi," say the stage directions, "who has listened to Sciarrone with increasing eagerness, finds, in his enthusiasm, the strength to confront Scarpia threateningly," while the orchestra gives out—*ff*, *tutta forza*—our example No. 6. "Vittoria! Vittoria!" he cries, soaring at once to the high A flat: "The avenging dawn has come that will make the impious, the inhuman tremble":

25

"Liberty raises its head once more; the tyrants go down in ruin! I rejoice in the martyrdom I have suffered; your heart quakes within you, Scarpia, hangman!" Tosca implores him distractedly to be silent. Scarpia merely laughs sarcastically; "Bluster, howl as you please," he says to Cavaradossi; "you are only showing me the depths of your criminal soul. Your last hour is nigh! The scaffold awaits you!"

Exasperated at last by Mario's outcry Scarpia orders the agents to remove him; they drag him off, in spite of Tosca's frenzied appeals. She would go with him, but Scarpia restrains her. He seats himself at the table again, composed and smiling, resumes his interrupted supper, and politely invites her to join him in a glass of Spanish wine, suggesting that perhaps between them they may after all find some means of saving Cavaradossi. Taking a seat at the table, leaning her elbows on it with her face cupped in her hands, looking at him with the profoundest disdain, she goes straight to the point. "How much?" she asks him: "your price?" He smiles imperturbably to the accompaniment of a suggestion of No. 6: "I know they call me venal," he remarks, "but I do not sell myself to beautiful women for money"; and he repeats the latter part of the sentence meaningly. He has long waited for this moment, he continues, has long been consumed by love for the great singer:

26

Andante appassionato

but more than ever does he desire her now that he has seen her weep; her tears were lava to his passion, and the look of hatred she had darted on him had added an agreeable ferocity to his appetite. He rises and approaches her with outstretched arms. She flies from him, first taking refuge behind the sofa, then running to the window. The idea occurring to her to go to the Queen for protection she makes for the door. Divining her intention he stands aside, knowing that he still holds the trump card. "You are free to go if you wish," he remarks ironically, "but your hopes would end in nothing: the Queen's grace would be bestowed only on a corpse." She collapses on the sofa again, directing on him a look of supreme hatred and disgust. "How you hate me!" he remarks complacently. "This is how I would have you—convulsions of rage, convulsions of love."

30

The psychological argument is degenerating into a physical pursuit round the sofa, chairs and table when distant drum beats, coming ever nearer, are heard. Scarpia explains them to her; it is the escort of some condemned men who are going to their doom. Tosca recoils from the window in horror as he tells her that down there a scaffold is being erected: her Mario, thanks to her, has only one hour to live. The tattoo dies away again in the distance.

Tosca, exhausted with grief and terror, sinks on to the sofa; and while Scarpia, leaning against the table and pouring himself a glass of wine, keeps his cool cynical gaze fixed on her, she breaks out into a lament over her shattered life. For art and love she had lived, she says:

27

without doing harm to a single soul; the griefs of others she had assuaged. Always, she continues, to the accompaniment of the melody of No. 9, her prayers had ascended to the saints, always she had decked the altar with flowers. She has given her jewels

for the mantle of the Madonna, her song had soared to Heaven.
Why then does God desert her in her hour of misery?

Scarpia's only reply is a pitiless "Decide!" She falls on her knees
before him, and to the accompaniment of a long orchestral lament
humbly begs for pity. "You are too beautiful, Tosca," he tells her,
with No. 6 making another appearance in the orchestra, "too
loving. I yield"—that is to say, he will grant Cavaradossi his
life: "a poor price for you to pay, but for me, a life." She repulses him with scorn. There is a knock at the door, and in response to Scarpia's cry of "Who is there?" Spoletta enters with
the news that Angelotti had taken poison when they found him.
"Ah well!" says Scarpia, "string him up on the gallows dead! [1]
As for the other prisoner, wait a moment." He turns to Tosca
with a laconic "Well?" There is another of those expressive Puccinian silences: then she moans "Yes!" and, bursting into tears,
buries her head in the cushions of the sofa. "But I must have him
set free this instant!" she interjects as Scarpia is about to give his
instructions to Spoletta.

He explains to her, *sotto voce*, that dissimulation will be necessary: the pardon must be kept secret; it must be believed by everyone that Cavaradossi is dead. "This trusty man"—indicating Spoletta—"will see to it." To prove his good faith he will give the order
in her presence. "Spoletta," he says, while the orchestra plays in
sinister fashion on No. 1, "I have changed my mind: the prisoner
is to be *shot*, like Palmieri: listen carefully—a fictitious execution,
as in the case of Palmieri. You understand?" Spoletta has already
conveyed by a glance that he has divined his Chief's sinister intention; now he gives his verbal assurance. Tosca's request that
she shall be the one to tell Cavaradossi of the plan is granted. "At
four in the morning," says Scarpia as he dismisses Spoletta, who
goes out with a meaningful "Like Palmieri!"

[1] For the reason for this we have to go back to Sardou. The Queen, it will
be recalled, had threatened Scarpia with the King's displeasure if he were
cheated of the satisfaction of having Angelotti recaptured and hanged; the
Roman mob too had been clamouring for the Chief of Police's head. So in
Sardou's fourth act, Scarpia, for his reputation and his safety's sake, orders
Spoletta to conceal the fact that Angelotti had tricked him by taking poison,
and to hang the dead man on the scaffold: "leave the body there, in the view
of all, until the hour of High Mass."

Scarpia now turns, full of passion, to Tosca: "I have kept my promise," he tells her. "Not yet," she replies; "I want a safe-conduct out of the Roman States for myself and him." The dramatic atmosphere now darkens, in a way that is possible only to music among the arts, by the whispering in the orchestra of a new motive that warns us to look beyond Scarpia's smooth perfidy to the tragic end of the drama:

The poignant sequel to this:

becomes of particular importance later. It is to repetitions of this motif that Scarpia seats himself at the desk and writes out a safe-conduct—"*via* Civita Vecchia,"[1] as she insists. While he is thus engaged she goes to the supper table and with a trembling hand takes up a glass of wine. But as she does so her glance happens to fall on a sharp-pointed knife; and a sudden startling surge in the orchestra suggests that a plan has occurred to her. Carefully concealing the knife behind her as she leans against the table, she waits until Scarpia, having signed and sealed the safe-conduct, brings it to her with arms outstretched to embrace her. He has barely time to ejaculate "Tosca, mine at last!" before she strikes the knife into his heart: "This is Tosca's kiss," she tells him. Writhing in agony he calls raucously, incoherently, for help. (The orchestral turmoil here is curiously suggestive of the furious outburst that follows the slow movement of the Ninth Symphony.) She gloats over his death agonies: "Your blood chokes you? You

[1] Where the Roman writ does not run.

have tortured me enough: now you die, killed by a woman! Die damned! Die! Die! Die!"

The sombre No. 28 coils and uncoils itself still in the orchestra as she washes her right hand in water from a carafe, adjusts her hair before a mirror on the wall, runs to the desk and searches feverishly for the safe-conduct, only to discover in the end that it is still in Scarpia's hand. She nerves herself to loosen the grip of the dead fingers on it, and as she gazes down on the body she ejaculates, on a note in the lowest part of her voice, "And this was the man before whom trembled all Rome!"; then she takes two candles from a bracket, lights them from the candelabra on the supper table, and extinguishes the latter. While the Scarpia motive (No. 1) repeats itself three times in ghostly orchestral tones that harmonise with the darkened atmosphere of the room she lays a candle on either side of the head of the corpse: then, catching sight of a crucifix hanging on the wall, she takes it down, kneels by the dead man, and slowly drops it on his breast—a last supremely ironic tribute to the loathsome piety of the satyr: then she stealthily steals out, closing the door noiselessly behind her. So ends the most macabre, and the most impressively macabre, scene in all opera.

32

Between the terrific tension of the second act and the even greater tension of the final stage of the drama the spectator's nerves would obviously need a little rest; and this Puccini supplied in full measure in the opening scene of the third act. Before the curtain rises, however, there is a short orchestral introduction —sixteen bars only—the tragic significance of which will not be manifest until later: the horn quartet gives out fortissimo, in unison, a melody which Cavaradossi and Tosca will sing later in the last few delusive moments of their life together on earth.

The curtain opens on a parapet in the castle of Sant' Angelo. On the left of the stage is a casemate, and in front of it a table (with writing materials, a large register, and a lantern) and a chair; in the background is a bench. On one of the walls of the casemate is a crucifix, with a hanging lamp in front of it. On the right we see the top of a small staircase that communicates with the courtyard below. In the far background the Vatican and St.

Peter's are visible. The air is clear, the night sky studded with stars: it is the early morning after the murder of Scarpia.

A series of descending thirds and fifths in the orchestra:

30

conveys a curious sense of morning freshness and serenity: towards the end of the prelude, however, there are sinister suggestions of No. 1. In the distance, growing fainter and fainter, we hear a tinkling of cow-bells; and to the accompaniment of the tranquil pastoral No. 30 a shepherd boy, far away, sings a simple little song in the vernacular. The first grey of dawn appears, and a distant sound of morning bells at different pitches trembles for a while on the quiet air, over a subdued, slow-moving strain in the orchestra, one phrase of which:

31

is particularly insistent.

An immense early morning peace is still brooding over the scene as a gaoler comes up the staircase with a lantern from which he lights first the lamp at the foot of the crucifix, then the one on the table; then he goes to the end of the parapet and looks into the courtyard below for the military picket he is expecting, bringing with it Cavaradossi. He exchanges silent greetings with a sentry on patrol, then seats himself outside the casemate and falls into a doze. All this time the strain of which No.·30 is part persists in the orchestra, with a faint reference at one point to the theme of the duet between Cavaradossi and Tosca in the first act (No. 12).

While the bells sound nearer and nearer, the picket, accompanied by a sergeant, appears on the parapet, bringing Cavaradossi with it, and the orchestra gives out the main phrases of the aria he will shortly sing:

At the sight of the sergeant the gaoler rises and salutes; the former gives him a paper which he reads; then he opens the register and enters the interrogatories and the replies: "Mario Cavaradossi? You have an hour to live. A priest is at your service if you desire one." The sergeant, having signed the register, goes out with the picket by way of the stairs.

33

Cavaradossi rejects the offer of the consolations of religion, but begs, to the accompaniment of No. 12 in the most poignant tones of the violoncellos, the granting of a last request. He is leaving a dearly loved one behind him: will the gaoler deliver a last message to her? He offers the man his sole possession, a ring; the gaoler, after a moment's hesitation, gives a sign of assent, takes the ring, and retires to the bench in the background. Cavaradossi seats himself at the table and begins to write, the violoncellos once more singing the tender No. 12.

He begins his famous aria, "E lucevan le stelle," at first reciting the substance of it as he writes, then abandoning the pen as memories of Tosca overwhelm him: the orchestral tissue is built up out of the examples shown above as Nos. 32, 33, 34. He recalls his ecstatic hours in the villa with Floria: No. 34, to which he sings of her kisses and caresses, is of particular importance; it becomes the expression of his passionate grief at the shattering

271

of all his hopes of happiness, and will be chosen later for the final summing-up of the tragedy. No. 33 is more especially associated with his cry of "I die despairing."

No. 12 is heard again in soft tones in the orchestra as Spoletta enters by way of the staircase, bringing with him the sergeant (carrying a lantern) and Tosca: with a silent gesture to the latter, indicating where she will find Cavaradossi, he goes out again, taking the sergeant and the gaoler with him, leaving the sentry, however, and bidding him keep an eye on the prisoner. There is a passionate outburst in the orchestra as Tosca runs to the weeping Mario, and, unable to speak for joy, raises his bowed head and shows him the safe-conduct. He takes it from her and they read it together: "Permission for Floria Tosca and the Cavaliere accompanying her. . . ." The signature awakes a slight suspicion in him. "This is Scarpia's first act of grace," he says. "And his last," adds Tosca grimly, for with the help of the Madonna and the saints she had killed him after procuring the safe-conduct, in the very moment of what he thought was his triumph over her; and we hear again in the orchestra the sinister strains of No. 28.

In an access of gratitude and admiration Mario takes her hands in his—the white hands that had been dipped in blood for his sake: "dear hands, so gentle, so pure, made for caressing children, for culling roses, for raising in prayer":

35

At the words "You dealt him death, victorious hands," we hear another brief reminiscence of No. 28 in the orchestra.

She tells him of the arrangements she has made for their flight —a carriage, money, jewels—and of the plan agreed upon with Scarpia for a sham execution. The guns will not be loaded; as they fire, he is to fall and simulate death; the soldiers will go away, and they two will make straight for Civita Vecchia, where a vessel will carry them across the sea to safety. They revel for a while in imagination in the joys of freedom and a new life together; then, recalling themselves to reality, she gives him his instructions once more: he must act the death fall realistically, but without injuring himself, just as she herself, with her experience of the stage, would do!

34

As the firing squad under the command of an officer emerges from the stairway the lovers indulge in a final ecstasy of love and hope—a repetition of the unison melody for the horns with which the act had begun; there it had had a certain sombre impressiveness; here, sung by soprano and tenor alone, without any supporting harmonies in the orchestra, it reveals itself as one of Puccini's least distinguished inventions. While the officer is marshalling his men in the background the sergeant, the gaoler and Spoletta appear, and the police agent gives the myrmidons of the law their instructions. A lugubrious prison bell tolls the hour of four; whereupon the gaoler removes his cap, and, going up to Cavaradossi, points to the officer and then descends the stairs, taking the register of condemnations and executions with him. Laughing quietly to herself Tosca reminds Mario once more to be sure to fall flat the moment the volley is fired, and, himself smiling, he promises to do so "like Tosca on the stage"; then they remind each other of the necessity for a façade of seriousness.

At that moment the orchestra strikes in softly with the most tragic theme in the work, the motive of the *real* execution—"as in the case of Palmieri":

36

Cavaradossi, having bidden Tosca a last farewell, follows the officer and the sergeant to the spot by the wall pointed out to him. Tosca places herself opposite, by the casemate, the better to observe him. The sergeant would bind his eyes, but Mario motions him away with a smile. It is now almost day. Tosca becomes impatient at the tedious slowness of it all; "Why this delay?" she asks them; "I know it is all a comedy, but you make this suffering seem endless. Come, present arms!"; and No. 36, which has been repeating itself incessantly, maddeningly, in the true Puccini manner, modulates and rises to a climax of anguish [1]:

37

35

The officers and the sergeant arrange the procedure of the execution, giving each man his separate instructions. As the officer is about to give the order to fire by lowering his sword, Tosca puts her hands over her ears, impulsively murmuring, however, "How splendid my Mario is!" and as the volley rings out she cannot help adding "See, now he is dying! What an artist!" And she sends him a kiss with her hand.[2] The sergeant inspects the

[1] There can hardly be the least doubt that when Puccini wrote the music for this episode he was subconsciously recalling the Transformation Music in *Parsifal*: apart from the basic resemblances of manner between the two—certain similarities of melodic and harmonic procedure, the cumulative effect of persistent repetition, etc.—we have only to compare our No. 37 with this passage from the climax of the Transformation Music:

Puccini's admiration for Wagner knew no bounds. A friend who called on him in his last years found him hypnotically absorbed in the score of *Tristan*: he put it aside with the resigned comment, "After this, what are we all but a lot of mandoline strummers and dilettanti? . . . This terrific music reduces us to nothingness. . . ." His greatest admiration was for *Parsifal*; we are told that he would play the Prelude, the Transformation Music and the Good Friday Music without the score for hours on end. The amazing thing is that in spite of this powerful German influence his genius went its own appointed way in perfect self-assurance from first to last, always Italian and never anything but Puccini.

[2] In no other opera of Puccini, with the exception of *Madam Butterfly*, are the stage directions so numerous and so detailed as in *Tosca*. Many of them

body carefully and is about to give the *coup de grâce* when Spoletta restrains him.[1]

All this while the orchestra has been thundering out Nos. 36 and 37. The officer, the soldiers, the sergeant, the sentry and Spoletta having all left the stage by the stairway, Tosca rushes to Mario's body and bends over it: her consuming fear is that he may be imprudent enough to move too soon. She looks cautiously over the parapet, then returns to him, with a warning "Not yet! Do not move!" At last, her fears allayed, she tells him to rise: "Mario! Up! Quick!" Touching him, she realises the horrible truth and throws herself in desperation on his body, sobbing "Mario! Your poor Floria!" From below there now come the muffled exclamations of Spoletta, Sciarrone and the soldiers: "It is true . . . Stabbed! . . . Tosca!"; for the murder of Scarpia has been discovered. "She must not escape! Watch the stairs!"

The sobbing Tosca has the prostrate body in her arms when they pour upon the scene from below. Spoletta, shouting "You shall pay dearly for his life!", tries to seize her, but she pushes him away violently towards the staircase. "With my own life!" she cries: "Oh Scarpia, before God!" She hurls herself over the parapet, leaving Spoletta and the others gazing after her in blank incredulity; and half-a-dozen bars devoted to a fortissimo enunciation of No. 34 in the orchestra bring the blood-curdling scene to a close.

There cannot be many operas in which the mortality rate is so high as in *Tosca*; not one of the principal characters is left alive at the finish. Sardou's appetite for slaughter seems to have grown with what it fed on. "He wants that poor woman dead at all

are taken directly from Sardou, who, like the first-rate craftsman he was, always gave his actors every possible assistance in this line. In the play, however, Tosca leaves the stage at the moment of firing, her feelings being too much for her; she returns, when all is over, to find Spoletta bending over the body. We shall probably not be far wrong in assuming that the copious stage directions for the scene in its changed operatic form were Sardou's work. They are from first to last in his vein.

[1] This little stroke of stagecraft, which is not in the play, is surely Sardou's; he had not forgotten that in the opera Tosca is still on the stage, and that the comedy of the mock execution has to be played out to the end with this last cruel refinement of suspense.

costs," Puccini wrote humorously to Giulio Ricordi in January 1899. "Now that Deibler's [1] sun has set, the Magician insists on being his successor. . . . On Tuesday morning I must go to see Sardou again. . . . Perhaps he will insist on killing Spoletta too. We shall see." However, Spoletta was allowed to survive.

[1] The famous Paris executioner of the period.

Madam Butterfly

GIACOMO PUCCINI [1858–1924]

PRINCIPAL CHARACTERS

Cho-Cho-San (Madam Butterfly)	Soprano
Suzuki	Mezzo-soprano
Kate Pinkerton	Soprano
Lieutenant B. F. Pinkerton	Tenor
Sharpless	Baritone
Goro	Tenor
Prince Yamadori	Baritone
The Bonze	Bass
Yakuside	Baritone
The Imperial Commissioner	Bass

1

Puccini's Muse was a lady with a passion for travelling. She took him first of all, in *Le Villi*, to the German Black Forest, and abandoned him at the last, in *Turandot*, in China, having meanwhile whisked him through Paris, Florence, Rome, the Wild West of America and Japan; and it was only by resolute evasive action on his part that he prevented her from carrying him off to India (in quest of the Buddha) and various other places—for no composer has ever considered and rejected a greater multiplicity of opera schemes than he. In 1900 it became the turn of Japan. In the early summer of that year he happened to be in London, helping Covent Garden to produce *Tosca*, and friends took him to the Duke of York's Theatre, where he saw the American David Belasco's *Madam Butterfly*, which had been based, with many alterations, on a story by another American, John Luther Long. He was unable to understand a word of the text;

277

but the story and the effective theatrical handling of it struck deeply into his artistic subconsciousness. For one thing, here was yet another incarnation of the type that always fascinated him, the woman who suffers cruelly through love. For another, the drama gave him a change of milieu that was a life-long necessity to him if his creative imagination was to be continually re-fertilised. Finally, there was much in the play which he must have instinctively felt called out for musical treatment, especially the moving episode of Butterfly's lonely vigil between the first and second scenes of the one-act American drama, fourteen minutes of miming and clever scenic effects without a word being spoken. Puccini no doubt felt that with his music he could make that interlude even more emotionally telling than Belasco had done, master of "theatre" as he was.

There followed, in course of time, the usual struggles with his librettists—in this case Illica and Giacosa—and with his own self-doubts and technical difficulties. One of these latter, which beat him for a long time, was the length of the second (the final) act of the opera, which, as it turned out, went against the work at its first performance. It was not until near the end of 1903 that he finished his score, and the opera was given for the first time, with Rosina Storchio, a fine singer and actress, as Butterfly, at the Scala, Milan, on the 17th February 1904. (Giuseppe de Luca was the Sharpless: the conductor was the experienced Cleofante Campanini.) It was a complete fiasco; never before or since, in all probability, has an audience, even an Italian operatic audience, treated the world to such an exhibition of bestial malignity towards a composer; the only valid explanation of it all is that the opposition was organised by some of Puccini's rivals and personal enemies.[1] The composer and his publishers withdrew the work next day. Puccini proceeded to make sundry alterations to it, the most drastic of which was to divide into two acts the overlong second, which originally ran to something like an hour and a half. In its revised form the work was given at Brescia on the 28th

[1] It is sometimes urged that it was the length of the second act that exhausted and exasperated the audience; but it is clear from contemporary accounts that the hostility of a large section of it had been evident from the beginning of the performance.

May 1904, with Salomea Krucenisca as Butterfly, Storchio not being in Italy at that time. It was now a resounding success, and quickly became popular in one country after another.

The minor changes in the score consisted for the most part in the excision of a number of details insignificant in themselves but theatrically harmful, slowing down the main action as they sometimes did. They had crept into the original score because of Puccini's over-anxiety to impress the Japanese milieu of the work on the audience. As he was to do years later in the case of *Turandot*, he had laboured conscientiously during the gestation of *Madam Butterfly* at getting the exotic milieu of the work thoroughly into his blood and bones, reading a good deal about Japan and Japanese customs, getting hold—with the assistance of the wife of the Japanese Ambassador to Italy—of such fragments of Japanese music as he could, and so on; and the knowledge he himself had found necessary he thought equally necessary to the audience.[1] We must disabuse ourselves, however, of the notion that he was trying to be authentically "Japanese" in his opera, any more than in *Turandot* he tried to be specifically "Chinese"; it was simply the Italian composer Puccini expressing himself within a framework of Japanese characters and Japanese surroundings.[2] When, at a later date, he was producing *The Girl of the Golden West* in New York, he said, somewhat naïvely but quite sincerely, that he believed the work to be really American. After assuring an interviewer that "the music cannot really be called American, for music has no nationality," he went on to say, "For this drama I have composed music that, I feel sure, reflects the spirit of the American public, and particularly the strong, vigorous nature of the West. I have never been West, but I have read so much about it that I know it thoroughly." So it had been with the "Japan" of *Madam Butterfly*, and so it was to be again with the

[1] Mme Ohyama, the Ambassador's wife, criticised adversely some of the Japanese names in the libretto. "Yamadori," for instance, she declared to be "feminine."

[2] Or rather pseudo-Japanese. The general European view of the Japanese in general and Japanese women in particular at that time was largely derived from Japanese prints and Pierre Loti's *Madame Chrysanthème*. "Japanese" musical comedy had come into fashion in the London theatre in the late nineties; *The Geisha* dates from 1896, *San Toy* from 1899.

"China" of *Turandot*. He would have agreed, had the point ever been put squarely to him, that what he "knew thoroughly" was not the actual Japan or the actual China, but the Japan or China of his own imagination. He was perfectly within his rights as an artist in giving his music here and there—by means of unusual scales, unconventional harmonies, quaintly-turned melodies, orchestral colouring, piquant effects and so on that would have been out of place in an opera less exotic—a shape and a tinge appropriate to the "Japanese" milieu as he imagined it. All we in our turn are asked to do is to play the musical game on his terms, as we play it on Verdi's terms in the "Egyptian" *Aïda*.

2

The opera has no formal overture: it begins with a quasi-fugal elaboration of an animated theme first heard in the violins:

which, with a later pendant:

defines for us at once the main outlines and the dimensions of the world in which the drama is going to be played, a small and, in the amused eyes of a young American naval officer, a quaint world, in which small quaint people are fussily occupied with small quaint things.[1] When the curtain rises we see a Japanese house with its little terrace and garden on a hill overlooking Nagasaki, the town itself and the harbour being visible below in the background. From the house emerges the marriage broker Goro, bowing and scraping obsequiously as he points out the vir-

[1] It becomes evident from some of his later uses of our No. 2 that Puccini wishes us to associate it more or less specifically with Nagasaki.

tues of the house to the new lessee, Lieutenant B. F. Pinkerton [1] of the United States Navy. Goro shows how a sliding partition can transform the aspect and the utility of the place, how the rooms can become whatever the occupant may desire at any given moment: here is the nuptial chamber, there the hall, though everything can be changed at will, the inside becoming the outside and vice versa, the view from the terrace being open or closed by a mere touch of the finger on a partition. All this explanation goes on to the incessant chattering of No. 1 and No. 2 in the orchestra, and with many bows and genuflections, graphically represented in the music, on the part of the deferential Goro. Pinkerton is enchanted with the novelty and the convenience of everything.

There is a change in the music as the broker reveals other amenities of this desirable suburban residence. He claps his hands three times and a woman and two men enter and make deep obeisances to the Lieutenant: they are (1) the devoted maid (Suzuki) of the new mistress of the house, (2) the cook, (3) the man-of-all-work, and bear respectively the poetic names of Miss Gentle Cloud of Morning, Ray of the Rising Sun, and—even the respectful Goro permits himself a discreet smile at this—Aromatic Odours. [2] Pinkerton decides that it will be simpler for him to call them "Mug One," "Mug Two," and "Mug Three." Suzuki politely ventures to remind him of the value of a smile in all human relations; but as Pinkerton looks bored with her flowery language Goro claps his hands thrice and the servitors all run off into the house.

Goro now prepares Pinkerton for a number of expected visitors—the bride, her relations, the Official Registrar and the American Consul; the bride's relations will include her mother, her grandmother, cousins male and female, about a couple of dozen other collateral branches, and an uncle, the Bonze (Priest), who, however, is hardly likely to grace the proceedings with his august

[1] In performances in English he becomes F. B. Pinkerton. This inversion of the initials is quite inexplicable; what *could* B. F. be taken to stand for but "Benjamin Franklin"?

[2] There was once a Japanese heavyweight boxing champion with a knockout punch on whom his countrymen bestowed the poetic name of Plum-Blossom Fist.

presence. So much for the ascendants; as for the descendants, Goro, with a smirk, leaves all that to the Lieutenant. Running through all this colloquy is a dainty theme:

to which Puccini gives a quiet little touch of the exotic by the simple insertion at one point of a B flat into a melody that is otherwise C major pure and simple.

A voice is heard at a little distance; it is that of the American Consul, Sharpless, who enters to the accompaniment of two new conjunct themes, each on the miniature scale of all that has gone before:

The Consul, rather out of breath after his climb, looks out admiringly at the town and the harbour and the sea below. While Goro and a couple of servants are setting out two wicker lounge chairs, two glasses, and the materials for whisky and soda, Pinkerton, very pleased with himself, tells Sharpless how he has acquired this fantastic little dream-place on a nine hundred and ninety-nine years' lease with the option of terminating the agreement any time at a month's notice, legal contracts in Japan, he says, being apparently as elastic as the houses.

3

So far the music has all been on an appropriately miniature scale, a number of tiny motifs being woven skilfully into a continuous texture. (This would be a virtue in the score which a first-night audience would hardly be likely to appreciate.) But with the passage of the action into what may be called the American zone a change comes over the musical idiom; the melodies are now more sweeping, the harmonies less exotic, the whole texture more solid. Pinkerton expounds for the Consul's benefit his own hedonist philosophy of life. The Yankee, he says, wanders over the earth:

5

Do-vun- que al mon-do   lo Yan-kee va-ga-bon-do

intent on business or pleasure, casting anchor where and when it suits him, until he runs into a squall, and then—as is apparently the case with him just now—life isn't worth living unless he can solace himself with the best of the pleasures and the loves of the country in which he happens to find himself; this he now means to do, marrying "in Japanese fashion" for nine hundred and ninety-nine years (with a monthly escape clause). From time to time the Consul, an older man, breaks in with a word of friendly criticism of "this easy-going gospel," to a phrase that impresses itself on our memory:

6

The Lieutenant, however, brushes aside the counsels of prudence with a toast of "America for ever!", in which Sharpless joins him as in duty bound.

The music reverts imperceptibly to the dainty "Japanese" manner, with a repetition of the tiny motifs shown in our No. 4, as Pinkerton enlarges poetically on the beauty and charm of his bride—"and all for a bagatelle," Goro interjects, "a matter of a mere hundred yen." He offers his professional services as marriage broker to the Consul, who laughingly declines them.

At a peremptory order from the impatient Lieutenant, Goro goes down the hill to usher in the bridal company, and Pinkerton seizes the opportunity to rhapsodise once more about the fragile beauty, the butterfly lightness and simple charm of his bride,

Puccini, with consummate art, striking a middle course in his music between the everyday reality of the American human element and the exotic pseudo-Japanese. The former predominates as Sharpless tells how Butterfly had called at the Consulate a few days ago; though he had not seen her, he had been struck by a mysterious something in her voice that seemed to breathe sincerity of affection; it would be a pity, he says, to break those delicate wings, and with them a trusting heart. The irresponsible young Lieutenant brushes the well-meant counsel of the older man aside; he does not propose to break those wings but to launch them on a flight of new love; so there is nothing for Sharpless to do but to toast bride and bridegroom and wedding in another whisky and soda.

We revert to the more exotic idiom again:

7

as Goro returns with the news that the bridal cortège is in sight. Before we see Butterfly we hear her voice in the near distance soaring above the chorus of the accompanying women, and, in the orchestra, the soft tones of a motif that will henceforth be characteristic of her:

8

a melodic and harmonic germ that is rich in possibilities of modulation and sequential treatment. "One more step to climb," she sings; "over earth and sea a vernal breeze is blowing, and I am the happiest girl in Japan, nay, in the world, for I have obeyed the call of love." Her song, which rests upon a soft choral accompaniment, reaches its height of ecstasy in a great cry of "at the call of my heart I stand now upon the threshold of the house where all blessings, be they of life or death, await me":

It is manifest at once that she is of a different, a superior substance not only to Goro and the rest of her compatriots, but to the thoughtless, devil-may-care young American who has acquired her. Cunningly interwoven with her ardent solo are the congratulations of her female friends; but this choral accompaniment has to be taken in by the ear alone, as part of the total musical fabric, for little of what they are saying is intelligible on its own account.

4

At last the little company debouches on the stage, all carrying open sunshades of gay colours. At a word of command from Butterfly they close their parasols and go down on their knees to Pinkerton; and for a moment we revert to the "Japanese" idiom in a motif that will become of importance later:

Butterfly pays her new lord and master some pretty compliments, and gravely assures him, to the strain of No. 10, that she has many more at her command if he cares to hear them. In reply to Sharpless she says she is from Nagasaki (here No. 2 comes out quietly in the orchestra), but as her family, at one time rich, had met with misfortune she had had to go as a geisha to earn her living. Her mother, she says, is very poor. To a question from Sharpless as to her father she replies curtly "Dead!", and her friends fan themselves furiously to hide their embarrassment. There is a moment of painful silence; then Butterfly goes on to say proudly, to the melody of No. 10, that she has another relation, an uncle who is a Bonze, whom her friends eagerly declare to be a veritable fountain of wisdom. There is yet another uncle, it appears; about him, however, the less said the better, she hints, for he is of rather weak intellect and a frequenter of pot-houses. All this Pinkerton laughs off as delightfully quaint.

While he is talking to her Goro is busy introducing some of her friends to the Consul. He turns after a while to Butterfly and asks her age, and with an archly apologetic air she admits she is rather old—no less than exactly fifteen: at this he is rather horrified, while Pinkerton, who never strikes us as abundantly blessed with either brains or tact, treats it as quite a charming joke. At his order, Goro in his turn bids the three house servants hand round sweetmeats and wines of the comical sort that presumably appeals to the quaint Japanese taste in such things. While this is being done a reminder of No. 2 in the orchestra is presumably intended to direct our attention once more to Nagasaki, from which fresh arrivals are now beginning to appear; among them are the Imperial Commissioner and the Official Registrar. Pinkerton takes Sharpless aside and laughingly draws his attention to the comical crowd of Butterfly's relations, who, for their part, for all their kowtowings, regard the two Americans somewhat suspiciously. To Pinkerton it is all a huge joke—Japanese relations acquired, like his house and his bride, on monthly terms; he is pretty sure he has a mother-in-law somewhere among those present. The women comment rather unfavourably on Pinkerton's appearance and general eligibility, one of them going so far as to swear that Goro had offered him to her before planting him on Butterfly. All this and other chatter takes place mostly to the accompaniment of the tripping No. 3; it is clear that some of Butterfly's companions are very jealous of her and hope the marriage will not last long. Her mother, on the other hand, who does her best for a while to keep out of sight, quite approves of Pinkerton's looks, while Uncle Yakuside, the family disgrace, the nitwit and toper, is already on the trail of something alcoholic. Mainly on the foundation of No. 3 an animated ensemble is built up, in which Pinkerton and Sharpless join, each according to character, the former fatuously certain that he is in for the best of luck with this charming bride of his, the latter warning him of possible trouble, for Butterfly is obviously in love and takes the union with the utmost seriousness.

5

The relations, including the mother, are duly presented to the condescending Pinkerton, who is particularly amused at the tipsy Uncle Yakuside. Like the experienced craftsman he was, Puccini weaves all his threads together with a masterly hand, and we who now know the opera well can see how all this detail fits neatly into the general plan. But there was much more of it in the first version, Puccini being over-anxious to make the exotic milieu convincing; and the first-night audience may be excused for wondering now and then when the real drama of Pinkerton and Madam Butterfly, with the expected tally of big emotional moments and vocal high lights, would get going. And Puccini has some way to travel yet before this can happen.

First of all the Consul, the Commissioner and the Registrar go with writing materials to a table and draw up the formal marriage contract. Heralded by the typical Butterfly motif (No. 8) there now follows a colloquy between Butterfly and Pinkerton in which the former is the principal source of interest; she is to be allowed to exhibit for a while the more kittenish side of her character— for she is only fifteen. Childlike she brings forth from her ample sleeves a number of the little objects she treasures most. She is a little afraid of offending him by all this, and Pinkerton, in a brief moment of comprehension of her, asks "But why, my lovely Butterfly?", to a tiny phrase in the orchestra that shows him to be sincerely touched by her affectionate simplicity and innocence:

11

Her few possessions consist of some handkerchiefs, a pipe, a girdle, a small silver clasp, a mirror, a fan and a little jar of carmine: this last she throws away because Pinkerton appears to disapprove of it. Finally she produces first of all something which she gravely declares she holds sacred—a knife sheath; and it falls to Goro to explain that the weapon was sent to her father by the Mikado with an invitation, which he had dutifully obeyed, to suicide. The sinister significance of the story is emphasised by a harsh figure in the orchestra:

12

Next come out of her sleeve the Ottoké, small figures representing the souls of her ancestors. Humouring her in this quaint fancy, Pinkerton pays the Ottoké his respects; but she goes on to explain that, unknown to her friends and relations, she had gone yesterday to the Mission, abjured her own religion, and adopted that of her lover, who has generously paid no less than a hundred yen for her. This confession becomes important in the action a little later.

Silence having been imposed on the crowd the Commissioner reads out the contract of marriage between Lieutenant Pinkerton, of the American gunboat *Abraham Lincoln*, and the spinster Butterfly, of the Omara quarter of Nagasaki. Bridegroom, bride and relatives all sign; and after the usual congratulations the Consul, the Commissioner and the Registrar depart.

The matter of Butterfly's abjuration of her own faith had obviously been introduced to prepare the way for a dramatic later episode in which her uncle the Bonze was to call down the wrath of his gods on her for her apostasy—the basic reason of it all being to emphasise the completeness of Butterfly's abandonment to her love for Pinkerton. But this further episode could not well be inserted immediately; so Puccini fills in the necessary brief interval with a scene which from the dramatic point of view could well have been dispensed with, in which, urged on by the Lieutenant, the toper Uncle Yakuside shows what he can do in the way of potations. Then the atmosphere is rent by a raucous cry of "Cho-Cho-San!" from the path that leads to the hill. At the sound of the dreaded Bonze's voice the friends and relations huddle together terror-stricken; Goro alone has courage enough to ask petulantly why this spoil-feast could not have spared them his presence, but even he thinks it prudent to make himself scarce. Soon the strange figure of the fanatical Bonze appears, holding out his hands threateningly towards Butterfly and breathing fire and slaughter. The sinister motif of the Curse:

13

dominates most of what follows. The Bonze had learned that Butterfly had renounced the religion of her fathers, and now he calls down on her the maledictions of the gods of Japan. The angry Pinkerton quells him with a single curt sentence and he deems it wise to retire, taking with him the relations and friends, all shouting "We renounce you!" at the dazed Butterfly, who all this while has stood apart, immobile and silent. The lovers are now alone and everything is set for the great closing rhapsody of the long act. Evening steals over the scene. Pinkerton takes the fainting and weeping Butterfly in his arms and whispers tender consolations, while in the background Suzuki is heard murmuring in her own tongue her evening prayers.

6

Drawing Butterfly towards the house Pinkerton begins the final duet with a deeply-felt melody:

14

to which Butterfly sings of her happiness in spite of her renunciation by her kindred. Suzuki and some servants enter for a moment and silently slide some of the partitions of the house, giving point to Butterfly's murmured words, "Yes, now we are alone, the world shut out!" Suzuki puts Butterfly's night robe on her, and at a sign from Pinkerton she and the others retire. The unvarying theme of Butterfly is her profound happiness in becoming Pinkerton's wife, in spite of everything, even the angry curses of the Bonze, whose motif (No. 13) cuts menacingly at one point across her ecstatic song. She tells of her reluctance to listen to Goro when first he had come to her with an offer of marriage from a barbarian—she hastily apologises for the thoughtless word—a man from America; but she had liked him from the first moment, and now he is all the world to her, for he is so tall, so strong, his laugh so frank. "Love me a little," she begs him, "just a little, as you would a baby, for I come of a people accustomed to and grateful for little."

When he calls her "Butterfly" it reminds her of something she has heard—that in his country when a man captures a butterfly he runs a pin through it and fastens it to a board; and the menacing Curse motif (No. 13) thunders out again in the orchestra. Pinkerton tells her soothingly that it is only that the man wants to make sure of possessing the lovely thing forever, as he will her. The passion of the music grows steadily, one ardent theme following straight on the heels of another. Finally Butterfly, to the accompaniment of No. 8, sings rapturously of the beauty of the starlit night, and the climax comes with an ecstatic elaboration, in unison, of No. 9, the melody with which she had made her appearance on the scene a little while before. The song ends, the pair go slowly from the garden into the house, and the last word is left to the orchestra, which dies down from a fortissimo to a pianissimo as the curtain falls on a chord that seems less a conclusion than a question to which the answer must be sought in the future.

7

The second act of *Madam Butterfly* is a masterpiece of invention, style and craftsmanship, working hand in hand. Puccini never surpassed it as a musical-dramatic unity; it is a mosaic of a hundred small pieces, but greater as a whole than in any of its parts. Most masterly of all is the art with which he passes by the most natural transitions from the music of the "quaint" pseudo-Japanese milieu to that of the larger operatic utterance; we are always conscious of the psychological difference between the two, but never of any break in the consistency of the musical style as a whole.

Three years have elapsed since the close of the first act: Pinkertion has long ago sailed away, leaving with Butterfly the child of the marriage and never communicating with her; yet her love for him is as ardent, her faith in him as profound as ever. The second act—as it is still called in the score—is played within the little house on the hill. When the curtain rises after a short orchestral introduction we see the room in semi-darkness, with Butterfly standing motionless by a screen, and the faithful Suzuki, before an image of the Buddha, murmuring a prayer in her own language and from time to time ringing a ritual bell: "Grant that Butterfly may weep no more," she prays. In the orchestra we hear again and again, in the following enlarged form:

15

the tragic motif (No. 12) associated with the suicide of her father, as Butterfly reproaches the gods of Japan for their indifference to her; surely the American God should be more accessible to those who call upon Him as she does, but alas, He seems not to be aware of her. Motif after motif is woven smoothly into the texture as she asks Suzuki how much money now stands between them and starvation, and learns that only a few small coins remain. Yet her belief that Pinkerton will return is unshakable; had he not intended to do so would he have fitted the house with locks as he had done, to keep out her pests of relations and to provide protection for his wife (No. 8), his little Butterfly? When the devoted but more worldly-wise Suzuki remarks that she has never yet heard of a foreign husband returning to his Japanese nest Butterfly turns upon her angrily, and in a tender melody in which she tries to imitate Pinkerton's loving accents:

16

Lento ♩=34

pp O But-ter-fly, pic-ci-na mo-gliet-ti-na, tor-ne-rò col-le ro-se

tells how, when he left her, he had promised to return when the roses bloomed again and the robin redbreasts—whose twittering is charmingly suggested in the orchestra—were building their nests once more. She brushes Suzuki's scepticism aside; one of these days, she insists in her well-known aria, limning the whole scene with her gestures, they will see a thread of smoke on the far horizon, and a white ship making for the harbour, and she, Butterfly, will stand on the brow of the hill, waiting unweariedly for the return of the man she loves. Soon a speck will appear in the distance, coming from the town. It will be he; and when he reaches the top of the hill he will call out "Butterfly!", and she will not answer at once, half in play, half so that she shall not die of happiness:

17

Andante

ff   *p*   *p*   etc.

and he, a little troubled at heart by her silence, will cry out to her as he used to do, "Dear little wife of mine, my little verbena blossom!" And so let Suzuki banish her fears, for he will come, of that she is sure; and No. 17 rings out passionately in the full orchestra, only to fade away in a pianissimo almost immediately. She sends Suzuki away, looking after her sadly.

8

The substance and the colour of the music change in a moment, reverting temporarily to the idiom of the childlike Butterfly of former days, as Goro and Sharpless enter from the garden, accompanied by the "Nagasaki" motif (No. 2) which we have learned to associate also with the Consul. Butterfly greets him joyously, and Suzuki returns to arrange a stool and cushions and set out a table with smoking materials. In the long scene of varied musical expression that follows, the embarrassed Sharpless tries to communicate the contents of a letter he has received from Pinkerton. But in her joy at hearing the beloved name she interrupts him time after time, so that his story never gets fully told, or even fairly begun. She asks when the robins nest in America, for it was then that Pinkerton had promised her he would return; here in Japan they have nested three times since he left, but perhaps they do so more rarely in America? She tells how, as soon as the Lieutenant had gone away, Goro had begun to pester her with other offers of marriage; and latterly he has been trying to tempt her to wed a rich simpleton, for her relations have all cast her off and she is in the depths of poverty. This latest suitor, Goro explains to Sharpless, is one Yamadori, who now enters in pomp, attended by servants bearing gifts of flowers. Goro and Suzuki greet him obsequiously, and the latter places a stool for him between the already seated Butterfly and the Consul. Butterfly twits Yamadori unmercifully on his hopeless passion for her in spite of the many wives he has had already and divorced. Goro is out of patience with her for refusing so rich a suitor, and yet more for deluding herself that she is still married to Pinkerton. She replies that it is true that in Japan a marriage can be ended by the husband opening the door and turning his wife out; but in America that cannot be done, and she is an American now.

While Butterfly goes aside with Suzuki for a moment Goro manages to whisper to Sharpless and Yamadori that Pinkerton's ship has already been sighted. Yamadori remarks distractedly "And when she sees him again . . ."; but the Consul tells them that the Lieutenant does not want to meet Butterfly; indeed, it was to break this news and that of Pinkerton's American marriage to her as gently as possible that he has come to the house. Sadly Yamadori turns to depart, Butterfly laughing unkindly at the piteous figure he cuts. One does not quite know what Puccini's intentions were with regard to Yamadori: his stage directions make it clear that he wants him to appear almost as ridiculous in our eyes as he does in Butterfly's, yet he characterises him musically throughout the scene in a motif of deep feeling, which rings out passionately in the orchestra as he and his servants finally leave the stage, followed by Goro.

9

Now that Sharpless is alone with Butterfly he tries once more, with deepening gravity, to tell her the contents of Pinkerton's letter, which she eagerly takes from him and kisses before he can begin to read it. Having regained possession of it he begins to read it to her, but only broken phrase by phrase because of her constant ecstatic interjections. The reading is accompanied by a persistent motif in the orchestra to which it is difficult to attach any precise label, though frequent use is made of it in the present scene and later: perhaps it was connected in Puccini's mind in some way with the simplicity of Butterfly's soul, and her pathetic obsession with the idea of Pinkerton's return:

18

In its later stages it appears topped by a broad melody in octaves:

19

The letter, the reading of which Sharpless is never allowed to finish, begins thus: "Dear Friend, please seek out that lovely flower. Three years have gone by since she and I were happy together, and perhaps Butterfly remembers me no more. If she still cares for me and expects me, I rely on you to prepare her discreetly for the blow. . . ." As she evidently senses nothing sinister behind these last words he resignedly puts the letter away again and tries another line of approach. What would she do, he asks her gravely, if Pinkerton were never to return to her? Sobered at the very suggestion of that calamity, she bows her head like a child submissive under punishment, and stammers, "Two things I might do—go back to where I came from and entertain people with my singing, or else—and better—to die!" As the Consul holds up his hands in sheer helplessness Butterfly summons Suzuki and bids her show him out, then repents of her harshness and draws him back and begs him to forget what she had said under the first shock of the wound he had dealt her. All through this episode there runs an orchestral figure, insistently repeated, of the kind which Puccini so often relied upon to create a cumulative effect of mental suffering.

Butterfly repudiates the idea that Pinkerton can have forgotten her, and to a rapturous outburst in the orchestra runs into the inner room, returning with her baby on her shoulder. She shows Sharpless the child, asking him if ever a Japanese baby was born with such blue eyes and golden curls. Sharpless admits the resemblance to Pinkerton, and asks if the Lieutenant had ever been told of the coming of the child. No, Butterfly replies, but surely when he knows he will hasten back to Japan; and in a great lyrical outpouring she asks the baby if he understands what the Consul has had the hardness of heart to suggest—that she should take her little one in her arms and go through the city in rain and tempest, trying to earn her keep and his by singing and playing and dancing. Her excited imagination running away with her, she sees the crowd open and the Emperor appear at the head of his warriors, and she will say to him, "Great Ruler, tarry a moment and deign to look at these blue eyes, blue as the heaven from which the Emperor himself has come." The vision is accompanied in the orchestra by a strongly accented motif:

20

of which Puccini will make powerful dramatic use at the end of the opera.

"And the good Emperor will stop," she continues, addressing the child in a strain at once tender and exalted, "and graciously create you the greatest prince of his kingdom," and she presses him passionately to her heart. Sharpless is on the verge of tears.

Feeling that it is hopeless to try any longer to pierce through Butterfly's mystical exaltation with anything in the nature of sober fact he takes his leave, she asking him to convey a message to Pinkerton from the child, whose name now, she tells him, is Grief, which on the day of his father's return shall be changed to Joy—this to a reminiscence of the rapturous No. 17 in the orchestra.

10

When Sharpless has gone Suzuki returns, dragging in the terrified Goro, whom she is threatening to murder; she has caught him, it seems, at his usual game of spreading the tale in the town that no one knows who is the father of Butterfly's baby. The marriage broker tries to explain that all he meant was that in America a child born under such conditions lives under a curse, rejected and scorned by all from birth to death. Blind with fury Butterfly takes down the paternal dagger that is hanging up by a shrine and rushes at Goro, who howls with fright. Suzuki carries the child to an inner room; and Butterfly, quickly repenting of having allowed herself to be betrayed into taking part in such a degrading scene, allows the howling Goro to escape. Putting away the dagger again she turns once more in thought to the child, pouring out her heart to it in a flood of tenderness: soon, she says, his father will come and take them both away with him to his own country.

Suzuki runs in excitedly as the distant boom of the harbour gun is heard. In soft strains the orchestra takes us back to the music of Butterfly's rapturous account of how some day Pinkerton will return. Trembling with excitement she takes a telescope from the table and runs out on to the terrace; and the reminiscent music soars to a great climax as she reads the name of the ship— the *Abraham Lincoln*. Triumphantly she turns to Suzuki; now, she says, the maid will see the folly of doubting; just when everyone was counselling her to weep and despair, love and faith had triumphed; "he has returned, and he loves me!" Now begins the charming episode in which the two women prepare the house for the home-coming of the beloved: "Shake the cherry-tree," Butterfly bids Suzuki:

21

Scuo-ti quel-la fron-da di ci—lie-gio e m'in-non-da di fior—

"till it drowns me with its blossom and drenches me with its perfume." Will he be here in an hour? Two hours? The house is to be gay with flowers to greet him, peach-blossoms, violets, jessamine and whatever else they can find; though this may strip the garden bare as in winter, within the house it shall be spring. Excitedly they strew flowers everywhere, to one happy little melody after another, the climax coming with:

22

as the two women sing, "Let us scatter in handfuls violets and tuberoses and verbena, petals of every flower."

Butterfly, looking sadly at her worn face in a mirror, bids the tenderly caressing Suzuki make her beautiful for the home-coming of her lord; the baby's cheeks too are to have a touch of carmine, lest the vigil before them make him even paler than he is now. A suggestion of the Curse motif (No. 13) is heard in the orchestra as Butterfly angrily recalls the Bonze and his prophecies of evil, giving way to the Yamadori music as her mood lightens and she remembers half-humorously the piteous pleadings of that rejected suitor; soon will come her triumph over them all. The music of the love duet in the first act (No. 14) steals in for a moment as she dons her wedding garment and puts a scarlet poppy in her hair, while Suzuki wraps the baby up in light loose fabrics.

Suzuki closes the shosi (the sliding shutters) at the back of the room, and Butterfly punches three small holes in them, the highest one for herself to see through standing up, a lower one for the crouching Suzuki, and the lowest one of all for the baby, seated on a cushion. So the three look out into the deepening darkness, through which the moon is now beginning to steal, and wait for the dawn and the coming of Pinkerton; the orchestra, however, envelops the rigid silent figures in a phrase expressive of grief and ending with a muttered hint of the Curse (No. 13), thus playing something of the part of a Greek chorus: it knows what Butterfly as yet does not, knows how her hopes of happiness will all end, and it communicates its sad prescience to us who are listening and watching. This First Part of the act is played out to complete silence on the stage, the orchestra alone continuing with the strains of No. 18 and its companion No. 19. The baby is the first to fall asleep and drop down on his cushion as the vigil goes on; then Suzuki succumbs to fatigue and she too sleeps; Butterfly alone remains as motionless as a statue, staring out into the night as the curtain slowly falls.

11

Before the Second Part opens on the stage there comes in the score an orchestral interlude in which Puccini plays in masterly fashion on motives old and new, the impression we get being one of ecstatic reminiscence shot with foreboding. At this point a little explanation is perhaps due to the reader who is accustomed to seeing *Madam Butterfly* played in *three* acts. The original plan of the librettists had been for an opera in the customary three acts; and included in the scheme was a scene in which Butterfly, calling at the Consulate, encountered the American Mrs. Pinkerton there, whereas in the present version the whole action, after the first act, takes place in Butterfly's house. Towards the end of 1902 Puccini became convinced that the opera ought to be in two acts only. "The Consulate," he wrote to his publisher Ricordi on the 16th November, "was a great mistake. The action must move forward to the close without interruption, rapid, effective, terrible! In arranging the opera in three acts I was making for certain disaster. You will see that I am right." Three days later, evidently in reply to some objections on Ricordi's part, he writes "Have no fear; I am sure of my ground . . . that the opera, with the division which I have adopted [i.e. the orchestral interlude] will be very effective indeed. The dilution of the work with the Consulate act is a mistake. This [opera] is a little drama which, once begun, must proceed without interruption to the end. . . . Illica agrees with me, and makes the same suggestion of cutting out the Consulate act; only he would like to keep the three acts—but to drop the curtain and raise it again on the same scene does not seem to me desirable." When the score was completed except for the orchestration Puccini felt that "it has turned out splendidly, the action moving forward straight and logically in the most satisfying way. Ah, that act at the Consulate was ruining everything!"

It was thus that the long second act came to assume its present form in the score—two parts linked by an orchestral interlude. In most performances, however, the interlude does not link the two parts but separates them: the curtain comes down on the First Part at the point where Butterfly, Suzuki and the baby have begun to look through the holes in the shosi; then, after an interval, the audience returns for the "third act," to which the interlude forms a prelude. All this is purely and simply a concession to the poverty of human endurance in the average audience—or supposed poverty, for today people manage quite well to keep their unbroken attention on such long one-act works as the *Rhinegold, Salome* and *Elektra*. From the artistic and the dramatic standpoint Puccini was right; we should remain in our seats while darkness gradually descends upon the room, and, under the guidance of the interlude, live imaginatively with Butterfly through those night hours of weary waiting.[1]

12

We have arrived, then, at the point where, after the orchestral interlude, Butterfly's long vigil is nearing its end. From far away

[1] The constant references to "three acts" in any study of *Madam Butterfly* is apt to confuse the reader. He should remember that when Puccini himself speaks of "three acts" in his correspondence he is referring to the *original form of the libretto*, of which the "Consulate act" formed an integral part; by insisting on this being cut out he reduced the opera to the two-act form on which his heart was set. The present three-act lay-out did not come into being until the Brescia revival, and it amounted to no more than a simple division, for theatrical convenience, of the long second act into a second and a third. It is therefore rather misleading to speak, as some analysts have done, of Puccini having "gone back to the original plan of three acts." There was no "going back to the original plan," which had included the "Consulate act." All that happened at Brescia (and afterwards) was that at the point where the orchestral interlude occurs an interval was made in order that the audience might relax for a while. The published score of 1906 was not "in three acts" but in (1) act one, (2) act two, first part and second part.

in the bay come inarticulate human calls and murmurs, accompanied by the clanging of ships' chains and anchors from the harbour; and when at last the curtain rises again we see the first rays of dawn stealing into the room, with Suzuki and the baby asleep by the shosi, and Butterfly still like a figure carved out of stone. The orchestra swells to a blaze of light and colour as the sunshine gradually floods the room. Butterfly is the first to move; she wakens Suzuki with a touch on the shoulder and then takes the baby tenderly in her arms. The recurrence of a motif that had been heard previously at the point where she had held the child up for the Consul's admiration tells us that it is the little one that is in the forefront of her mind as she now confidently assures herself that soon Pinkerton will come:

23

"Sleep, my love," she croons to it as she carries it off to a room above; "you are with God and I with my sorrow," to which Suzuki adds a reflective "Poor Butterfly!"

A grave motif to be later associated with the thoughtful, good-hearted Sharpless (see No. 24) is dwelt on for a little time by the orchestra as we enter upon the next vital stage of the action. Suzuki, opening the door to the Consul in response to some knocking, is staggered to see that he is accompanied by Pinkerton; the pair enter with an air of stealthy secrecy. Suzuki informs the Lieutenant that not merely has her mistress been waiting and watching the whole night for him but not a ship has entered the harbour during the last three years without her anxiously scanning its flag and colours; while last night, in the sure expectation of his coming, she had insisted on having the room strewn with flowers. Suddenly Suzuki catches sight of a foreign lady in the garden, and she asks the men anxiously who this may be. Pinkerton, who never cuts an impressive figure in the drama, dares not tell her: all he can bring himself to say is "She has come with me." It is left to Sharpless to tell her, quietly but resolutely, that this is Pinkerton's wife, whereupon Suzuki breaks into a wild cry of despair—"Souls of my ancestors, for my little one the light of the sun has gone out!", and she sinks on her knees with her arms raised to heaven and her face turned to the ground.

In vain the Consul tries to comfort her; they had come so early in the morning, he tells her, in the hope of finding her alone and being able to count on her guidance and support. In grave, sympathetic tones:

he breaks it to the dazed and anguished Suzuki that while they all know how Butterfly must suffer they feel that their first care must be for the child.[1] The voices unite for a moment in a trio in which Pinkerton muses sadly on the unchanged appearance of the room in which he and Cho-Cho-San first plighted their love, and Suzuki, the one who feels most deeply for Butterfly, bemoans the new turn of events: "Souls of my forefathers," she wails, "this is the end of all for my poor little one!"

13

Pinkerton sends her out into the garden to join Kate. The Lieutenant, unable to bear up under this load of misfortune for them all, decides to follow Suzuki: Sharpless, reverting for a moment to the music of his fatherly talk with him in the first act, reminds him of his disregarded warning on that occasion. Pinkerton abjectly admits his own recklessness and heartlessness, but can get no further in the way of redemptive action than to give Sharpless some money for the support of Butterfly. Taking up the strain of No. 24 he bids a mournful farewell to what had once been the scene of his love:

[1] As the reader will remember, Butterfly had told Sharpless that she had never sent Pinkerton news of the birth of a child. We must therefore presume that the Consul had given the Lieutenant this news after his return from his interview with Butterfly; in which case Mrs. Pinkerton's resolution to adopt the child must have been rather sudden.

Ad—di—o fio-ri-to a-sul di le—ti-zia e d'a-mor.

Then he goes out with bowed head, leaving to Sharpless the task of disclosing the whole dreadful truth to Butterfly. He is decidedly not a "sympathetic" figure anywhere in the opera, and least of all here; but it is difficult to see in what other guise the librettists could have presented him to us, the original drama being what it was.

The Lieutenant having left, Suzuki and Kate Pinkerton enter from the garden, a conversation there having evidently been just concluded. "You will tell her, then," says the latter, "and advise her to trust me, for I will tend him as a son of my own"; to which Suzuki mournfully assents, stipulating, however, that she shall be alone with Butterfly when the blow falls on her, for her heart will be broken. Just then Butterfly is heard calling from a room above, and presently we see her at the head of the staircase and beginning to descend. In vain the maidservant tries to hold her back. She has come in the confident expectation of finding Pinkerton there, but seeing only Sharpless and Kate she begins to be alarmed. "Who are you?" she asks the American woman. No one dares to answer her, but the orchestra fills the stage silence ominously, some descending phrases in the whole-tone scale being particularly expressive. At last Kate Pinkerton ventures to speak to the dazed Butterfly; "I am the innocent cause of all your woe. Forgive me." "How long is it since he married you?" asks Butterfly. "A year," is the reply, "and will you not let me do something for the child? I will give him the most loving care." Motif eloquently succeeds motif in the orchestra (No. 23, No. 6, No. 15, No. 13), to which is entrusted all the delineation of what is going on in the stunned soul of poor Butterfly. Sadly she felicitates Kate on her marriage to Pinkerton; "Under the great vault of heaven there is no woman happier than you. May you always remain so. Feel no sadness for me; but do this for me—tell him I shall find peace"; and she declines, though not unkindly, the friendly hand the other woman proffers her. She has always been pathetic; now we see her in process of becoming inwardly great.

Overhearing an enquiry addressed to Sharpless, Butterfly tells Kate that Pinkerton shall have his son if he will come for him—in half an hour from now, she adds meaningly: her great resolution has been already formed. Suzuki having shown Kate and the Consul out, Butterfly, mastering herself with a great effort, bids her shut out the sunlight that is now flooding the room: spring has died within her, and she wishes to forget its presence in the world. Suzuki closes the curtains and doors until the room is in almost total darkness, the orchestra meanwhile enveloping the scene in an ominous twilight of its own. When Suzuki proposes to bring the child to Butterfly she tells her to go and join him in his play; but the weeping maid cannot bring herself to obey. There comes one of those long Puccinian silences to which the conductor should give the utmost possible value; then Butterfly murmurs the words of a sad mysterious old song: "He came through the closed gates; then he went away, and left us with nothing, noth-ing—but death!"

Imperiously she bids the sobbing Suzuki leave her. Then she lights the lamp in front of the large image of Buddha, before which she bows her head for a few moments. She shudders convulsively as she recalls the Bonze's prophecies of woe (No. 13 in the orches-tra), then goes to the shrine, draws the white veil from it and throws it over the screen, takes the dagger out of its sheath on the wall near the Buddha, holds the haft in her two hands, kisses the blade, and reads out softly the words engraved on it—"Better to die with honour than to cling to life in dishonour." The tempo and colour of the orchestral music change for a brief spell as the door on the left opens and Suzuki appears with the child, who, at her urging, runs towards his mother. In a convulsion of tenderness and grief Butterfly kisses him and holds him to her breast: "You must never know," she cries, "that it was for you, for your dear innocent eyes, that Butterfly died, so that you may go away be-yond the sea and not recall with regret the mother who abandoned you." She sings a last passionate invocation to him, this angel who had come to her from Paradise, to look well at his mother's face for remembrance in days to come:

Andante sostenuto ♩ = 50

O a me, sce—so dal tro-no del -l'al-to Pa—ra—di-so,

"Farewell, my love, my little love," she ends her cry, "and now go and play."

She seats the child on a stool, gives him the American flag and a doll to play with, and tenderly bandages his eyes; then with her own eyes fixed on him she goes behind the screen. The dagger is heard falling to the ground, and the white veil that was on the screen is snatched away. Butterfly comes tottering from behind the screen, the veil wound round her throat. She gropes her way to the child, gestures to him with her hand, gives him a last embrace, and falls beside him. The voice of Pinkerton is heard off-stage, calling "Butterfly!", and the orchestra crashes in with a phrase of climactic poignancy:

27

The door is flung open; Pinkerton and Sharpless enter and run to Butterfly, who points feebly to the child as she dies. Pinkerton falls on his knees, while the sobbing Consul picks up the child and kisses him. Then Puccini's genius finds the right musical ending to the drama; the orchestra thunders out the motif (No. 20) that had accompanied Butterfly's ecstatic vision of the Emperor some day catching sight of the child, and, moved by his beauty, making him the foremost of the princes of his empire. It is a masterstroke of tragic irony, of a type of which music alone among the arts has the secret; but it is in the nature of the case one of which a first-night audience could not be expected to be conscious. It is only after long acquaintance with *Madam Butterfly*, indeed, that we become fully aware of the many subtleties that have gone to the making of it.

Gianni Schicchi

GIACOMO PUCCINI [1858–1924]

PRINCIPAL CHARACTERS

GIANNI SCHICCHI	*Baritone*
LAURETTA	*Soprano*
ZITA	*Contralto*
RINUCCIO	*Tenor*
LA CIESCA	*Mezzo-soprano*
NELLA	*Mezzo-soprano*

1

ɴ 1915, while he was engaged upon what was to prove the least successful of his works — *La Rondine*, produced in Monte-Carlo on the 27th March 1917 — Puccini felt an urge to try his hand at a one-act opera. Hence arose in the course of time the so-called *Trittico*, three short works in contrasted genres — tragedy, sentiment and comedy, as Puccini described them — consisting of *Il Tabarro*, *Suor Angelica*, and *Gianni Schicchi*. The triptych received its first performance at the Metropolitan Opera, New York, on the 14th December 1918. The first Italian performance was at the Costanzi Theatre, Rome, on the 11th January 1919. Since then *Il Tabarro* and *Suor Angelica* have been unjustly neglected by the theatres; *Gianni Schicchi*, however, has become a repertory piece.

The libretto of this, by Gioachino Forzano, is based upon a historical episode in Florentine life during the Middle Ages. (The date of the action of the opera is 1299.) The hopes and fears of the expectant relatives of rich, or supposedly rich, testators have long been a favourite theme for comic art: in our own day we have been given, in addition to Puccini's masterpiece, a bright comedy by Zola — *Les héritiers Rabourdin* — and Lord Berners' ironic

Funeral March for a Rich Aunt, in which the sparkling eye of the
gratified heir can be seen peeping out of the black-edged handkerchief. Perhaps the best swindle in actual history connected with a
last will and testament is that recorded of a Florentine rogue,
Gianni Schicchi, who placed his gifts as a mimic at the service of
certain relatives of old Buoso Donati, who had just died, and whose
wealth was worth taking a bit of extra trouble to secure. Concealing for a while the fact of the death, they placed Schicchi in Buoso's
bed, where the consummate comedian dictated to a lawyer, in
proper form, a will of the required type, which included a bequest
to himself of a valuable mare known as "the lady of the stud."

As if Schicchi's achievement of itself were not sufficient to ensure a humorous immortality for his name, Dante must needs
empty the vials of his wrath on him in the 30th Canto of the *Inferno,* placing him in the Eighth Circle among a crowd of thieves,
panders, swindlers, barrators and other gentry of that type. Dante
describes

> *due ombre smorte e nude,*
> *che mordendo correvan di quel modo*
> *che 'l porco quando del porcil si schiude.*

(Two pallid, naked shades which ran biting like the hog let out
from the sty). One of these was Myrrha, who had loved in illegiti-
mate fashion her own father, the King of Cyprus. The other

> *giunse a Capocchio, ed in sul nodo*
> *del collo l'assannò, sì che, tirando,*
> *grattar li fece il ventre al fondo sodo,*

(came at Capocchio and buried its teeth in the nape of his neck,
and then dragged him so that he made his belly scrape on the hard
bottom). It is explained to Dante that

> *Quel folletto è Gianni Schicchi,*
> *e va rabbioso altrui così conciando;*

(that goblin is Gianni Schicchi, and he goes raging and dealing in
this manner with the rest). It appears that just as Myrrha had
counterfeited for her own ends the form of another, so Schicchi
had stooped,

per guadagnar la donna della torma,
falsificare in sè Buoso Donati,
testando e dando al testamento norma.

(to impersonate Buoso Donati, making the will in due form, that he might get for himself the lady of the stud).

It is evident that the tight-lipped Dante, who probably never saw a joke in all his life, felt particularly venomous, even for him, towards Gianni Schicchi; and were he writing a supplement to the *Inferno* today he would no doubt find a place for Puccini in it, — probably in the section of the Eighth Circle of hell reserved for the makers of discord.

2

The curtain rises on a bedroom in the house of Buoso Donati. It is nine o'clock on an autumn morning in Florence: the light in the room is part sunlight, part candle-light. On the right is the big bed in which the old man has just died. On the left are a large window giving a view of the tower of Arnolfo, and a smaller window opening on to the terrace. There are staircases right and left. A table with various silver objects on it catches the spectator's eye. Through the half-closed curtains of the bed we get a glimpse of the red coverlet under which is supposed to be the body of Buoso. Beside the bed are four candelabra with lighted candles, and in front of it another with three candles that have gone out. To these candelabra we shall owe a couple of rich comic touches later.

With hope and fear contending for mastery in their hearts, the relatives of the dead Buoso are on their knees in front of the bed. They have lost no time in coming to the house when the news has gone round that the rich old man is dead. Their ages range from seven to seventy or more, from little Gherardino, the son of Gherardo, a nephew of Buoso, and his wife Nella, to old Simone, one of Buoso's cousins. Simone's son Marco is there, with his wife La Ciesca. The very old woman present is Buoso's cousin Zita, who is accompanied by her young nephew Rinuccio. The company is completed by Betto di Signa, a brother-in-law of the deceased, a ruin of uncertain age, and obviously a very poor relation. Buoso seems to have left behind him no more direct relatives than this miscellaneous collection of interested mourners. All are behaving themselves in a conventionally proper way, moaning and mumbling prayers, except little Gherardino, who is obviously bored by the proceedings: with his back to the others he is amusing himself with some wooden balls. Soon he upsets a chair, and the mourners suspend their lamentations for a moment to "Sh!" him. A little later he plucks his father by the sleeve and whispers something to him; whereupon the exasperated Gherardo runs him out of the room.

There is no formal prelude to the opera — merely a preamble of some twenty-five bars during which we hear a phrase that runs through most of the opening scene and recurs frequently later:

It begins at a great pace, but by the time the curtain rises it has slowed down to a *largo,* and it suffers a further change by passing from major to minor now and then. It is a curious phrase, in that it keeps us perpetually suspended between the comic and the tragic: the merest trifle of exaggeration in this direction or that during the playing of it would suffice to make it either. It is accompanied in the preamble by a little figure:

which is also much used later. No. 1 we may perhaps call the death motive. It begins, as has been said, at a great speed — the composer's marking is *tumultuoso* — suggestive of the frantic haste with which the expectant relatives have made their way to old Buoso's house, while the slower tempo later and the switch over to the minor show them composing their features to the proper degree of affectionate concern as they enter the death chamber. Example No. 2, which keeps on insinuating itself into the texture every now and then, suggests, apparently, the shadow of Gianni Schicchi already playing impishly over their hopes and fears.

Even while they are assuring the shade of the departed Buoso that they will not cease weeping for so good a man for the rest of their lives it is evident that their minds are not on his past but on their own future. While the others cease their wailings for a moment to gabble a prayer or two Betto and Nella begin whispering to each other about "what they are saying at Signa," where the deceased had some property. Gradually we learn what it is that the gossips have been saying lately at Signa — that if Buoso dies the monks will do well, while others know for certain that everything has been left to a convent. The mourners begin to be a trifle worried. They ask Simone's advice, he not only being the oldest among them but having been at one time mayor of Fucecchio. After profound deliberation Simone gives his verdict — if the will is in the custody of a notary, that may be good for the monks but bad for them, but if by any chance it has been left in this room, that may turn out bad for the monks but promising for them.

New hope springs up in their hearts, and especially in that of young Rinuccio, who breathes a prayer that the document will turn out to be just what they would all like it to be, so that he may marry his adored Lauretta, the daughter of Gianni Schicchi. The tempo of No. 1 changes to *allegro vivo* again as the relatives, now in a state of high fever, begin to turn the place upside down in the search for the will. Old Betto does not take part in this search, but furtively tries to pocket some of the valuable silver articles on the table. The others pull out drawers, open lockers, look under the bed. Soon the room is littered with papers. One false alarm succeeds another. At last Rinuccio opens a parchment which he thinks may be the will, and we hear in the orchestra a suggestion of a melody:

3 *Allegro coll'8va*

that will later be associated with him and his Lauretta: if all goes as well as he hopes it will, they can marry next May-day. He gives the document to old Zita, and all gather round to see what it contains. Zita looks about for the scissors that were on the table a few moments ago, but cannot find them, for the excellent reason that they are in Betto's pocket. In the end she tears off the ribbon with her hand. Inside the parchment is yet another parchment, and inside this the will — at last.

Zita reads the inscription on it — "To my cousins Zita and Simone." The sap of hope rises high in them both: Simone, overcome by his pleasurable emotions, lights again the three candles that had gone out; nothing could be too good for this excellent Buoso. The others begin to speculate as to what the old man may have left each of them — the house, perhaps, or the mills and the mule at Signa, or, who knows, all these and more. Zita now stands in the centre of an excited group, all of them with their eyes turned eagerly on the fateful parchment; and the solemnity of the occasion is marked by a theme of almost legal deliberation in the orchestra — the "will" motive, we may perhaps call it:

It shows to what excellent use the notes and the simplest harmonies of the scale of C major can still be put, all modern developments notwithstanding. No. 2 is heard fluttering ironically round it.

The lips of the relatives move as they read the will. Their faces register first of all anxiety, then incredulity, and finally rage as they realise what has happened to them. They throw themselves, exhausted, wild-eyed, despairing, into any seat that presents itself. Simone alone has a bit of action left in him: he puts out not only the three candles he had lit a few minutes ago but all the others — a richly humorous touch in performance. Now they know! they say bitterly: the monks are going to get rich and fat at their expense; out there at Signa heaven knows what *they* will be drinking while the monks are doing themselves well with the products of the vineyards; Rinuccio's happiness will have vanished for the benefit of the scheme for reconstructing Santa Reparata. They all shake their fists and heap curses on the heads of the frairs, whom they call by every opprobrious name they can think of, the orchestra all the while pouring out a flood of rage exceeding even their own in volume.

Gradually fury gives way to depression once more. Some of them begin to shed tears of self-pity: who would ever have believed this of Buoso? And the worst of it is that there's no altering it now. Once more they appeal to old Simone as the doyen of the family and the former mayor of Fucecchio: surely he can think of something? But the old man merely shakes his head sadly and hopelessly. Rinuccio comes forward. There is only one man, he says, who can advise and, perhaps, help them — Gianni Schicchi. They are all about to swear that, as members of a respectable family, they will have nothing to do with that rascal or his daughter when Gherardino rushes in, shouting "Here he comes!" At the commencement of the scene of the search for the will, Rinuccio, without saying anything to the others, had sent the boy with a message to Gianni to come to the house at once. The relatives continue to abuse Gianni, and to cry out at the idea of a Donati marrying the daughter of a man like that; but Rinuccio reasons with them. Gianni is artful, he says; there isn't a nook or cranny of the law that he doesn't know. He is a jester of the first order; why, they have only to look at those shrewd eyes of his, at his great nose like an old ruined tower, to see that he is capable of carrying any trick through to the end, and only a trick of the cleverest kind is going to be of much use to them now. Enough of this silly talk about his being a rustic! Florence itself, that lofty, lovely tree, with its branches reaching almost to heaven itself, Florence, with its palaces and towers, does it not renew its roots in the valleys? Rinuccio's song in praise of Florence, its arts, its sciences, its great men:

has something of the flavour of a popular melody. It ends with a cry of "Enough of these miserable animosities and recriminations:

good health to the new breed and Gianni Schicchi! " A broad orchestral phrase that occurs in the middle of Rinuccio's song:

becomes of importance later.

3

As the strains of the aria die away, Gianni himself enters, followed by Lauretta. The arch-rogue pauses on the threshold, amazed at the woe-begone looks of the relatives, which the man of the world in him can account for only on the theory that Buoso has had the bad taste to recover. While Rinuccio and Lauretta are greeting each other affectionately to the strains of No. 6, Gianni, who has observed the candles round the bed, and now guesses what has happened, hypocritically assures the relatives, to the accompaniment of No. 1, that he knows why they are grieving. Still, death is an everyday matter, and there is always the deceased's estate. They break it to him that this has gone to the monks, every bit of it; and Zita swears that now there is no money in the family she will not allow her nephew to marry a penniless girl like Lauretta. A lively ensemble is built up, Lauretta and Rinuccio vowing eternal fidelity to each other, Gianni Schicchi calling Zita, among other things, a sordid, miserly old curmudgeon, Zita returning his insults in kind, and the others interjecting every now and then a remark to the effect that what they ought to be thinking about is the will. As the dispute mostly concerns the lovers, it is naturally accompanied by a broad version of No. 3:

The indignant Gianni is for leaving the scene, and it takes all the persuasive powers of Rinuccio and Lauretta — the latter in a

charming little appeal to her father which she sings on her knees
to the tune of No. 6 — to get him to change his mind: Lauretta's
trump card is the assurance that unless she can go to Porta Rossa
and buy the ring she will throw herself into the Arno.

"Give me the will," Schicchi says at length. He strides up and
down studying it, with the relatives following him mechanically,
while the lovers, forgetful of all the rest, bid a sad farewell, to the
melody of No. 3, to their dream of a wedding on May-day. At first
Gianni has no hope that the will can be got round. Then we see from
his face, as the agonised relatives do, that an idea has struck him.
He gets rid of his little Lauretta by telling her to go out on the
terrace and give the bird some crumbs. Then he asks the company
if anyone except themselves knows that Buoso is dead. Their reply
is "No." Then no one must hear of it just yet, he says. But what
about the servants? Zita tells him that no one except themselves has
entered the room since the end came. And now Gianni becomes
the man of action. He orders them to carry the body and the
candelabra into an adjacent room and to remake the bed; which
they do.

A knock at the door makes everyone's heart jump into his
mouth. "It's Maestro Spinelloccio, the doctor!" says Zita in a scared
whisper. While the others crowd round the barely open door and
hold the doctor in conversation, and Betto darkens the room by
closing the window shutters, Gianni conceals himself behind the
bed-hangings. Spinelloccio, speaking in a nasal tone with a
Bolognese accent, asks after his patient, and is assured that he is
going on nicely. He tries to approach the bed, but the others block
his way, and from behind the curtains comes a thin, weak, tremu-
lous voice begging the physician not to insist. Perhaps Spinelloccio
can call again in the evening. Buoso is much better, but he needs
rest, and he is feeling very drowsy. At the sound of what for the
moment they take to be the voice of Buoso himself, so good is the
imitation of it, the relatives almost jump out of their skins: but as
soon as they realise that it is only Gianni speaking they manage to
steady themselves — all except old Betto, who, in his fright, lets
fall a silver dish he had been hiding in his sleeve; Zita picks it up
and replaces it on the table, giving Betto a nasty look and threatening him with her finger, but saying nothing. The doctor lets himself
be edged out of the room, attributing, as he goes, this marvellous

recovery to the well-known skill of the Bologna school of medicine. (In the old Commedia dell'arte the Doctor was generally a Bolognese.)

As soon as he has gone, Betto reopens the shutters, once more letting in the light of day, and Gianni comes into sight again. " Was the voice anything like correct? " he asks them. They assure him that it was absolutely right. " Victory! Victory! " he cries, but still they do not understand. He tells them to send to the notary and bid him come without a moment's delay to old Buoso Donati, who has got much worse and wants to make his will. When he arrives, he, Gianni Schicchi, lying in the bed, concealed behind the curtains in a darkened room, will impersonate the dying Buoso: the orchestra gives humorous point to what he says by harping on the death motive (No. 1) of the genuine Buoso. In a passage of the utmost slyness he describes how all the notary will see will be a head with a nightcap on it and a face covered with a kerchief, except for a nose that will look like Buoso's but will be his, Gianni Schicchi's; and in that guise he will dictate a will, a proper will! His head is bursting with the brightest, maddest joke that ever was, a joke that is a challenge to heaven itself. The others think it is a magnificent idea, which could only occur to a genius like him. While Rinuccio rushes off for the notary the others crowd round Schicchi, kissing his hands and his clothes and blessing the day when he thought of this scheme for circumventing the monks. They even go to the extent of embracing each other and singing the praises of love among relations.

Then they give Gianni instructions as to the dictating of the will. Simone wants the Fucecchio farms; others claim those of Figline, or Prato, or the property at Empoli, and so on. But the most valuable of all are the mills and the mule at Signa, and everyone wants these. Simone thinks they ought to come to him because he is the oldest and because he has been the mayor of Fucecchio; the others stake out their own claims. They are all shouting each other down when the tolling of a funeral bell is heard. It strikes dismay into them: the whole town knows, then, that Buoso is dead! Even Gianni Schicchi's nerve fails him for a moment. " All's lost! " he says. It is precisely at this critical moment that simple little Lauretta chooses to come back from the terrace with the information that the bird won't eat any more. " Then give him something to drink," says her father tersely: at all costs she must be out of the way while he is putting his fraud through.

As Lauretta goes out, Gherardo, who has gone to see what is happening in the street, rushes in panting for breath, only just able to gasp out that it is a false alarm; it is only the Moor baptised by the captain who has come to grief. "Requiescat in pace!" sing the relieved relatives cheerfully; and immediately the mills and the mule and the house at Signa come uppermost in their thoughts again. This time, instead of wrangling about the matter, they agree to leave it to the decision of Gianni Schicchi. He consents to act as arbiter. Zita, Nella and La Ciesca dig out for him one of Buoso's nightgowns, a kerchief and a nightcap. While he is putting these on, the relatives in turn edge up to him and whisper into his ear promises of bribes if he assigns the house, the mule and the mills to them. His reply to each of them is "All right!", but the typical motive of his slyness (No. 2), peeping out in the orchestra through it all, bodes ill for the relatives. Each of them, however, retires well satisfied, rubbing his or her hands.

While Simone goes to the window to look out for the notary and Gherardo clears the table for the latter, the others sing the praises of Gianni's lifelike impersonation of Buoso — nose, voice, everything is perfect. The ensemble reaches its climax of ecstasy in a great cry of "O Gianni Schicchi, our saviour!":

They push him towards the bed, but he halts them with a solemn gesture. He has a warning for them. They know the law, he hopes: "If anyone substitutes himself for another in a matter in which a legacy is concerned, both he and his accomplices shall lose one hand and then be exiled"; and in that case, farewell for every one of them to beautiful Florence! The relatives, thoroughly sobered,

repeat his final words: none of them can bear the thought of dragging out existence under another sky than that of Florence, and
with only one hand at that.

4

A knock at the door sends Gianni scurrying to the bed, while
the others darken the room, place a lighted candle on the table,
and make other preparations for the notary, who, with Rinuccio
and a couple of friends of Buoso, Pinellino the shoemaker and
Guccio the dyer, enters to the motive of No. 4 in the orchestra.
This makes way for the death motive (No. 1) as the pseudo-Buoso
greets the newcomers and thanks them for coming to witness his
will. The notary seats himself at the table and spreads out his
parchments and seals, the two witnesses standing by him. Schicchi,
in a feeble voice, explains that it had been his intention to write
out his will with his own hand, but his paralysis having made
that impossible for him he has sent for this worthy notary. To
demonstrate his paralysis, Gianni raises a trembling hand to the
accompaniment of the mocking No. 2, the relatives registering
compassion and murmuring "Poor Buoso!" At the sick man's
special request the relatives are allowed to remain in the room
during the making of the will, which is carried out to a development of the motive quoted as No. 4. The notary gabbles the long
Latin preamble as he gets it down on the parchment — he, Amantio
di Nicolao, a notary of Florence, on this first day of September 1299,
inscribes at the request of Buoso Donati this last will and testament, which revokes and annuls all preceding ones — a clause
which meets with the warm approval of the relatives.

First of all the notary asks about the funeral. Does Buoso wish
it to be an ostentatious one? No, no, says Gianni; it is not to cost
more than a couple of florins. Once more the relatives thoroughly
approve. Then Gianni begins his dictation of the will. At his opening words — " To the Frati Minori and the fund for Santa Reparata
I bequeath" — the relatives start up in terror; but they sit down
again, with a sigh of relief, when he continues, "five lire." They
commend his charity and his piety alike; good works should always be remembered in one's will. The few florins in ready money
left by the deceased are next bequeathed to the relatives in equal

shares. Other legacies follow in quick succession – to Simone the property at Fucecchio, to Zita the farms at Figline, to Betto the Prato fields, to Nella and Gherardo the property at Empoli, to La Ciesca and Marco that at Quintole. Each beneficiary in turn murmurs his grateful thanks. And now, they say under their breath, for the things that really matter, the Signa mule, house and mills! The mule, the testator continues, the best mule in Tuscany, which cost three hundred florins, he leaves to – his devoted friend Gianni Schicchi. While the notary is getting that down in his Latin the relatives jump up in affright. Simone, forgetting himself, asks what on earth Gianni Schicchi can want with the mule; but the testator cows him with the rejoinder that Gianni Schicchi knows perfectly well what Gianni Schicchi wants; and poor old Simone subsides, muttering "Ah! the rascal!"

The house in Florence is next bequeathed by Buoso to his dear, devoted, affectionate friend Gianni Schicchi. This is too much for the relatives, who cry out in a wild chorus against such injustice; but he brings them to reason by singing a line or two of the farewell to Florence and its divine sky, with its reminder about the loss of one hand. The sentiment seems to the notary beautifully appropriate to the dying Florentine, but the relatives understand its darker significance. Anyhow all is not yet lost; there are still the mills to be disposed of. The rogue leaves these also to his dear, affectionate friend Gianni Schicchi; but between each phrase of his dictation he inserts another subtle reminder to the relatives of the penalties attaching to complicity in the making of a false testament. Caught in their own net, they can do nothing but groan.

Rinuccio now slips out to join Lauretta on the terrace. Adding insult to injury, the testator directs Zita to give twenty florins out of her own purse to the two witnesses, and a hundred to the notary. The three go out expressing their gratitude to this excellent Buoso and regretting that soon they will see him no more. When they have gone, the relatives rush in force towards Gianni Schicchi, calling him a rascal, thief and traitor. They tear off his nightgown. He leaps from the bed and assails them with Buoso's staff, ordering them out of his house. They begin to pillage the place, each going off with as much as he can carry, while he pursues them with the stick. When they have all gone, Rinuccio opens the great window from outside, revealing Florence in all its beauty in the full sunlight; and the lovers pour out their hearts to each other and to the city they love to the broad melody of No. 3.

Gianni Schicchi returns from the fray loaded with things he has retrieved from the marauders. As he throws them down in triumph he catches sight of Rinuccio and Lauretta. His heart melts: he smiles understandingly, removes his cap, and turning to the audience asks them, in a speaking voice, if Buoso's money could have come to a better end than this. For this little pleasantry of his he has been consigned to the Inferno; but, by permission of the great Dante, if they have been amused he will ask them for a verdict of extenuating circumstances. He starts the applause with his own hands, and bows to the audience as the curtain descends. And of course he carries us with him; for whatever Dante may have to say on the subject, and however regrettable it may be from the point of view of the moralist, the world has generally found its rogues more companionable than its saints.

Turandot

GIACOMO PUCCINI [1858–1924]

PRINCIPAL CHARACTERS

TURANDOT	*Soprano*
ALTOUM	*Tenor*
TIMUR	*Bass*
THE UNKNOWN PRINCE	*Tenor*
LIÙ	*Soprano*
PING	*Baritone*
PANG	*Tenor*
PONG	*Tenor*

1

HE READER who has seen Puccini's *Turandot* on the stage will remember three curious Chinese figures, bearing the perhaps not wholly authentic names of Ping, Pang and Pong, who seem to be always round and about the main action though rarely at the core of it, and who speak a musical language somewhat different from that of the leading characters. The explanation is that these three figures are descendants of the "masks" of the old Italian genre of improvised play, the commedia dell'arte.

Before Puccini's opera appeared, Richard Strauss and his librettist Hugo von Hofmannsthal had already made, in *Ariadne auf Naxos,* an attempt to combine these so-called masks organically with a serious dramatic action — an attempt which, on the whole, has to be written off as a failure, but at all events a noble failure. Puccini and his poets, Giuseppe Adami and Renato Simoni, have succeeded better in effecting this fusion in *Turandot,* partly because they have not ventured on the psychological subtleties and

symbolisms so dear to the German mind, partly because excellent
Italian models for the particular kind of fusion they desired lay
ready to their hand. The master of this blend of serious drama and
the commedia dell'arte was Count Carlo Gozzi (1720–1806), one
of the last scions of a noble Venetian family that had become im-
poverished by the time of Carlo's birth. About the middle of the
eighteenth century a new orientation had been given to the Venetian theatre by the "modern" plays of Goldoni and one or two
other dramatists. Gozzi's passion for the ancient genre of improvised drama led him to associate himself with one of the still surviving companies of masks, and to write for them between 1761
and 1765, in a mixed genre of his own, ten plays which he called
"Fiabe" — stories with a touch of unreality. The most famous of
them all, perhaps, is *Turandot* (1762); but several of the others
have also served as the basis for later plays or operas. The fiaba
of *La donna serpente* was drawn upon by Wagner for his youthful
opera *Die Feen*, and that of *L'amore delle tre melarance* by Pro-
kofieff for an opera with the same title. The interesting central
theme and the vivid incidents of *Turandot* have always made it
a special favourite. In 1802 Schiller produced a German version
of his own of Gozzi's play, for which Weber, seven years later,
wrote an overture and some incidental music. Among modern
operatic treatments of the subject the most notable are those of
Busoni (1921) and Puccini (1926).

Gozzi seems to have derived his material mostly from a story in
a Persian collection of tales which had been made known to Western Europe, in a French translation, towards the end of the seventeenth century. This version skilfully weaves into a unified tissue
various motives that had been popular among story-tellers from
time immemorial — that of the obstinately virgin princess who con-
demns her unsuccessful wooers to death, that of a trial for life or
death by means of three enigmas, that of an Unknown who ripostes
with an enigma of his own, and so on.

In Gozzi's five-act play, the kingdom of Astrakhan has been overcome by its enemies, and the old King (Timur), his queen, and
his son (Calaf) driven into exile. Calaf, after enduring all kinds
of privations and degradations for several years, finds himself at
last in Pekin, where he comes upon another refugee from Astrakhan, the faithful Barach, who has settled down in Pekin under

the name of Assan and there taken to himself a wife. Calaf learns from Barach that all China groans under the cruelty of the man-hating Princess Turandot,[1] who sets each of her would-be lovers three enigmas to solve, and, on his failing to do so, remorselessly has him executed. The latest victim is the Prince of Samarcand, whose miniature of the lovely Turandot happens to come into Calaf's hands. He at once falls madly in love with her, and presents himself for the usual trial.

Everyone tries to dissuade the seeming madman, especially Turandot's father, the Emperor Altoum, who is sick of all this bloodshed and entirely out of sympathy with his daughter's whim-sey, though he abides by his promise to her never to force her to marry under any other conditions than those she herself has laid down. At the public trial Calaf, to everyone's astonishment, solves all three enigmas. Turandot is furious, and, womanlike, at once demands a replay of the game, on the ground that the three enig-mas solved by the Unknown were far too easy: owing to the trial having been sprung on her so suddenly, it appears, she has had insufficient time in which to think up three posers really worthy of her and of the occasion. Altoum refuses to listen to her: she her-self had framed the rules of the game, she has lost, and she must now abide by the result. Thereupon Turandot tries a bit of charac-teristic feminine blackmail: if the Unknown Wooer and her cruel parent really insist on it she will go to the altar, but only to plunge a dagger into her heart when she gets there. Never, she swears, shall any man possess her.

The Unknown thereupon chivalrously gives her another chance. He wants her to come to him willingly, he says, or not at all. So he stakes not only his bride but his life on a last and supreme throw. *He* will set Turandot a single enigma: if by the next day she can discover his name and that of his father, she can have him slain like his predecessors. She accepts, and at once proceeds, of course, to do all she can to discover, by fair means or foul, the identity of

---

[1] The correct pronunciation of the name is with the main accent on the first syllable and the final "t" sounded: Gozzi, indeed, sometimes spells it as a four-syllable word — Turandotte. Singers, however, have found it convenient to omit the final "t," and so we arrive at "Turan*doh*" as the now customary pronunciation of the word. The strong accent, however, must still be on the first syllable, with the suspicion of a fainter one on the third.

this original and exceptionally audacious wooer. In this she succeeds, by a series of intrigues and accidents that need not be told in detail here. At the public divan next day she triumphantly announces the name — Calaf, son of Timur. But alas, from the first sight of him she has felt secretly drawn towards him, and still more so since he made his generous gesture; and so she magnanimously spares his life, but bids him depart from Pekin for ever. In his despair at losing her he tries to kill himself. This certain proof of his disinterested love breaks down the last defence of her virgin pride, which had suffered a severe blow when, for the first time, her three enigmas had been solved. Confessing that he has conquered her, she voluntarily gives herself to him as his bride; and Gozzi's play ends with an assurance on her part that she deeply repents her former obstinacy and cruelty where the male sex was concerned.

2

The exigencies of a three-act opera necessitated some compression of Gozzi's five-act drama, the omission of several characters and scenes, the transformation of others, and the invention here and there of a new character or a new episode. Puccini and his poets, however, retain Gozzi's Italian masks in the Chinese milieu in principle, though, of course, with considerable modifications. In Gozzi there are four of these stock figures of the commedia dell'arte — Pantalone, Tartaglia, Brighella and Truffaldino. These he had to have, indeed, because the four male members of the Sacchi company of actors, with which the playwright was associated, specialised in them: the head of the troupe, Antonio Sacchi, was always the Truffaldino, Atanagio Zanoni the Brighella, Agostine Fiorelli the Tartaglia, and Cesare Darbes the Pantalone. In *Turandot* Gozzi elevated Pantalone to the post of the Emperor's Secretary, and Tartaglia to that of Grand Chancellor, in which exalted capacities, however, they still have only subsidiary parts to play. But Brighella, who is made Master of the Pages, and Truffaldino, who is at the head of Turandot's slaves, remain, in Gozzi's play, genuine figures of the commedia dell'arte. They take no part in the major events of the drama; they exist in a separate little world of their own, in which, as the tradition of the genre dictated, they *improvise* their lines (in dialect), and occasionally indulge in hearty popular humours.[2]

Puccini, in his turn, finds the masks useful for moving incessantly about the fringes of the main action, supplying illuminating comment on it, and now and then furthering it a little. He makes Ping the Grand Chancellor, Pang the General Purveyor, and Pong the Chief Court Cook. The three invariably appear as a sort of tripartite entity, speaking, thinking and acting in concert; and their music is in a lighter, more everyday conversational style than that of the leading characters of the drama, whose terrific emotional tension demands a more exalted manner of speech.

The one really new character in the opera is the somewhat enigmatic little girl Liù, who, it appears, has been the guide and solace of old Timur during his miserable wanderings over the earth after the loss of his kingdom and the disappearance of his son. In a sense, she is superfluous so far as the essentials of the action are concerned, though she contributes very effectively to the emotional range of the music, and, near the end, helps to increase the tension of it considerably. The librettists seem to have dimly felt the necessity for reinforcing their text with a character corresponding in some degree to the Adelma of Gozzi's drama. This Adelma is a Tartar princess who, after the destruction of the royal house to which she belongs, has become the favourite slave of Turandot. In the days of her prosperity, however, she had felt a sympathetic interest in a young man, of whom no one knew anything, who used to perform menial tasks at the court of her father: this young man, of course, was the fugitive and anonymous Calaf. She recognises him again at the trial at the divan, realises that she

[2] Each of the Italian masks represented a familiar type. Harlequin was a nimble, extravagant, saucy rogue. The Captain was a swashbuckler and braggart of the Ancient Pistol species. Pantalone was an absurd old man, Scaramouche a gay roisterer, Tartaglia a ridiculous fat stutterer, Brighella a coward, boastful, dishonest and sycophantic, Truffaldino a universal butt; and so on. These general characteristics were of course susceptible to all kinds of nuance and modulation according to the subject and the milieu of each particular play. In the genuine commedia dell'arte the actors were provided only with a scenario of the action: their words and by-play were improvised. In Gozzi's *Turandot* this precedent is followed where Brighella and Truffaldino are concerned.

loves him, becomes madly jealous of Turandot when she sees the possibility of the Unknown winning her, and, informing him that Turandot is plotting to have him killed, tries to induce him to flee with her. It is she who, partly by accident, partly by artifice, discovers Calaf's name and that of his father: these she discloses to Turandot, hoping in this way to ensure, to her own benefit, the failure of the Prince's wooing in that quarter.

Adami and Simoni having dispensed with Adelma, they transfer to Liù something of the motive — vital to Gozzi's play — of the former's love for Calaf. In the opera, it is clear, the Prince does not even know by sight this little companion of his father when he stumbles upon the forlorn couple in the square at Pekin. We learn that in the distant past he had chanced to smile, at his own court, on the humble little slave Liù, who, we gather, is still no more than a child at the period at which the action of the opera takes place — an important point which is generally obscured for the spectator in the theatre by the obvious physical maturity of the singer taking the part. This smile has remained ever since as a golden memory in the heart of the child. She loves Calaf in her simple way; and towards the close of the opera she makes the supreme sacrifice of her own life to him and to his passion for Turandot by refusing to reveal his identity to the myrmidons of the savage Princess, who is determined to have the name if everyone in Pekin has to perish in the quest of it. Naturally one expects, after this, Liù's self-immolation to have a vital bearing on the dénouement of the opera, especially when we remember how that dénouement is brought about in Gozzi's play by the somewhat parallel character of Adelma, who is also in love with Calaf. But whereas Adelma is directly instrumental in bringing about the conjuncture of events leading to Turandot's discovery of the name of the Unknown, and so to the ultimate unravelling of the tangled psychological threads, the heartrending self-sacrifice of little Liù is entirely without influence, or, indeed, bearing, on the dénouement of the opera. For Liù dies without having revealed the Prince's name, even under torture; and the final situation — in which Turandot, knowing the name at last, and, being able to revenge herself, if she wishes to do so, on the man who has humiliated her, decides that after all her new love is more potent than her old pride — has to be brought about by the device of

Calaf himself disclosing his name to her as the climax of his ecstatic bravado.

This ending is not without a certain ingenuity, but it has neither the force nor the dramatic conviction of Gozzi's. Yet in the opera, after the death of Liù and the departure from the scene of the mourning Timur with the body, there remains nobody but the Prince to answer, for Turandot's benefit, his own enigma, and so bring the drama to its appointed end. We are left, then, wondering a little just *why* Liù has been allowed to play the relatively large part she does in the penultimate stage of the work. The answer seems to be that the horrible episode of the torture of Liù fascinated Puccini purely for its own sake. Strictly speaking, the opera could have managed, psychologically and dramatically, perfectly well without Liù. But episodes of super-suffering, and, at a pinch, of actual torture seem to have had a curious fascination for Puccini. We may conjecture that while the peculiarly pathetic character of Liù attracted him as a musician, the emotional appeal of this sympathetic little figure writhing under the crudest physical torture was simply irresistible. And so the child occupies an amount of space in the dramatic canvas of *Turandot* that is hardly justifiable on purely rational grounds.

3

After the completion of the triptych — *Il Tabarro, Suor Angelica* and *Gianni Schicchi* — in 1918, Puccini spent several months in an agonising search for a subject for a new opera. It was not until 1919 that Renato Simoni suggested looking for what he wanted in Gozzi. Oddly enough, Puccini seems to have made his first acquaintance with the story of Turandot through an Italian version, by Maffei, of Schiller's play. He soon realised that he had found his long-desired subject; but the way was long and dolorous before he and his poets could give it the shape he desired. His keen dramatic sense told him that two acts would be enough: but that plan seems to have been given up solely for reasons connected with the convenience of theatrical audiences.

The drafting of the first act presented few difficulties. But it was a long time before a satisfactory design for the remainder could be worked out; and Puccini had virtually completed the music for the first act before the words for the other two were ready. His letters show both his librettists and himself to have been in considerable and continuous perplexity as to the best way in which to end the opera; and one gathers, from a hint here and there, that it had not been the original intention to dispose of Liù after the fashion finally adopted in the opera. As late as November 1922 Puccini told Adami, " I think that Liù must be sacrificed to some sorrow, but I don't see how to do this unless we make her die under the torture. And why not? Her death could help to soften the heart of the Princess." This suggested psychological motive, however, is *not* incorporated in the libretto. When we read, indeed, of the long struggle of the composer and his poets against the difficulties of the last act we are not at all surprised at its showing a slight constructional weakness here and there.

Puccini's letters make it clear that he attached the utmost importance to the final duet between Turandot and Calaf. This was to be not only dramatically but musically the peak-point of the work: the music, we may surmise, was to elucidate triumphantly in its own way whatever might have been left a trifle unclear in the drama. By one of the bitterest ironies of fate under which any musician has ever suffered, he was destined never to complete this duet — the main outlines of the music of which he had long had in his head — because his poets failed to supply him with the necessary words in time. In the spring of 1924 a malady of the throat that had vaguely troubled Puccini from time to time became more insistent: though he was never allowed to know it, it was cancer. In the autumn of that year he consulted a Belgian specialist, and in October went to Brussels for an operation. This appeared, at first, to have been successful; but a couple of days later the heart failed unexpectedly, and on the 29th November Puccini was dead. Not long before the operation he said forebodingly to a friend: " The opera will be given incomplete, and someone will come to the front and say, ' At this point the Master died.' " It happened precisely as he had foreseen. At the first performance, in the Scala Theatre, Milan, on the 25th April 1926, under Toscanini, an abrupt ending was made at the last page to be completed in the score by Puccini himself: and Toscanini, turning to the profoundly moved audience, said quietly, " At this point the Maestro laid down his pen." The work is always given now with an ending written by

Franco Alfano, based on the composer's own sketches for the final scene.

4

The action of the opera takes place in Pekin, in legendary times. There is no orchestral prelude.

When the curtain rises we find ourselves in front of the great wall that surrounds the city, which glows in the distance in the rays of the evening sun. On the right a big bronze gong is suspended. Here and there on the wall are stakes on which are impaled the heads of some of Turandot's unsuccessful suitors. A vast crowd stands before the wall, silent and motionless.

The horror that broods over Pekin whenever Turandot is in one of her merciless moods is vividly suggested by the orchestra in the half-dozen bars that precede the rising of the curtain. The effect is mainly harmonic, with many reiterations of the type of chord shown in the following quotation:

1

and colouristic, with gong and xylophone breaking into the texture with barbaric tints and clangours of their own. At intervals there appears, above these harmonies, the melodic figure shown in the second bar of the above example. The crowd is listening to a mandarin reading, from the top of the wall, the latest decree: Turandot the Chaste will be the bride only of one of royal blood who shall solve the three enigmas she sets him; if he fails, he must lose his head. The Prince of Persia having lately tried and failed, he will die this day at the rising of the moon.

The mob, crazed with this incessant shedding of blood, cries out frantically to the executioner, Pu-Tin-Pao, to begin his work at once; and they make as if to storm the wall with a shout of "To the Palace!" The guards get to work among them with whips and drive them away, to a clamorous melody in the orchestra:

Above the shrieks of the frenzied crowd we hear the despairing voice of Liù, begging for help for the old man with her, who has been knocked down by the stampeding crowd. A youth among them bends over the old man and recognises him as his father. There is an affectionate scene between the two, accompanied throughout by No. 2. The youth — the Unknown Prince — entreats Timur not to call him publicly "My son," as the usurper of their throne pursues them implacably everywhere.

By this time the crowd has re-formed. It goes mad with excitement as the executioner's assistants, their garments stained with blood, appear on the wall with an enormous sword, which they begin to sharpen on a whetstone, singing a savage sadistic chorus in praise of their profession and of Turandot; wherever she may reign, they say, there will always be work for them to do! They gloat over the many victims, past and future; the enigmas are three, they repeat, but death is only one. Meanwhile we have learned from the old man's lips how, after the battle that had sealed the fate of his kingdom, little Liù had come to him and dragged him away. Since then she had been his guide and support in all his weary wanderings, comforting him, begging his bread for him. "Who art thou, Liù?" asks the Prince Calaf. "I am nothing, my lord — only a slave," the child replies. He asks her why she has taken on herself so great a burden of suffering. She returns the ecstatic answer, "Because one day, in the palace, you smiled on me!"

And that is all the light we get upon the antecedents and the mind of Liù, for now our attention is wholly taken up by the crowd once more. This has gradually re-gathered in front of the wall. Its lust for blood increases as the sky grows darker and the first pale rays of the moon begin to appear, heralding the death of the latest victim. The whole lighting of the scene gradually changes, and with it the colour and the harmonic texture of the music. At first the mob is almost calmed by the spectacle of the golden sungleam fading before the coming of the moon: then, as the sky becomes a livid silver, a monstrous cry of delight goes up from the crowd. " Pu-Tin-Pao! Pu-Tin-Pao! " they shout again and again, until from the distance comes the dirge of the children at the head of the approaching procession:

About this melody more will be said later.

Soon the procession comes into view along the wall – first the executioner's assistants, the priests with funeral offerings, various mandarins, and last of all the Prince of Persia, followed by the gigantic executioner. The Prince is so handsome and so young, his bearing so dignified, and his gentle eyes so full of his dream, so unheeding of everything around him, that at the sight of him the crowd's blood-lust dissolves into pity. A funeral march in the orchestra accompanies him on his slow way across the wall, and to the strains of this the crowd calls louder and louder on the Princess Turandot to show him mercy. The Unknown Prince joins in this appeal. At last he cries to the cruel one, " Oh, that I might see thee, that I might curse thee! " And at that moment Turandot herself appears on the imperial loggia to the right of the wall. The cold moonlight playing on her face seems to intensify the expression of proud indifference on it. The crowd, awed by the majesty and the conscious power that stream from this statuesque figure, falls on its face before her. On the wall there remain erect only the Persian Prince and the executioner; in the forefront of the stage only the Unknown Prince. At the sight of Turandot's beauty he has covered his dazzled eyes.

Even while the crowd is still murmuring its broken appeal for mercy, Turandot raises her hand in an imperious, conclusive gesture. The executioner understands, and the cortége moves on again and at last disappears, with the crowd following it. Turandot slowly re-enters the palace, while the priests, to the last echoes of the funeral march, offer up a prayer to great Kung-tze to receive the soul of the man who is about to die. By now the light has faded still further, and on the stage we see only the Unknown Prince, Timur and Liù. Calaf has realised, at the sight of Turandot, that the hour of his destiny has struck. After a brief ecstatic invocation to her beauty he stands absorbed in silent reflection, until a word from Timur unlocks his lips again, only for him to rave of the vision he has just seen. Timur, in terror at the sinister enchantment that has fallen on his son, bids Liù take his hand: she does so, urging him to come away with them, to where life is. " Life is here, where Turandot is! " is his only reply. The name of Turandot strikes upon our ears from afar also: it is the last invocation of the merciless beauty by the Prince of Persia as the axe falls and the crowd gives a cry of horror.

Timur's appeals have no effect on Calaf, who moves towards the great gong that is flashing in the moonlight. He is about to strike it, thereby announcing himself as a new wooer of Turandot, when three strange figures suddenly fling themselves across his path. They are Ping, Pang and Pong. In urgent phrases they advise him to go away from this door that leads only to butchery, to return to the country whence he came and lose his head there if he will, but not here, not here! Pekin and China are full enough of fools who want to die: why should he add to their number? And for what? For one who, when all is said, is merely a woman, a thing of common flesh and blood. He can find elsewhere a hundred wives if he wants them. Although the three masks speak a musical language different from that of the tragic characters of the opera, Puccini, here as elsewhere, succeeds in making them all appear as part of the same dramatic milieu.

Ping, Pang and Pong are still gesticulating around the Unknown Prince and obstructing him, and he is making violent efforts to get past them, when from the balustrade of the imperial loggia comes a soft chorus of female voices — Turandot's maids, bidding them all be silent, as their mistress is asleep. But the three masks take no notice of them. They renew their entreaties to the crazy Unknown to listen to reason. Turandot's enigmas, they assure him, are all insoluble. But he hardly hears them, for now there come to his ear, out of the darkness and the distance, not voices but the

mere shadows of voices. They are those of the dead lovers of
Turandot; they tell him to delay no longer but to call on her of
whom they still dream, and she will appear to him. As the ghostly
visions and voices fade from sight and sound, the Unknown cries
out that he alone loves Turandot. Again the tolerant, cynical masks
reason with the madman. All is illusion, they say: nothing really
exists, neither he nor Turandot, nor God, nor man, nor the kings of
this earth. As their last argument they point to the gruesome spectacle now visible on the ramparts, where the executioner is placing
the head of the Prince of Persia on a stake. The white moonlight
beats down upon it; even so, say Ping, Pang and Pong, will the
moon one of these nights kiss Calaf's face.

Timur, in a pathetic monologue, tries to recall his demented son
to the world of reality. Liù follows with a still more moving appeal.
She confesses that everywhere in her wanderings his image has
been in her heart, his name on her lips; if now he persists in his
folly, old Timur will lose his son, and she will lose " the shadow of a
smile." She breaks down and weeps at the young man's feet. He
looks sadly and compassionately at the little figure, and in a long
monologue in which concern for Liù is blended with a kind of
pity for himself, he bids her remember that smile of his of long
ago of which she had spoken, and to devote herself henceforth
to old Timur, who now will need her more than ever. The three
masks, Timur and Liù unite in a last despairing appeal to Calaf, in
a big ensemble that works up gradually from the following theme:

to an outcry of the most frenzied kind. But appeals and force are
alike unavailing. The gong once more gleams in the moonlight, and
catches Calaf's eye. He tears himself loose from Ping, Pang and
Pong. It is death, they tell him. " No! It is life! " he replies. In a
sheer delirium of ecstasy he cries out three times the name of
Turandot, seizes the hammer, and strikes three tremendous blows

on the gong. The orchestra thunders out the majestic theme that symbolises Turandot (No. 3). Old Timur and Liù cling to each other in despair. The three masks fly in horror, leaving the madman to his fate. The curtain descends on Calaf standing before the gong, staring at it as if obsessed.

Puccini uses some genuine Chinese melodies in *Turandot*. That quoted as our example No. 3 is one of these: it will be found in the chapter on Chinese music in the *Travels in China* of John Barrow (London, 2nd ed., 1806), who had accompanied the Earl of Macartney in his mission to that country. According to Barrow, the tune was even at that time fairly familiar to the Western world, it having been arranged by one Mr. Hittner and published in London, but " with head and tail pieces, accompaniments, and all the refined arts of European music," says Barrow, " so that it ceases to be a specimen of the plain melody of China." He himself prints it in what he calls " its unadorned state, as sung and played by the Chinese ":

The title of the song is " Moo-Lee-Wha." In 1862 the German his torian of music Ambros quoted the melody in the chapter on East-ern music in the first volume of his great History. He condemned Chinese music in general as being " singular " and " unbeautiful," apparently never pausing to ask himself whether Chinese stand-ards of beauty might not be different from those of the Western world. How completely he misconceived Chinese music in general and "Moo-Lee-Wha" in particular is shown by his harmonising the latter on the tonic-dominant-subdominant principles of European music, which are entirely alien to it. Some idea of the absurdity of Ambros' harmonisation may be had from the following quotation of the first four bars, and more especially from the "accompaniment" to the fourth bar:

It is strange that a writer of such learning should have failed to see that as the tune is one of those, so frequent in exotic or primitive music, that avoid the seventh of the scale, this "leading note" should also be avoided in any harmonisation of it, otherwise the whole character of the melody is changed. Puccini was perhaps no scholar; but he was a man of genius, and his intuition told him that if "Moo-Lee-Wha" was to sound at all Chinese in *Turandot* it would have to be harmonised with the "flat seventh," i.e., with a whole tone, not a semitone, before the tonic. The following quotation:

is from the big scene of the divan in the second act. It will be seen at a glance how Puccini's method of harmonisation not merely preserves unimpaired but heightens the non-European element in the melody, which is utterly dissipated by Ambros' class-room harmonies.

5

The opening scene of the second act is given up entirely to the masks, who once more illuminate the psychological situation for us in a musical language of their own. We see the front of a pavilion — a great curtain curiously decorated in the Chinese style, with a door in the middle and one at each side. We seem, for the moment, a long way from the tragedy of the first act when Ping pops his head through the centre opening and, turning first to the right, then to the left, calls out Pang and Pong. Their entry is formal enough — three servants follow them, each with a different-coloured lantern, which they ceremoniously place on a low table, round which are three stools, in the very middle of the stage. The servants then retire to the background.

The three masks have met to discuss in their own fashion the unpleasant situation created by the latest challenge to Turandot. It will end, they foresee, in either a wedding or a funeral; and they humorously profess to be prepared for either, whether it be a gorgeous palanquin they will have to follow or a handsome catafalque. They fall to musing on the China of old and the China of their own day. For seven thousand centuries the country slept the sleep of profound peace, everything proceeding tranquilly according to ancient rule. Then came Turandot with her cursed riddles and all that these have brought in their train — suitors, challenges, hopes, fears and beheadings in unending succession. They read out the melancholy record of deaths from three scrolls which the servants have left on the tables. And they are weary of it all, weary of being little more now than adjuncts to the executioner. Each of them is racked by a nostalgia of his own. Ping has a little house on a lake in Honan to which he longs to return and dream his life away: Pang thinks wistfully of his garden at Kiù: Pong has forests somewhere the grateful shade of which he has almost forgotten: and here they are in Pekin, all three of them wasting their lives poring over the sacred books, saddened by the interminable spectacle of human folly. Their weariness and their heart's longing are finally crystallised in an exquisite after-refrain in the orchestra:

Love and sweetness have vanished from the world: there is nothing but frenzy and decapitation: the end of China itself must surely be near:

Would that the day might come when it will fall to them to prepare the nuptial couch for Turandot, to escort the bride and groom with lanterns, and to sing in the garden until dawn of day of the coming back of love and light to spectre-ridden China!

From the dream in which they have gradually lost themselves more and more completely they are wakened by a volley of trumpets and trombones and drums from within the palace. For the town is alive again with the sound of people hastening to the great divan that is to be held that same day, at which yet another lover will try to vanquish the ice-cold Turandot. At a sign from Pong the servants remove the lanterns as ceremoniously as they had placed them on the tables, and with their hearts heavy within them the three masks go out to face the torture of the new trial.

When the curtain rises again it is on the huge square in front

of the palace. An immense marble staircase with three landings
stretches up from the centre of the stage. At the top of this stand
the eight Wise Men, sages of great age and still greater dignity, if
not, indeed, pomposity. Each has in his hand three sealed scrolls
containing the solutions of Turandot's latest enigmas. Various
officials and notables pass up and down, among them Ping, Pang
and Pong, now in the yellow robes they wear only on important
public occasions. At the foot of the staircase, on one side, is the
Unknown Prince. On the other side are Timur and Liù, almost lost
in the crowd. The people comment softly on it all, while the orchestra pours out a flood of ceremonial music, which increases in power
and brilliance as the preparations for the divan advance towards
their climax. This arrives when, the mists of incense having rolled
away, the Emperor Altoum becomes visible on his throne at the
highest central point of the scene, and the multitude greets him
with a cry of " May you live ten thousand years! " and prostrates
itself with its face to the ground. The Emperor is so old and venerable that he has the air more of an ageless religious symbol than
of a mere human being.

Addressing the assembly in a thin blanched voice that betokens
his years, he speaks of the oath by which he is bound to his daughter, but counsels the young Unknown to depart and so avoid the
further shedding of blood. The Prince replies that he asks only to
be put to the trial. In vain does old Altoum plead with him: the
young man's resolution is immovable, and in the end there is nothing for it but for the Emperor to bid the trumpets sound and the
ordeal that is certain to end in death begin. As it is essential that
the Emperor's words shall be clearly heard, in spite of the weakness of his voice, Puccini makes him intone them without accompaniment; and as it would sound odd if the Prince's brief replies
were delivered in another medium, these also are sung unaccom-
panied, the orchestra being restricted throughout the episode to
an occasional interjection between the vocal phrases. The effect of
it all is to concentrate our attention on the warnings and the challenge to an extent that could not have been achieved by any other
means: the limitation imposed on the musician by the character of
the old man's voice has been converted by Puccini into an instrument of extraordinary dramatic power.

A number of Turandot's women come out from the palace and

take up a position on the staircase. They are followed by Turandot herself, beautiful, cold and aloof as usual. She throws a glance of proud indifference at the Unknown, who only by an effort at self-mastery can look at her with composure. To the accompaniment of the harmonies shown in No. 1, with a strong colouring of gong and xylophone as before, a mandarin recites the terms of the coming contest. A chorus of children in the distance intones once more the hymn in praise of Turandot (No. 3). Then, without any preamble, Turandot, from her place at the foot of the throne, begins her address to the Prince. She tells the story of how in that very palace, thousands of years ago, there lived in peace and purity the Princess Lo-u-ling, till one day the barbarian descended on China, the empire was lost, and Lo-u-ling slain in a night of atrocity by a man — a man such as the stranger who now braves Turandot. Long brooding on that story had bred in her a loathing of men and a consuming desire to avenge the innocent Lo-u-ling; never shall any man possess her, she cries, to one of the great themes of the opera:

Her own words working like an intoxicant on her as she utters them, her song rises to a climax of resentment against the man who now stands before her at the foot of the steps. "The enigmas are three," she cries, "death is one":

He answers her with "The enigmas are three, life is one," repeating her own melody higher in the scale, as if at once capping her words and confuting them. Then, at a still higher pitch, they repeat together their respective cries, each of them, as it were, bent on bearing down the other by sheer weight of asseveration.

The crowd urges Turandot to accept the challenge of this bold

Unknown. The trumpets having imposed silence, she propounds her first enigma, the orchestra adding a tension and a poignancy of its own to the atmosphere of the scene:

10

Without a moment's hesitation the Prince replies: the thing that is born each night only to die next day is Hope. The eight Wise Men, having unrolled their scrolls, solemnly declare the answer to be correct. For a moment Turandot is abashed. Recovering her poise, she remarks menacingly that Hope flatters only to deceive; and to increase the terror of her next question she descends to the midway landing of the staircase, where, with her eyes burning into the Prince, she launches the second enigma. This is more difficult than the first one: the Unknown hesitates for a while, and both the Emperor and the crowd eagerly encourage him. But the solution comes to him in time: the thing that is like a flame yet is not a flame, that grows cold when life is lost and burns when life is won, is Blood. Once more the Wise Men confirm it from their scrolls.

The joyous cries of the crowd anger Turandot, who orders the guards to chastise them. She descends the remainder of the steps, halting in front of the Unknown, who sinks on his knees before her. A raging fury now, bending over him like a beast of prey, with her face almost touching his, she hurls at him the third enigma, and gloats ferociously over his seeming discomfiture. Suddenly a great light comes to him: he leaps to his feet to deliver his reply: this thing of ice that begets in him fire is TURANDOT.[3] Again the Wise Men pronounce him to be right, and the assembly gives out the typical Turandot melody (No. 3) in the form of No. 5, in a tremendous outburst of voices and orchestra, and to the words " Glory to the conqueror! "

[3] Each of the enigmas has been condensed into as few words as possible for the purposes of this analysis.

Turandot refuses to accept defeat: she implores her father **not**
to throw her into the arms of this stranger, and turning with a **blaze**
of fresh hatred towards the Unknown she swears that neither **he**
nor any man shall ever possess her. The Emperor's only reply **is**
to declare that his oath is sacred: the crowd, too, is all on the **side**
of the Unknown who has ventured and conquered where so **many**
had failed, and lifted from the city the horror that has **brooded**
over it so long. It is the Prince himself who offers Turandot a **way**
out. He will release her from her bargain, he says, on one **condition.**
Three enigmas she has propounded to him, and three he has **solved.**
One only he will now put to her. She does not know who he is: **if**
before dawn she can tell him his name, then at dawn he is **willing**
to die. Turandot signifies by a gesture that she accepts:

11

Altoum and the crowd unite in singing the praises of this **generous**
victor, and the curtain falls on a massive chorus of homage to **the**
Emperor, to the melody of the Imperial Hymn.

6

The first scene of the third act shows us the great garden of **the**
palace, with a pavilion on the right, which is supposed to lead **into**
Turandot's chambers.

It is night. Turandot has lost no time in getting to work: all **Pekin**
is being searched for someone able to give her the name of the Unknown. Mournful harmonies well up from the orchestra, convey-
ing a sense of tension and of mystery, and we hear the voices **of**
the heralds proclaiming that by command of Turandot no one **in**
Pekin is to sleep that night. On pain of death for all, the name **of**
the Unknown must be brought to her before dawn. From the **far**
distances of the unhappy city come faint echoes of the heralds'
words — " Nessun dorma! . . . Pena la morte! "

The " Nessun dorma " is taken up by the Unknown Prince, who all this while has been reclining on the steps of the pavilion, sunk in dreams and visions of his own. Softly — more softly than the average Italian tenor can generally manage to sing the passage — and reflectively, to some of the most beautiful music in the score, he sings, over harmonies of this type:

12

Andante sostenuto

his message to Turandot. She, like the others, he says, shall not sleep. No one but himself knows his name; and from his lips alone shall she learn it at break of day, learn it in a kiss that will melt the frigid beauty and make her his. The orchestra repeats his final phrases in an ecstasy of passion; and it is remarkable with what perfect naturalness this tense strain merges into the lighter one that accompanies the irruption of the three masks into the scene, at the head of a number of dim figures that gradually define themselves, against the darkness, as the people of the town. They have come, with the masks at their head, to try to induce the Unknown to save the city. Despairingly the three ministers call on him to leave his star-gazing and listen to them. Death threatens every house in Pekin. What is it he wants? Is it love? They surround him with beautiful maidens, whose blandishments he rejects. Is it riches? Gold and gems are displayed before his eyes, and Ping, Pang and Pong sing the praises of them. Is it glory? they will help him to found empires, if only he will be content to know himself to be the only one to have vanquished Turandot, and leave Pekin for ever.

Every temptation of the body, every blandishment of the spirit having failed, the exasperated ministers resort to threats. He does not know this Turandot of theirs, they tell him: she is infinitely crafty, infinitely cruel, and China is rich in subtle, fantastic tortures unknown to the rest of the world. Turandot, frustrated, will

never forget and never forgive: he himself will die a horrible lingering death if he remains in the city and does not divulge his
name. The crowd, now maddened with fear, surges round him,
cursing him for his obduracy and threatening him with their knives.
His sole reply to appeals and threats is that he wants Turandot, and
her alone.

Suddenly a commotion and cries of " Here is the name! " are
heard from the direction of the garden, and some guards rush in,
dragging with them Timur and Liù. The drama has reached its
highest point of emotional tension. The startled Prince calls out
that these two know nothing: he alone knows his name. But Ping
remembers them as the two with whom the Unknown had been
seen talking the day before. He hurries towards the pavilion, calling, with the crowd, " Princess! Princess! " Turandot, accompanied
by her motive (No. 3) in triumphant and terrible trumpet tones,
appears on the threshold of the pavilion. Bending low before her,
Ping informs her that they have discovered two people who know
the name, and that they have hooks with which to tear the secret
from their lips if the Princess commands. Ignoring all the others,
she addresses herself with cold irony to the Prince, to the accompaniment of No. 2 in the orchestra. He is pale, she says tauntingly.
It is her own fear, he replies, that she sees reflected on his face in
the pallid light of dawn; and he swears again that the old man
and the maiden do not know him. "We shall see!" is Turandot's
answer. She orders Timur to speak; but the old man, frightened
and bruised and bleeding, only turns on her a look of mute misery.
The ministers seize him to torture him; but before they can get to
work Liù turns to Turandot and declares that she alone knows the
name the Princess is seeking. The crowd utters a jubilant cry, which
changes to one of baffled fury as Liù goes on to say that the name is
her secret and will remain so.

The Prince breaks out into threats against the mob. He is seized
and bound by the guards, and the horrible scene of the torture of
Liù begins. She is forced by the guards to her knees, and as she
still refuses the name, her arms are twisted at the command of the
maddened Ping. The torture increases till the child can bear no
more, but still she will not yield. As she falls almost dead near the
steps of the pavilion, something in Turandot seems to break. She
is faced by a mystery beyond her understanding: what gives her,

341

she asks Liù, the strength to suffer like this? It is love, the child
replies, a love for her lord which she has never yet confessed to
anyone. She bids the guards torture and destroy her: she glories
in her pain, which is the last and greatest sacrifice she can make to
the being she loves.

It is only for a moment that Turandot has weakened. They are
to tear the secret from the girl, she says; and the crowd cries out
for Pu-Tin-Pao and more and worse torture. When the sinister
figures of the executioner and his assistants loom up through the
darkness, Liù's resolution fails her. The demented child — the spectator should never forget that Liù is supposed to be only a child —
runs to Turandot, calls out that she, the ice-cold Princess, will yet
love the Unknown as she loves him, and that her death will be his
triumph:

13

then snatches a dagger from the belt of one of the guards and
plunges it into her heart. She dies, with a last fond look at him, at
the feet of the Prince. The orchestra repeats sadly the melody of
No. 13, to the strains of which Timur pours out a pitiful lament
over his " little dove." The body is carried away, the old man walking beside it, holding the little hand in his.

The three masks, the crowd, and even Turandot — after a spasm
of rage in which she snatches a whip from one of the executioner's
assistants and slashes the face of the soldier who has allowed his
dagger to be taken from him — have been moved to pity and remorse by these horrible happenings and their still more horrible
ending. The superstitious mob is afraid that the dead girl's spirit
will haunt them. Ping, Pang and Pong feel something human surg-
ing up within them the very memory of which had almost faded
from their minds during these long years of cruelty. Turandot's
attendants have covered her face with a white veil. When the last
of the crowd has disappeared, following the body of Liù, and only
the Prince and Turandot are left on the stage, he tears her veil
aside, bidding her forget her coldness and be a woman again. She

repels him with scorn: she is divine, she says, and he must not profane her even by touching her veil. But he takes her in his arms and kisses her. At this her defences break down; tremblingly she begs him to leave her — she is afraid of this new something that life has brought her. The old Turandot, she laments, is no more: "The dawn is here," she stammers, "and Turandot's sun is setting." Yes, replies the Prince; it is indeed the dawn — and the coming of a sweeter, purer day.

Now she has fully found her new self. Transfigured, exalted, she confesses that at the first sight of him she had loved him, and, with the memory gnawing her of those who had been sacrificed to her, her hate of him was only her love for him making her dread for him the fate that had overtaken the others. She hated him, too, for very pride: she had to conquer or be conquered. Now that he has triumphed, she begs him to be content with his victory and to leave her, taking his mystery with him. He replies that his mystery is his no longer, now that Turandot is his. His name he gives into her keeping, and with it his life — he is Calaf, the son of Timur. For a moment she becomes almost the old Turandot once more, as she realises that he has placed himself utterly in her power. But he has no fear of her; and as the trumpets sound to proclaim that the appointed hour has come, he goes with the still proud beauty to the supreme trial.

After a brief orchestral interlude the curtain rises on the exterior of the palace, glowing in the red light of dawn. The Emperor is sitting among his court, awaiting, as the vast crowd in front of the palace is doing, the last fateful act of the long-drawn drama. The Prince and Turandot enter. She ascends the staircase at the top of which the Emperor is sitting, and says, "I know the stranger's name: it is — Love!" Calaf rushes to her and folds her in his embrace, while the crowd gives a great cry of joy and strews flowers around them.

The musical world will never cease to regret that Puccini died before he could complete this his greatest score. He laid down his pen at the point where, after the death of Liù, Prince Calaf begins his appeal to Turandot to descend from her lonely ice-cold heaven to the warmth of earth with its human love. Alfano has done his loyal best with the material available to him; but nothing can compensate us for the loss of the Master's touch. It is evident that the librettists had considerable difficulty with the last stages of the drama, and indeed the dénouement they finally decided on is not wholly convincing; but we have the feeling that Puccini's music to the duet between the Prince and Turandot would have carried a conviction of its own.

La Bohème

GIACOMO PUCCINI [1858–1924]

PRINCIPAL CHARACTERS

RODOLFO	*Tenor*
SCHAUNARD	*Baritone*
BENOIT	*Bass*
MIMI	*Soprano*
PARPIGNOL	*Tenor*
MARCELLO	*Baritone*
COLLINE	*Bass*
ALCINDORO	*Bass*
MUSETTA	*Soprano*
A CUSTOM HOUSE SERGEANT	*Bass*

1

THE FIRST thing to note in connection with *La Bohème* is that neither in its original nor its operatic form has it a real "dramatic action": there is no strictly logical sequence of events from one scene to another, no evolution of character under the impact of circumstance; all we have in the opera is four cameos of bohemian life in Paris. This peculiarity of structure, indeed, told a little against Puccini's work at first in some quarters.

The *Scènes de la Vie de Bohème* of Henry Murger (1822–1861), from which the material for Puccini's opera was drawn, is not a continuous novel but a series of sketches of Murger himself and some of the other bohemians and the grisettes among whom his short life was spent, and the adventures, partly authentic, partly fictitious, that befell them.[1] Some of the characters figure in the book in different surroundings, and at times under different names; and the Italian librettists further linked and fused them in a way of their own for the purposes of the opera. For instance, the pathetic little episode of Mimi's muff in the last act of the opera belongs not to Murger's Mimi but to one Francine, whose lover is not the author Rodolphe, but a sculptor, Jacques D. . . . In Murger it is the four men only who always stand for the same types; Rodolphe is always the man of letters, Marcel the painter, Schaunard the musician, and Colline the bookworm and philosopher.

About Schaunard we know, by good luck, more than Murger has told us. In real life he was Alexandre Schanne, who published his memoirs in 1887 under the title of *Souvenirs de Schaunard*. From him we learn that the original of Rodolphe was Murger himself; Colline was an amalgam of a philosopher named Jean Wallon and one Trapadoux, and Marcel a fusion of a Marcel Lazare and a certain Tabar. Schanne's immense nose earned for him among the bohemians of his youth the nickname of Marshal Nez. In some of the early sketches of bohemian life in *Le Corsaire* Murger had slightly disguised him as Schannard: by a printer's error this became Schaunard: and as nobody troubled to correct it, it remained Schaunard ever after. He was born in December 1823; his father was a maker of toys and woolly animals; his mother had a shop in the Passage des Panorames, round the corner from what became later the rue Vivienne. He himself followed painting as a profession, but took up music as a hobby and earned a few francs occasionally by singing in the chorus at small theatres; later he became proficient enough on the viola to play that instrument in the orchestra of the Théâtre-Lyrique. He seems to have had some skill also on the trombone. Between 1850 and 1860 he did various journalistic jobs and wrote a couple of one-act plays; the Paris bohemians of that epoch had to be versatile and agile to

---

[1] The sketches began in the Paris journal *Le Corsaire* in 1848. In November of the following year Murger collaborated with Théodore Barrière in a play, *La Vie de Bohème,* that was produced with great success at the Variétés Theatre and ran for some years: Rodophe, Marcel, Schaunard and Colline all appear in it. The play still makes good reading for opera-goers who wish to construct for themselves the bohemian milieu of Puccini's opera.

keep body and soul together. "Prosperity," for Schanne, meant two meals a day; if he earned as much in a year as a minor book-keeper—say 4,000 francs (about £160 at that time)—he thought himself well off. In 1850 he managed to get a picture exhibited in the Salon, and he published a song or two now and then; but in his last years he was still making toys like his father before him.

2

Puccini's Schaunard, of course, is basically that of Murger. There he is a bit of a painter as well as a musician, but chiefly the latter; he has composed a number of symphonies, including one with the intriguing title *On the Influence of Blue in the Arts*. One of his few lucrative engagements is with a rich Englishman bearing the not quite credible name of Mr. Birn'n, whose sleeping and waking hours are made a misery by a parrot that keeps on reciting speeches from classical tragedies in the best Dramatic Academy style of elocution. The bird belongs to an actress in the apartment below the Englishman; by listening to her rehearsing her rôles it had learned them so thoroughly that it could have deputised for her, if necessary, in the theatre. Several of the inhabitants of the building had terminated their tenancies in despair; but the Englishman was made of sterner stuff. First he tried to buy the bird, with the intention of wringing its neck; but the actress would not part with it. Then Mr. Birn'n had the bright idea of using the piano as a counter-irritant; "the most disagreeable of instruments might be strong enough to contend against the most disagreeable of winged animals," he thought. So he engages Schaunard to play a single scale on the piano from five in the morning until the evening at a fee of two hundred francs a month, rejecting the musician's suggestion that he shall poison the bird with parsley, which the chemists agree in declaring to be "the prussic acid of these animals"; let the Englishman just scatter some bits of parsley on his carpet, says Schaunard, and Coco will meet his death as surely as if he had been dining with Pope Alexander VI (the father of Cesare and Lucrezia Borgia). This episode of the parrot makes a fleeting appearance in the opera, though most spectators miss the point of it.

In Puccini neither Schaunard nor Colline has any feminine encumbrance, the composer and his librettists no doubt feeling that they had enough love interest on their hands already with the Rodolfo-Mimi Marcello-Musetta pairs. In Murger, Schaunard has for mistress a certain Phémie, whom he used to correct, when necessary, with a cane; but discovering one day that one of her knees did not quite match the other his artist's sense of symmetry was outraged and he was compelled to discharge her; however, he generously presented her with the cane as a souvenir of his affection.

Schanne tells us that the authentic Tabar had begun to paint a picture of the Red Sea which he could not complete because of the cost of models, costumes and so on; so he converted it into a less expensive "Niobe and her children slain by the arrows of Apollo and Diana," which was exhibited in the Salon of 1842. This gave Murger his cue for the marvellous history of that picture of *his* Marcel the acquaintance of which we make again in the opera. For five or six years Marcel had been working at a great picture of "The Passage of the Red Sea by the Israelites," which was refused so often by the Salon jury that in the end it knew the way to the Louvre by heart, and could have found its way there alone if put on wheels. But Marcel never lost faith in his own genius or in what he was sure was his masterpiece. He began by altering it a little and sending it in to the Salon again as "The Crossing of the Rubicon"; but the jury was sharp enough to see that Caesar was only Pharaoh painted over. The next year he put a lot of snow in the picture, planted a fir-tree in one corner, transformed an Egyptian into a grenadier of the Napoleonic Guard, and renamed the picture "The Passage of the Beresina." Once more it is recognised and rejected. He now plans to make it the "Passage des Panorames" (a street in Paris). Before he can carry out his design a Jewish art dealer, Salomon, offers him the miserable sum of 150 francs for the picture, in spite of Marcel's anguished protest that the cobalt in Pharaoh's robe alone had cost him more than that. In the end he lets it go for that amount plus a dinner for the four bohemians. Salomon had flatteringly assured him that he was buying the picture for a rich connoisseur who proposed to tour Europe with an exhibition of masterpieces. But a week later, joining a crowd in the Faubourg St. Honoré that is admiring the sign over a provision dealer's shop, Marcel finds that the attraction is none other than his "Passage of the Red Sea"; a boat has been added by another hand, and it is now entitled "The Port of Marseilles." Going away with the enthusiastic comments of the crowd ringing in his ears, Marcel murmurs "Vox populi, vox dei."

3

In Murger both Marcel and Rodolphe fight their way out of bohemia in the end. Marcel gets two pictures into the Salon, one of them being bought by a rich Englishman who had been one of Musette's lovers; with the proceeds the painter pays off some of his debts and treats himself to a real studio. Rodolphe's success was with a book that interested the critics for as long as a month; and even Schaunard had scored a hit with an album of songs. But at the time when we first meet with Rodolphe in bohemia he is starving like the others, though, again like them, he is always gay. At one period his night address is the Avenue de Saint-Cloud, fifth branch of the third tree on the left as you come out of the Bois de Boulogne. His play *Le Vengeur* has been refused by every theatre in Paris. This is the masterpiece we find him burning in the first act of the opera to keep his fingers warm on a winter's day. There is a great deal of manuscript, for it has been copied and re-copied many a time: in Murger he keeps only the latest copy. "I always knew I would manage to place you somewhere some day," he says as the huge manuscript goes into the stove; "but if I'd known what use it was going to be put to I would have added a prologue." When we first meet with him he is ekeing out a living of sorts by editing two fashion magazines, *L'Écharpe d'Iris* and *Le Castor*. Like all the young romantics of the epoch he was Shakespeare-mad. One day Colline met him on the boulevard carrying a rope ladder and a bird-cage with a pigeon in it. It appears that having acquired a new love whose name was Juliet, he had as a matter of course to transform himself into Romeo; he would be obliged, indeed, if Colline would address him only by the name now on his cards—Romeo Montague. One of his first duties will be to kill some Tybalt or other. His Juliet having informed him that there was a balcony outside her apartment, he needs the ladder he is carrying to surmount this. He has done his best also to procure a nightingale to sing when he would have to quit his lady at dawn, with Juliet murmuring

Wilt thou be gone? It is not yet near day:
It was the nightingale, and not the lark,
That pierced the fearful hollow of thine ear;

. . . .

Believe me, love, it was the nightingale.

In his passion for fidelity to the original he had gone so far as to try to obtain a Nurse for his Juliet. His explanation of the pigeon to Colline is that this was the best the bird-seller could do for him, he being out of nightingales at the moment: but pigeons, he had assured Rodolphe-Romeo, also burst into song at dawn. When he calls on Juliet that night complete with ladder and cage, he finds, to his annoyance, that the ladder is superfluous; she had omitted to tell him that her balcony was on the ground level, so that all Romeo had to do to ascend was to throw his leg over it. The pseudo-nightingale wakes them up at an inconveniently early hour the next morning. Juliet, who is as poor as a church mouse, can find nothing for their breakfast but some onions and a bit of bacon, bread and butter. Romeo looks at Juliet: Juliet looks at Romeo; then both look at the pigeon, which is "singing optimistically on its perch." "He was very tender," Romeo remarks appreciatively an hour later: "he had a nice voice," says Juliet. It always heightens our enjoyment of the first act of the opera if we can see each of the four bohemians imaginatively against the Murger background of poverty and gaiety.

4

Colline, in Murger, was the scientist and philosopher of the brotherhood; he was good at mathematics, scholastics, botanics and anything else ending in "ics." Though not of an amorous disposition he had as *amante* a tailoress who spent her days and nights copying out his philosophical works. By the time the book comes to an end we find him inheriting money, marrying well, and giving "evenings," with music and cakes.

Puccini's male characters, then, correspond closely to those of Murger. It is a different matter when we come to the women: Puccini's Mimi and Musetta are composite figures.

In the first act of the opera, when Rodolfo asks his new acquaintance her name, she replies, "They call me Mimi, but my name is Lucia." This is completely meaningless to the audience. It has found its way into the libretto only because one of Murger's sketches tells the story of Rodolphe and a certain Lucille, who went in the bohemian quarter by the name of Mimi. Rodolphe had taken her over as a going concern from one of his friends and fallen madly in love with her. She, however, was an incurable coquette and gold-digger, like virtually all the ladies who figure in the *Scènes de la Vie de Bohème*; she deceived him right and left, only returning to him when it suited her purpose. Schanne tells us that she was a combination of "profound egoism and immense sensibility," "without a vestige of moral sense." Nothing less like the modest, shrinking little Mimi of the first act of the opera could well be imagined.[1] The charming episode of the loss of Mimi's door-key and the artful strategic concealment of it by Rodolfo is taken from another of Murger's stories, that of a certain Francine, a poor little consumptive seamstress who had run away from home to escape the malice of a stepmother and found six months of happiness with the sculptor Jacques D . . . (Puccini transfers her cough to his Mimi of the third act.) It was Murger's Francine, not Rodolphe's Mimi, who had come to Jacques' room one night to light her candle, and, when the last match had gone out, dropped her key and could not find it, because Jacques had had the presence of mind to kick it under a piece of furniture. Both she and her lover come to a horrible end. Puccini further transferred from Francine to Mimi the pathetic episode of the tiny muff brought to warm her hands when she is dying. From another story, *Epilogue des Amours de Rodolphe et de Mademoiselle Mimi*, he took the moving little motive of the broken Mimi, now at death's door, seeking refuge with Marcel, and Colline selling his books and Schaunard his scanty wardrobe

---

[1] We learn from Schanne that in Murger's Mimi there is something also of a cousin of his named Angèle, a good bourgeoise who married respectably, and of a friend of hers named Marie, who, though married, had a soft spot in her heart for Murger. She seems, like so many of the Frenchwomen of that period in and out of Murger's pages, to have had the poor health that made the type so attractive to poets of *l'école poitrinaire*. The younger Dumas' Marguerite Gautier (Verdi's Violetta) is a later representative of the type.

to buy a few comforts for her before she is taken to the hospital, where she dies in misery.[1]

In Murger, as in Puccini, Musette is Marcel's mistress. It was he who had given her the name of Musette, because she was always singing; her notes were clear, we are told, but not always in tune; some of the Musettas we hear in the theatre imitate her all too conscientiously in this latter respect. She was intelligent, but an incurable man-hunter and gold-digger, reckless, spendthrift, self-indulgent, preferring silks to cottons, driving about in her carriage one week and taking the omnibus the next, according to the state of the purse of her lover of the moment. As in the opera, her barefaced infidelities are a perpetual exasperation to Marcel. In Murger she ends by settling down as the wife of a respectable postmaster, the guardian of a former lover of hers. "She is going to marry," Marcel tells Rodolphe one day. "Contre qui?" asks the latter. From Schanne we learn that Marcel's "singing Musette" was derived from a certain Mme. Pierre Dupont.[2] Schanne describes the real Musette in terms that confirm Murger's delineation of her. She was always "on the make," and always perfectly frank about it. She did very well, till one day in 1863 she set out in the "Atlas" from Marseilles for Algiers, taking with her 40,000 francs, and was drowned.

5

By the time that Puccini's *Manon Lescaut* was off his hands and on the stage, in February 1893, he was in hot pursuit of another subject. According to his friend Fraccaroli he had virtually decided in that same February on Murger's *Scènes de la Vie de Bohème*. But soon there arose that complication with Leoncavallo—

[1] According to Schanne, the Teinturière Phémie with whom Murger endowed Schaunard was one Louisette, who worked in an artificial flower factory and also did some dyeing—hence the "Teinturière." After an illness of three months she lamented that she had no frock to go out in on New Year's Day, and so worked on Schaunard's emotions that to buy her one he sold his new overcoat for thirty francs. She went out gaily in it and never returned to him. This is probably the authentic source of the moving episode of the sale of the coat in Murger and in the opera.

[2] As we have seen, a painting by Schanne was exhibited in the Salon in 1850. It bore the title "Portrait of Mme. Pierre." This was no doubt the Mme. Pierre Dupont who sang. It would be interesting if that picture of the "singing Musette" could be found today.

whose *Pagliacci* had appeared in May 1892—the details of which are still rather obscure, though the main facts are not in dispute. At a chance meeting of the two composers, who were acquaintances rather than friends, they began to discuss their future plans. Puccini happened to say that he had the Murger book in his mind for his next opera; whereupon Leoncavallo leaped from his seat, shouting, "But that is the subject *I* have chosen!" After that, neither of them let the grass grow under his feet. The next morning *Il Secolo,* which belonged to Leoncavallo's publisher Sonzogno, announced that the composer of *Pagliacci* was now engaged on an opera based on Murger's famous work; the same afternoon Ricordi's paper *Il Corriere della Sera* informed the world that Puccini had a *Bohème* in hand. Leoncavallo's *La Bohème* was produced in Venice in 1897, with considerable initial success; but by that time Puccini's work had become well established, and Leoncavallo's proved less and less able to stand up to the competition.

The music of *La Bohème* occupied Puccini all in all, allowing for interruptions, for no more than about eight months, from some time in 1894 to November 1895; but hammering out the libretto had meant two years of hard labour on his part and that of his librettists, Luigi Illica and Giuseppe Giacosa. As usual, Puccini, who was rarely in the least doubt as to what he wanted as dramatist, drove his collaborators to near suicide with his demands for fresh reconstruction, modification and condensation. Giulio Ricordi, who was a fourth in some of the discussions, has left us a lively description of the sorrows of the two devoted librettists, and of the frenzied Puccini gnawing his nails down to the flesh, so that after each conference he had to pay a visit to his manicurist. We will deal with some of the constructional difficulties of the trio as occasion arises in our analysis of the opera.

La Bohème was given for the first time at the Teatro Regio, Turin, under Toscanini, on the 1st February 1896. It had a cool reception from most of the critics, who lamented what one of them called the "degradation" the composer had inflicted on his Muse; but the public warmed to it more and more at each performance, and at Palermo, in April of the same year, it scored a complete success, in spite of the superstitious conviction of Mugnone, the conductor, that no good would come of a production on the 13th of the month, and a Friday at that. For a while, indeed, it seemed that his forebodings would be realised, especially when the oboist did not turn up until half-past nine. The final curtain did not fall until one in the morning, but the audience, instead of leaving, clamoured for more. It ended with the last act being repeated from the entry of Mimi, with as many of the orchestra as had not gone home by then, a Rodolfo without his wig, and a Mimi whisked from her dressing room and pushed on to the stage with her hair down.

The biographers have been at pains to recall that Puccini himself and his fellow-students at the Milan Conservatoire had lived a life of gay poverty closely resembling that of Murger's characters, and have opined that the bohemian scenes of *La Bohème* are so excellent because here the composer was "drawing upon his personal experiences." That assumption is somewhat unnecessary. Shakespeare surely did not have to liquidate Anne Hathaway with a bolster to realise just how Othello felt after the murder of Desdemona. Wagner did not need to have trodden the actual meadows of Monsalvat one Good Friday morning to write the Good Friday music of *Parsifal*, nor to have suffered the worst pangs of conscience, aggravated by a painful wound in the groin, before he could find the right accents of anguish for his maddened Amfortas. Puccini himself had had no first-hand experience of police third-degree methods when he wrote the music for the torture scene in *Tosca*, nor had any female relative of his been deserted by an American naval officer before he could limn his broken-hearted Butterfly. No creative artist worthy of the name is very much dependent upon "personal experiences" in order to place himself inside the skin of a character and speak with the veritable tongue of that character; all he needs is an imagination protean enough to assume for a moment any one of a hundred forms, and a faculty of expression on a par with his imagination. So we need not jump to the innocent conclusion, as more than one biographer has done, that Puccini, thanks to his youthful experiences in Milan, is himself Rodolfo, Marcello, Colline and Schaunard rolled into one; any more than we need suppose that Strauss could never have written his orchestral masterpiece unless he himself had been as crazy as Don Quixote at some time or other.

6

Puccini was fully aware that his characters called for a little explanation on his part; so to each of his four acts he prefixed a few lines taken from Murger's book. The preamble to the first act runs thus: "Mimi was a charming girl of a type that made a peculiar appeal to Rodolphe's plastic and poetic susceptibilities. She was twenty-two, slight, dainty, roguish. Her face suggested a sketch for some aristocratic beauty; her features, the last word in refinement, were softly lit up, as it were, by her limpid blue eyes; [*but in moments of boredom or ill-humor they gave a hint of an almost savage brutality, which a psychologist would probably have read as the sign of a profound egoism or utter insensibility. As a rule, however, her face was charming, with its fresh young smile, its air now tender, now imperiously coquettish*]. The warm lively blood of youth coursed in her veins, giving her complexion a rosy tint underneath its camellia-like whiteness and transparency. This sickly beauty had a great attraction for Rodolphe. . . . But what made him most madly in love with Mimi were her hands, which, despite her domestic duties, she managed to keep whiter than the hands of the Goddess of Idleness." The passage in italics in this quotation was omitted by Puccini: the Mimi he wanted us to take to our hearts in his first act was to have no darker side to her character; she was to be all innocence, aspiration, fragility, patience and pathos.

Puccini thought it further necessary to reproduce the gist of Murger's description of bohemia and its inhabitants. The type, said the French novelist, has appeared in one form or another in all ages, with Villon as one of its supreme representatives: but it is only in Paris that bohemia now exists or can exist. Your genuine bohemian believes in art for art's sake; according to his lights he obeys the imperious call of art, indifferent to failure, poverty, suffering or ridicule. Few even of the best of them win recognition until it is too late; many of them die young. There is a particularly tragic fringe of them, young bohemians who, in addition to being duped by the world, are their own self-dupes: "they mistake a fancy for a vocation . . . and die either the victims of perpetual accesses of pride or the idolators of a chimera." There is another sub-species—the weaker ones who give up the fight against

hardship and privation, return to the comfortable paternal fire-
side, marry their cousins, become small-town notaries, and in
their well-fed middle age tell and re-tell with supreme complacency the story of their one-time sacrifices and sufferings for art.

For Murger the bohemians *pur sang* are those of his own type,
the young fellows with something in them who, given a bit of
luck, will one day make good. "Rain or dust," begins the passage
from the *Scènes de la Vie de Bohème* which Puccini has chosen as
introduction to his score, "sun or shadow, nothing can stop these
bold adventurers. . . . If need be, they will practice abstinence
with all the rigor of an anchorite; but let a tiny bit of fortune
come their way and they will ride a cock-horse on the most ruin-
ous fantasies, falling in love with the youngest and fairest women,
drinking the best and oldest wines, and never finding windows
enough to fling their money out of. Then, when their last crown
is dead and buried, they start dining again at the table d'hôte of
chance, where their cover is always laid, and go marauding in all
the industries that have any connection with art, hunting from
morn till eve the wild animal known as the five-franc piece. . . .
Bohemians speak among themselves a dialect of their own, the
product of the studios, the stage and the editorial office. . . .
This vocabulary is the hell of rhetoric and the paradise of neolo-
gism. . . . A delightful life, and a terrible one. . . ."

This, then, is the milieu, these the character types, that Puccini
would have us keep in mind during his first act.

7

The curtain rises on the bohemians' attic in the Latin Quarter
of Paris. The scanty furniture consists of a table, a cupboard, a
small book-case, four chairs, and an easel. On the right is a stove
that shows no sign of giving out any heat. A few books lie about,
for Rodolfo and Colline are men of letters; some packs of cards
suggest occasional lighter interests. Through a great window we
get a side glimpse of roofs and chimneys covered with snow, for
it is Christmas eve.

Rodolfo is not working—he is too cold and hungry for the
ideas to flow—but staring moodily out of the window. Marcello
is at the easel, making an heroic effort with his frozen fingers to

add a touch or two to his painting "The Passage of the Red Sea."
The motifs given out by the orchestra, such as:

1

and

2

are those which will always characterize the bohemians in their
collective aspect.[1] "This Red Sea Passage takes it out of me,"
Marcello grumbles; "it chills me to the bone." He steps back a
little to get a better view of his work, ejaculates "By way of
revenge a Pharaoh I will drown," and puts in a few vicious
strokes at the canvas.[2] What is Rodolfo doing? he asks over his
shoulder. The poet has been lost in depressed contemplation of
the view from the window: he sees chimneys pouring out their
smoke by the thousand, he says, but this lazy old fraud of a stove

[1] In 1883, towards the end of his three years' course at the Milan Conservatoire, Puccini wrote a *Capriccio Sinfonico* for orchestra which was performed with considerable success at a Conservatoire concert in the July of
that year. The full score has never been published, but there exists a contemporary arrangement of it for piano duet by one Giuseppe Frugatta.
Puccini not only used two of the themes of this early work for his *Edgar*
of 1889 but fashioned out of the main theme of the central allegro section of
it the opening bars of *La Bohème*, transposing it a major fourth down, and
altering the outline of it at some points. In the *Capriccio* it runs thus:

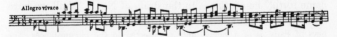

Readers who possess a score of the opera will find it interesting to compare
the two versions. It will be seen that in bar 12 of the above quotation we
have a pendant to the theme that reappears in bars 12–19 of *La Bohème*.
[2] Whenever Marcel felt inspired and energetic, Murger tells us, he would
engulf another Egyptian.

of theirs does no work—just takes its ease like a gentleman of leisure: [1]

3

Nei cie-li bi—gi guar-do fu-mar dai mil—le co—mi-gno-li Pa-ri—gi

Marcel makes excuse for the delinquent; after all, he admits, it is their fault, for they never feed him, never pay his dues. "And those imbecile forests, what are they all doing underneath the snow?" asks Rodolfo. "Let me communicate a profound thought that has just occurred to me," rejoins Marcello: "I am cold to the marrow"; and he blows on his fingers again. "Nor will I conceal from you," says Rodolfo, "that I no longer believe in the sweat of my brow"; and No. 1 pounds out with humorous impatience in the orchestra. "My fingers are as frozen," continues Marcello, "as if they were embedded in that big block of ice, Musetta's heart," and with a sigh for his lost illusions he puts palette and brushes aside. Rodolfo, as befits a man of letters, becomes philosophical and metaphorical: "Ah, love's a stove that consumes too much fuel." ("And too quickly," interjects Marcello); and the fellow-sufferers from love go on each capping the other's imagery: "where the man is the faggot"—"and the woman does the blowing"—"as the one burns down and out"—"the other stands and looks on." "But meanwhile here we are freezing"—"and what's more, dying of hunger." "Something must be done about it"—"Let's sacrifice a chair"—and Marcello seizes one of them and begins to break it up.

Rodolfo restrains him: he has a better idea. "Eureka!" he cries, taking a bulky manuscript from the table. "Genius will tell: ideas flame forth!" he continues to the strain of No. 3. "Shall we burn

[1] Our No. 3, to which Rodolfo sings of the "grey sky" and smoking chimneys of Paris, is of a gaiety quite unexpected in the circumstances. The fact is that it was originally written in praise of the blue sky of Sicily and the smoking Mount Aetna. Puccini had originally intended it, in 1894, for an opera with a Sicilian setting, *La Lupa* (based on a play by Giovanni Verga), the plan for which he had soon dropped. He had gone to Sicily, however, to get local colour, and this melody was one of the fruits of his stay there.

the Red Sea?" asks Marcello. "No," says Rodolfo, "think how
the paint will smell! My drama, my ardent drama, shall give
us heat." "You are not going to read it?" protests Marcello in
mock terror; "I'd prefer to freeze!" "No, let the paper burn to
ashes, and the poet's inspiration ascend to the heavens whence it
came. The age will suffer an irreparable literary loss, but Rome
is in peril! Here goes the first act!" Charmingly descriptive music
accompanies the tearing up of the first act of the play, the lighting
of a candle by flint and steel, and the commission to the stove of
the sheets of the dramatic masterpiece that has been refused by
every theatre in Paris.

With No. 3 pursuing its eager course in the orchestra—for even
cold and hunger cannot quench the spirits of our young bohemians—poet and painter draw up their chairs to the stove and
joyously warm their hands. They are in this attitude when the
door at the back is flung violently open and the clumsy bookworm
Colline steps in:

4

and furiously throws a bundle of books on to the table. He is in
a very bad temper: what has happened to the world, he asks
angrily, when the pawnbrokers won't make a man a bit of an
advance on Christmas eve?; and No. 1 gives a comically peevish
point to his grievance. The unaccustomed sight of a fire in the
stove, however, cheers him up a little. This drama of Rodolfo's
is really scintillating, he assures the author; its only fault is that
it is too short. "Brevity is the soul of wit," Rodolfo assures him
complacently. Claiming the right to a complimentary seat at this
unexpected first performance of the play Colline takes Rodolfo's
chair from him and warms his hands at the stove. Marcello
grumbles about the excessive length of the entr'actes, for these
yield no warmth; like a true dramatic critic he clamours for more
action, so Rodolfo bundles the second act into the stove, the
orchestra suggesting a fresh gust of flame. Colline congratulates
him on the profundity of thought displayed in the drama; and
Rodolfo, while lamenting so sad an end to his great love scene,

heroically sends the remaining three acts after the first two. But the flames soon die down and finally sputter out, and then, like critics at the first performance of a play, Marcello and Colline rush at him crying "Down with the author!"

Before they can hurl him too into the stove a joyous new theme to be associated with Schaunard is heard in the orchestra:

5

and their attention is drawn to two shop boys who enter from the back, one bearing provisions, wine and cigars, the other a faggot of wood. The three bohemians delightedly take possession of these unexpected reinforcements, Colline carrying the wood to the stove, Marcello giving an exultant shout of "Bordeaux!" as he examines the label on a bottle of wine. Now they can celebrate Christmas in proper fashion! But why these generous gifts of the gods? The mystery is solved by the exuberant entrance of Schaunard, scattering gold coins on the floor and singing to the melody of No. 5, "All the wealth of the Bank of France is yours!" The others stare incredulously at the money. "Pieces of tin?" suggests Marcello. Schaunard shouts at him to take a closer look at the coins: whose image and superscription do they show? "King Louis Philippe's!" says the awed Rodolfo; and he makes a profound obeisance to his beneficent Majesty.

8

Schaunard explains how he discovered this El Dorado. An English gentleman—he may even have been a Milord—had engaged him on the strength of his reputation as a musician; when Schaunard asked when the lessons were to begin he was told "At once." Pointing to a parrot in a cage outside the first floor of the building, the Englishman had instructed him to keep on playing the piano until the bird dropped dead. After enduring this outrage on his dignity as an artist for three long days, says Schaunard, he turned his famous charm on the servant girl, fascinated her, wheedled some parsley out of her, and gave it to

Lorito, who at once fell dead. The other bohemians take no notice at all of his long tale, for the one thought in their minds is food. Rodolfo lights another candle; the faggot is flung into the stove; Colline's books are swept off the table and a copy of the "Constitutional" spread on it by way of a tablecloth—"a splendid paper; one can eat and devour the supplement at the same time"; the viands are laid out—a fine pie, cold roast beef, etc.; and the four chairs are drawn up. Schaunard, still unable to get a hearing for his story, at last loses his temper; he snatches away the pie the others have started on, removes the other eatables, puts them in the cupboard, and tells them that all this must be stored up for leaner days that are sure to come. This is Christmas eve, when no one in the Latin Quarter with any sense dines at home. Puccini builds it all up into an enchanting vocal quartet, the main threads of which are No. 5 and another joyous theme:

6

Out there in the street, Schaunard continues, there is the savoury odour of fritters:

7

girls are singing with their lovers; religion itself demands that though they may drink at home on Christmas eve they must eat outside. His enthusiasm infects the others. They lock the doors and are opening a bottle of wine when a knock is heard: they know only too well who it is—the landlord, old Benoit, come for his rent. At first they are for pretending that they are not at home, but in the end they decide they will have to admit him. He comes in with an ingratiating smile and hands Marcello his bill. They greet him with the most effusive cordiality, insist politely on his joining them at table, pour him out a glass of wine, and drink his health, to the accompaniment of a charming new motive:

8

Andantino ♩. = 100

They keep pressing wine on him, but after each potation he returns like a homing pigeon to the point he started from—the quarter's rent is due, and he looks to Marcello to redeem his promise to pay it. The others nearly faint when the painter draws Benoit's attention to the gold coins spread out on the table. They think he must have taken leave of his senses; but Marcello knows what he is about. The money is convincing proof of their solvency; but he asks the landlord to put aside all thoughts of mere mammon for a few minutes and be one of their festive company.

9

In another delightful ensemble they play artfully on the old man's vanity. They refuse to believe that he is older than they: did not Marcello see him the other evening at the Bal Mabille with a pretty young blonde? "Old rascal!" says one approvingly. "Seducer!" says another; "the man's an oak-tree, a cannon"; the maiden's ardour had been nothing to his. Benoit, who by now has been made to swallow more wine than he can carry, melts into a mood of senile self-satisfaction. He may be getting on, he tells them, but he is still robust. In his youth he had been timid with women, but now he's the very devil among them. Complacently he describes his feminine ideal: he likes them neither as big as a whale or a map of the world and with a face like a full moon, nor on the skinny side, for the lean ones are often very trying, too full of grievances, "like my wife, for example."

The bohemians are scandalised. In a lively quartet they express their horror of this elderly Casanova polluting the chaste atmosphere of their attic; the place must be decontaminated forthwith. Marcello rises to his full physical and moral height; the others follow him, and the bewildered Benoit is hustled to the door and thrown out on to the landing, with their best wishes for a happy Christmas eve.[1]

That little matter of the quarter's rent having been thus satisfactorily settled, the bohemians, to the tune of No. 7, turn to the more important question of where to spend the evening. The voting is in favour of the Momus, the famous café in the Latin Quarter where all the bright young spirits of Paris used to foregather to wrangle about literature and art and politics and set the world in general to rights. (Schanne tells us that it was located at No. 15 in the rue des Prêtres-Saint-Germain l'Auxerrois; it had a great vogue between about 1843 and 1848, numbering notabilities like Baudelaire and Gérard de Nerval among its patrons.) The bohemians divide the money on the table among them, and Colline, on Marcello's advice, promises to make himself more presentable by having a hair-cut and a shave.

As the Rodolfo theme (No. 3) steals out softly in the orchestra the conscientious man of letters announces his intention of staying behind for a little while to order to finish the leading article for one of his papers, the "Beaver," a matter of a mere few minutes for a practised hand like his. So the other three leave him, Schaunard giving him a final playful exhortation to "cut short the Beaver's tail."

Blowing out one of the candles, Rodolfo clears a space on the table and sits down to write. But the ideas will not come; he tears up what he has written and throws down his pen. Just then a timid knock is heard at the door: the Mimi theme, breathed softly by the orchestra:

tells us who is without. Rodolfo opens the door for her; in her hand she has a candle and a key. The candle having gone out, she

---

[1] The episode of the bamboozling of the landlord who has called, full of optimism, for his rent is condensed from a similar one in Murger.

has come to get a light from this neighbour of hers. No sooner has she entered the room than she is seized with a fit of coughing—the ascent of the stairs has been too much for the fragile, underfed creature. Rodolfo solicitously places her in a chair, where she swoons, dropping key and candlestick as she does so. He revives her by sprinkling water on her face,[1] which gives him an opportunity to observe—and to inform the audience—that while very beautiful she is also very pale. She apologises for being so troublesome; but he manages to persuade her to sit nearer the fire and take a sip of wine.

He lights her candle, gives it to her without speaking, and accompanies her to the door; but just as they are bidding each other good evening she finds, to her dismay, that she has lost her key:

10

Andante moderato ♩= 88

p Oh! sven—ta—ta, sven—ta—ta! La chia-ve del-la stan-za

As the draught from the open door has extinguished her candle again he relights it from his; but that too fails, and the room is now in darkness. He manages to locate her by the polite apologies she is making for all the trouble she is giving; and now the attention of both of them centres on the lost key. Rodolfo gropes for it on the floor and at last finds it, but checks the impulse to give it to Mimi and slips it into his pocket. The music to this little cameo has been throughout the perfection of quiet simplicity and naturalness; now it is time for Puccini to brace himself for the big lyrical close to his first act.

10

As they still grope in the darkness Rodolfo's hand touches Mimi's, and he is shocked by the coolness of it: "How very cold your little hand is," he says: "let me warm it":

[1] There is a charming bit of realism in the orchestra at this point; the trouble is that the sprinkling by Rodolfo and the sprinkling in the orchestra rarely coincide in performance.

11

Andantino ♩ = 58

pp Che ge-li-da ma-ni-na, se la la-sci ris-cal-dar etc

Bass: Ab —————— Eb ———— Ab ———— Db

What is the use of searching for the key? he asks. They will never find it in the dark, but soon the moon will be up, and then they will have better luck. To reassure her as she timidly tries to withdraw her hand he begins to tell her all about himself, who and what he is and how he lives. He is a poet. What does he do? He writes. Is that a living? Hardly. Anyhow he lives; and though he is poor he is as happy as any grand seigneur, he declares to a reminiscence of No. 3, writing hymns to love, luxuriating in his dreams, building castles in the air, a pauper in the flesh but in soul a millionaire. Sometimes, though, his coffers are raided by two thieves—two beautiful eyes such as hers; yet he does not regret his loss:

12

Andante lento ♩ = 52

Ta—lor dal mio for-zie —re--- ru-ban tutti i gio-

iel——li due la-dri: gli oc-chi bel-li

Hope is springing to life in his breast again, he assures her. And now that he has told her his story, will she not tell him hers?

To the simple strain of No. 9 she replies, "They call me Mimi, but my name is Lucia." Little has she to tell him about herself. At home or in a shop she embroiders on cloth or silk, and after her simple fashion she is happy, for into the fabrics she weaves the roses and lilies of her dreams: "these things are full of enchantment for me, for they speak of love and spring":

13

Andante calmo ♩ = 54

pp   Mi piac-cion quel-le co-se, che han si dol-ce ma-li-a, che par-la-no d'a-mor

and her simple confession ends with a phrase, sung to the words
"All this is poetry. Do you understand me?":

14

pp

of which Puccini will make fine use later. "They call me Mimi,"
she repeats, "but I know not why." She leads a very lonely life
in a tiny chamber that looks out over the housetops; but when
spring comes it gets the sun's first kiss, she assures him to a melody
at once passionate and pathetic, that is the emotional high light
of the score thus far:

15

Andante molto

pp   Ma quan-do vien lo sge—lo il pri-mo so-le è mi-o----

She loves the scent of flowers, but those she makes, alas, are
odourless. "More than this I cannot tell you about myself," she
concludes with a touch of naïveté, dropping from melody into
simple speech; "I am just a neighbour of yours who comes to
bother you at an inopportune moment."

Just then, to Rodolfo's annoyance, Marcello, Colline and
Schaunard call to him from the street below, urging the sluggard
to hurry up with his article and join them. Opening the window
and thus admitting the first rays of moonlight into the gloomy
room, he assures them that he has only another three lines to
write, and then he will be with them at the Momus; nor is he, as
they assume, alone. Turning to Mimi, whom now, at last, he
really sees as she stands bathed in the moonlight, he sings, to the
melody of No. 12, an ecstatic hymn in praise of her beauty: she
answers with equal ardour, and for the first time their voices

blend in harmony. He kisses her; she would fain disengage herself and send him out to join his companions, but, thinking better of it, shyly asks whether she may come with him. He tries to get her to see that they would be much cosier all by themselves in the attic; but her reply suggests that she will be not unwilling to return there with him after the festivities. And so, to the whispered strains of No. 11, she gives him her arm and they go out together, as befits an operatic hero and heroine, on a C *in alt.*

11 .

The second act is staged in the heart of the Latin Quarter, where Paris is enjoying itself on Christmas eve. The third act takes place at the Barrière d'Enfer—the toll-gate at which the custom-house officers deal with the provisions brought in from the country; and nothing could be more indicative of the lack of real dramatic evolution in the structure of *La Bohème* than the fact that for a long time Puccini intended his Barrière scene to constitute his *second* act and the Latin Quarter scene his third. (About the fourth act there could never be any doubt; it would obviously have to centre in the death of Mimi.) How the composer and his librettists proposed to handle their original plan for the second and third acts with any appearance at all of dramatic probability is beyond our understanding; but it evidently took Puccini a long time to decide on the present order. His correspondence shows him insisting, as against Illica's wishes, that there must be a Latin Quarter scene that would include the Musetta episode, which latter, he claims, was *his* idea. By what process of reasoning, and exactly at what time, he decided on the present order for acts 2 and 3 we do not know; but we may congratulate ourselves that, as usual, his excellent sense of the theatre pointed out the right course to him in the end.

In his prose preface to the second act he condenses for our benefit some passages from Murger that describe the inseparable attachment to each other of the four bohemians—to whom the Café Momus had given the name of the Four Musketeers—and supply us with the background for an understanding of the new character soon to be introduced—Musetta. She was a fine girl of twenty, we read, coquettish and egoistic, very ambitious but wholly illiterate, taking the revolutions of fortune's wheel philosophically, one day flaunting it in her carriage in the rue Bréda, on the next content with an omnibus in the Latin Quarter.

It is now later in the evening: there has been time for Colline to get groomed for a public appearance, and for Rodolfo and Mimi to join the other three for the great celebration at the Café Momus, which we see, when the curtain rises, on the right-hand side of a square formed by the convergence of various streets. A few citizens are seated at tables outside the café, which is illuminated by a huge lantern. Shopkeepers are touting for the patronage of the miscellaneous crowd circulating in the streets—boys, girls, children, soldiers, servant girls, working girls, gendarmes and so on. Rodolfo and Mimi are strolling up and down arm in arm, obviously preferring each other's company to that of anyone else in the world. Colline stands near a rag shop; Schaunard is bargaining for a pipe and a horn that have taken his fancy in a tinsmith's shop; Marcello is making his way with some difficulty through the milling crowd.

12

The general atmosphere of gaiety is established by a few bars of the Momus theme (No. 7) in the orchestra (the strain to which, in the first act, Schaunard had sung the praises of the odour of fritters and the gay crowd in the street outside the attic). It is upon this theme and one first allotted to the hawkers:

16

that the lively opening chorus is constructed. Everyone is bawling at once, the hawkers trying to sell their various wares, the townsfolk and the street arabs commenting on the uproar, the people outside the café clamouring for service. Schaunard is still bargaining for the tinsmith's horn; the D is out of tune, he declares, and to prove it he blows some D flats that are alien to the E flat scale in which No. 16 is now heard. While Colline is confabulating with a clothes dealer about a coat—"It's rather worn," he says, "but still quite good and cheap"—Rodolfo and Mimi come well into view, to the accompaniment of a tender phrase in the orchestra:

17

They disappear into a milliner's shop, for Mimi has seen a bonnet in the window that takes her fancy. Marcello, jostled by the girls, is doing his best to enjoy himself despite his recent desertion by Musetta: but he is quite unable to share Colline's enthusiasm over an almost unique copy of a Runic grammar which the philosopher has just picked up on a stall.

When Mimi reappears she is wearing the new bonnet, and Rodolfo is telling her how wonderfully its rose trimming suits her complexion; and a little phrase wells up in the orchestra:

18

that will acquire a strange poignancy in the last act. But the appetite of the innocent Mimi whom we have seen in the first act is evidently beginning to grow with what it feeds on: she draws Rodolfo's attention to a pretty coral necklace. By now, perhaps, he is beginning to appreciate the wisdom of Ovid's advice to the young lover—"Don't call on her on her birthday; you'll find it too expensive"; but he manages to side-track her by telling her he has an old uncle who is a millionaire, and if it should please God to take the old gentleman to a better world he will buy her a much finer necklace than this. For a few moments they are lost once more in the crowd at the back of the stage; and when we see them again an exchange of glances between Mimi and some students calls for a little mild comment on Rodolfo's part. The fleeting episode is apt to go unnoticed by the spectator. He should be aware of it, however, for here Puccini is quietly preparing us for the main psychological motive of the third act—the proneness of Rodolfo to accesses of jealousy.

The happy pair light upon the other bohemians just after Marcello, Colline and Schaunard have come out of the café carrying a table, for although it is the depth of winter they are determined to dine out of doors; some worthy citizens seated near by resent the intrusion of these noisy newcomers and move away in a huff.

Having introduced Mimi to his friends, Rodolfo becomes poetical in praise of her charms, and the others chaff the poet for being so high-falutin. But before the feast can begin and the tempestuous Musetta enter to change the whole face of things, Puccini and his librettists, finding themselves with a little space on their hands, insert a delightful interlude in which the children besiege one Parpignol—a toy-seller who enters with his barrow from the rue Dauphin—and pester their mothers to buy them something. Marcello, Colline and Schaunard, after studying the menu, have to shout their orders—turkey, lobster, wine, etc.— to make themselves heard by the waiters. Schaunard puts on considerable dog to impress the latter; Mimi having timidly suggested that she would like some custard, Schaunard, with an air of tremendous importance, bids the waiter bring "The best you have! For a lady!"

13

Parpignol having left the scene, drawing after him, like another Pied Piper, all the children, Mimi tells Marcello of the pretty pink bonnet Rodolfo has bought her, to a theme:

19

out of which, in conjunction with another given to Marcello ("Oh beautiful age of illusions and utopias, when the heart still believes and hopes!"):

O bel-la e-tà d'in—gan-ni e du-to—pi — e!

Puccini proceeds, as usual, to make a charming vignette, musically self-contained and self-sufficing yet fitting neatly into the general frame.

Rodolfo's and Mimi's rhapsodies on love begin to get on the nerves of Marcello, who becomes more and more pessimistic as he thinks of his faithless Musetta. But just as the bohemians are about to drink a toast there is a diversion that gives the act a totally new turn. From the rue Mazarin there bursts on the scene like a tornado the rip-roaring Musetta herself:

21

having in tow her latest protector, a rich, pompous, fussy, over-dressed old beau of the name of Alcindoro, whom, however, she addresses by the pet-dog name of Lulu. She is very pretty, very coquettish, very artful, knowing all the tricks of the trade. Poor Alcindoro is already near the end of his patience with her tyrannical caprices. He wants to dine unobtrusively inside the café; but Musetta, having at once recognised her bohemian friends, insists on having the table lately vacated by the little group of townsfolk. "The naughty Elder," says Colline, looking critically at Lulu. "With the chaste Susanna!" Marcello adds contemptuously. "What fine clothes she wears!" says Mimi enviously; to which Rodolfo rejoins sententiously, "The angels go naked." Before Rodolfo can reply to her query "Who is she?" Marcello supplies the information: "I'll tell you. Her name is Musetta: her surname is temptation: as for her vocation, she is like a magnetic needle, so often does she change her direction in love [1]: she is a screech-

[1] The English version of the text—"as to her vocation, like a rose in the breezes she changes her lover for lovers without number"—is based on a

owl, that most bloodthirsty of birds, whose favourite morsel is the heart. For my part, I've no heart left, so pass me the ragout."

While the others are chattering together, Musetta, to a motive as expressive of her restless vitality as No. 21:

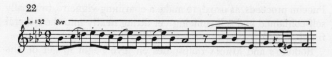

22

goes on railing at everyone and everything. (Perhaps No. 21 is Musetta herself, No. 22 Musetta as seen through Marcello's eyes.) She is furious because Marcello so pointedly ignores her and Schaunard laughs at her tantrums; and she has no one to back her up, she complains, but this old pelican of a Lulu! She could scratch everyone's eyes out. She complains to the waiter that the plate he has put before her smells of onions; and before he can remove it she dashes it on the ground. Some working-girls who are crossing the stage point her out to each other and laugh: she is evidently well known in the Quarter. Poor old Alcindoro tries in vain to pacify her: "Manners! Manners!" he keeps ejaculating; "Try to behave! What will all the people say?"

14

"Now the fun is at its height!" says Schaunard, during another of those miniature ensembles of which Puccini is so fond in *La Bohème*. Colline agrees. Rodolfo gives Mimi a quiet hint that he would never forgive her if *she* were to behave as Musetta has done; she protests that she loves him too much for the question of forgiveness ever to arise between them. Marcello, though he still refuses to take the smallest notice of Musetta, is visibly weakening, and she changes her strategy accordingly. For the benefit of them all, but mainly of Marcello, she launches, in what is virtually an aria in waltz time, into a flattering description of herself:

---

misunderstanding of the Italian words, "Per sua vocazione fa la rosa dei venti; gira e muta soventi d'amanti e d'amore." "La rosa dei venti" is literally "the rose of the winds," but its idiomatic meaning is the card beneath the magnetic needle, showing the points of the mariner's compass.

Wherever she goes, she assures them, all masculine eyes are drawn to her. ("Tie me to my chair!" Marcello implores his friends.) She is conscious of her power, and simply *must* exercise it over men. "Why do you"—she addresses Marcello directly, "you who were once in love with me, try so stupidly to fly from me now? I know you don't want to speak your grief; but I know also that you are dying of it." [1] While she pauses for a moment for breath Rodolfo explains to Mimi that Musetta was once Marcello's love, but the fickle creature had deserted him for a more luxurious life with another. Mimi understands it all at last, and her sympathies seem to be with poor Musetta, for in her opinion great love means in the end great sorrow. Alcindoro manages to get in an occasional "Softly! Softly! Manners!" Colline and Schaunard philosophise aside on the sad case of Musetta and Marcello; the former finds the girl not unattractive, but finally, much in the spirit of Kipling's "A woman is only a woman, but a good cigar is a smoke," he decides that for his part he'd rather have his pipe and a Greek text.

Musetta, now sure of her triumph, approaches Marcello, who is too hypnotised to take flight as he would obviously like to do. She sees that in order to play her last card she must get rid of Lulu, which she does by howling that she is suffering agonies from a tight shoe and packing him off with it to a neighbouring shop to get her another pair. Marcello is quite melted now; his heart is not dead, he assures her, and is hers any time she likes to come for it. At the height of the big ensemble she throws herself into his arms to a thunderous outburst of No. 23 in the orchestra.

[1] Musetta's song was originally a piano piece the idea of which had come to Puccini one day when he was being gently rocked in a boat on the waters of a lake. Later he was asked, along with Mancinelli and Franchetti, to write something for the launching of an Italian battleship at Genoa; and his contribution was this waltz-melody! Thinking it too good to be wasted, he decided later to put it into the mouth of Musetta; and his correspondence shows him demanding from Giocosa a text that would go with the rhythm of it.

The enthusiasm of the bohemians wanes as the waiter approaches them with their bill; each turns it over to the other for settlement, and each finds, to his dismay, that he has no money in his pockets; even Schaunard's purse has mysteriously disappeared. Fortunately for them a diversion now occurs. In the distance a tattoo is heard, and the populace pours upon the stage to welcome the military band that soon arrives, headed by a gigantic drum-major.[1] Puccini builds up a big finale in the simplest way imaginable: he introduces just one new melody—Musetta's ironic goodbye to the still absent Alcindoro:

24

but for the rest he merely fastens, in the orchestra, one familiar tune to the tail of another—the tattoo, No. 5, No. 16, No. 21, etc.—without any conceivable rhyme or reason, and on top of the orchestra brings the whole of the vocal resources of the company into play. It is a brazen evasion of the problem of dramatic composition, but somehow the dodge works to perfection. While this hullabaloo is going on Musetta places the bohemians' bill and that of Alcindoro on the latter's plate before she and her friends decamp in the rear of the departing tattoo and the crowd, Musetta, unable to walk in only one shoe, being carried out by Marcello and Colline to the cheers of the multitude, Rodolfo and Mimi following arm in arm, and Schaunard, blowing his horn, at the tail of the procession. The stage is completely empty by the time Lulu returns with a carefully wrapped up pair of new shoes for Musetta. The waiters make a combined rush at him: and as he realises that he has not only lost his mistress but has a double bill to pay he collapses in a chair.[2]

---

[1] The fanfare is a French one, dating from the time of Louis Philippe. It was found for Puccini by his publisher Giulio Ricordi.

[2] This seems to be Puccini's final version of the scene just before the fall of the curtain. There are at least two vocal scores of *La Bohème*, differing from each other in some small respects, as in the present instance.

15

When next we meet the bohemians it is towards the end of February. Much has happened since the joyous racketing at the Café Momus. Rodolfo, we are asked to believe, is now insanely jealous without the virtuous Mimi having given him much justification for being so; she has also developed consumption. Musetta has been at her old tricks again, and her relations with Marcello are once more those of cat and dog.

Conscious that he is not evolving his action dramatically but only depicting a series of isolated episodes that follow each other in no inevitable sequence, Puccini prefixes to his third act a few sentences taken from Murger's account of the ups and downs of the love of Rodolfo and Mimi, the breaking of Rodolfo's heart, the brief periods of reconciliation during which their love for each other was as ardent as ever. We are given also a thumbnail sketch of Musetta—her genius for elegance, her love of luxury, her invincible egoism, her slavery to her caprices.

The scene of the third act is at the Barrière d'Enfer, on an outer boulevard. On the left is a small open space with a tavern facing the closed toll-gate, on the right a road leading from the rue d'Enfer to the Latin Quarter. Over the tavern hangs a sign-board, Marcello's masterpiece "The Passage of the Red Sea" (now bearing the inscription "The Port of Marseilles"), which the painter has had to sell in order to pay for his and Musetta's board and lodging. On either side of the door of the tavern are bold frescoes of a Turk and a Zouave—further commercial products of Marcello's art. Lights are showing in the lower room of the inn; every now and then we hear shouts, roars of laughter, and the clinking of glasses. Round a brazier is seated a group of sleepy custom-house officials; another comes out of the tavern with wine. Gaunt plane trees, with marble benches between them, stretch out towards the boulevards. It is early morning, cold and dreary, of a day near the end of February; snow is falling steadily.

Over a shuddering open fifth in the 'cellos that persists as a ground bass for more than a hundred bars we hear, as the curtain rises, a succession of hollow fifths in flutes and harp:

25

that match the bleak desolation of the place and the hour. Now and then there comes from inside the tavern a song, in thirds and sixths, which is no doubt intended to be that of joyous topers toasting their lasses, but actually does no more than add an extra touch to the melancholy mood invoked by No. 25:

26

Even a fragment of a song from Musetta, to the tune of No. 23, does nothing to dispel the prevailing gloom.[1] Outside the gates the scavengers, stamping their feet and blowing on their fingers, are clamouring to be admitted, but it is a little while before one of the officials opens the gate to allow them to pass through to the rue d'Enfer.

16

Later a sergeant, coming out from the guard-house, gives the sign for the toll-gate to be opened, and as the first faint streaks of daylight appear and the snow ceases to fall the people waiting outside pour through—milk-women, peasant women with their butter, cheese and eggs, and so on. When they have all moved away, Mimì enters furtively, as if unsure of her direction, from the rue d'Enfer, to the soft accompaniment of No. 9 in the orchestra. She is seized with a fit of coughing: Puccini is determined at the outset to secure our sympathies with her in her latest metamorphosis. She asks the sergeant where she can find an inn in which a painter is working: he points it out to her. Then she

[1] It was Ricordi's suggestion, gladly adopted by Puccini, that Musetta should sing this fragment from her song of the second act. It is an excellent way of letting us know that she is in the tavern with Marcello, and that her frivolous, inconstant character remains unchanged. She does not appear in person until much later in the present act.

accosts a servant girl who has come out of the tavern, asking her in broken accents if she can find for her a painter named Marcello and tell him that Mimi is waiting outside. The girl goes back into the inn, and soon Marcello emerges. Day has now dawned, drear and murky; the bell of the Hospice Sainte Thérèse rings softly for matins; and—quite unnecessarily, one cannot help thinking—Nos. 1 and 2 are repeated a few times in the orchestra.

Marcello, running to Mimi, explains, for our benefit more than hers, that he and Musetta have been located in the inn for a month or so, he keeping the pot boiling by painting the figures of the Turk and the Zouave on the façade, Musetta contributing something to their finances by giving singing lessons to the frequenters of the place. Mimi learns that Rodolfo is in the tavern, but she refuses to enter. In despairing accents:

27

she pours out her woes to Marcello: Rodolfo, madly jealous, avoids her though he still loves her. This little episode makes one of those self-contained and entirely convincing musical wholes in which Puccini is seen at his best. The psychology of the situation, however, is not so convincing, partly because the librettists and the composer feel that at all costs, in view of the impending fourth act, we must be entirely on Mimi's side. She implores Marcello's help. He points out to her, like a sensible man of the world, that when two people feel about each other as she and Rodolfo now do and are only making each other wretched, the best thing they can do is to part. She agrees in theory, but pleads rather inconsequently that without the aid of Marcello a solution of the problem is impossible; for she and Rodolfo have often tried to separate, but in vain. "I get on with Musetta, and she with me," Marcello assures her, "because we love gaily: song and laughter, that is the secret of love that does not change"; and once more Mimi agrees with him.

"Well, well," says Marcello, "I will waken him," for it now appears that Rodolfo had arrived at the tavern an hour before dawn and fallen into a sleep of utter exhaustion; and Marcello invites Mimi to look through the window and see for herself. After another spasm of coughing she explains that she has done nothing but cough since the time last night when Rodolfo left her, saying that all was over between them. At daybreak she had hurried here in the hope of finding him. "He's awake now; he has risen and is looking for me," says Marcello; "come with me."

But she only ejaculates "He must not see me": she is too well aware that the big scene is coming that must be played not inside the tavern but in view of the audience. Marcello sensibly suggests that she shall return home and not make a scene there; but apparently she makes at once for the cover of one of the plane-trees. One says "apparently" because the earlier and the later editions of the score differ from each other at this point. In the former, after Mimi's "He must not see me," Marcello says "In that case hide yourself over there," and he points to the tree. She does so as quickly as she can, the orchestra giving out half-a-dozen bars of quiet reminiscence of Nos. 1 and 2 that are obviously intended to give her time to scuttle across the stage before Rodolfo, according to the stage directions, "comes out of the tavern and hastens to Marcello." But in the later score Marcello's reply to her "He must not see me here" is "For mercy's sake, Mimi, return home; don't make a scene here." Nothing is said about her hiding herself. The orchestra merely plays softly for eight bars on a contrapuntal combination of No. 12 and No. 3, which are followed by the five or six bars of the bohemians' music referred to above. Then Rodolfo enters from the tavern.

The librettists obviously did not quite know how to manage the situation, what words to put into the characters' mouths. Marcello's "Hide yourself over there," with the stage direction "pointing to the plane-trees," makes sense in itself, as does the later direction, "Mimi cautiously approaches [from the cover of the trees] to listen" to the dialogue between the two men; but in the later edition the first and only hint of Mimi having withdrawn to the trees, and of the reason for this, is a direction later on, "Mimi cautiously approaches to listen": from where she listens we are not told just then, though we read further on that she "comes closer and closer, under cover of the trees."

28

The whole thing is a piece of bad stage construction. Without a moment's warning to us, without a moment's hesitation on his part, the Rodolfo who only a minute or two before has been sleeping the sleep of the exhausted is suddenly awake in full possession of his faculties and "comes out and hastens towards Marcello," crying, "Ah, Marcello, at last [I've found you]." The "At last" implies, surely, that he has been looking for Marcello for some time. The orchestra—rather inconsequently, but then Puccini rarely pauses to ask himself whether the circumstances in which he now wants to revive an old tune have any relevance to the circumstances in which it is now to appear—accompanies the remark with No. 10, the melody to which Mimi, in the first act, had sung "How stupid I am! Where can I have left the key of my room?" Then Rodolfo gets to the point with extraordinary abruptness: "No one can hear us here; I want a separation from Mimi"; [1]

[1] This is perhaps the feeblest piece of construction in the whole work. "Finalmente" may be taken as meaning either "At last I've found you"— which is the translation given in the English edition—or "At last we can talk without being overheard." The episode is equally ridiculous whichever way we take it. My conjecture is that there had been a change of mind on the part of the librettists and the composer at this point. Mimi and Rodolfo having had their crucial quarrel the night before, naturally the librettists had sent the poet off in the early hours of the morning in search of his old boon-companion Marcello. If we imagine him, at the point of the drama now in question, rushing in *from the town* and conveniently lighting on Marcello at the tavern, the words put into his mouth are quite plausible: he bursts out at once with the thought that has been uppermost in his mind for hours. But no doubt the librettists and Puccini realised at this point that all this would simply be a duplication of the entry of Mimi; so to avoid that they hit on the device of making Rodolfo arrive at the tavern *before* the scene opens. But then a new problem arose—how to get him on to the stage in time for Mimi to overhear his conversation with Marcello; and it was here that their invention broke down. It is asking too much of us to believe that the fuming, desperate Rodolfo, after finding his friend an hour before dawn, had said nothing at all to him then about the reason for his visit, but had flung himself on to a bench ("sopra una panca," Marcello tells Mimi),

and he launches into a story of how he had thought his love for her was dead, but her blue eyes had revived it.

17

This interests the eavesdropping Mimi, who approaches warily to listen to what may follow. Marcello takes a common-sense line with his friend—why try to bring the dead past back to life again? If love does not laugh and sparkle it is nothing but weariness. "The trouble is that you are jealous, choleric, fantastic, chockfull of prejudices, tiresome, pig-headed." Nothing we have so far seen of Rodolfo in the opera has given us any suspicion of these elements in his make-up, apart from the almost imperceptible hint to which reference has been made on page 62; but since Puccini will have it so for the pathetic purposes of the present act and the next, the poor fellow pleads guilty to at any rate the first item of the indictment. But he insists that his jealousy is justified. "With bitter irony," as the stage direction puts it, he tells Marcello that Mimi is a coquette who flirts with everyone:

29

Allegro moderato ♩ = 126

Mi—mi è u—na ci—vet — ta--- che fra—scheg—gia con tut—ti.

let any miserable little puppy of a Vicomte make eyes at her and she does all she can to lure him into her toils—which is true enough to Murger but not at all congruous with the opera as we have seen it evolving thus far—if the word "evolving" is at all suitable to the series of episodes that is *La Bohème*.

Marcello doubts whether all this is true, and Rodolfo agrees with him. "In vain I try to hide my torment: I love her above all things in the world. But I live in fear," he concludes—and Mimi, still in the cover of the trees, creeps a little nearer to hear what is coming. Mimi, he says, to the accompaniment of some sombre chords in the orchestra that are like a presage of funeral bells:

and slept the sleep of the utterly exhausted for a couple of hours; and now, a mere twenty-three bars after Marcello, looking through the window, has seen him stretching himself, he rushes into the open, shouting "I want a separation from Mimi!"

"Mimi is sickly; every day she grows weaker; the poor little creature, I fear, is doomed. Every day she is racked with coughing, and her cheeks betray her malady." And the only shelter he can offer her is a squalid fireless garret through which the north wind blows cruelly. Yet she smiles and sings, while he is consumed with remorse. "She is a hothouse flower; poverty has wasted her, and to bring her back to life more is required than love." We may feel that Rodolfo's self-indictment is psychologically a trifle overdone for the purposes of the situation, but there can be no doubt as to the power of Puccini's musical handling of it, especially when he launches a melodic and harmonic complex:

31

that keeps reiterating itself, in the best Puccini fashion, throughout the description of Mimi's malady. The artist in Puccini, as we all know, delighted in scenes of suffering, with a touch of torture in them for preference; and there being no opportunity for anything of that kind anywhere else in *La Bohème* he makes one here, Rodolfo abandoning himself to the very luxury of self-torture as he thinks of all that Mimi has suffered and is now suffering, and Mimi, lost in self-pity, coughing and sobbing "Ah! I must die!" from the cover of the plane-tree. It is her coughing that in the end reveals her presence. The repentant Rodolfo runs to her—the orchestra giving out a tender reminiscence of No. 9 —and embraces her affectionately. He would take her into the warmth of the tavern, but the poor creature, mindful as ever that the big scene must be played out to the end in full view of the audience, refuses the invitation, declaring that the odour of the place would stifle her.

18

It is now time the lovers were left alone for a while; so the librettists give Marcello a pretext for leaving the stage. And here we come upon another of the sundry little discrepancies between the two vocal scores of the work. The frivolous No. 12 flares out in the orchestra, and Musetta's brazen laugh is heard from within the tavern. "That's Musetta laughing," Marcello cries, looking through the window; "with whom? Ah, the coquette! I will find out!" Having said which, in the earlier score he runs in a frenzy into the tavern, leaving the stage to Rodolfo and Mimi. But in the later score there is no mention of his going into the tavern, though later we find him speaking "from within," and later still we find him on the stage again.

Mimi, now alone with Rodolfo, would bid him a last farewell; she will return to the room of her own which she had left in the first act at the call of love, there to embroider as of old and die. In pathetic accents she makes her last request to him: her few clothes and trinkets and the prayer-book Rodolfo had given her— if he will wrap them up in an apron she will send the porter for them: the final point is given to her appeal by the motive (No. 14) associated in the first act with her dreams of simple happiness. Under her pillow, she continues, he will find her little rose-pink bonnet; perhaps he would like to keep it in remembrance of her. "Farewell!" she sings:

32

Andante con moto ♩ = 92
dolcissimo

𝆑 Ad-di-o dol—ce sve-glia-re al--la--- mat--ti--na.

"Farewell the sweet awakenings in the morning; farewell rebukes and jealousy, farewell the anguish of suspicion." [1] Rodolfo takes

---

[1] This is another case of Puccini's "lifting" from an earlier work. The music of Mimi's "Addio dolce svegliare alla mattina" ("Farewell the sweet awakenings in the morning") and of the quartet that follows is taken bodily from a song, "Sole e amore," written by Puccini in 1887. The librettists, of course, had to provide the old music with new words.

up the strain: "Farewell the life of dreams in your smiles, the kisses of the true poet"; and their voices unite in a despairing final cry of "To be alone together in the winter is death—but when spring comes, with it comes the sun."

But apparently all this, while serious enough as far as the music is concerned, is not to be taken quite at its face value, for according to the stage directions Mimi's "Farewell rebukes and jealousy" is spoken "playfully." The act might well end here, with the reconciliation of the lovers; but Puccini has now to provide us with the key to the situation in the fourth act, where we find Marcello once more abandoned by the volatile Musetta. From the tavern comes the sound of smashing plates and glasses; a little later the pair emerge and break out into a spate of recriminations. Marcello accuses Musetta of flirting with one of the men in the tavern, and threatens to teach her better manners. She replies that as they are not married he has no husband's rights over her, and swears she will do as she likes whenever and where-ever she likes. It ends with her saying she is going away, to which Marcello replies "Good riddance!"; and with a final exchange of diplomatic courtesies—"Viper! Witch!" "Shop painter! Toad!" —they part once more, Musetta going off into the town, Marcello returning to the tavern.

All this while Rodolfo and Mimi have been tranquilly col-loguing on their own account about lilies and roses and the twit-tering of the birds in their nests. They have now arrived at the stage of assuring each other that they will not part until the spring comes again with its flowers, and so, "Would that winter might last for ever!"; and they move away hand in hand as the curtain falls. These last words of theirs seem to be an attempt on the librettists' part to work in a reminiscence of one of the most charming episodes in Murger, in which Marcel presents Musette with some flowers. She promises to be faithful to him as long as the flowers last. "But they will be withered in a couple of days," he protests; "if I had known I would have bought immortelles."

19

We have seen Puccini, in the preamble to the first act, suppress-ing a passage in Murger that showed a less likeable side to the character of Mimi. In the third act of the opera she is still all

innocence, sweetness, pathos; if she has been unhappy with
Rodolfo that is because he is insanely and unjustifiably jealous.
But now in the fourth act we have a Mimi who is obviously of the
same type as Musetta; yet Puccini gives us no light at all on what
has presumably happened between the third act and the fourth;
his paraphrase of Murger in his preface to the last act merely tells
us that for some months the poet and the painter have been living
miserably alone, having had no word for a long time of Mimi
and Musette.

The librettists based their last act on the final chapter but one
of the *Scènes de la Vie de Bohème*, rejecting, however, the gruesome ending to that. In Murger, Marcel is still mourning over the
desertion of Musette, while Mimi has left Rodolphe for a certain
Vicomte Paul. Painter and poet now occupy two rooms in the
same building. It is Christmas eve once more. The two friends,
sobered by experience, discuss their past, present and future; they
realise it is time they ceased brooding nostalgically over the past
and made an effort to give some conscious direction to their lives.
They will begin by burning all the little souvenirs of their lost
loves—ribbons, letters, faded flowers and so forth. But Marcel
cannot find it in his heart to destroy an old bouquet that Musette
had once worn. So he thrusts it furtively into his waistcoat, and,
happening to turn round at that moment, finds that Rodolphe is
similarly saving from destruction a little night-cap that had once
been Mimi's. "He's as weak as I am," Marcel murmurs to himself.

Just then the door opens and Mimi enters. She has been abandoned, we learn, by the Vicomte, who has even sold the furniture
and trinkets he had given her. In the last stages of hunger and
exhaustion, and knowing she has not long to live, she begs a
night's shelter from the two friends. The next day Colline and
Schaunard call on them, the latter in a summer overcoat, for
having heard that Mimi is ill he had sold his winter clothes and
given the money to Rodolphe. Colline, for his part, has sold his
dearly-beloved books. A doctor is called in, who sends Mimi to
a hospital, where the friends visit her. One day Rodolphe gets a
letter from a friend, a student in the hospital, informing him that
No. 8—Mimi—is dead. Rodolphe is plunged into the depths of
despair. A week later the pair meet by chance, and the student
informs Rodolphe that he had been in error. It appears that when

he wrote his letter he had been away from the hospital for a couple of days, during which Mimi, unknown to him, had been removed to another ward; in No. 8 another woman had been placed, who had died; Mimi was still alive yesterday, neither better nor worse but very unhappy, thinking that Rodolphe must be ill because he had not come to see her. The two men go at once to the hospital, where they learn that Mimi had died at four o'clock that morning. "She is there," says the student, pointing to a great cart in the courtyard: poor friendless Mimi is on her way to the common grave reserved for corpses that no one has claimed.

Puccini, of course, could not let *his* Mimi come to so miserable an end as this; at least she would die surrounded by her bohemian friends. For the rest, however, he keeps fairly closely to the lines of Murger's story, and puts to a new and dexterous use the episode of Colline's sale of his coat. Apart from the little song the philosopher sings on that occasion there is comparatively little that is new in the music of the fourth act: this roused the resentment of some of the Italian audiences in the early days of the opera's appearance; they felt they had been cheated—they had paid for four acts of music and had been fobbed off with not much more than three. It took them some time to realize that the fourth act of *La Bohème* is one of Puccini's most exquisite creations.

20

The curtain having risen again, to the strains of No. 1, we see the attic once more as in the first act, with Marcello at his easel and Rodolfo at his writing-table, each trying to give the impression that he is hard at work, whereas what really interests them is the conversation in which they have evidently been engaged for some time. At the point where we are allowed to eavesdrop Rodolfo is telling his friend that he has just met Musetta, riding in a carriage and pair, with servants in livery, as irresponsibly gay as No. 21 in the orchestra would lead us to expect. He had enquired about the state of her heart, and had been informed that she was blissfully unconscious of its activities, thanks to the velvet that covered it. Marcello, professing to be delighted at the news, slams the paint vigorously on the canvas, not hearing Rodolfo's aside—"Rubbish! You're laughing, but on the wrong side of your face!" But the painter, in turn, has some news for the poet. He has seen Mimi; and now it is Rodolfo's turn to stop writing, bite his lip, and do his best to look unconcerned. Strange as it may seem to us, the virtuous Mimi of our second and third acts was also riding in her carriage, dressed like a queen. "Splendid!" says Rodolfo; "I'm enchanted to hear it"; and now it is Marcello's turn to comment, aside, "You liar, you're eating your heart out for love." They try to work, but it is useless. Rodolfo puts down his pen, Marcello flings away his paint-brush; the latter takes a bunch of ribbons from his pocket and kisses it; later, Rodolfo brings out from a drawer an old bonnet of Mimi's; and each of them lets his memory play, half sweetly, half sadly, on the days that are no more. Their brief duet, which begins with Rodolfo's lament over the lost white hands and fragrant tresses of Mimi:

is one of those exquisite vignettes, musically complete and shapely in itself yet blood of the blood of the surrounding dramatic tissue, bone of its bone, a procedure of which the secret is Puccini's. Marcello, brooding upon the dark eyes and saucy lips of Musetta, answers with a countertheme; then their voices blend to the strain of No. 33, Marcello calling to Musetta, Rodolfo pressing to his heart the little rose-pink bonnet which Mimi had left under her pillow when she forsook him. It is a pity that this tender, quiet episode should always be ruined in performance by the necessity the tenor feels himself under to shout the baritone down, and vice versa: what was intended to be a duet degenerates into something like a vocal duel.[1]

---

[1] It seems to have escaped the notice of everyone concerned that Puccini has enclosed the whole vocal line of this longish episode (four whole pages of the score) within brackets. Manifestly he intended it to be presented to us as a sort of psychological parenthesis: Rodolfo and Marcello, momentarily abstracted from outward crude reality, are lost in their individual nostalgic memories of the happy vanished past. The prolonged pause in voices and orchestra that precedes it is itself significant. The singing of the episode should convey unmistakably this sense of temporary inward abstraction—

As No. 33, the voices having ceased, sings itself out quietly in the upper reaches of the orchestra, the two bohemians make another attempt at a show of indifference. "What time is it?" asks Rodolfo. "Time for our yesterday's dinner," replies Marcello. "Hasn't Schaunard returned yet?" Rodolfo enquires; and No. 5 in the orchestra prepares for the exuberant entry of the musician, flourishing four rolls of bread; he is accompanied by Colline, who carries a paper bag from which he extracts a herring—"a dish worthy of Demosthenes," he assures them.

21

The four seat themselves at the table and profess to be dining like Lucullus. "Now the champagne goes on the ice," says Schaunard, putting a water-bottle into Colline's hat. Addressing Marcello with old-world courtesy as "Baron," and offering him a slice of bread, Rodolfo asks him whether he prefers trout or salmon; another slice, when offered to Duke Schaunard, becomes that great delicacy a parrot's tongue. The Duke politely declines it—"I dare not; I shall be dancing this evening." Colline, having devoured his roll, rises solemnly and begs them to excuse him: he is a Minister of the King, who requires his attendance; he has also to see Guizot. They all bow respectfully to him. Schaunard, feeling he is being neglected, declares that the muse has taken possession of him; but the others shout him down. His suggestion of "something in the choregraphic line," however, is received with enthusiasm—"a dance to vocal music."

They clear away the table and chairs and prepare for the dance. Colline is for a gavotte, Marcello for a minuet, Rodolfo for a pavanella; but Schaunard insists on a fandango, and the orchestra backs him up. In the end they decide on quadrilles. Schaunard, as the musician of the party, gives the beat with an air of professional importance. Rodolfo, approaching Marcello in gallant fashion, bows deeply and addresses him as "Fair Lady": Marcello, putting on a female falsetto, begs the bold man to respect his modesty. Soon they become critical of their partners: Schaunard accuses Colline of dancing like a lackey, which the philosopher regards as an insult that can be wiped out only in blood. They fight a fero-

but it never does. The brackets are even omitted from the first English edition of the score.

cious duel, one armed with the poker, the other with the tongs. Schaunard exhorts Rodolfo and Marcello to bring a stretcher for Colline; the latter, more liberal in his ideas, orders a cemetery for Schaunard. Behind and around them Rodolfo and Marcello dance a rigadoon.

The gaiety is at its height when the door is flung open, to the accompaniment of a crashing chord succeeded by an almost inaudible drum-roll, and Musetta enters in great agitation with the news that Mimi is following her, so ill that she has hardly the strength to climb the stairs. Rodolfo catches sight of his former love seated on the top stair and rushes towards her, followed by Marcello. The lovers fall into each other's arms with cries of "O my Rodolfo! You will have me here with you?" and "My Mimi, for ever!" To the accompaniment of the typical Mimi theme (No. 9), now with darker harmonies, the bohemians lay her gently on the bed, draw the coverlet over her, and adjust the pillow under her head. Musetta hurriedly explains that having chanced to hear that Mimi had left her Vicomte she had sought her far and wide and at last found her, dragging herself along with difficulty, knowing she was dying, but longing to see Rodolfo once more. The orchestra dwells mournfully on No. 13, lingering with profound pathos on the original cadence to this (No. 14), as Mimi tells them how happy she is now, feeling that she may still live, never to be parted from Rodolfo again. But all are painfully aware that she is cold and hungry, and that there is no food in the room, no warmth for her poor little body. "In half an hour she'll be dead," Schaunard whispers to Colline. "I feel so cold," Mimi complains. "If only I had a muff! I feel that my hands will never be warm again!" she stammers feebly, the orchestra still pouring out Nos. 13 and 14 in wave on wave. Rodolfo takes her hand in his. She calls the bohemians to her side by their names, one by one: to Marcello she says, "Listen, Marcello; Musetta is a good soul"; and he murmurs "I know, I know."

22

Schaunard and Colline drift helplessly away: the musician sits at the table, burying his face in his hands; Colline is lost in thought; Musetta takes off her ear-rings, gives them to Marcello to sell, and bids him bring some cordials and a doctor for Mimi, who has now become drowsy. Rodolfo still sits beside her, holding her hand. "You will not leave me?" she murmurs: "No," he assures her, and the orchestra dwells with infinite poignancy on the theme—No. 18—associated with their hour of happiness at the Café Momus.

Musetta declares that she will go in search of a muff, to gratify what may be Mimi's last request; Marcello accompanies her. Meanwhile Colline prepares to make his own great sacrifice for Mimi's sake. He takes off his overcoat, the old comrade that has shared good times and bad with him:

34

Allegretto moderato ♩ = 63

p   Vec-chia zi-mar-ra, sen-ti,   io res-to al pian, tu a-scen-de-re

"never have you bent your shabby back to rich man or mighty; in your pockets philosophers and poets have found a tranquil refuge. Now that our joyous days together are over I bid you farewell, faithful old friend; farewell, farewell!" Slowly and sadly he folds the coat up and is about to go, but seeing Schaunard sunk in misery he approaches him, pats him on the shoulder and tells him there are two, and only two, acts of kindness it is now in their power to do: "this is mine"—pointing to the coat he is going to sell—"the other, to leave these two together." Schaunard mournfully agrees with the philosopher: as pretext for his departure he takes up the water-bottle. The pair go out, gently closing the door behind them, to the accompaniment, for the last time, of Schaunard's No. 5, its old ebullience now modulated to an expressive andante.

The lovers are now alone. The melody of No. 5 merges imperceptibly into that of No. 12—Rodolfo's outpouring of love to Mimi in the first act. She opens her eyes, sees that the others have left, and lays her hand on Rodolfo's, who kisses it affectionately. She has only been feigning sleep, she says quietly, because she wanted to be alone with him:

35

Andante calmo

pp fin-ge-vo di dor-mi-re--- per-chè vol-li con te so-la re-sta-re

There are many things she wants to tell him, but one in particular,
something vast and profound as the sea—that he is her love and
her life. Her arms go round his neck for a moment, then fall
weakly again, and with a last pathetic touch of coquetry the
wasted creature asks him, "Am I still pretty?" "Lovely as the
dawn," he assures her. But she cuts him short: his comparison is
wrong—he should have said "as the sunset"; and the sombre
No. 30 strikes in with its sinister suggestion of death. Her mind
wanders back into the past: "They call me Mimi," she murmurs,
"but I know not why." He compares her to a swallow returning
to its nest, and shows her the bonnet. She hails it with childlike
delight, and motions to him to place it on her head. "Do you
remember," she asks him to the melody of No. 10, "the day when
first I came to your room?"; and they remind each other of everything that had happened then—how frightened she was, the
mislaying of the key, the search for it in the darkness, how
Rodolfo, guided by Fate, as he now assures her, had found
it, how her blushes were invisible in the gloom, and how he had
clasped her hand and found it so cold that he had to warm it
into life.

Just then a spasm seizes her and her head falls back. Schaunard
enters and hastens to the side of the alarmed Rodolfo, and, with
the orchestra giving out No. 9, they lower her gently, she assuring
them that she feels better now. Musetta and Marcello steal in, the
one bearing a muff, the other a phial. As Mimi appears to be
sleeping they converse in low tones that add to the gradually
increasing tension of the scene. The doctor is on his way, says
Marcello; meanwhile here is a cordial. Mimi opens her eyes, sees
the muff, and fastens on it with childlike glee: "how soft and
warm it is," she says; "now my hands won't be white with cold";
and the orchestra gives out in the merest whisper, but with a new
poignancy of harmony and colour, a phrase that had accompanied
Rodolfo's first touch of Mimi's frozen hand in the first act:

36

She thanks him as the supposed donor of the muff. "Here for
ever with you, dear," she murmurs: "my hands are warm now,
and I shall sleep." Her head falls back, and indeed she appears
to be sleeping. Musetta, warming the cordial over a spirit-lamp,
breathes a prayer to the Madonna for her. The others move away
from the bed and talk in low tones, Rodolfo now and then going
back on tip-toe to look at the silent figure, hopeful that it is only
sleeping. But Schaunard, in a hoarse whisper, suddenly says,
"Marcello, she is dead!"—at the very moment when Colline
returns and gives Musetta the money that is now useless. Rodolfo
has not heard Schaunard's ejaculation: he is at the side of the
room, stretching Musetta's cloak across the window to shut out a
shaft of sunlight which he thinks may incommode Mimi. "How
is she?" Colline asks him. "You can see," he replies; "quite tranquil." But as he turns round he sees something in the faces of
Marcello and Schaunard that frightens him. "What is the meaning
of this coming and going?" he asks them, "and why do you look at
me like this?" Marcello can only embrace him and murmur
"Courage!" Rodolfo raises Mimi, takes her hand in his, and then,
realising what has happened, falls sobbing on the bed, while the
orchestra seizes upon the simple melody (No. 35) to which, earlier
in the scene, Mimi had assured Rodolfo that she had only been
feigning sleep, and converts it into a passionate threnody that
gradually dies out in silence as the curtain falls:

37

Pelléas and Mélisande

CLAUDE DEBUSSY [1862–1918]

PRINCIPAL CHARACTERS

PELLÉAS	*Tenor*
MÉLISANDE	*Soprano*
GENEVIÈVE	*Contralto*
GOLAUD	*Baritone*
ARKËL	*Bass*
YNIOLD	*Soprano*
A DOCTOR	*Bass*

1

PELLÉAS AND MÉLISANDE was the product of a coincidence unique in musical history. Between 1890 and 1892 the young Belgian Maurice Maeterlinck had been feeling his way towards a new type of expression in drama. In the latter year he found himself in the five-act play *Pelléas and Mélisande*. This seemed to many readers to cry out for musical treatment; yet the current idiom of neither French, German nor Italian music was quite appropriate to the shadowy theme or the peculiar diction of the play. During precisely the same period the young Debussy had been reaching out towards a new musical language to the mastery of which he could at last feel that he had attained at the very time when the Belgian dramatist's play was published. The composer's dilemma was that of the playwright reversed: he felt that with his new musical idiom he could create a new type of opera, yet he did not know where to look for a libretto that would match the fluidity and the finesses of that idiom.

Goethe used to maintain that each man's mental life would have been something fundamentally different from what it was had he been born ten years sooner or later. He would have rejoiced at the confirmation of this theory of his supplied by the case of Maeterlinck and Debussy. The two men were born within a week of each other in August 1862. The appearance of one of them in the world ten years before or ten years after that date would have meant that by 1892 he was either too far ahead of the other or too far behind him. What happened in that year was that a new form of dramatic expression, aiming at suggestion rather than statement, at showing not so much character in action as characters in the grip of a fate against which action was futile, found ready for it a new language of music that in its turn shrank in horror from the obviously assertive in melody, in harmony, in colour and in design. Debussy was bent on breaking up the old four-square type of melody, in which a phrase of two, four or eight bars is balanced symmetrically by correspondent phrases of the same length. Instead of promptly resolving dissonances in the traditional manner he prolonged and enchained them, thus giving an impression of endless harmonic fluidity. The language thus created was the only one appropriate to the expression of personages so shadowy, moods so vague, as those of Maeterlinck's play. The gods had brought it about that living within a few miles of each other there were two artists speaking the same tongue, nourished by the same culture, aiming at the same refinements of expression; each of them preferring, as it were, the soft pedal to the loud. It may have been a miracle that these two should have instantaneously found each other, but it was one of those miracles that are occasionally bound to happen. And that the coincidence of the orbits of the two men at the particular time and place of 1892 was one of those things that can happen only once in a century is shown by the subsequent history of both of them. Maeterlinck never again found a musician who understood him as Debussy had done, while Debussy, though he longed to write another opera, never again found a dramatic subject to suit him as *Pelléas and Mélisande* had done.

Maeterlinck's drama was published in Brussels in May 1892. Debussy came across it in Paris a few weeks later, and at once conceived the notion of setting it to music. It must have seemed to him as if it had fallen from heaven into his lap. Some three years before that date he had described to his friends the sort of play he had more or less dimly in mind for the only kind of opera he could imagine himself writing. There were to be no long acts, condemning him to write more music than was necessary, merely to fill up a prescribed mould. Stereotyped symmetries of "poetic" construction were to be avoided, so that his vocal music could model itself more or less on prose speech. People *sang* too much in opera, he thought: singing, in the fullest sense of the term, should be reserved only for the most highly-lit moments of the drama, and in general the vocal line should fluctuate between a melodic recitative and full lyricism, according to the emotional intensity of the situation: operatic characters should no more *sing* sober statements of fact than they should merely *say* things that rose from the very bottom of their heart. The conventional forms of music should not be allowed to determine the structure of a drama even to the extent they do in Wagner; on the contrary, it is the drama that should lead and music that must follow. When he added that in the ideal opera poem as he conceived it the personages would not "discuss" but "submit to life and destiny" he anticipated in the strangest fashion the contribution that Maeterlinck was to make to the solution of his own problem of opera; for if ever there was a world in which men and women do not "discuss" but are helpless corks on the sea of fate it is that of *Pelléas and Mélisande*.

Debussy began by making sketches for a few of the more salient features of the play. He saw a stage performance of the latter in Paris in May 1893, and it was presumably this that determined him to set to work systematically at his opera. He went to Ghent and saw Maeterlinck. He found him completely ignorant of music, but perfectly willing to turn his play over to the composer for his own purposes: he not only authorised him to make whatever cuts he liked but even suggested a few on his own account. The composition progressed slowly, Debussy ruminating over almost every bar and often rejecting later what he himself had imagined to be the definitive form of an episode. He perhaps laboured too long and too hard at this passage or that because he was almost morbidly anxious that every bar should unmistakably bear the Debussy sign manual. He was not getting on as fast with the music as he could have wished, he told a correspondent in 1893. Here and there it reminded him too much of some other composer; more especially did "the phantom of old Klingsor, alias R. Wagner," keep popping out at all sorts of inconvenient moments, necessitating, he thought, tearing up what he had just written and setting out afresh in search of something more " personal."

However, by 1902 the orchestral score was complete. Long before that, André Messager had become interested in the work. He in his turn secured the interest of Albert Carré, the director general of the Paris Opéra-Comique, and it was in that house that the first performance was given, on the 30th April 1902, with Jean Périer as Pelléas, Mary Garden (whose English accent was not precisely an asset) as Mélisande, Dufrane as Golaud, Vieuille as Arkël, and Mlle Gerville-Réache as Geneviève. Messager conducted. In the first performances the part of Yniold was taken by a little boy, one Blondin. Just before the production an unfortunate impression was created in Paris by a letter from Maeterlinck to the director of the *Figaro* which was unworthy of the author of *Wisdom and Destiny* and *The Life of the Bee,* and for which the only possible excuse was the ancient one of the woman in the case. Maeterlinck seems to have taken it for granted that the part of Mélisande would be played by his recently acquired wife, Georgette Leblanc. When he realised that it was not to be so he suddenly discovered that he totally disagreed with the modifications of his text for which he had given Debussy carte blanche ten years earlier. The listener, he said, would be able to hear for himself " the extent to which the text of the Opéra-Comique production differs from the authentic one." The performance of the opera would be given " in spite of him." " In short," he went on to say, " the *Pelléas* in question is a work that has become foreign, almost inimical to me; and, deprived as I am of any control over my own work, I am reduced to hoping that its failure [i.e., that of the opera] will be immediate and resounding." Far from being a failure, however, the opera was a success from the start.

2

Debussy did not take over Maeterlinck's text just as it stood. His most notable omissions were the opening scene of the servants (which it would have been impossible to realise properly on the stage), the first scene of the fifth act, in which the servants discuss the tragedy that has just happened, the first scene of the third act (Yniold with Pelléas and Mélisande), and the fourth scene of Act II, in which Arkël dissuades Pelléas from leaving the castle. Here

and there the composer has dovetailed a couple of settings or has omitted some of Maeterlinck's words: in the fourth act, for instance, he cuts out everything between Mélisande's "Si, si, je suis heureuse, mais je suis triste" and Pelléas's "Quel est ce bruit? On ferme les portes!" There are several occasions when the text of the opera differs in some small detail from that of the play; but whether these alterations were made by the composer or the poet we do not know.

Though certain of the themes in the opera can safely be identified with certain characters, Debussy's use of the leit-motif device is hardly in the least like Wagner's. The modifications which the themes undergo in this situation or that are so many and so subtle that endless quotation would be necessary to show the intimacy of the connection between the action and the music of the opera. The following analysis, therefore, will mostly confine itself to a description of the action, with an occasional citation of a motive only in its first form, or some form near the first.

The place and time of the drama are legendary. In an ancient castle by the sea sits an old half-blind King, Arkël by name, wise with age, mellow with pity for the sorrows of men. With him is his daughter Geneviève, the mother of an elder son, Golaud, and of a much younger one, Pelléas, by a different marriage. Golaud's father is dead; the father of Pelléas, though he does not appear in the play, we know to be sick somewhere in the castle.

The opera opens with a brief orchestral prelude which sets before us clearly three of the principal motives. It is difficult, if not impossible, to attach a definite label to some of the themes of the work. The solemn opening theme:

is heard again, some twenty-four bars later, at the entry of Golaud; but it appears in such different circumstances and carries so many implications in the course of the work that only for convenience' sake can we venture to call it a Golaud motive. There is more warrant for applying that term to the wavering theme which succeeds No. 1 at the fifth bar:

This is undoubtedly to be associated with Mélisande. Nos. 2 and 3 are instantly presented in combination, a symbol, as it were, of the strange blending of the destinies of Golaud and Mélisande.

The curtain rises, revealing the frail, elfin figure of Mélisande by a stream in a forest. Golaud enters to No. 1: he has lost his way in pursuit of a beast he has wounded. He is on the point of retracing his steps when he hears sobbing. Turning round, he sees what looks hardly more than a child sitting by the water's edge. He draws nearer, and at last touches her on the shoulder. She starts up and shrinks from him with a cry of " Do not touch me!," threatening to throw herself into the water if he does so. To all his questions he can get nothing but the vaguest answers. She has been hurt, but she does not know by whom. She has run from somewhere long ago, but does not know where she wants to go. She is lost and frightened. Gleaming at the bottom of the water is a golden crown that has fallen from her head while she was weeping. It was given to her by " him," but who " he " is Golaud does not learn. She will not let Golaud recover it: she will throw herself into the water if he tries. He tells her who he is — Golaud, grandson of Arkël, the old King of Allemonde; of her he learns no more than that her name is Mélisande. She looks at him with child-like curiosity and comments on him with a child's frankness: he seems to her a giant, and his hair and beard are beginning to grey. It is characteristic of Debussy's entirely non-Wagnerian way of handling his motives that he should use the motive of Mélisande (No. 3) to accompany both her own words descriptive of Golaud, " Oh, your hair is so grey," and Golaud's remark about herself, " I am looking at your eyes. Do you never close your eyes? " Wagner would have shuddered at the thought of employing the Mélisande motive when it was a case of describing Golaud!

No. 3 accompanies also Golaud's reply, " Yes, a few, here, at the temples," but his own motive (No. 2) is heard in counterpoint with it in the orchestra. This counterpoint, however, is not disclosed in the piano score.

Golaud is fascinated and troubled by Mélisande's eyes, which never seem to close. At last he persuades her to go away with him for safety, but whither he himself cannot tell her just then. " I do not know," he says in answer to her question: " I too am lost." The words are a symbol.

The scene changes to a hall in the castle. As usual while the many simple changes of scenery are being effected, the composer carries on with a few bars of orchestral interlude. These interludes, many of which are of extraordinary suggestiveness, seem to have been suggested to Debussy by Albert Carré after his first tentative hearing of the work with the composer at the piano. The present one begins with the wavering Golaud motive (No. 2), and merges into another in the brass:

4   *Molto moderato*

The later uses of this authorise us, perhaps, to regard it as the motive of Destiny.

In the castle hall, Geneviève is reading to Arkël a long letter to Pelléas from his brother Golaud, describing how he has found a terrified girl in the forest, and married her. That was six months ago, and he still knows no more who the baffling, mysterious creature is and whence she came than on the day when he saw her first. Golaud desires Pelléas to prepare Arkël for his home-coming with Mélisande. (It is made clearer in Maeterlinck than in Debussy that by this inexplicable marriage Golaud has brought to naught Arkël's schemes for his kingdom; though we do discover in the opera, as well as in the play, that at the time of his meeting with Mélisande in the forest Golaud was on a mission to ask, at his grandfather's bidding, the hand of a certain Princess Ursula in marriage). If all is well, the letter continues, Pelléas is to light a lamp at the top of the tower that overlooks the sea. If Golaud does not see it there on the third night after the receipt of his letter he will sail away again and never return. Geneviève finishes her reading, and the orchestra comments upon the situation in three bars of lacerating sadness:

Arkël gravely consents. Age has taught him wisdom and tolerance: what Golaud has done may seem strange, but which of us has the right to judge the deeds of others and determine their destiny for them? Geneviève is more troubled, though she sees that since the death of his first wife Golaud has withdrawn more and more inwards upon himself and gradually become almost a stranger to them. While she is speaking Pelléas enters, to the accompaniment of his characteristic theme:

He has been weeping. He has received, he says, at the same time as the letter from Golaud, another one informing him that his friend Marcellus is very ill and longs to see him before he dies. Arkël, reminding him that his own father is also ill, here in the castle, persuades him to delay his journey; and as the old King and Geneviève go out, the latter utters the decisive word: Pelléas is to light the lamp in the tower that same evening. Arkël has unwittingly pronounced the doom of Pelléas and Mélisande.

After a few bars of interlude, based on No. 3, a new scene opens before us. We see Geneviève and Mélisande in front of the castle; and it is characteristic of Debussy's indifference to ordinary realistic probability that this scene follows upon its predecessor after less than ten bars of interlude. We are in a world where the writ of everyday reality does not run.

Geneviève and Mélisande are discussing the sombreness of the old castle and its surroundings when Pelléas enters. The three watch, in the waning light of evening, a great ship leaving the harbour down below. Mélisande realises that it is the ship that brought her there. "Why is it leaving tonight?" she asks: she fears it will be wrecked in the storm that seems to be brewing. Geneviève having gone into the castle, Pelléas leads Mélisande by the arm down the rough steep path, which is now almost completely dark. "I am perhaps going away tomorrow," he says. "Oh! why are you going?" asks Mélisande; and the orchestra brings the scene to an end with a most moving reminiscence of No. 3:

It is like an unanswered question, a question to which there *can* be no answer. Already we sense Debussy's power to achieve the maximum of poignancy by the very simplest means, without any of that "insistence" that made him turn his back on so much even of the greatest German music. Thus ends a first act in which all the main threads of the drama have been dexterously introduced by the dramatist, and dyed by the composer in tints no less tragic because of their extreme delicacy.

3

The setting of the first scene of the second act is a shady spot in the castle park. Pelléas and Mélisande are sitting by a spring, the waters of which, he tells her, are credited by ancient legend with the power to open the eyes of the blind; but no one seems to resort to them now that the King himself is almost blind. (Pelléas's description of this "blindman's well," and Mélisande's question, "Does it open the eyes of the blind no more?" obviously have a symbolical significance that appears to have escaped the notice of the commentators. It is by the waters of this well that the blind eyes of the fated boy and girl are partially opened to the destiny towards which they are being inexorably driven).

The profound emotion of the scene expresses itself against an orchestral background of the most exquisite pastoral beauty. The pair seat themselves on the edge of a marble basin, in the shade of a great lime tree. Mélisande tells Pelléas of her first meeting with Golaud in the forest, of which she remembers little now except that he wanted to kiss her and she would not, though she does not know why. Childlike she is fascinated by the clear water of the spring. She plays thoughtlessly with the ring that Golaud had given her, throwing it high above the water and catching it as it falls, till at last another symbol casts its shadow over the play: the ring slips through her fingers and falls into the water. "We shall never find it again, nor shall we ever find another," she says. "I thought I had it in my hands. . . . I had already closed my hands, and it fell in spite of all. . . . I threw it too high, towards the sun." And what are they to say to Golaud? she asks. "The truth," replies Pelléas, "the truth!"

After the usual orchestral interlude the scene changes to a room in the castle. Golaud, whose horse, he does not know why, had taken fright, bolted madly, thrown him and fallen on him while he was hunting — at the stroke of midday, which was the very time when the ring had been lost in the water — is lying on his bed, tended by Mélisande. She bursts into tears, unhappy for no reason that she can give. He questions her affectionately. Is it the King? Is it Geneviève? Is it Pelléas, who has always been strange, and now is sad that he cannot go to his dying friend Marcellus? Is it the gloomy castle, the sunless forest around it — for the place is very cold and gloomy, and those who live in it are well on in years. The sombreness of which Golaud speaks is painted in a few chords in the orchestra:

Mélisande does not know; she knows only that she is wretched. The sun never shines here; this morning she saw it for the first time

— and we hear the briefest and softest of reminiscences, in a flute, of a melody which, in the scene before this, had described the soft plashing and rippling of the water of the stream.

As Golaud takes her little hand in his to comfort her he notices the absence of the ring. She stammers confusedly that it had slipped from her finger that morning in the cave by the sea, where she had gone to gather shells for little Yniold. In great agitation Golaud tells her she must find it immediately, before the sea rises and carries it away. He would rather lose everything he possesses than this ring. If she is afraid of the cave, she must ask Pelléas to accompany her. But she must go at once: he will not sleep until he has his ring again. She goes out weeping.

The scene changes to the entrance to a gloomy cave: Mélisande, accompanied by Pelléas, has gone there at the bidding of Golaud, though she knows well enough it was not there that the ring was lost. She is terrified at the darkness of the cave, which Pelléas describes to her. It is so vast and dangerous that no one has ever explored it to the end: ships have entered and been wrecked there. But the roof is beautiful with its incrustations of salt and crystal, which gleam fitfully when the light of the sky happens to strike on them. When at last the moon pierces the clouds and floods the entrance, three white-haired old beggars are seen, sitting side by side against a ledge of rock. There is a famine in the land, Pelléas explains, and the old men have crept inside the cave to sleep. As the beggars become visible the harmonies go strangely hollow, taking a form for which Debussy was certainly indebted to his studies of Moussorgsky:

Mélisande flies from the sinister scene in terror, followed by Pelléas, saying "We will return another day."

Debussy ends his second act here; but in Maeterlinck there comes now a short scene between Arkël and Pelléas — in a room in the castle — which we are surprised that the composer did not set to music. Pelléas again wishes to leave the castle, and once more the old King dissuades him from doing so. It is true, he says, that Marcellus is dead, but there are other duties for Pelléas, as for all men, than the visiting of graves. Pelléas's father is so gravely ill that almost certainly he will not recover. The land is threatened by enemies; the people are dying of hunger; is this the time for Prince Pelléas to go far away? Still, says Arkël, he will leave the decision to the young man himself — " for you must know better than I what events you ought to offer to your being or your destiny. I ask you only to wait until we know what is to happen." " How long shall I have to wait? " asks Pelléas. Thus for the second time, and in a scene in which every word seems heavy with fate, Arkël pens the boy within the narrow plot of earth where danger and death lurk for him: Arkël, who claims to have learned from life at least one lesson of wisdom, that none of us has the right to put himself in the way of the destiny of another, becomes unconsciously the main instrument for withholding Pelléas from finding another destiny than the one awaiting him in the castle. Had the profound significance of the scene escaped Debussy, one wonders? Did he think a second scene of this kind superfluous? Or had he, in fact, missed the deep symbolism of the " letter " scene also, and taken this into his own plan only because, with its explanation of certain material things, it seemed to him essential to the elucidation of the action? It is impossible to say.

4

In the cruder theatrical sense very little " happens " in *Pelléas and Mélisande*, yet the drama mounts to its tragic dénouement with consummate art. All that has taken place so far has been a preparation for the warmly lyrical third act, in which the hapless lovers at last, and unexpectedly, find each other. In the fourth act, tragedy comes swift on the heels of ecstasy; and in the fifth the waves of destiny close over the heads of these pitiful creatures, in the soul of none of whom was any evil.

Maeterlinck's first scene — that of Mélisande, Pelléas and Yniold (Golaud's little son by his first marriage) in a room in the castle — is omitted from the opera, which begins with the second scene of the play. The setting is one of the castle towers, where Mélisande is combing her hair at a window. The introductory orchestral music is calm and sweet. Mélisande sings a snatch or two of a simple song,

"Saint Daniel et Saint Michel, Saint Michel et Saint Raphaël, Je suis née un dimanche, Un dimanche à midi."[1]

Pelléas appears on a sentry path that runs below the tower window. The enchantment of the night soon works upon them both. At Pelléas's request Mélisande leans out of the window, and he strains upward to her. He begs her to give him her hand to kiss, for he intends to leave on the morrow. She implores him to delay his departure, and as she bends lower and lower to him to reach his hand with hers, her long hair suddenly descends upon him, inundating him with its glory.

This marks the commencement of the great scene that is the lyrical high-light of the opera. It is characteristic of Debussy's horror of the insistent that after one swift surge of tone in the orchestra, — at the moment when Mélisande's hair descends — lasting no more than a couple of bars, both voices and orchestra are immediately hushed. It is now that the pair pour out their overloaded hearts to each other, and what they have to say is at once so profound and so intimate in its emotion that, paradoxical as this may seem in opera, it cannot be said in any but the quietest tones. Only rarely in the course of the long duet does the tone rise much above *piano,* but within the narrow scale of dynamics which Debussy permits himself there is plane after plane of passion. There comes a *fortissimo* gush of sound when Pelléas, intoxicated with the beauty of Mélisande's hair, which is in his hands, about his arms, around his neck and in his mouth, cries out that her tresses are like living birds in his hands, "and they love me, they love me more than you!" Then once more his emotion, precisely because of its intensity, expresses itself in a new lowering of the voice.

At the height of their rapture they are startled by a sudden fluttering of doves about them, flying from the tower; and while Mélisande, sensing the approach of evil, tries in vain to raise her head, for her hair is entangled in the branches of a tree, footsteps

[1] The song that appears in all the editions of the play since about 1895 — five stanzas commencing,

> *Les trois sœurs aveugles,*
> *(Espérons encore),*
> *Les trois sœurs aveugles*
> *Ont leur lampes d'or,*

— is a later addition by Maeterlinck to his original text.

are heard approaching. "It is Golaud!" says Mélisande, . . . "I believe it is Golaud! He has heard us!" . . . and a whisper and an expressive chord or two are all that Debussy needs to make us hold our breath with apprehension, as Pelléas and Mélisande do:

10

C'est Go - .laud!

Almost invariably Debussy's quietude of manner increases in proportion to the gravity of what he has to say.

"What are you doing here?" Golaud asks. Pelléas is too confused to answer. "You are children," continues Golaud. "Mélisande, do not lean so far out of the window: you will fall. . . . Do you not know that it is late? It is close on midnight. Do not play thus in the dark." And then, with a nervous laugh, "You are children. . . . What children! What children!," and he goes away with Pelléas.

The orchestral interlude that follows is one of the most moving episodes in the opera: Debussy distils the last drop of poignancy out of the succession and apposition of the motives of Golaud, Mélisande and Pelléas (Nos. 2, 3 and 6).

The colouring of the interlude gradually darkens as we make our way, in imagination, to the castle vaults, where Golaud and Pelléas are discovered when the curtain rises. Perhaps Golaud does not quite know himself why he has brought his brother to this gloomy, infected place, where a stench of death comes up from the stagnant water. Pelléas walks circumspectly in front of Golaud, who carries a lantern. The older man holds the younger by the arm, ostensibly to keep him from slipping over the abyss. But the light that the lantern casts on their path is a flickering one, for Golaud's hand is trembling, like his voice. A strange episode, the force of which resides in the fact that, while not a word is said on either side about what happened outside the tower, we feel it to be the one matter really occupying the mind of each of them. At length they leave this sinister place, with its stifling odour of death, for the clean upper air.

The transition to the sunlit terrace, where the fresh morning breeze blows in from the sea, and the scent of newly watered flowers rises from the beds, and the bells are ringing as the children go down to the beach to bathe, is skilfully managed in the usual orchestral interlude. It is only now that Golaud can speak of what is uppermost in his mind. He knows, he says, that what happened yesterday evening between his brother and Mélisande was only child's play, but it must not be repeated. Mélisande is very young, very impressionable, and about to become a mother: she must be handled very delicately, lest misfortune befall her. Pelléas must avoid her as much as possible, though not markedly. Pelléas does not reply. In the play, Golaud at this point sees something in the distance that turns out to be a flock of sheep being led to the town. "They are crying like lost children," he says; "one would say they already smelt the butcher." It is curious that Debussy should have neglected to set these few lines, with their obvious tragic symbolism.[2] Maeterlinck knew well what he was doing when he ended the scene with them.

Golaud and Pelléas go out in silence, and the scene changes to a space in front of the castle. Golaud takes his little Yniold on his knee and gets him to talk about his Uncle Pelléas and his little mother Mélisande. Are they often together? the tortured man asks. What do they say to each other? Do they ever speak of him, Golaud? Do they kiss? He raises the child on his shoulders to the height of the window that looks into Mélisande's room; and in an amazingly dramatic scene — it is characteristic, by the way, both of Maeterlinck and Debussy that it is through the medium of the child's innocent prattling that the tragic tension is brought to its breaking point — Yniold describes how Pelléas is there with little mother, and they are saying nothing, only looking with fixed eyes

[2] Perhaps he did not do so because he wanted to set in full the later episode (act IV, scene 3) of the sheep being driven to the butcher. But three or four bars would have sufficed for the handling of the half-dozen suggestive lines which Maeterlinck puts into the mouth of Golaud.

at the light, as if they were expecting something to happen. At last terror seizes on the child, and he calls to his father to let him down. Golaud has learned nothing of what he so desires and so fears to know; and as he and Yniold go out together, No. 2 in the orchestra paints the anguish of which he cannot speak to anyone.

5

In the fourth act events move more swiftly.

Pelléas and Mélisande meet in a passage in the castle. Pelléas has come from the sick room of his father, who seems now to be out of danger. But the young man has a foreboding of catastrophe. His father had taken him kindly by the hand and said, looking at him strangely, " Is that you, Pelléas? Why, I never noticed it before, but you have the grave, friendly face of those who have not long to live. . . . You must travel; you must travel." Pelléas has resolved to obey him; this is his last evening in the castle, and he and Mélisande will never meet again. But he must see Mélisande alone before he goes; and they agree to meet by blindman's well in the park.

Pelléas having left, Arkël enters. Now that Pelléas's father is out of danger, he tells Mélisande, he hopes that sunlight and joy will visit the ancient place again. He has pitied Mélisande ever since she entered the castle, pitied that bewildered look of hers as of one who is expecting some great misfortune. He believes that young and beautiful things have the gift of shaping about themselves events that are warm with youth, beauty and happiness. But Mélisande remains silent, her eyes turned to the ground; and the old man's heart goes out to her in a fresh surge of pity.

Golaud enters, visibly distracted, and with blood on his forehead: " I have been through a hedge of thorns," he explains, in one of the many sentences in the play that carry a sinister double meaning. Mélisande would wipe his brow; but he repulses her roughly and orders her to bring him his sword. His pain of soul drives him on to a crescendo of fury and brutality. Why does she look at him as she is doing? he asks her; and he calls Arkël's attention to those fixed, wide-open eyes of hers. " I can see nothing in them but a great innocence," says the old King. " Great innocence ": Golaud repeats: " they are greater than innocence! They are purer than the eyes of a lamb. . . . They could give lessons in innocence to

God!" Yet he will know the secrets of the other world before he can read the secret of those eyes. "Close them! close them!" he stammers, "or I will close them for long." He takes her hands, then lets them go in an agony of physical repulsion. He seizes her by the hair and forces her to her knees, now to the right, now to the left, raging, laughing hysterically, then suddenly growing calm again and affecting indifference. "You shall do as you please," he tells Mélisande. "I attach no importance to it. I am too old, and then, I am not a spy. I shall wait to see what chance brings, and then . . ." Arkël stands amazed at the half-insane outburst. Mélisande bursts into tears after Golaud has gone: "He does not love me any more," she moans. "I am not happy! . . . I am not happy!" "If I were God I should pity the heart of men," says the old King quietly; and after that it is left to the orchestra to probe the pathos of the situation to its depths.

The scene changes to the park, where Yniold is vainly trying with his little hands to raise a big stone under which his ball has run. In the distance he hears the bleating of sheep. He runs to the edge of the terrace and watches them advancing in the dying light of the sun — so many of them that he cannot count them, all huddled together as if they were afraid of the dark. They run fast till they reach the big cross-road, and from there they do not know where to go. They seem to want to go to the right, but the shepherd throws earth at them and makes them turn aside. But why are they now so suddenly silent? And the invisible shepherd gives him the answer — "Because it is no longer the way to the fold." Something seems to constrict the heart of the child, who runs out to look for someone who may comfort him. It is a great pity that this moving episode should be omitted as it is in many performances.

Pelléas enters. Soon, he muses, he will have left the castle, leaving behind him everything that binds him to life. But he must see Mélisande first, to look into the depths of her heart and say what he has not yet said. When she comes he draws her out of the edge of the moonlight into the shade of a great lime-tree, where they cannot be seen from the tower window. He bids her farewell and kisses her. "I love you," he says; and she replies, in the lowest of voices, "And I love you too." That is all! The drama has at last reached its climax, and this is all the pair have to say to each other

— and they indeed say it rather than sing it, without even a supporting note from the orchestra:

It is a violation of all the centuries-old rules of opera, which lay it
down that when lovers find each other there shall be no limit to
their rapture. But it is one of Debussy's supreme strokes of genius:
there are few things in the whole range of opera that catch at the
heart as these half-dozen simple unsung words do. This is the veritable triumph of reticence: at what any other dramatist and composer would have seen to it was the peak-point of impassioned
statement Maeterlinck and Debussy lead us to the very verge of
silence, but what a silence! A silence which, so far from being
empty, seems to hold all the immensities within it.

The young pair lose themselves in tender poetic memories and
images:

Pelléas, in his great happiness, would draw Mélisande into the
light, but it is now she whom a dim instinct bids remain in the
shadow of the tree, though there they cannot see each other's eyes.
"I am happy," she says, "but I am sad." From the castle comes a
dull sound of doors being closed and chains being fixed and bolts
being shot. It is too late now for them to re-enter. All is lost, says
Pelléas, yet all is saved! For now there can be no going back in any
sense. As they embrace madly, Mélisande hears a stealthy footstep
and the crackle of dead leaves. Pelléas will not listen to her warning; he hears nothing but the beating of her heart and his own. But
Mélisande's eyes, piercing the gloom, see Golaud crouching behind a tree, no further from them than the tip of their shadows: his
sword is drawn, and Pelléas is without his. "Do not move," Pelléas
whispers, "do not turn your head. He will rush out upon us!" They

embrace distractedly for the last time as Golaud rushes on them
sword in hand. He strikes Pelléas, who falls dead beside the spring.
Mélisande flies in terror, pursued by Golaud in silence.

6

With the deletion of Maeterlinck's scene of the servants at the
commencement of Act V, only one scene remains to bring Debussy's opera to a close.

The setting is a room in the castle. Mélisande is lying on her bed,
while in a corner of the room Golaud, Arkël and a Doctor are seen
in conversation. (From the talk of the servants we have gathered
that Golaud and Mélisande had been found lying in front of the
castle door, he with his own sword still sticking in his side, she
wounded nearly to death. But Golaud is strong and is now all but
cured, while Mélisande, on her deathbed, has been delivered of a
puny child). It is not of so small a wound — one not big enough
to kill a bird, — that Mélisande can be dying, says the Doctor,
therefore Golaud need not distress himself, for it is not he who has
killed her. She was born for no reason but to die, and now she is
dying for no reason. But Golaud breaks out into bitter reproaches
against himself. " They had simply kissed each other like little children, as if they had been brother and sister. And I . . . I did it in
spite of myself."

Mélisande awakes and asks Arkël to have the big window
opened, that she may see the sun going down on the sea. Never
has she felt better, she tells him, but it seems to her as if she knew
something. What that something is we learn from a sad little
phrase in the oboe which will afterwards be associated with the
new-born child:

She is told that Golaud is in the room, and she wonders why he
does not come to her. He drags himself to the bed, and at his request the other two leave him alone with her for a while. He begs
Mélisande to forgive him, but she asks him what there is to forgive.

He has done her great wrong, he moans. He sees it clearly now. All that has happened has been his fault, but he loved her so! And now they are both about to die, she first, then himself; and to a dying man one must speak the truth. Did she love Pelléas? "Yes," she murmurs: "I loved him. Where is he?" But that is not what he wants to know. Did she love him with a forbidden love? Were they guilty? "No, no," she replies; "we were not guilty. Why do you ask that?" But only one answer, the one he desires and yet fears, and desires all the more because he fears it, will satisfy the self-tortured man. He implores her, for the love of God, to tell him the truth. Then, baffled once more, he recalls Arkël and the Doctor. He bewails the ignorance in which he is to be left: "I shall never know!" he cries; "I shall die here like one blind!"

Is it true that winter is coming? Mélisande asks the King, for she is so afraid of the cold. They place by her the child, of which till now she knew nothing; but she is too weak to take it in her arms. The servants enter one by one and range themselves along the walls of the room in silence — a sign that death is near at hand. Golaud breaks out in impotent rage against them, but they answer nothing. He turns again to Mélisande in a last passionate desire to speak alone with her once more. But Arkël bids him leave her in peace, for the human soul, he says, is timid and silent and loves to steal away alone. Suddenly the servants fall on their knees at the further end of the room. The Doctor approaches the bed and touches Mélisande. "They are right!" he says. Golaud breaks into sobs. Arkël leads him away, trying to comfort him: "She needs silence now. It is terrible, but the fault is not yours. She was a gentle little soul, so timid, so silent, a poor little mysterious creature, like all the world. She lies there as if she were her child's big sister. . . . The child must not stay here. . . . It must live now in her stead: it is the poor little one's turn." The theme of the child (No. 13) threads its way delicately through the texture, and the curtain falls to a last murmured suggestion of the Mélisande motive (No. 3).

Wozzeck

ALBAN BERG [1885–1935]

PRINCIPAL CHARACTERS

WOZZECK	*Baritone (and Speaking Voice)*
THE DRUM-MAJOR	*Heroic Tenor*
ANDRES	*Lyric Tenor (and Speaking Voice)*
THE CAPTAIN	*Buffo Tenor*
THE DOCTOR	*Buffo Bass*
MARIE	*Soprano*
MARGRET	*Contralto*

1

UNTIL Berg's *Wozzeck* was launched in 1925 the literary world in general outside Germany knew little or nothing of Georg Büchner, on whose drama with the same title the opera is founded.[1] He was born on the 17th October 1813 at Goddelau, near Darmstadt, where his father was a doctor. The young Georg studied science, in particular anatomy and zoology, at Darmstadt, Strassburg and Giessen, with a view to adopting his father's profession. Becoming involved in the widespread political unrest of the period, he saw several of his young companions thrown into prison, and escaped a similar fate himself only by flying to Strassburg. There he continued to work hard not only at science but at philosophy and history, the epoch of the French Revolution having a special attraction for him. In Strassburg he wrote an essay "On the Nervous System of the Barbel" which

---

[1] He is not so much as mentioned in the latest edition of the Encyclopaedia Britannica, though there is an article there on his younger brother, Ludwig (1824–1899), the author of the *Force and Matter* (1855) that made something of a sensation in the scientific world of its own day.

brought him not only the dignity of a corresponding membership of the Strassburg Society for Natural Philosophy but a doctor's degree from the Philosophical Faculty of Zürich, in which latter town he settled in December 1836 as a teacher in the High School. On the following 2nd February the first signs showed themselves of a disease that was probably typhus. Nineteen days later he was dead.

He had crowded a great deal of thinking and feeling into his life of little more than twenty-three years. In 1833 he had written *Danton's Death,* a remarkable drama dealing with the leading personalities of the Revolution. His other literary works consisted of a comedy, *Leonce and Lena,* the fragment of a psychological novel, *Lenz,*[2] and the drama *Wozzeck.* The world has seldom seen a more precocious talent. There is naturally a good deal that is merely young-mannish in some of his work, more especially in *Leonce and Lena,* where, in common with so many of his contemporaries, Büchner tries to philosophise in a style half-cynical, half-profound, imitated from some of Shakespeare's clowns. But there is also in all Büchner's work a knowledge of human nature quite astounding in a man of his years, an impatience with sacrosanct literary forms and subjects that lends him a peculiar interest today, and above all a sympathy with human suffering, especially that of the underdog, that makes *Wozzeck* in particular one of the most moving documents of its genre and its period.

The boy was from the first in full revolt against the romanticism in which so many fine spirits at that time sought a refuge from the hard realities of life. The after-crop of the Napoleonic wars had been an exhaustion and a disillusionment that were already heralding, in the early 1830's, the attempts at a political revolution that came to a head everywhere towards the end of the 1840's. In Germany in particular the discontent was great: the people had rallied devotedly to the side of their princes in order to shake off the Napoleonic yoke, only to find, when victory had been achieved, that the princes, for the most part, made use of their new security only to forge fresh chains, material and spiritual, for their subjects. Büchner was one of those who felt that the time for romantic dreaming was past, but one also who saw clearly that for the mo-

---

[2] i.e., Reinhold Lenz, the poet who in his early years was so closely associated with Goethe. He became mentally deranged some years before his death. The problems of his mind and fate evidently had a peculiar attraction for Büchner.

ment, as he wrote to his family in 1833, any attempt at open revolution was doomed to failure. And of course his conviction of the futility of action only deepened his sense of the curse that lay upon the majority of the human race. " I have been studying," he wrote to his fiancée in 1833, about the time he was engaged on *Danton's Death,* " the history of the Revolution. I felt utterly crushed under the horrible fatalism of history. I find in human nature a dreadful sameness, in human affairs a fatal force, that is in all of us and in none of us. The individual is merely foam on the wave, greatness a mere accident, the authority of genius a puppet show, a ludicrous struggle against an iron law, which we can at most recognise, but to master which is impossible."

Like other highly-strung youths of the period — Berlioz and Flaubert, for instance — who had studied anatomy and practised in the dissecting-room, Büchner felt at once a macabre contempt for the human body and mind and an ironic pity for them. Something of all this, of course, was merely a conscious distillation from Shakespeare in his Hamlet mood: it was fatally easy for the disillusioned youth of the romantic epoch, French and German, to strike a picturesque " Alas, poor Yorick! " attitude. But in Büchner, as *Wozzeck* was to show, the sense of burning pity for poor humanity finally submerged the ironic amusement over it. " People call me a scoffer," he says in one of his letters. " It is true that I often laugh, — never, however, at *what* a man is, but only *because* he is, which he cannot help in any way, and I laugh at myself, as sharing the same fate. . . . In a sense, indeed, I mock, not from disdain but from hatred. To hate is as permissible as to love, and I cherish hatred in the fullest measure against those who scorn. . . . Aristocracy is, at most, shameful contempt of the holy spirit in man: against it I direct its own weapons, pride against pride, mockery against mockery. . . . I hope I have always turned upon suffering, down-trodden creatures more glances of compassion than I have expended bitter words on the cold hearts of those in authority."

Evidently the world as he found it hurt his generous young heart grievously, but he could not bring himself, like so many of his contemporaries, to take refuge from it in a world of romantic make-believe: the evil inherent in the scheme of things, if it could not be overcome, should at any rate be courageously faced. " When

I am told," he says in one of his letters, " that the poet must show the world not as it is but as it should be, I reply that I have no desire to improve on the good God, who assuredly has made the world as it must be. As for the so-called idealistic poets, my feeling is that for the most part they have created nothing but marionettes with sky-blue noses and affected pathos, — not creatures of flesh and blood whose joys and sorrows I can feel as my own, and whose actions inspire me with abhorrence or admiration. In a word, I lay much store by Goethe and Shakespeare, but very little by Schiller." The German romanticism that turned its gaze backwards to the idealised Middle Ages because it could find no foothold in the brutal present had no attraction for him, he said.

He raised the banner of revolt against not only the conventional literary subjects but the accepted forms of his epoch. One of the most salient features of *Danton's Death* and of *Wozzeck* is the rapid succession of scenes, some of them so short as to consist of only some half-dozen lines. This technique, which of course makes a modern stage production of either of the dramas a matter of some difficulty, he perhaps derived from Lenz. The classical drama being supposed to proceed on the assumption of the " unities " of time and place, many of the younger rebels against authority regarded it as a point of honour to flout these imaginary rules by presenting a dramatic action with the complete freedom, the absence of manufactured symmetries, that it would have in real life. The last scene but one of *Wozzeck*, for example, shows a few children playing in the street in front of the house door of the murdered Marie. Only some forty words in all are spoken: then the scene changes to the last scene of all, the dissecting-room of a hospital. There are present a doctor, a surgeon and a magistrate; the only words spoken are by the last-named, and they amount to no more than this — " A good murder, a real murder, a first-rate murder! As fine as anyone could wish for. It is a long time since we had one so fine! " Many technical difficulties of this kind, however, which are insoluble on the ordinary stage, can be overcome in opera, where the music can prolong the shortest of scenes to the full stretch of its emotional possibilities, or can supply, by means of orchestral prelude, postlude or interlude, what the poet has not given his characters sufficient time to say, or even what is better left unsaid in words. On the whole, Berg has been able to take over Büchner's text as it stands, with only a few omissions or slight adaptations, some of which will be noted in the course of our analysis of the opera.

The finer spirits of the early nineteenth century felt a burning sympathy with the appalling lot of the German poor. Heine, for instance, had sung in passionate accents the sorrows of the over-worked and starving Silesian weavers, sitting at their looms with their eyes filled with bitter tears, cursing the God who created them and to whom they pray in vain, cursing the King who extorts the last groschen from them in their misery and has them shot like dogs when they complain, cursing the " false fatherland where prosper only infamy and shame, where every flower is blighted in the bud, where rottenness and decay regale the worm, while we go on weaving, weaving — day and night weaving the old Germany's winding sheet, with a threefold curse woven into its threads." Büchner's Wozzeck is the German under-dog of the period in his most pitiable aspect. Officially he is Johann Franz Wozzeck, thirty years, seven months and twelve days old at the time of his death, militiaman and fusilier in the second regiment, second battalion, fourth company. Uneducated, uncomprehend-ing, he is the slave and the butt of everyone, not only of the Cap-tain of his regiment, whose regimental servant he is, but of the Doctor, who laughs at him to his face, regards him merely as an interesting subject for scientific experiment, and uses him for demonstration purposes to the students. His one thin ray of sun-shine in a dark world is the trull by whom he has had a child; and she is stolen from him by the boastful Drum-Major, who makes use of his physical superiority over the wretched Wozzeck to humili-ate him in the eyes of the other soldiers. Over almost everyone and everything of first-line significance in the drama there broods the shadow of something like incipient madness: no one is wholly nor-mal. It would have been impossible for any composer to treat such a subject in the traditional idiom of music: the attempt could in the nature of things only be made when many of the old conven-tions of opera had to some extent broken down.

2

Berg, who was the most gifted of Schönberg's associates and pupils, took about six years over the composition of *Wozzeck*. In any six years a fertile and vigorous mind is bound to outgrow its old self at various points; so it is not surprising to find indications in the final stages of the opera that the composer had outgrown the Berg of the first stages. It is useless to look in the work for a self-consistent idiom from the first page to the last: some parts of it represent a deliberate exploitation of the atonal theories of Schönberg in their most extreme form, while other parts are just a normal extension or subtilisation of the traditional German musical speech.

In his handling of the voices Berg has not always been conspicuously happy. In a foreword to the score he tells us that the vocal principle on which he has proceeded in certain episodes has been that of Schönberg in his *Pierrot Lunaire* and *Die glückliche Hand*. Though the notes are written in the usual way on lines and in spaces, they are not to be *sung* at these definite pitches. The business of the actor is merely to *suggest* the pitch while achieving what Berg calls " speech-melody"; he must convey neither the impression of singing nor that of the " realistically-natural " speech of everyday usage. We may grant the validity of a compromise of this sort in theory without being able to agree that so far it has worked out particularly well in practice. It is not merely that now and then the voices in *Wozzeck* do things that are both painful to the musical ear and provocative of irreverent laughter. A more serious hindrance to our whole-hearted acceptance of this would-be " speech-melody" is that it so often fails to do the very thing it sets out to do. It fails to carry conviction either as song, as speech, or as a fusion of the two; it is neither speech achieving melody nor song biting like speech, but a bastard by-product of speech and song, which neither captivates the ear nor commands the assent of the intellect. That a new compromise between song and speech will be effected in the opera of the future — or in certain portions of certain operas — can hardly be doubted: theory points in that direction, while Debussy has triumphantly demonstrated some possibilities of the genre in *Pelléas and Mélisande*. But the proof of the pudding will always be in the eating: if the concoction is not agreeable to the palate no amount of theorising will make us swallow very much of it.

Berg seems to have made the acquaintance of Büchner's drama for the first time in a Vienna production of May 1914, and to have resolved there and then to write an opera on the subject: a period of war service, however, made it impossible for him to proceed with the plan until the summer of 1917. The orchestral score was complete in every respect by April 1921. The piano arrangement (by Fritz Heinrich Klein) was published two years later. On the 11th June 1924 three extracts from the opera were given, under Hermann Scherchen, in concert form in Frankfurt-am-Main. The first stage performance of the complete opera took place at the Berlin Staatsoper, under Erich Kleiber, on the 14th December 1925.

The musical form of *Wozzeck* is original and peculiar. There is nothing eternally sacrosanct about any of the forms in which opera has so far realised itself, neither that of Monteverdi, nor that of Gluck, nor that of Mozart, nor that of Wagner, nor that of Debussy. Each of these forms was born of the general mentality of a particular epoch and the totality of the resources of music in that epoch; and their perfect validity for their own day inevitably makes them to some extent invalid for a later day. Once more, the proof of the pudding is in the eating: any form is good that makes it possible for the combined dramatic and musical conception to realise itself clearly and effectively. Wagner, for the purposes of opera, took over from instrumental music, especially that of Beethoven, the procedure we call symphonic development. There is not the slightest *a priori* reason why the opera composer of the future should not take over from instrumental music other devices, other forms, other textures. Berg has shown considerable originality and ingenuity in this respect. Practically every one of his fifteen scenes is cast into a recognised instrumental " form " — the suite, the passacaglia, the fugue, the rondo, sonata form, and so on. Fuller reference will be made to these in the course of the following exposition, though it is impossible in a book of this kind to analyse the musical texture in close technical detail.

The few musical quotations given here must not be looked upon as " motives " in the Wagnerian sense of that term, in spite of the fact that some of them crop up afresh in this scene or that. Finally, the best, if not the only, way for the plain man to approach *Wozzeck* for the first time in the theatre is to concentrate mainly on the drama and let the music, mostly atonal, take hold of him as and when it can.

3

Each of the three acts of the opera falls into five scenes. We see first the Captain's room in the early morning; he is sitting in front of a table, looking into a mirror as Wozzeck shaves him. From the outset we get the impression that practically everyone in the strange work is going to prove, in some way or other, to some degree or other, a trifle abnormal, if not half or wholly crazy. The Captain is philosophising after his own fashion, for in his vacant way he is a bit of a thinker: he has just made the remarkable discovery that Time is now an eternity, now only a moment, and he shudders when he reflects that the earth turns on its axis once in every twenty-four hours. From Wozzeck he gets, in answer to all his speculations, little more than a laconic " Jawohl, Herr Hauptmann! " This is even his resigned assent to the Captain's sly remark, made to test him, that the wind seems to be south-north. The Captain laughs at the man's simplicity, and proceeds to point out that Wozzeck has no morals. ("Moral," he condescends to explain, "means when a man has morality "). Wozzeck, it appears, has a child who has come into the world "without the blessing of the Church, as our highly respected garrison chaplain puts it." Wozzeck replies to this at what is for him unusual length. "Herr Hauptmann, the good God will not ask the poor little brat whether the Amen was said over it before it was made. The Lord said, ' Let little children come unto me.' We poor people! Money, money! What it is to have none! If I were a gentleman, and had a hat and a watch and an eyeglass and could speak properly, I would be virtuous all right! There must be something fine about virtue. But I am just a poor devil, and our sort are unlucky in this world and the next. No doubt if we got to heaven we would have to lend a hand with the thunder! " The Captain is a trifle disconcerted by all this: Wozzeck is a decent fellow, he says, but he thinks too much. A man should not think too much; it pulls him down. The shaving finished, he dismisses Wozzeck, telling him not to run as he generally does, but to go slowly, and exactly in the middle of the street — " Slowly, remember, nice and slowly! "

The musical form of this scene is that of the suite — prelude, pavane, gigue and gavotte with two " doubles." The opening phrase of the opera (there is no overture):

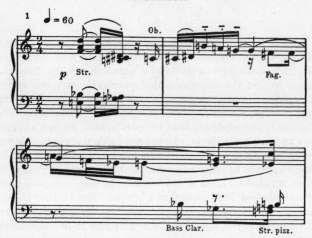

recurs at intervals during the conversation, as does the theme of the Captain, which is heard in the cor anglais, in the fourth bar, immediately after No. 1:

Wozzeck's remark "We poor people!" is sung to a phrase used a good deal in the course of the work:

3

Wir ar-me Leut!

After an orchestral interlude, which allows time for a change of scene, we see Wozzeck and another soldier of the regiment, Andres, cutting sticks in a copse: the time is the late afternoon of the same day. The musical form of this short scene is described by Berg as that of the rhapsody. Wozzeck's first remark, after some chords in the brass that convey the uncanny atmosphere of the milieu:

is, "This place is accursed!" His already slightly unhinged mind sees strange lights streaking across the grass among the fungi: he imagines a head trundling along the ground at night and turning into a hedgehog when someone picks it up. The stolid Andres, who is not subject to these disordered whimsies, tries to amuse himself and his companion by singing a simple little hunting song which is couched musically in something resembling a folk-idiom. (In this scene both men employ the "speech-melody" from time to time, singing of the ordinary kind being mostly reserved for more formal musical utterances such as Andres' ditty).

The eeriness of the place and his own morbid fancies work more and more upon Wozzeck. He babbles about the Freemasons, stamps on the ground, cries out that a chasm is yawning and the earth rocking beneath him, and sees strange shapes moving about. At last his nerves snap; he staggers about blindly, imploring Andres to fly with him. Andres tries to steady Wozzeck's rambling mind. When the rapidly sinking sun lights up the wood harshly for a moment, Wozzeck sees in imagination a fire mounting from earth to heaven, and hears the blaring of trombones and strange clashings and janglings around — all of which is graphically illustrated in the orchestra. Andres, becoming, in spite of his phlegm, a trifle unnerved himself by his companion's fancies, assures him that what he hears is merely the drums sounding at sunset in the barracks: he gathers up his sticks and persuades Wozzeck to return to the town with him.

An impressive orchestral interlude, with hints of military music in the background, prepares us for the following scene, which is set in the humble room which Wozzeck occupies with Marie. When the curtain rises we see her at the window, playing with their little child. The regiment marches down the narrow street, with the Drum-Major at its head; and one of Marie's neighbours, Margret, looking up, sees Marie lost, like herself, in admiration of the Drum-Major — a fine figure of a man, they agree. He waves his hand to Marie as they go by, and she returns his greeting. Margret having commented maliciously on her neighbour's evident interest in soldiers, the two women bandy reflections on each other's virtue for a moment or two. The exchange of compliments ends with Marie shrieking an offensive epithet at her neighbour and closing her window with a bang.

As a result of this closing of the window the military music becomes inaudible inside the room. Marie takes her poor brat in her arms and sings over it a lullaby which balances matters rather happily between the German folk song and the new melodic and harmonic idiom of the Schönberg school, as may be seen from the " Eia popeia " refrain:

The child falls asleep, and Marie loses herself in dreams from which she is roused by a knock at the window. It is Wozzeck. He cannot come in, he tells her, for he is due at the barracks after having cut the sticks for the Major. From his confused speech she senses that all is not well with him: it appears that he has seen and heard strange things in the wood, and now he feels something sinister to be impending. In the hope of quietening him she holds out the child to him, but his thoughts are elsewhere and he does not look at it. He leaves hurriedly. Marie gazes anxiously at the sleeping child. " Ah, we poor people! " she moans as the room grows quite dark: " I cannot endure it! " And she runs to the door in terror.

After another brief orchestral interlude the curtain rises on the fourth scene. The time is the next day, and the setting the Doctor's study. This scene is constructed musically in passacaglia form — a series of twenty-one variations on a ground-bass given out by the 'cellos at the rising of the curtain:

The Doctor is as mad as the rest of them; and Berg has told us
that his object in choosing the passacaglia form for this scene was
to stress the fact that the man is suffering from an *idée fixe*.
Wozzeck, for him, is simply a subject for speculation and experiment. He has observed him coughing in the street, actually bark-
ing like a dog, in spite of his, the Doctor's, demonstration that
the human diaphragm is controllable by the will. Wozzeck must
eat nothing but beans till next week, when he can have a little
mutton; for a revolution is taking place in the science of dietetics,
and the Doctor tells off a few items on his fingers — white of
egg, fats, carbon hydrates, oxyaldehydanhydride. Mixed up with
it all are further fretful complaints about Wozzeck having coughed.
From time to time the Doctor gains control of himself for a moment, only to lose it again as suddenly. Wozzeck tries to pacify
him by pointing out that there is no going against nature. But
as he proceeds he becomes more and more obsessed, more and
more incoherent, talking of the world going so dark in front of
a man that he has to feel his way about blindly with his hands,
with everything slipping through his fingers like a cobweb; and
yet, though all is dark, there is a red glow in the west, as it might
be from a forge; and sometimes in the middle of the day, when the
world seems to be going up in fire, he hears a fearful voice speaking
to him.

"Wozzeck, you have an *aberratio*," says the Doctor; but before he can get any further with his scientific lucubrations Wozzeck breaks in on him with "And the fungi! Have you seen the
rings they make on the earth — circular lines, figures? What do
these mean?" The Doctor warns the man that he is shaping for
a madhouse. "You are suffering from a fine fixed idea, a first-rate
aberratio mentalis partialis of the second species, already well
developed." Wozzeck, apparently neither seeing nor hearing him,
groans "Oh, Marie, Marie!" while the Doctor rubs his hands
in ecstasy over the interesting case with which this poor fellow

provides him. "Oh my theory! my fame!" he cries: "I shall be immortal! immortal! immortal!" And with each repetition of the word — which is always underlined by the trombones — his vocal line becomes more and more extravagantly absurd, till his megalomania culminates in a crazy trill:

Then, suddenly resuming his solemn professional manner, he goes up to Wozzeck and bids him let him see his tongue. Wozzeck obeys, and the curtain falls.

Berg now skips a couple of Büchner's scenes — those outside and inside a booth. The fifth scene, which opens with a flowing theme in flutes and violins (the marking is *andante affettuoso*):

is set in the street in front of Marie's door. It is evening. Marie is admiring the Drum-Major, who is posturing like a peacock before her. Never has she met a man who is so truly a man as he, she confesses; she is bursting with pride that he has condescended to take notice of her. But as he is now, he assures her, is nothing to what he is on Sunday parade, with his white gloves and his great plumes. It all ends with her flinging herself into his arms and disappearing with him through the open house door. As No. 8 recurs frequently in one form or another during this scene, the form may be described as that of the rondo.

4

The official explanation of the opening scene of the second act is that it is in sonata form, which, apparently, of all musical forms corresponds best to the interaction of the three characters. No. 3 plays a large part in the texture.

Once more we see Marie in her wretched room, the time,

presumably, being the morning after. She is almost simultaneously engaged in admiring herself in a shabby little fragment of mirror, trying to get the child to sleep — now and then, for this purpose, she flashes the reflection from the glass across the wall — and envying the women who are better off than she though their mouths are no redder than hers. When Wozzeck enters she instinctively presses her hands to her ears. But he has caught the gleam of something in her hair, and she has to tell him what it is — merely a pair of ear-rings which, she assures him, she had found. Apparently he has his suspicions; but he masters himself and turns with his heart full of pity to the uneasily sleeping child, whose forehead is moist. "Wir arme Leut!" he ejaculates once more: "nothing under the sun but work: even in our sleep we sweat!" He gives Marie his scanty earnings and goes out, leaving her musing sadly on her wicked self and the evil there is in the world.

Common chords are exceedingly scarce in the atonal score of *Wozzeck*. When the poor fellow hands over his money to Marie, however, we hear in the orchestra a long-held chord in C major, which attracts our attention all the more strongly because it follows abruptly on a passage of great harmonic and contrapuntal complexity. Berg's somewhat naïve explanation of the intrusion of this obvious chord is that it symbolises as no other combination of notes could do the commonplace nature of money!

The usual orchestral interlude terminates in an upward harp glissando, which runs into the Captain's theme (No. 2) as the curtain rises. The Captain and the Doctor meet in a street. The latter is in a great hurry, and the Captain has much difficulty in getting him to stop for a chat. When he does so, he scares the life out of the Captain by telling him of the number of his patients who have died recently, some of them in agony. He runs an appraising professional eye over the Captain. Looking none too good, he says: bloated, neck too thick, threats of an *apoplexia cerebri* that will probably carry him off, though with luck it may paralyse him on one side only. He is certainly a most interesting medical case, and if it should happen that, by God's will, his tongue is partly paralysed, they will make experiments on him that will immortalise them. The next four weeks will probably decide. The Captain goes white with terror. Only four weeks!

Already he sees the mourners wiping the tears from their eyes; at any rate they will be saying "He was a good man!" The passage in which the Doctor dwells gleefully on the possibility of the Captain having an apoplectic seizure:

is typical of Berg's vocal line at its most peculiar. The slither down from the High E to the low E flat, we learn from a note in the score, is intended to suggest the hee-haw of an ass.

Wozzeck appears, in a nervous hurry as usual. The precious pair detain him and make him the butt of their malicious humour. The Captain introduces the subject of Wozzeck's profession of regimental barber, and asks him slyly if he has not found a hair from someone's beard in his plate — a sapper's beard, for example, or a corporal's, or — who knows? — a Drum-Major's? Wozzeck has certainly a fine wife. Even if he does not find hairs in his soup, perhaps sometimes, as soon as he has turned the corner, they may be found on a certain pair of lips. Poor Wozzeck goes deadly pale. He is no match for these more educated men in innuendo and irony. All he can do is to say, "Herr Hauptmann, I am a poor creature! I have no one else in the world! If you are joking . . .", and then he wanders off into incoherencies. The Captain assures him that he means him no ill. The Doctor feels his pulse and pronounces it feeble and irregular — "optic muscles rigid," he continues professionally, "tense, eyes staring! Hm!" With a despairing cry Wozzeck tears himself loose from his tormentors and disappears. The Captain feels a trifle disconcerted: the Doctor merely remarks, "A phenomenon, this Wozzeck!" Then, seeing that the Captain is on the verge of another lapse into maudlin self-pity, he hurries away, with the other chasing him.

The musical form of this scene is that of a fantasia and fugue, three principal themes coming into play — that of the Captain

(No. 2), one symbolising Wozzeck, and a third, derived from the passacaglia, which may be taken to represent the Doctor.

The next scene is once more the alley in which Wozzeck lives. Marie is standing outside her door. Wozzeck enters. He is visibly a stage nearer the mental breaking-point: he talks incoherently about sin, and Marie, and Marie's red mouth, and asks about "him," and whether "he" has stood there where he now stands. Marie replies that many people pass up and down, and she cannot forbid the street to anyone. For a moment she is terrified as she thinks he is going to strike her. "Better a knife in me than a hand on me," she says; "when I was ten years old my father did not dare that." She goes into the house. Come to himself again, Wozzeck repeats softly "Better a knife! . . . A man," he continues below his breath, "is an abyss; his brain reels when he looks into it. . . . My head is swimming!" He goes slowly down the street.

In this scene, which corresponds in its musical form to the largo of a symphony, Berg employs only a chamber orchestra of one flute (also piccolo), one oboe, one cor anglais, two clarinets, a bass clarinet, one bassoon, a double bassoon, two horns and a solo string quintet.

A slow Ländler:

introduces the next scene, which takes place in a beer garden packed with soldiers, youths and girls, some of whom are dancing, others promenading. A few are tipsy and betray the fact in their conversation. A new dance is begun — a waltz:

in which Marie and the Drum-Major, the former swimming in ecstasy, take part. They are watched by Wozzeck. Crazy with jealousy, he is on the point of rushing among the dancers when the waltz comes to an end and the couples leave the floor. He sits

down again. Andres, the soldiers and some apprentices burst into
a lusty song: and when this is over, Wozzeck starts a conversation
with Andres the gloom and incoherence of which on Wozzeck's
side soon bore Andres, who leaves him for more congenial company. One of the apprentices climbs on to a table and preaches a
burlesque sermon in the best German pseudo-philosophical style;
but he soon tails off into the drunken-maudlin, and is taken away
by some of the others. While the company in general resume their
singing and waltzing (No. 11 once more), a personage described
as the Fool approaches the lonely and moody Wozzeck, and,
whether by accident or by design, sets the poor man's brain whir-
ring insanely again by telling him that he smells blood. The figures
on the dance floor, among whom are Marie and the Drum-Major,
suddenly seem to Wozzeck to be going round and round in a crim-
son sea.

The musical form of this scene is described as a scherzo with two
trios.

The transition to the fifth scene is made by way of a development of the waltz (No. 11). The new setting is the guard room of
the barracks. As the curtain rises we see the soldiers sleeping all
around with half-open mouths, and hear them snoring melodically
and harmonically (in five parts) in the twelve-tone scale. Wozzeck wakens Andres with his moaning. He cannot sleep; if he
closes his eyes he sees Marie dancing and hears the fiddles playing, and a knife keeps flashing before him. "O Lord, lead us not
into temptation," he wails, as he tries to sleep again. But just then
the Drum-Major enters, announced by a theme:

which becomes the principal factor in the rondo that follows.

The Drum-Major, fatuously pleased with himself as usual, begins to brag of his latest conquest. If they want to know the name
of the ardent beauty, let them ask Wozzeck. Taking a nip from the
flask he draws from his pocket he offers it to Wozzeck, inviting him
to drink with him. Wozzeck merely looks away and whistles. Thereupon the Drum-Major, losing his temper, hurls himself savagely

on the physically inferior Wozzeck, who is soon beaten to the ground and nearly strangled. The vainglorious Drum-Major having left, after another swig from the flask, Wozzeck, his face bleeding, raises himself and staggers to his plank bed again. He sits down and stares into vacancy, while Andres and the others, after a cynical comment or two, resume their interrupted slumbers. The music ebbs away into silence as the curtain falls.

5

The first scene of the third act presents us with seven variations and a fugue on a theme: [3]

given out, as soon as the curtain rises, by various solo instruments one after another.

Marie is sitting in her room at night, reading aloud from the Bible, by the light of a candle, the story of the woman taken in adultery, and bemoaning her own frailty. She thrusts the child from her, saying, " The boy gives me a stab in the heart!," then draws him to her tenderly again and tells him a little story: " Once upon a time there was a poor child who had no father and no mother . . . it was hungry and wept day and night. . . ."[4] She breaks off, wondering why Wozzeck had not been to see her

---

[3] The official description of the form of the third act is " Six Inventions," distributed thus:

    Scene 1. Invention on a Theme.
    Scene 2. Invention on a Tone.
    Scene 3. Invention on a Rhythm.
    Scene 4. Invention on a Six-tone Chord.
              Invention on a Key. (Orchestral Interlude).
    Scene 5. Invention on a Rhythm in Even Quavers. (Perpetuum mobile).

[4] This, the fifth variation on the theme, contrasts effectively with the others by being quite tonal; it is as if Marie were taking pains to speak to the child in a language simple enough for his undeveloped intelligence to understand.

yesterday or today; then she turns once more to the Bible and reads out, " And she knelt before His feet and wept and kissed His feet. . . ." She beats her miserable breast and cries, " Saviour, I would anoint Thy feet; have pity on me and mine as Thou hadst pity on her! " The fugue commences with the words " And she knelt at His feet," which Marie gives out in a style that is at least as near to speech as to song:

though the vocal tones are sufficiently definite in pitch to offer themselves for imitation in the orchestra. A solo viola takes the subject up at the second bar, a solo violin at the third, and a solo double bass at the fourth. Marie's cry of " Saviour! I would anoint Thy feet . . ." which is also developed fugally, is " wholly sung," as the directions in the score put it.

The orchestral meditation on the theme of No. 14 dies away to a soft B natural deep down in the double basses; and this note, in one form or another, pervades in the most curious way most of the next scene. The curtain rises to show us a pond in a wood. It is growing dark. Wozzeck enters with Marie. She is anxious to get back to the town, and urges him to quicken his steps. But he makes her sit down beside him, sympathises with her for having walked so far, and assures her that her feet will not hurt her much longer. He likes the darkness and the quiet all round them. How long is it that they have known each other? he asks. " Three years at Whit-suntide," she replies. " And how long do you think it will last? " he continues. Her only answer to that is to leap to her feet with a feverish " I must go! " He forces her to sit down again, and his talk takes a sinister turn. He compliments her ironically on her good-ness, her piety, her fidelity; then his mood changes suddenly and he speaks of the sweetness of her lips, for which he would give heaven itself. But soon his madness steals over him again. Marie shivers in the night air; whereupon he tells her that when the morning dew falls she will not feel the cold.

Silence falls on them both: the moon rises, and a long-held B natural persists like an obsession through all the harmonic changes in the orchestral tissue. " How red the moon is! " says Marie. For Wozzeck it is the symbol of blood. He draws a knife and plunges it into her throat, stoops for a moment over the body, ejaculates " Dead!," straightens himself nervously, and at last steals away in silence. The inexorable B natural is still sounding when the curtain falls.

A long crescendo on the B leads into a quick polka, played on an out-of-tune piano behind the scenes. The curtain rises on a room in a poor tavern, where a number of people, among them Margret, are dancing. Wozzeck is sitting at a table, feverishly urging the others to dance and dance again, as a means to make him forget his crime. Losing his self-control he ousts the piano music with a song of his own, and dances a few steps with Margret; then he draws her to his table, seats her on his knee, and embraces her. She sings for him a little song the burden of which is that long frocks and pointed shoes are not for serving-women. Something snaps in Wozzeck's brain. He leaps up, shouting " No! No shoes! One can go to hell barefoot! . . ." Margret sees blood on his hands, and her startled cry brings the others to the table. He stammers out that he has cut himself, an explanation which the others deride, as the blood is on his right hand and arm. At last, with a wild cry of " Am I a murderer? " he rushes out.

After a quick change of scene we see Wozzeck by the pond again in the moonlight. Terrified and remorseful, he has come straight from the tavern to search for the knife. He stumbles over Marie's body. What is that red necklace she is wearing? he asks crazily: was it, like the ear-rings, the price of her sin? He searches frantically for the knife, fearing it may betray him. At last he finds it and throws it into the pond. Just then the moon shows blood-red through the clouds, and he sees in it another witness and discloser of his crime. All nature seems to be proclaiming it! And the knife: where it fell will it not be found by some bather? And he plunges into the water, in part in search of the knife, in part to wash away the blood he feels to be still upon him. But the water itself turns to blood as he laves himself with it!

431

He gets out of his depth and drowns. His last choked cry is heard by the Doctor and the Captain, who enter just then and sense that someone is drowning, but are too terrified by the un-canniness of the spot, the red of the moon, and the grey of the clouds to think of doing anything to help. After the final groan from Wozzeck they hurry away; "Come, Doctor," says the Captain, tugging at his companion, "this is not good to hear!"

The orchestral interlude that follows, beginning with an *adagio* for strings:

is one of the finest sections of the whole work; it passes in review much of the material we have by now learned to associate with Wozzeck, so that it may be regarded, perhaps, as an elegy over him. (The *adagio* prelude is said to be derived from a symphony on which Berg was working in 1913–14). When at last the curtain rises for the short final scene we see again the street before Marie's house door. It is morning, and in the bright sunshine Wozzeck's tiny child is riding its hobby-horse while all the other children play about and sing an old rhyme:

Rin-gel, Rin-gel, Ro-sen-kranz, Rin - gelreih'n!

But a sudden end comes to both song and play as children come running in with the cry that something has happened to Marie. "Your mother is dead," says one of them to the child; but all he does is to ride his hobby-horse faster with a delighted "Hopp! Hopp! Hopp!" The older children all rush away to the pond to see the body; and after a moment's hesitation Marie's child follows them, still crying "Hopp!"

Büchner's final scene — the one in the dissecting-room, already referred to — has not been used by Berg. For operatic purposes the scene of the children certainly makes an effective curtain: and yet one wishes that the composer had seen fit to show us Wozzeck on the dissecting table, with the orchestra, in a last and greatest effort, summing up the pitiful life and death of the poor fellow in a way that only music could achieve.

Index

Ernest Newman was born in 1868. Educated at Liverpool College and Liverpool University, he was intended for the Indian Civil Service, but when his health broke down he went instead into business in Liverpool, carrying on musical and literary work concurrently. In 1905 he became music critic of the Manchester Guardian *and subsequently of the* Birmingham Post. *Since 1920 he has acted as music critic for the* Sunday Times (London). *During his long career Mr. Newman has written, translated, and edited numerous books, the most celebrated of which is his monumental four-volume biography* The Life of Richard Wagner *(1933, 1937, 1941, 1946).*

THIS BOOK has been set on the Linotype in CALEDONIA, *a style of type-letter that printers call "modern face." The "modern" part of the classification marks a change in fashion in printing types that took place during the last years of the eighteenth century, under the influence of such "modernizing" printers as Baskerville, Didot, and Bodoni.*

The typographic scheme of the book is the work of W. A. Dwiggins, who also designed the type-face. Lithography by THE MURRAY PRINTING COMPANY, *Forge Village, Mass., on paper manufactured by* S. D. WARREN COMPANY, *Boston, Mass. Bound by* THE COLONIAL PRESS INC., *Clinton, Mass. Cover design by Muni Lieblein.*

Vintage Books

Vintage Books